T0383923

PHARMACEUTICAL INNOVATION

The pharmaceutical industry worldwide is a rapidly burgeoning industry contributing to growth of gross domestic product and employment. Technological change in this field has been very rapid, with many new products being introduced. Partly for this reason, health care budgets throughout the world have increased dramatically, eliciting growing pressures for cost containment. This volume, written by well-known students of health economics, explores four important issues in pharmaceutical innovation: (1) the industry structure of pharmaceutical innovation, (2) incentives for correcting market failures in allocating resources for research and development, (3) competition and marketing, and (4) public evaluation of the benefits and costs of innovation. The lessons are applicable to countries all over the world, at all levels of economic development. In countries with larger markets, market mechanisms will generally provide adequate incentives. In countries with small markets, however, especially those with low incomes, some form of government intervention may be required. This collection discusses existing evidence and proposes incentive arrangements to accomplish social objectives.

Frank A. Sloan has been the J. Alexander McMahon Professor of Health Policy and Management and Professor of Economics at Duke University since 1993, where he holds faculty appointments in the Department of Economics, the School of Public Policy, the Fuqua School of Business, and the School of Nursing. Before joining the faculty at Duke, he was a research economist at the Rand Corporation and served on the faculties of the University of Florida and Vanderbilt University. His current research interests include alcohol use and smoking prevention, long-term care, medical malpractice, and cost-effectiveness analyses of medical technologies. Professor Sloan also has a long-standing interest in hospitals, health care financing, and health manpower. He has served on several national advisory public and private groups, including the Physician Payment Review Commission. He has been a member of the Institute of Medicine of the National Academy of Sciences since 1982, recently chairing committees on vaccine financing and cancer in low- and middle-income countries. He recently received a Merit Award from the National Institutes of Health and an Investigator Award from the Robert Wood Johnson Foundation. Professor Sloan's most recent books include *The Smoking Puzzle: Information, Risk Perceptions, and Choice* (2003) with Drs. V. Kerry Smith and Donald H. Taylor, Jr., and *The Price of Smoking* (2004) with Drs. Jan Ostermann, Gabriel Picone, Christopher Conover, and Donald H. Taylor, Jr.

Chee-Ruey Hsieh is a Research Fellow in the Institute of Economics at Academia Sinica, Taipei, Taiwan. He received his Ph.D. in economics from Vanderbilt University in 1990. Dr. Hsieh has a long-standing interest in health economics and health policy. He is the coeditor of *The Economic Analysis of Substance Use and Abuse* and *The Economics of Health Care in Asia-Pacific Countries.*

Pharmaceutical Innovation

Incentives, Competition, and Cost-Benefit Analysis in International Perspective

Edited by

FRANK A. SLOAN

Duke University

CHEE-RUEY HSIEH

Academia Sinica, Taiwan

CAMBRIDGE
UNIVERSITY PRESS

University Printing House, Cambridge CB2 8BS, United Kingdom

One Liberty Plaza, 20th Floor, New York, NY 10006, USA

477 Williamstown Road, Port Melbourne, VIC 3207, Australia

4843/24, 2nd Floor, Ansari Road, Daryaganj, Delhi - 110002, India

79 Anson Road, #06-04/06, Singapore 079906

Cambridge University Press is part of the University of Cambridge.

It furthers the University's mission by disseminating knowledge in the pursuit of education, learning and research at the highest international levels of excellence.

www.cambridge.org
Information on this title: www.cambridge.org/9780521874908

First published 2007

A catalogue record for this publication is available from the British Library

Library of Congress Cataloging in Publication data
Pharmaceutical innovation : incentives, competition, and cost-benefit analysis in international perspective / [edited by] Frank A. Sloan, Chee-Ruey Hsieh.
p. ; cm.
Includes bibliographical references and index.
ISBN-13: 978-0-521-87490-8 (hardback)
ISBN-10: 0-521-87490-4 (hardback)
1. Pharmaceutical policy. 2. Pharmaceutical Industry. 3. Drug development – Technological innovations – Economic aspects. I. Sloan, Frank A. II. Hsieh, Chee-Ruey. [DNLM: 1. Drug Industry – economics. 2. Cost-Benefit Analysis. 3. Economic Competition. 4. Health Policy. 5. Pharmaceutical Preparations – economics. 6. Vaccines – economics. QV 736 P5323 2007]
RA401.A1P43 2007
338.4′76151–dc22 2006031632

ISBN 978-0-521-87490-8 Hardback
ISBN 978-1-107-46001-0 Paperback

Contents

Tables

Figures

Contributors

Ernst R. Berndt
Sloan School of Management, MIT

William S. Comanor
UCLA School of Public Health

Pierre-Yves Cremieux
Analysis Group, Boston

Michael Drummond
University of York

Charles E. Eesley
Sloan School of Management, MIT

Henry Grabowski
Duke University

Aidan Hollis
University of Calgary

Yichen Hong
Chinese Culture University, Taipei

Chee-Ruey Hsieh
Academia Sinica, Taipei

Denise Jarvinen
Independent Scholar

Frank R. Lichtenberg
Columbia University

Kuang-Ta Vance Lo
National Chengchi University, Taipei

Genia Long
Analysis Group, Boston

Stephen M. Maurer
University of California at Berkeley

Phil Merrigan
University of Quebec at Montreal

Mark V. Pauly
University of Pennsylvania

Uwe E. Reinhardt
Princeton University

Ya-Chen Tina Shih
University of Texas

Frank A. Sloan
Duke University

Acknowledgments

Technological change in pharmaceuticals has been a major driving force in improving the health of populations in many countries throughout the world. Gains in health have been achieved at the cost of high spending on personal health care services. Financing health services is closely linked to incentives for research and development. Thus, countries face a dilemma of providing access to pharmaceuticals, preserving incentives for research and development, and controlling their health care budgets. At the same time, countries view growth of local pharmaceutical industries as highly desirable for their overall economic development. This book is motivated by these complex issues associated with pharmaceutical innovation and aims to communicate and disseminate the findings of research on this topic.

Early drafts of the chapters (except for the introduction and concluding chapter) were presented at the International Conference on Pharmaceutical Innovation held in Taipei, Taiwan, May 26–27, 2005. We are grateful for the financial support for this conference, which came from various sources, including the R.O.C. Department of Health; the Bureau of National Health Insurance; the Institute of Economics, Academia Sinica; and the International Research-Based Pharmaceutical Manufacturers Association (IRPMA). The organization of the conference benefited from an excellent support staff. We thank Carol Cheng, chief operating officer of IRPMA, who led the team that organized the details of the conference.

Having multiple contributors is a strength in that they are excellent authors. On the other hand, edited books can be uneven, and our editorial work sought to make the book more even. In addition to reviewing the papers, giving our comments to authors, and performing substantial edits to make the book read like a single-authored volume, we collaborated in writing the introduction and concluding chapters. Editorial work on this book was conducted when the second editor was on a sabbatical leave at the Center for Health Policy, Duke University. We would like to thank Kate Whetten, the director of the Center, for providing office space and research facilities to make our collaboration very productive, and Khuwailah Beyah for assisting us with the manuscript. Finally, we wish to thank the contributors for making both the conference and this book a success.

Frank A. Sloan

Chee-Ruey Hsieh

PHARMACEUTICAL INNOVATION

ONE

Introduction

Frank A. Sloan and Chee-Ruey Hsieh

I. Context

The pharmaceutical industry serves a dual role in modern society. On one hand, it is a growing industry, and its output makes a direct contribution to gross domestic product (GDP). On the other, prescription drugs, this industry's major output, are an input in the production of good health. These products make an important contribution to the improvement of population health.

The purpose of this book is to investigate public policy issues in pharmaceutical innovation. In Section II we first describe the important characteristics of prescription drugs. We emphasize that these characteristics deviate from the standard conditions in a competitive market. In Section III we discuss the current performance of the pharmaceutical market. In Section IV we investigate market failures that persist in allocating research and development (R&D) resources and in the utilization of prescription drugs. In Section V we analyze the policy conflict between the economic and health sectors arising from pharmaceutical innovation. The final section discusses the structure of the book and the major content of the chapters.

II. Characteristics of Prescription Drugs

Prescription drugs have many complex characteristics, which, when taken together, have led to major controversies in public policy arenas, including pricing, patents, and incentives for research and development, as well as excess industry profits. Each characteristic is not unique to pharmaceuticals, but rather it is the characteristics, taken in combination, that make the industry unique.

Probabilistic Nature of Demand and Effectiveness

Prescription drugs are inputs in the production of good health. Individuals' demand for such drugs is not because they enjoy consuming them, but rather for their potential effects on their health. Thus, the demand for a drug is a derived demand stemming from the demand for good health. Since individuals face uncertainty in their health status, the demand for a drug is probabilistic, depending in large part on the person's health state. People take drugs as a treatment when they are acutely ill or have some chronic health problem, either to ameliorate the symptoms or to reduce the rate of progression of diseases. Not only is disease onset uncertain, but, as Arrow (1963) mentioned, the effectiveness of therapy is uncertain as well. For biological reasons, people differ in whether and the extent to which a drug produces the desired outcome as well as in adverse side effects of the drug. Also, although the efficacy (effectiveness in ideal use) is a condition for drug approval by government regulatory authorities, the environment in which randomized clinical trials are conducted to test for drug efficacy is often different from the environment in which the drug is actually used in the community. In practice, drugs are used for off-label indications and for populations other than those included in trials (e.g., racial or ethnic minorities, the elderly, and children).

Ideally people would be able to purchase insurance to protect against the possibility that a medical intervention is not successful. But as Arrow (1963) stressed, there is no market for insuring against such risk. Rather, health insurance covers the expense arising from the use of medical services. As a result, such organizational arrangements as nonprofit hospitals have arisen as imperfect substitutes for this missing market. The basic idea is that organizations not oriented toward the profit motive would be willing to devote the needed resources to care for patients, which profit-seeking organizations may not be prone to do. Arrow did not specifically mention prescription drugs, which, in any case, in 1963 were much less important than they are today. The pharmaceutical market is dominated by firms organized on a for-profit basis. This creates a potential conflict between pursuing profit and pursuing health and has led to some proposals for public production of pharmaceutical products, especially vaccines.

Financial Risk

The demand for prescription drugs is less predictable on an individual basis than is the demand for many other consumption goods, such as transportation and housing. Uncertainty in demand in turn creates a financial risk to individuals; spending on prescription drugs may be considerable, especially for elderly persons and those with chronic diseases more generally. Unlike the missing market for insuring against the risk of an unsuccessful outcome of therapy, there is an insurance market to protect against financial loss arising from illness. Much spending on prescription drugs is covered by health insurance in high-income countries. Although insurance coverage for prescription drugs provides a social benefit in terms of risk protection, it also imposes a social cost from moral hazard that arises when drugs are covered. The socially optimal level of consumption is at the consumption level where the marginal social benefit equals the marginal social cost of such consumption. However, with complete insurance coverage, consumption may rise to levels far higher than this – to levels at which the marginal social benefit is far less than the marginal social cost.

The theory underlying the concept of a socially optimal level of consumption is static. That is, it does not account for the possibility that shifts in demand may increase rates of product innovation and hence future product demand as well. Widespread insurance coverage coupled with such secular changes as the aging of the population may induce firms to invest more in research and development than they otherwise would, and the resulting innovation may itself be a source of increased demand. In such a dynamic context, as a consequence of pharmaceutical innovation, many new drugs are introduced into the market each year, and individuals often opt for the newest drugs, especially when they have insurance coverage. The new drugs tend to be more expensive on average, leading to increased expenditures. The expenditure increases in turn have led to various forms of private and public cost containment, including price controls, drug formularies to restrict the drug choice set individuals face, and limits on total drug expenditures. Although cost-containment programs may reduce demand in the short run, in the longer run, they may also reduce the rate of product innovation.

Physicians as Agents for Patients

By definition, the notion that a prescription is required before a drug can be purchased means that physicians act as front-line professional agents, making consumption decisions on behalf of patients. The underlying rationale for requiring prescriptions is that patients possess insufficient information to know when specific drugs are appropriate for treatment. Conceptually and ideally, physicians would be perfect agents for their patients, prescribing in a way that patients would if they were fully informed about treatment appropriateness.

However, in the real world, except for professional ethics and guidelines, there is no effective institutional arrangement to deter physicians from acting as imperfect agents. In many Asian countries, physicians both prescribe *and* dispense drugs. Thus, they are in a position to profit directly from the sale of prescription drugs, whether or not a well-informed patient would want to purchase such drugs. In Western countries by contrast, although the separation of prescribing and dispensing drugs has long been widely accepted by all parties, physician prescribing may be unduly influenced by pharmaceutical advertising and detailing as well as various inducements, such as free trips to attractive tourist spots where pharmaceutical companies provide opportunities for learning about their products as well as for various recreational activities. The existence of imperfect agents creates a potential conflict between pursuing health and pursuing profit: patients care about their health, but physicians may care about their financial well-being as well as their patients' physical and mental well-being.

Cost of Pharmaceutical Research and Development

Research and development for prescription drugs is a lengthy and costly process. Although there is no consensus about how to calculate the cost for research and development in the pharmaceutical market and on the actual size of the cost, there is a consensus that the mean R&D cost associated with introducing a new prescription drug is in the range of hundreds of millions of dollars (see DiMasi, Hansen, and Grabowski 2003; Light and Warburton 2005). The high cost is attributable in part to the strict criteria for drug approval set by government agencies (Grabowski, Vernon, and Thomas 1978; Cockburn and Henderson 2001). Governments in most countries require manufacturers to demonstrate both safety and efficacy before a drug can be approved for sale. Consequently, clinical trials for testing have become the most costly process in the development of a new drug.

If manufacturers sold drugs at the marginal cost of production and distribution, they would have no way to recoup the cost of R&D. To allow these firms to recoup such cost, in most countries, patents confer market power on new products, and monopoly profits provide the cash flow to cover and generate a return on investments in R&D. However, the patent system is a double-edged sword: it preserves the incentive for R&D on one hand, but on the other, it creates a barrier to entry in the pharmaceutical market. The barrier to entry results in higher prices and expenditures as well as lower levels of consumption of the new drugs than would prevail under competition. This has led some experts to suggest alternatives to the patent system, such as patent buyouts and advanced payment mechanisms that would preserve the incentive for product development, while at the same time eliminating or mitigating the negative effects of monopoly pricing under the patent system.

Deviations from the Competitive Norm

A basic tenet of economics is that competitive markets lead to efficient outcomes, that is, consumption at the level at which society's willingness to pay or, equivalently, the marginal benefit from consumption of the good, equals the marginal social cost of producing and distributing it. The market is indeed the best way to allocate resources if the market environment satisfies preconditions of competitive markets: (1) both buyers and sellers have full information, (2) the products in the market are homogeneous or heterogeneous but easily compared, and (3) entry into and exit from the market is free. Even dynamically, one expects under competition that investments in new products should be made up to the point at which expected rates of return equal the cost of capital. But the goal of equity is conceptually distinct from that of efficiency. A competitive market may not lead to an equitable outcome, and equity is an important consideration in health policy around the world.

The market for pharmaceutical products clearly deviates from these preconditions in important respects. Product heterogeneity is the least critical of these preconditions since competitive markets would require only that consumers be able to assess differences in value (or quality) between goods with different products. Inadequacy of information, however, is a major problem, not only for consumers of prescription drugs, but for physicians in their roles as prescribers as well. Furthermore, whatever its merits may be, the patent system precludes free entry.

In spite of these deviations, many countries rely on markets to allocate resources for prescription drugs. The market may not be an ideal solution, but this approach must be compared with the alternatives.

III. The Performance of Pharmaceutical Markets: The Four "Highs"

Critics of the pharmaceutical industry as it operates in major industrialized countries base their evaluations in large part on four "highs": (1) high R&D cost, (2) high marketing expenditures, (3) high prices, and (4) high profits.

That research and development for new drug is a lengthy and costly process is universally accepted. Pharmaceutical firms typically allocate a relatively larger share of their resources on R&D than do their counterparts in most other industries or relative to spending by the public sector. For example, R&D expenditures as a percentage of GDP ranged from 2% to 3% in major developed countries, such as the United States, Japan, Germany, and France, during 1988–2002 (National Science Council 2004). By contrast, pharmaceutical manufacturers of patented drugs consistently spent over 10% of their sales revenue on R&D during the past two decades. Furthermore, the share of R&D expenditures as a percentage of sales revenue in this industry has increased over time. Taking the top 10 pharmaceutical firms in the United States as an example, the share of sales revenue spent on R&D increased from 11% in 1990 to 14% in 2000 (Kaiser Family Foundation 2001).

However, taking the high cost of R&D as a given, critics have noted that pharmaceutical firms spend an even larger share of their sales revenue on marketing. The largest U.S. pharmaceutical firms spent over one third of their annual sales on average on "marketing and administration" during 1990–2000 (Kaiser Family Foundation 2001).

Unlike other industries, until recently when direct-to-consumer advertising has emerged in the United States and in New Zealand, market efforts of pharmaceutical firms have not been aimed at consumers directly, but at physicians. The rationale is that the physician acts as a professional agent for the patient in the market for prescription drugs. Pharmaceutical manufacturers justify their expenditures on marketing to physicians on grounds that they are educating physicians about appropriate uses for the drug. The critics, while acknowledging such marketing efforts have some educational value, argue that marketing exerts an undue influence on physicians for the financial or other reasons already discussed. Many of the differences between products highlighted in marketing and advertising efforts are not to inform physicians but to increase demand for their products beyond levels of demand that would exist if physicians were perfect agents for their patients and to make demand for their products more price inelastic than they would be, absent marketing efforts. Greater price inelasticity confers market power on sellers, permitting them to charge a higher price. Similarly, there is controversy about whether direct-to-consumer advertising improves consumer welfare by leading to more appropriate use of pharmaceutical products, or whether it simply leads to excess use of the advertised products.

The third high is the high price of pharmaceuticals, which is particularly observed in countries in which there are no government-imposed restraints on pricing. In the United States in particular, there is no direct government intervention in pricing; but at the same time, the market for generic drugs is highly developed. Generics provide some limits on what some sellers of branded products can charge. The rationale for high prices is that they permit an adequate return on the high investments on R&D. However, whether or not the return is adequate or more than adequate is a highly controversial issue.

There are appreciable price gaps between branded and generic drugs in the U.S. pharmaceutical market, ranging from 40% to 83% (Caves, Whinston, and Hurwitz 1991). Since the incremental manufacturing costs for branded and generic drugs are almost identical, the price difference between these two types of drugs is largely attributable to the difference in price markup over marginal cost. Entry into the market for generic drugs is not completely free since generic manufacturers must demonstrate chemical equivalence and drug safety to public regulators; entry is relatively free. Thus, the market structure of generic firms resembles the competitive norm more closely.

Variation between countries in pricing and access to generics provide natural experiments to aiding our understanding about how countries' public stances toward the pharmaceutical sector affect market performance and consumer (patient) welfare. International comparisons of drug prices indicate that, on average, drug prices in the United States are higher than those in other developed countries with various forms of government regulation of pharmaceutical product prices (Danzon and Furukawa 2003). Whether or not this implies that prices in the United States are excessively high is a complex question; on the one hand, higher prices may lead to excess profits and returns that exceed the levels needed to elicit socially optimal levels of investments in research and development. Furthermore, high prices raise equity concerns, especially for less affluent persons, as do cross-subsidies by U.S. households of research and development that benefit users in other countries as well. On the other hand, profits and returns on R&D may not be excessive but rather represent the amounts required to generate socially optimal levels of R&D as well as employment opportunities in areas where the R&D takes place.

One measure used by economists to gauge profitability of a firm is the price-cost margin [(price-marginal cost)/price]. Scherer and Ross (1990) found that the price-cost margin in the pharmaceutical industry was 61.4%, compared to 30.5% on average for industries overall. In terms of price-cost margins, the pharmaceutical industry ranked sixth out of 459 manufacturing industries. Such evidence suggests that profits are high, but not necessarily that they are excessively high.

IV. The Performance of Pharmaceutical Markets: Market Failure in Pharmaceutical Markets?

Judging from the relatively larger share of R&D expenditures of total pharmaceutical firms' sales revenues, it would appear that the market mechanism functions fairly well in providing financial incentives for R&D. However, the distribution of R&D expenditures across disease groups is uneven, which could indicate a market failure in the allocation of R&D resources from a global viewpoint. The search for prevention and cure of some diseases, such as for infectious diseases that are highly prevalent in low-income countries, seems to be conducted at a far lower level, at least relative to the need, than is the search for new methods for preventing and curing diseases more common in higher-income countries, for example, development of a vaccine against malaria versus new drugs for fighting depression (Kremer and Glennerster 2004; Berndt et al. 2005). Kremer and Glennerster (2004) indicated that new molecular entities for treating tropical diseases in humans accounted for less than 1% of all new molecular entities licensed worldwide during 1975–1997. However, given the widespread incidence of tropical diseases in low-income countries, the drugs developed for treating these diseases could potentially yield important impacts on health outcomes. Empirical research has shown that market size, which reflects both populations with particular diseases and willingness to pay for drugs among those affected, influences the rate of pharmaceutical innovation (Acemoglu and Linn 2004; Finkelstein 2004). Low income is a determinant of market size.

With the market mechanism, the driving force that allocates resources for R&D is pursuit of profit instead of pursuit of health. The decision rule for R&D investment is to maximize profit, not to maximize health gains. In defense of pharmaceutical firms, they have an obligation to their shareholders to maximize profit. Further, for many diseases concentrated in poor countries, income is so low that effective demand for disease prevention and therapy is correspondingly low. Without financial assistance from outside the poor countries, treatments for these diseases are at a financial disadvantage. There is indeed a market failure in allocating R&D resources according to health needs. This type of market failure can be remedied only by intervention from private foundations and/or governmental organizations.

A case in point about underinvestment in R&D applies to vaccines, which may have both preventive and therapeutic uses. One reason for underinvestment in vaccine research is that vaccines not only prevent disease for specific individuals who are vaccinated but also prevent the spread of disease to others. Individuals' willingness to pay for vaccines may not reflect the external benefit from being vaccinated. Vaccines for major communicable diseases may have much larger social benefits than many drugs. Compared to drugs, firms earn fewer profits in the vaccine market (Kremer and Snyder 2003). Thus, private firms have less incentive to discover and develop new vaccines because of the low profits, although their potential value to population health is very high. Again, intervention from private foundations and governments is needed to deal with this type of market failure. Markets cannot accomplish desired social objectives on their own.

It has been alleged that much pharmaceutical innovation involves introduction of "me-too" drugs, which have therapeutic qualities similar to existing branded drugs. Although the patent system creates a legal barrier to entry in the pharmaceutical market, this barrier is not absolute. A patent is based on the molecular entity, not on a drug's therapeutic class. Thus, pharmaceutical firms can focus on developing new molecular entities that satisfy the regulatory authorities as being a new product. Randomized controlled trials are still needed for regulatory approval of a drug, and as already noted, trials are expensive. Current regulations do not require the new entrant to show that its drug is more effective than existing products (Angell 2004). According to the U.S. Food and Drug Administration (2005), 431 new molecular entities were approved by the U.S. government during 1990–2004. Of these, only 183 new molecular entities provided a substantial therapeutic advance as compared to existing products. Pharmaceutical firms devoted about 60% of their R&D resources to discovering and developing new molecular entities offering little therapeutic advantage over the existing products. The argument is that rather than focus research and development efforts on fundamental innovations, which could lead to major improvements in the public's health, firms are attracted to large existing markets, and R&D resources are misallocated as a result.

Although, in one sense, development of "me-too" drugs represents a misallocation of resources and hence a market failure, in another sense, a strong case can be made for them. For one, me-too products are common in virtually all markets. There is not just one midsize vehicle in the U.S. automobile market. In many ways, the midsize vehicles or the various laptop computers are all me-too's. Some people may prefer one of the me-two vehicles because they like the car's contours or its cup holders. Or they might prefer the durability of one brand of laptop computers if they are prone to dropping them. Similarly, drugs in the same therapeutic class may differ in certain ways, such as their side-effects profiles. Moreover, with multiple drugs in a therapeutic class, a private or public purchaser can bargain with sellers over price. A credible threat of excluding a drug from the purchaser's formulary gives it market power. Without me-too's, pharmaceuticals would have more market power under the patent system than they do currently.

Having good information is critical to making good choices in any market. Although the physician acts as an agent for the patient, the information possessed by the physician is often incomplete; clinical trials needed for regulatory approval do not require head-to-head (pharmaceutical product-to-product) comparisons. Without being required to do so, private firms lack incentives to provide public information on the relative effectiveness of their drugs since public information is just like other public goods that everyone can access it once it becomes available. Private firms have incentives only to produce private information that increases sales of their products. Incomplete information provision in turn creates possible misallocations, including underuse or overuse of specific drugs (Angell 2004; Newhouse 2004).

V. The Dual Roles of the Pharmaceutical Industry

Societies are interested in prescription drugs and pharmaceutical innovation in large part because of the potential health benefits obtained from drugs. But particularly in light of increased global competition in many sectors, many countries are looking for sectors in which they have a comparative advantage. Pharmaceuticals and biotech are viewed favorably in many higher-income countries because they rely on highly educated workforces, and production may be less likely to be outsourced to countries in which prevailing wages are lower. This dual role greatly increases the complexity of public-sector policy making.

The Pharmaceutical Industry's Role in the Economic Sector: Industrial Policy

Innovation is an engine of economic growth (Romer 1990). Innovation allows more output to be produced with fewer resources (labor, capital, etc.): that is, it increases productivity. To pursue economic growth, some countries, the United States for example, rely on market mechanisms to encourage innovation, whereas other countries, Japan for example, use industrial policy to pick the winner. Although strategies for encouraging product innovation are different between countries, existing empirical evidence consistently indicates that technological innovation is the leading cause of economic growth in developed countries (Kim and Lau 1994).

Scientific advances, the major source of technological change, occur at different periods in different fields. Major advances in information science in the 1980s and early 1990s led to substantial innovation in information technology. In the early twenty-first century, major advances are occurring in genomics, and, consequently, technological change in biotech and pharmaceuticals appears to be increasing. Compared to the innovation in information technology and in other fields, innovation in biotech and pharmaceutical has many different impacts on human society, not only increasing GDP directly through its employment effects in the short run, but also by improving the public's health and longevity (see, e.g., Murphy and Topel 2003a, b; Cutler 2004), such innovation increases long-term economic growth as well. Of course, a country can achieve much of the benefit of long-term growth through improved health by adopting policies that are not favorable to pharmaceutical firms, such as price controls, letting other countries do the innovating, and foregoing the favorable employment effects of having a healthy and innovative pharmaceutical sector but at the same time achieving savings in prescription drug expenditures to the extent that the country pays lower prices for prescription drugs. There is an important trade-off between a strategy that encourages drug innovation within the country and pharmaceutical cost containment on the other.

In addition, as the world becomes ever more interconnected, an exogenous shock resulting from the spread of new virus, such as the SARS epidemic in 2003, can have a major negative impact on economies globally. Pharmaceutical innovation enhances medicine's capability and provides means for preventing or at least mitigating such disease shocks. Under the threat of a new virus, the development of a new drug or new vaccine becomes a top priority of national security and economic stability. Thus, countries view growth of local pharmaceutical industries as highly desirable for their overall economic development. Moreover, small countries without a capacity to produce vaccines are particularly vulnerable to shutdowns of vaccine supply in the presence of a major pandemic and may want to have local manufacturing capacity for this reason.

The Pharmaceutical Industry's Role in the Health Sector: Health Policy

Although the health gains to be derived from pharmaceutical innovation are universally acknowledged, there have also been major increases in private and public spending on pharmaceutical products. Between about 1995 and 2005, the rapid increase in pharmaceutical expenditure has become the leading factor in accounting for the growth of overall health care expenditures in many OECD countries. Several empirical studies have shown that the increase in the use of new drugs is the major factor in the rapid growth of pharmaceutical expenditures (Addis and Magrini 2002; Berndt 2002).

The relationship between health care spending and health improvements is complex. Increased health care spending is realized in the short run;

however, many of the potential health benefits accrue in the long run. For example, higher expenditures on an improved drug for blood cholesterol may lead to reductions in heart disease several decades hence. Societies in general, and many elected public officials in particular, may be insufficiently patient to be willing to trade costs accruing currently for benefits in the far distant future. Also, since randomized clinical trials of drugs extend only over short time periods, the long-run effects of drugs cannot fully be assessed until long after they are introduced. Uncertainty of future benefits may also explain some decision makers' short-term orientations. In contrast to the benefits, higher costs associated with pharmaceutical innovation are already apparent in the short run.

Variations in the rate that future benefits are discounted to the present cannot fully explain policy differences between countries. For example, in the United States, there are virtually no public restraints on paying for a new drug, once it has received regulatory approval. In the United Kingdom, by contrast, new drugs are subject to economic evaluation that compares costs and benefits of the drug, and the findings of these evaluations affect insurance coverage for drugs (Box 1.1). It seems unlikely that citizens in the United Kingdom are more impatient than their counterparts in the United States. Casual impressions would suggest just the reverse. Rather and more importantly, the countries differ in the weights attached to efficiency versus equity objectives in general and in public acceptance of explicit calculations of benefit versus cost by a public-sector agency as a method for allocating resources in particular.

Box 1.1. "Britain Stirs Outcry by Weighing Benefits of Drugs versus Price"

Millions of patients around the world have taken drugs introduced over the past decade to delay the worsening of Alzheimer's disease. While the drugs offer no cure, studies suggest they work in some patients at least for a while.

But this year, an arm of Britain's government health care system, relying on some economists' number-crunching, issued a preliminary ruling calling on doctors to stop prescribing the drugs.

The ruling highlighted one of the most disputed issues in medicine today. If a treatment helps people, should governments and private insurers pay for it without question? Or should they first measure the benefit against the cost, and only pay if the cost-benefit ratio exceeds some preset standard?

The United States generally follows the first course. Even the most cost-conscious insurers say they'll pay the price if a drug works and there aren't other options. Britain openly and unapologetically adopts the second course. If a drug or type of surgery costs a lot and helps only a little, it says no.

"There is not a bottomless pit of resources," says Phil Wadeson, finance director for the National Health Service unit that oversees hospitals and doctors' offices in Liverpool. "We reached the point a while ago where there is far more medical intervention than any health-care system can afford."

Source: Jeanne Whalen, "Britain Stirs Outcry by Weighing Benefits of Drugs versus Price," *Wall Street Journal,* November 22, 2005, pp. A1 and A11, citation from p. A1.

The Conflict of Policy Goals

Mechanisms for resource allocation in the economic and health sectors are quite different in most high-income countries because the two sectors have different policy goals. The economic sector in these countries depends on markets to guide resource allocation, the policy goals mainly being macroeconomic in nature, such as increases in employment and national income per capita. By contrast, the health sector often relies on regulatory approaches to allocate resources. While markets are the best we have for achieving efficiency objectives, policy making in the health sector tends to be *more* highly weighted toward equity – which includes promoting access to personal health care services and improving the nation's health, including the health of the poor, disabled, children, and the elderly, groups typically not active in the labor force.

Innovation in pharmaceuticals can sometimes be consistent with public goals in both economic and health sectors. To the extent that technological change improves health and if R&D is conducted in the country, innovation promotes employment and income-increasing goals as well. Also, a healthy population is more likely to make for an economically productive workforce.

But for many and probably most countries, the dual roles of the pharmaceutical industry are likely to create a conflict in policy goals between the economic and health sectors. There is at least one specific example that illustrates a policy conflict between the different sectors. The health care cost containment and/or public budget control objective often means limited introduction of new technologies – done by a combination of pricing, formulary policies, and policies to encourage use of generic drugs. Since financing health services is closely linked to incentives for research and development, placing cost containment as a focus of health policy *may* create a time inconsistency problem between static efficiency and dynamic efficiency. Static efficiency, which refers to optimal allocation of resources at a point in time, may indicate pricing new drugs lower (near marginal cost) to achieve the goal of efficient resource allocation in the short run. Dynamic efficiency, which refers to efficient allocation over time, indicates pricing new drugs higher to preserve incentives for research and development at the level at which the expected social rates of return on R&D investments equal the marginal social cost of capital used to finance such investments. Dynamic efficiency thus refers to optimal resource allocation of investment effort in the long run.

The difference between static and dynamic efficiency poses several dilemmas for countries. First, and probably most important, why should a country not be a free rider, that is, focus on short-run budget considerations and let other countries worry about dynamic efficiency? After all, in a global economy, the new drugs can be imported later and possibly at lower prices than in the countries in which R&D takes place. This is certainly an option, especially for smaller countries. Each year as a result of technological advances in pharmaceuticals, many new prescription drugs are introduced into the world market. However, only a few countries in the world, such as the United States, United Kingdom, Germany, France, Sweden, and Japan have the ability to develop new drugs. Second, policy makers may understandably be more present-oriented in practice than, if all of the public's preferences were known, they should be. Or perhaps the public is short-sighted as well. Why pay the price of innovation when, it may be assumed, new pharmaceutical products will be available anyway? Or perhaps private returns to pharmaceutical R&D investments are excessive anyway, and a high rate of innovation can be obtained even if restraints on current pricing.

Eschewing considerations of dynamic efficiency, however, comes at a cost. While most countries are adopters of pharmaceutical innovation, as Danzon, Wang, and Wang (2005) noted, the expected price and market size are the most important factors influencing the timing of a new drug launch. Pharmaceutical companies increase the delay in launching a new drug in a country if the expected price is relatively low and the market size is relatively small. This suggests that populations of higher-income countries, which focus on static efficiency, and lower-income countries, which do not have a choice but to focus on short-run concerns, are at a disadvantage in obtaining access to new drugs.

VI. The Structure and Contents of This Book

Four Issues in Pharmaceutical Innovation

Following this chapter's overview of pharmaceutical innovation, our book highlights four important issues in pharmaceutical innovations: (1) the industry structure of pharmaceutical innovation, (2) incentives for correcting market failures in allocating resources for research and development, (3) marketing and market competition, and (4) public evaluation of the benefits and costs of innovation.

Industry structure refers to the interface between the public sector and industry, in this case pharmaceuticals, as well as the extent of competitiveness between firms in the industry and the presence or absence of preconditions for competition to occur.

As we have already documented, a major market failure is the absence of incentives to develop some drugs that potentially have important social benefits, but that are not currently being developed, in large part because pharmaceutical manufacturers lack an adequate incentive to engage in R&D to develop such socially beneficial products. Several types of vaccines are a case in point. Clearly the patent system has proven to be inadequate in providing a sufficient incentive. Perhaps other incentive plans can either replace or supplement existing incentives to correct this market failure.

The topic of marketing and market competition drills down further into topics raised in the first part of the book. As indicated above, branded drugs (both innovative and "me-too" products) and generics compete in the pharmaceuticals market. Policies that promote generics may be good for cost containment but not so good for product innovation. We have also emphasized the important role of information provision as a precondition for efficiency, both in the short and long terms. Yet some information efforts aimed directly at consumers or at physicians may not promote optimal use of resources. To the extent that prescribing patterns are adversely affected, there will be an impact of the types of pharmaceutical innovation that occur in the longer run.

More generally, any public policy that affects use of pharmaceutical products in the short run should affect innovation in the longer run. As discussed above, countries differ in their relative emphasis on cost containment by the public sector versus reliance on market forces to achieve socially desirable outcomes. A method for achieving cost containment and static efficiency in some countries has been public evaluation of the costs and benefits of new technologies.

Chapter Overview

Part I

In part one of this book, two chapters address the overall structure of the pharmaceutical industry from two different perspectives: (1) a broad overview of the role of pharmaceutical industry in the economy and in the health sector, and (2) a narrower but more in-depth review of the research and development for new drugs. In Chapter 2, Uwe Reinhardt begins with a review of the various protections governments extend to the pharmaceutical industry. He then focuses on the industry's cost structure and the corresponding pricing strategies that this industry adopts in domestic markets as well as internationally. He concludes that performance of markets for pharmaceutical products worldwide is less than well balanced currently. Therefore, he discusses two approaches that if adopted simultaneously could introduce a better balance of power into the market for pharmaceutical products. The first is to increase the share of cost paid by patients for prescription drugs so that the demand side, either patients or their physicians, could act as more cost-conscious purchasers. The second approach is to establish an information infrastructure to provide potential users of prescription drugs with objective, science-based information on the prices and relative cost effectiveness of rival products being offered in the pharmaceutical market. Another major contribution of this chapter is Professor Reinhardt's discussion of price discrimination and how it applies to pricing of pharmaceutical products globally.

The way in which prescription drug R&D is organized and carried out has changed over the past few decades. In Chapter 3 William Comanor first describes how the structure of discovering and developing new drugs has changed since the mid-1980s. Historically, much R&D was conducted by large vertically integrated companies. More recently, the larger companies have not been as actively engaged in such research, but have increasingly funded research conducted by others, often smaller companies. Thus, rather than being concentrated in a few large firms, the new structure has involved an increasing degree of disintegration in the research and development process for new drugs. After describing these important changes, he considers the costs and benefits of the new structure in terms of economies of scope and scale. Scale economies would occur if efficiencies can be realized when R&D is conducted on a larger scale. Economies of scope would be realized if conducting R&D on a drug in one therapeutic class increases the efficiency of conducting R&D on a drug in another therapeutic class. For example, are firms that conduct research on a new antidepressant more efficient in conducting research on a new drug to control high cholesterol? More generally, he also explores the implications of current trends for the efficiency of the drug development process.

Part II

In the second part of the book, we include four chapters to address issues arising from the market failure in allocating R&D resources in the pharmaceutical industry. Chapters 4 and 5 deal with market failures for finding new drugs for the developing world in general as well as potential solutions for these failures. Chapters 6 and 7 focus on vaccines in particular.

In Chapter 4 Aidan Hollis examines three proposals in considerable detail. The first is an Advanced Purchase Commitment by sponsors, who offer an explicit subsidy in advance for innovative products. The subsidy offer includes a fixed-dollar amount per unit as well as a commitment to purchase a specific number of units at that price. The second proposal is that sponsors pay annual rewards based on the therapeutic effectiveness of innovative drugs. The third approach is to offer a patent extension on patented products to pharmaceutical companies if they successfully developed a vaccine for a disease such as HIV/AIDS that is highly prevalent, particularly in some low-income countries. Hollis concludes that the third approach is an extremely inefficient way to reward innovation. By contrast, the second approach could correct the market failure directly by rewarding innovative drugs according to their therapeutic effectiveness, which is measurable by cost-effectiveness analysis, a topic discussed later in greater detail in Chapters 10 and 11.

In Chapter 5 Stephen Maurer compares two approaches that could correct market failure by providing incentives to discovering and developing new drugs for diseases that prevail mainly in developing countries. The first approach he terms an "end-to-end" strategy: government or nongovernmental organizations in high-income countries (sponsors) offer a single reward for researchers who successfully complete the entire drug discovery pipeline. The second approach he terms a "pay-as-you-go" strategy: sponsors offer smaller but more frequent rewards at multiple stages along the drug discovery pipeline. After comparing the strengths and weaknesses of each approach, he further discusses the potential of a mixed strategy that combines the above-mentioned approaches toward the effectiveness of drug discovery in the developing world.

Vaccines are among the most socially valuable public health investments, yet structural and financial problems have resulted in recurring vaccine shortages in recent years. *Financing Vaccines in the 21st Century: Assuring Access and Availability*, the final report of the Institute of Medicine's Committee on the Evaluation of Vaccine Purchase Financing in the United States, was issued in August 2003 (Institute of Medicine 2004). The committee proposed a substantial redesign of the current system for purchasing and distributing vaccines and recommended its replacement by a vaccine *mandate, subsidy*, and *voucher* system.

In Chapter 6 Frank Sloan and Charles Eesley examine details of implementation not discussed in the report. In addition, some of the criticisms of the stakeholders as expressed to the National Vaccine Advisory Committee of the U.S. Centers for Disease Control are assessed. The focus of their chapter is primarily on details of the mechanism for setting the subsidy, and evaluation of the advantages and disadvantages of some alternative proposals. A number of complexities are considered in implementing a public subsidy along with a requirement that private and public insurers cover specific vaccines, as well as vouchers that promote both innovation and widespread use of vaccines.

In Chapter 7 Frank Lichtenberg compares two ways that can help to cope with the many shortages of vaccines that have occurred in recent years. First, the government can become a developer and producer of vaccines, as contemplated in the U.S. National Vaccine Authority Act. The second is to allow vaccine prices to adjust to market-clearing levels. He argues that the second approach – reducing disincentives, and enhancing incentives, for private vaccine development and production – is likely to be far more effective than initiating government vaccine development and production. In the end, this is a contentious issue about which experts from various countries will undoubtedly disagree. While markets promote efficiency in R&D and public producers may lack the incentive to develop and produce vaccines efficiently, the market size of some countries is likely to be too small to sustain a private vaccine production, especially when coupled with the goal that the producer also be innovative. Such small countries run the risk of being cut off from essential vaccine supplies during times of shortages and particularly in the case of pandemics. For such countries, public production of vaccines may be the desirable, albeit second-best, alternative.

Part III

The third part includes two chapters to address the issues of competition and marketing in the pharmaceutical market. In Chapter 8 Henry Grabowski examines determinants and characteristics of generic competition in the U.S. market. The U.S. generic drug industry has grown rapidly over the past two decades. The more generic entrants and more intense the degree of price competition, the more rapid the erosion in the brand product market share in units to the generic firms as well as the returns to R&D in brand products. Furthermore, outside the United States, generic competition has had a substantial effect on prices in countries that encourage generics through reference pricing, such as Germany, and in countries, such as the United Kingdom, that encourage physicians to prescribe generic products. A key driver of the growth of generics in the United States has been the 1984 Hatch-Waxman Act, which reduced the costs and times for generic entry, and the rise of managed care formularies, which strongly encourage generic drug utilization. Grabowski also analyses how both brand firms and generic drug firms have responded strategically to provisions in the law. Thereafter, he considers policy changes that could remedy some of the unintended consequences of the Act.

In Chapter 9 Ernst Berndt provides a comprehensive analysis of the determinants and impact of direct-to-consumer advertising (DTCA) of prescription drugs, which has become a new marketing strategy adopted by pharmaceutical firms in the United States and New Zealand and has raised various debates and controversies in recent years. Based on a detailed review of the existing literature, he concludes that although DTCA has grown rapidly in the United States, it is a relatively modest component of total prescription drug promotion spending, 13–15% between 2000 and 2003, and a much smaller proportion of sales, 2%. DTCA is relatively targeted to conditions where one would expect the elasticity of sales with respect to marketing efforts to be substantial. Generally, the evidence to date suggests that when DTCA has an impact, it is primarily on overall sales at the level of a therapeutic class rather than on individual brand market shares within a class. Furthermore, there is evidence that DTCA simultaneously mitigates underdiagnosis and undertreatment of depressive disorders, but also encourages ambiguous utilization for patients with marginal illness severity; there is limited evidence that DTCA is associated with greater patient adherence to recommended treatment.

Part IV

The last part includes four chapters that describe methods of public evaluation of the benefits and costs of pharmaceutical innovation as well as empirical evidence on the effects of the evaluation process. In Chapter 10 Mark Pauly criticizes many studies of cost-effectiveness analysis on pharmaceuticals that use an incorrect measure of cost, which when followed would lead to inefficient resource allocation decisions, distort the mix of funds for research, and reduce population health below what it would be if a more conceptually appropriate approach were followed. More specifically, he points out that cost-effectiveness analysis affects not only expenditures and use of existing products but also innovation for new products. He suggests health care decision makers pay attention to the effect of current reimbursement policies on the development of new drugs by conducting a cost-effectiveness analysis from a societal perspective. He examines 28 recent studies of cost-effectiveness analysis and finds none of them using marginal cost as a cost measure. Most studies measure cost by using average wholesale price or market price. This practice leads to a value for the cost of a drug substantially in excess of marginal cost. He then discusses a general approach for correct measurement of costs and summarizes that a theoretically correct measurement of cost depends on various factors, including regulation, administrated pricing by public insurers on a budget, patent protection, whether the R&D and production of drugs is domestic or foreign, and whether the welfare perspective is limited to own-country or global. A general conclusion from his analysis is that removing profit from the costing of a drug is an important step toward the conceptually appropriate measurement of cost. A practical approach to this conclusion is to measure cost by average wholesale price minus above-normal profits. Under this approach, more products will be judged to be cost effective than if the average wholesale price had been used.

In Chapter 11 Michael Drummond reviews the international experience with using economic evaluation in health policy decisions. He argues that the formal use of economic evaluation in making reimbursement decisions has proved workable. However, those jurisdictions considering adopting this policy should consider carefully the methodological and practical problems that tend to arise. The main methodological issues concern the synthesis of comparisons between treatments where head-to-head clinical trials do not exist, extrapolation of costs and benefits beyond the duration of clinical trials, and the incorporation of equity considerations. The main practical issues concern the prioritization of technologies for assessment and adapting data from other countries for use in one's own setting. The reimbursement decisions made, or the national guidance issued, in jurisdictions using economic evaluation do embody a cost-effectiveness logic, but other factors, such as equity and affordability, clearly come into play. There is also considerable speculation and debate about whether particular jurisdictions employ a societal willingness-to-pay threshold, above which technologies will not be funded. Finally, he offers some advice for countries contemplating the formal use of economic evaluation.

In Chapter 12 Pierre-Yves Cremieux and his coauthors review the current state of the literature on the value of pharmaceuticals and calculate the value of pharmaceutical spending in Canada. Although studies on quantifying the relationship between pharmaceutical innovation and health outcomes are subject to many difficult challenges, including many other determinants of health outcomes, heterogeneity in data, and methodological limitation, their review indicates that an increase in spending on pharmaceuticals in general would result in substantial increases in life expectancy. Following a review of the literature, Cremieux and his colleagues further calculate the rate of return on pharmaceutical spending in Canada. By applying the method developed by Murphy and Topel (2005) and the empirical results of their earlier study (Cremieux et al. 2005), they find that the gains attributed to pharmaceutical spending generate nearly 59% of the value of total life expectancy gains realized over the period 1981–1998. This result indicates that gains from incremental pharmaceutical spending in Canada would outweigh expenditure by nearly 20 to 1.

In Chapter 13 Chee-Ruey Hsieh and his coauthors study the effect of new drugs on health outcomes. Specifically, they test the hypothesis that diseases associated with larger stocks of innovation in pharmaceutical treatment have better health outcomes than diseases associated with less pharmaceutical innovation. To test this hypothesis, they construct a disease-specific panel database obtained from Taiwan over the period 1985–2002 by using the correspondence of the classification systems between drugs and diseases. They use cumulative number of new molecular entities approved and launched in Taiwan as the measure of pharmaceutical innovation and longevity as the measure of health outcomes. They find that adoption of new drugs has a significantly positive effect on longevity. Their most conservative estimates suggest that a 10% increase in cumulative number of new molecular entities is associated with an increase in life expectancy at birth of approximately 0.1%.

Summing Up

Chapter 14 by Frank A. Sloan and Chee-Ruey Hsieh draws on major findings of the book and discusses the most important implications for countries that seek to promote and cope with the problems of pharmaceutical innovation. They distinguish between what is known and what is not known about pharmaceutical innovation and chart a course for future economic research on this important topic.

PART ONE

THE INDUSTRY STRUCTURE OF PHARMACEUTICAL INNOVATION

TWO

The Pharmaceutical Sector in Health Care

Uwe E. Reinhardt

I. Introduction

In 2004 total global pharmaceutical sales were reported to have been about $550 billion in U.S.-dollar equivalents (IMS Intelligence 2005), only a tiny fraction of total global gross national product (GNP) of about $35 trillion (FinFacts 2005).

Sales reported for 2004 in the United States, which spends more per capita and absolutely on pharmaceuticals than does any other country, amounted to only $200 billion, which is about 1.7% of U.S. gross domestic product (GDP in that year, or 11.1% of total U.S. health spending; Heffler et al. 2005). Assuming that drug manufacturers received about 75% of total retail sales and that their net after-tax profit margin was 16% on sales (*Fortune* 2005), their after-tax profits of about $24 billion in 2004 amounted to only 0.20% of U.S. GDP in that year, and about 1.3% of total U.S. national health spending.

These statistics, which portray the pharmaceutical industry as only a minor player in health care and an almost trivial player in the economy as a whole, belie the importance of the industry in terms of value added and in terms of the heated policy debate it triggers all around the globe.

The value that pharmaceutical research and products add to human existence can be appreciated by anyone who has used pharmaceutical products to reduce pain, eliminate potentially lethal infections, or control high blood pressure or cholesterol, not even to speak of other popular life-style drugs. That value has been more formally explored in a recent compendium of essays written by highly distinguished economists (Murphy and Topel 2003b). Addressing the question "Are we getting our money's worth?" from health spending in general and medical research, including pharmaceutical research in particular, the consensus among the authors was "From an economic perspective, the answer is a resounding 'yes': in fact, considering the extraordinary value of improvements in health, we may even be spending too little on medical research. . . . The average new drug approved by the FDA yields benefits worth many times its cost of development" (p. 2).

As the world looks anxiously at the possible impact of the bird flu virus on humans, that passage has added import: anxious policy makers do not look to surgeons or hospitals to solve this problem, but to the pharmaceutical industry.

Remarkably, while the pharmaceutical industry undoubtedly is one of the highest value-added industries in modern economies, that industry is not generally the focus of gratitude or affection. On the contrary, almost everywhere on the globe the industry is viewed with suspicion and often is the butt of vocal criticism and rancor. Relative to its size, it attracts a disproportionate share of attention from public policy makers and critical illumination from the media.

What can explain this seeming paradox – the evidently high value the industry adds to human life and the sharp criticism of which it so often is the focus?

Part of the apparent paradox stems from the industry's awkward position on the spectrum from publicly owned enterprise and pure private, investor-owned, and profit-driven enterprise. On the one hand, the pharmaceutical companies are structured as profit-seeking enterprises. Unlike many other profit-seeking industries, however, the research-based pharmaceutical industry cannot survive without government protection.

Another source of friction is the industry's widespread practice of price discrimination wherever government does not outlaw it outright. Price discrimination is a two-edged sword. On the one hand, it allows the industry to extract more revenue from society than a single-price policy would. On the other hand, however, it allows customers to be served who would be priced out of a single-priced market.

Yet other friction arises over the clash of national regulatory policies on drug pricing, on the one hand, and international attempts to place global trade more on free-market principles, on the other. This issue touches on the question of how the cost of pharmaceutical research and development (R&D) should be shared by nations. This debate has led in recent years to unwelcome attempts by the United States to engineer changes in the health systems of other countries through trade negotiations.

This chapter explores some of these issues in greater depth, at a general level that cuts across individual nations. It begins with a review of the various protections government extends to the industry. Next, the focus is on the industry's cost structure and the controversial pricing practices that structure begets. Thereafter follows an exploration of what it would take to introduce a more economically efficient, evenly distributed balance of power into the market for pharmaceutical products.

II. Government Protection of the Pharmaceutical Industry

Every research-based pharmaceutical company has two major product lines: (1) scientific knowledge and (2) pills and other pharmaceutical products. Both thrive on protection by government and could not survive long without it.

Intellectual Property Rights

The research findings produced by the pharmaceutical industry are inherently in the nature of a *public good,* because a public good exhibits two distinct characteristics. First, its consumption by one person does not detract from another's consumption of that same good. Clean air is a classic example, as is national security or scientific knowledge, such as a basic theorem. Economists call this characteristic "nonrival," in the sense that there need not be rivalry over the use of the public good. Second, unless government explicitly excludes potential users of the good from using it, for example, through patent laws, it is technically impossible to exclude would-be-users from using it. Economists call this property "nonexclusivity."

Ideally, according to economic theory, the production of goods that are nonrival and nonexclusive should be *collectively* financed through government, so that thereafter the government owns the rights to the public good and then can make it freely available to potential users. Basic scientific knowledge clearly falls into this class of goods. That approach will then lead to an *efficient* use of the public good, in the sense that no one willing to pay the incremental cost of using it is excluded from it. In the case of scientific knowledge, that incremental cost is zero.

Much, though not all, of the scientific knowledge produced around the globe has traditionally been handled in this fashion. One thinks here of the scientific research performed by government research facilities or of academic research funded either by government or by private donors who wish the product of that research to be shared, free of charges as widely as possible, on a global basis. One occasionally sees proposals to apply this approach also to pharmaceutical research. Various models could be used to that end.

For example, government could fund and conduct pharmaceutical R&D to the stage at which a product is ready for the market and then allow competing manufacturers to produce and market the products. Alternatively, government could contract with investor-owned research facilities to produce specified, targeted pharmaceutical R&D, just as it now does for military R&D, take ownership of successful R&D, and then make it freely available to competing manufacturers. Finally, government could simply stand ready to purchase from private R&D enterprises the property rights to successfully completed R&D and then make it available freely to competing manufacturers, leaving the private research facilities to decide what avenue of research to pursue.

One should expect these and similar proposals to emerge around the globe in the decades ahead, although it is not clear how easily they could be sold to public policy makers and to private industry. In the meantime, governments probably will continue to rely for pharmaceutical R&D on privately produced intellectual property whose right to private ownership will then be protected through patents. That approach by now has a proven track record of over a century, although it inevitably will remain an unending source of controversy, as the pharmaceutical industry and governments wrestle over the proper length of patent protection and over the disposition of intellectual property rights upon the expiration of patents, with a critical media reporting on the fight.

The central point to note, however, is that without patent protection the pharmaceutical industry as we know it could not long survive, because imitators could always quickly destroy its economic base. It would, of course, deprive the world of the highly valuable contribution that the research-based pharmaceutical industry makes to human well-being.

Protection of Quality

One could imagine a world in which pharmaceutical companies could develop, produce, and market their products without any government supervision whatsoever. If a particular product turned out to be unsafe in use, the market would quickly discover it and punish the producers economically. The coup de grace would be given by litigation that would punish the company's owners further. Some libertarian thinkers might imagine that such an arrangement would work. In a compendium, "Policy Medicine versus Policy Quackery: Economists against the FDA," for example, Daniel B. Klein (2005) quotes the libertarian Nobel laureate economist Milton Friedman as follows: "The FDA has already done enormous harm to the health of the

American public by greatly increasing the costs of pharmaceutical research, thereby reducing the supply of new and effective drugs, and by delaying the approval of such drugs as survive the tortuous FDA process." When asked "If you could do anything to improve health in America, what would you do?" Klein quotes Friedman as replying: "No more licensing of doctors. No more regulation of drugs. Not of any kind. Period."

In practice, no country follows that libertarian approach. Apparently reliance on private market forces and litigation as adequate safeguards in pharmaceutical therapy is viewed as much too risky. First, the protection of limited liability granted the owners of publicly traded companies severely limits the recourse injured parties would have to the personal wealth of the owners of pharmaceutical companies. The now universal principle of limited liability allows the owners of an enterprise to escape most of the financial consequences of even truly grievous mischief that a company may have visited on behalf of these owners on the rest of society, including grievous environmental hazard. Many corporate executives may not be aware that this protection actually is one of the earliest forms of social insurance. Second, no country is willing to countenance the human casualties that this approach to product safety would have. Although, using a human capital approach, economists probably could justify these casualties in many instances by the added lives saved, the general public and the politicians who represent them undoubtedly would not find the economists' collectivist calculus persuasive.[1]

It may well be that the public authorities who do attempt to safeguard the quality of pharmaceutical therapy in each country, for example, the U.S. Food and Drug Administration (FDA) in the United States, typically may be more averse to risk, and hence more restrictive, than would be the majority of the patients being protected. Even so, on balance, both the general public and the pharmaceutical industry probable benefit greatly from the existence of these public authorities. Pharmaceutical companies benefit from having a powerful external stimulus for internal quality control. Furthermore, approval of a product by the authorities can serve as a helpful, if not decisive, shield in litigation over product safety. Few pharmaceutical companies around the globe would be likely to prefer a world without such public supervision.

A question that arises in an international context is whether the quality and safety standards one nation imposes on products sold within its own borders necessarily should be binding upon products sold from pharmaceutical companies within its own borders to other nations. One could imagine, for example, that citizens in high-income country A (e.g., the United States or Taiwan) may be far more intolerant of side effects and be willing to pay a far higher price to eliminate them than might be citizens in poorer country B (e.g., a much poorer country in Latin America or Southeast Asia) who might be willing to countenance greater risk for the benefits expected from a drug at a lower cost. This issue is not much discussed in the literature, but is one worthy of debate. From the perspective of public image, of course, many pharmaceutical companies in risk-averse, high-income countries might be reluctant to observe different safety standards for lower-income countries.

Restrictions on the Resale of Pharmaceutical Products

Governments may prohibit the resale of pharmaceutical products between buyers for two reasons. First, and most frequently mentioned, is safety. If any buyer of a pharmaceutical product could resell it to anyone else, government would effectively lose its ability to assure citizens of the safety of drug therapy, and potentially dangerous counterfeit drugs would abound. Second, permitting unfettered reselling of pharmaceutical products between buyers inevitably would drive each product to a single price worldwide. As will be argued later under the rubric of "price discrimination," neither the pharmaceutical industry nor public policy makers should naturally aspire to a single-price policy for such products.

Ostensibly for the first reason, but also for the second, the open resale of pharmaceutical products between buyers is generally not permitted in countries with the ability effectively to prohibit such sales. Although mainly intended to protect the general public, it protects as well the revenues of pharmaceutical companies.

Quasi-Public, Quasi-Private Enterprises

Most pharmaceutical company executives probably view their enterprises as classic manifestations of free enterprise, in which private investors take enormous financial risks purely for the sake of private gain, but doing much good for humankind in the process. The reality is rather different. As the preceding discussion suggests, however, the industry is best thought of as a fragile little bird, sitting in the hand of government, which protects it from all manner of the market's dangerous economic buffeting, and, in return for that protection, is required from time to time to chirp songs that it would rather not sing. By the very nature of the protection granted the industry, it inevitably becomes the focus of the government's health and science policies. Pharmaceutical executives who understand this requirement usually know how to manage it well. Those who do not risk running afoul of both government and the general public.

As to the financial risk taken on by investors in publicly traded pharmaceutical companies, these are no larger than the risk one assumes in investing in a broad stock-market index, such as the Standard & Poor's 500 index, which reflects the risk and returns for some 500 publicly traded companies (Myers 1999), a point revisited below in the section on the economics of the industry.

III. The Industry's Cost Structure

The development of new pharmaceutical products, from basic research to approval for marketing, is a complex process everywhere and can span a decade or more. According to Pharmaceutical Research and Manufacturers of America, for example, "only one of every 10,000 potential compounds investigated by America's research-based pharmaceutical companies makes it through the research and development pipeline and is approved for patient use by the United States Food and Drug Administration," and "winning approval, on average, takes 15 years and research and development costs over $800 million dollars" (2005, p. 1; see also Dickson and Gagnon 2004).

Estimating the R&D Costs of Successful Products

Given the length and complexity of the R&D process, estimating the total R&D cost of a successful pharmaceutical product is a daunting methodological challenge that, therefore, has remained a source of controversy, even among economists.

For one, there is the question of what costs to impute to a particular, successful product. A research-based pharmaceutical company can be likened to an oil company that roams the world in search of oil deposits. Such a company will drill many holes that ultimately fail to yield oil. The cost of these dry holes then must be recouped from successful wells. Therefore, the costs of dry holes are routinely allocated to the cost of successful wells. It is so also with pharmaceutical companies. To the total R&D cost incurred directly for successful new products must be added the R&D costs of products that had to be abandoned somewhere along the lengthy R&D process. Making that cost imputation properly presents the first methodological challenge in estimating the R&D costs of new drugs.

A second methodological problem is how to convert monetary outlays for R&D that are made over the span of an entire decade or more into a single amount that is properly adjusted for both inflation and the time value of money. Even after adjustment for inflation, which is straightforward, $1 million spent today represents much more value than $1 million to be spent only a decade hence, because much less than $1 million would have to be invested now to have in hand $1 million a decade hence.

Monetary outlays spaced over time therefore are converted into one number with identical time value, either as of the beginning of the time-phased cash flow, the so-called *present* value of the cash flow, or at its end, the so-called *terminal* value of the cash flow. The conversion into present or terminal values is made with an interest rate that reflects the pharmaceutical firm's weighted average annual cost of debt and equity capital, the weights being the relative fractions of debt and equity used to raise outside financing. The interest rates used for that purpose reflect the outside investors' opportunity cost of investing their money in the firm rather than in some riskless asset, for example, a long-term government bond, plus a risk premium to compensate investors for the risk they assume by investing with this particular firm.

The fact that a given time-phased cash flow can be concerted either into its present or terminal value can easily confuse persons not familiar with economics or finance. To illustrate with a stylized example, suppose that the relevant R&D outlays for a product represent an even money flow of, say, $50 million a year for 10 years. If the firm's weighted average cost of financing were, say, 10% per year, then this cash flow would have a present value of $307 million as of the beginning of that money flow and a terminal value of $797 million at its end point, presumably when the product is about to launch in the market. At a weighted average cost of financing of, say, 8%, the two values would be $335 million and $724 million, respectively. At a weighted cost of financing of 15%, they would be $251 million and $1,015 million, respectively. Yet all of these different figures represent an identical cash flow.

One can think of the present value of the R&D stream as the sum of money the firm would have to have on deposit to finance the 10-year stream of R&D spending of $50 million a year, if the balance in the account could earn the firm's weighted average cost of financing per year. Alternatively, the terminal value would represent the total amount of money the firm has invested in the R&D project on behalf of shareholders to the date of launch, including accumulated interest equal to the firm's weighted cost of financing, the return the firm presumably could have earned on alternative projects. Which of these numbers is the most appropriate depends on the use to which it is put. For practical purposes, the terminal value probably is the more intuitively appealing, because at the time of the launch of a new pharmaceutical product, it is the amount that the present value of all future sales revenues from the product, minus production, marketing, and other future annual costs associated with the sale of the product, the firm must cover.

It was worth going into this methodological detail on the estimation of R&D costs because public estimates of those costs tend to be so controversial. DiMasi, Hansen, and Grabowski (2003) recently estimated the cost for U.S. pharmaceutical firms at between $800 million and $900 million. These estimates were promptly attacked as exaggerated by Light and Warburton (2005) in the same journal. Such arguments could arise over any or all of the following issues: (1) the estimates of the actual R&D outlays that should be properly attributed to a successful product, (2) the interest rate used to calculate the present or terminal value of that cash flow, and (3) whether, for policy purposes, the present or terminal value of that cash flow is the more appropriate figure. In the end, the only approach to settling such disputes would be to make the raw data used in making such estimates available to any researcher who would like to audit the calculations (Reinhardt 1997).

However those issues are settled, there can be no doubt that the up-front R&D costs incurred to launch a new pharmaceutical product is in the hundreds of millions of dollars, not only in the United States, but elsewhere as well.

The Risk of Investing in Pharmaceutical R&D

Because the R&D process leading to new pharmaceutical products is so long and may have to be abandoned at any time, investments in R&D may appear to be highly risky from a financial perspective. It is not so. Any sizeable research-based pharmaceutical firm invests simultaneously in many diverse R&D processes, many addressed to different illnesses, afflicting different parts of the human body. Many of these processes will fail to yield fruit; others will be successful to varying degrees. In a sense, then, a large pharmaceutical firm is not much different from a large mutual fund, except that the latter invests purely in diverse financial securities whereas a pharmaceutical company invests in the R&D for a diverse portfolio of new pharmaceutical products. From the viewpoint of an investor in the stock of a pharmaceutical company, the risk inherent in the overall flow of returns earned by a pharmaceutical company on its entire portfolio of R&D investments is not substantially different from the risk of an investment in a well-diversified mutual fund. That insight emerges from standard economic portfolio theory, but also from empirical research.

For example, Stewart Myers (1999) presented estimates of the financial risk and the associated weighted average cost of capital of large pharmaceutical firms. He found that the risk index of such firms, measured by the so-called beta coefficient, was close to the risk index of a broad market index, such as the Standard & Poor's 500, namely 1. The number suggests that, if the rate of return on the general market index rises or falls by, say, 10%, the rate of return of a large pharmaceutical company tends to rise or fall by about the same percentage. This risk index implies a corresponding weighted average cost of financing that is not purged of inflation of about 14% and an inflation-purged figure of about 10%. These are the interest rates one would use to convert time-phased R&D streams into their present or terminal values.

By contrast, Stewart estimated the beta coefficients for smaller biotech companies, organized around one or a few products, as anywhere from 1.5 to 2.3, suggesting that when the rate of return on the general market index changes up or down by 10%, the rate of return on biotech stocks tends to swing by between 15% and 23% up or down, which means that the stock certificates issued by biotech companies are much riskier from the perspective of investors and the associated weighted average costs of capital much higher.

Cost Structure and Pricing

Economists distinguish between annual *fixed* and *variable* costs. Fixed costs are those that do not vary with the volume of production and sales. Variable costs vary more or less directly with output volume. For purposes of analysis, it is convenient and generally realistic to assume that the variable costs per unit are constant over the empirically relevant range of output. What is a variable and a fixed cost, however, varies with the time frame. In the very short run, for example, a month or quarter, most costs are fixed. Over a year or more, costs that are fixed in the very short run become variable.

A distinguishing characteristic of the pharmaceutical industry is that its annual fixed costs (including an annual allocation of the cost of R&D) tend to be high relative to its variable costs in the sense that the variable or *incremental* cost of producing and packaging an additional batch of product tends to be quite small relative to the fully allocated average unit cost per unit of output, including the allocation of fixed costs.

A consequence of such a cost structure is that, in the short run, it will be profitable for the firm to sell output at prices that cover the lower *incremental* costs and yield some margin above those costs, but fall far short of *total average unit costs* (fixed and variable costs per unit of output). That shortfall may be acceptable if not all output is sold at such low prices, but only some batches, leaving higher-priced batches to help recover all fixed costs – in other words, if the firm can *price discriminate.* A controversial question is whether such price discrimination is in society's interest or whether it should be interdicted by public policy makers. That question is explored in the next section.

IV. Price Discrimination in the Market for Pharmaceuticals

Price discrimination refers to the practice of selling identical products to different sets of customers at different prices. Expressed another way, different customers pay different markups over the identical incremental cost of producing an identical product. Price discrimination is widely practiced in the hotel and airline industries, by universities in the United States that can vary their tuition through scholarships, by electric power companies, and in the health care industry. Hospitals in the United States, for example, routinely charge different payers different prices for the same services. In the U.S. pharmaceutical market, different prices are charged to different insurance carriers and to self-paying patients. Worldwide, the same pharmaceutical firms sell the identical product to different countries at different prices.

Industries that engage in price discrimination have three common features. First, their incremental production costs at any moment in time are low relative to fixed costs, which means that, in the short run, a price-discriminating firm with ample capacity can earn a positive contribution margin to overhead and profits by selling product at prices below fully allocated costs (fixed and incremental costs per unit), as long as price exceeds incremental costs. Low incremental costs can imply very low prices for some customers. Second, the practice of price discrimination presupposes that customers can be segregated into distinct groups, each with a different price sensitivity or degree of bargaining power. Third, for either technical or legal reasons, customers cannot resell purchased products to one another.

The Potential Benefits of Price Discrimination

Suppose a pharmaceutical firm had been granted a patent for a new product and, thus, enjoyed a degree of monopolistic power in its product market. Suppose that initially the firm were free to set the price of the product so as to maximize its profits, but had to charge all customers the same price. This arrangement would price out many customers willing to pay prices in excess of the incremental cost of producing the product but not a price as high as the single, profit-maximizing price. These customers would benefit if they could buy the product at a lower price, and the pharmaceutical company would gladly do so as long as that lower price exceeded its incremental production cost and did not oblige it to lower its price to customers willing to pay the higher, profit-maximizing price. This two-price policy would be a classic example of price discrimination. It would yield added profits to the manufacturer, but it would also benefit additional customers.

The two-part pricing strategy could be extended to a multiple-price strategy by selling successive batches of output at successively lower prices, as long as those prices exceeded incremental costs and as long as customers receiving the product at a lower price could not resell it to customers willing and able to pay a higher price. Each additional batch would enhance the firm's profits, but it would also benefit yet another group of customers.

At the limit, there might be one batch of output sold at a price equal to incremental cost. While the firm would not profit from selling that batch, it would serve customers (e.g., in a very low-income country) willing to pay only that very low price. The firm might willingly do so, especially if this enhanced its reputation as a good world citizen. Economists would call this outcome "efficient" in the sense that no customer willing to pay a price equal to at least the incremental cost of producing the product would be left unserved by the pharmaceutical firm.

The preceding analysis can be modified to include as a starting point not a profit-maximizing single price, but a single price constrained by government to a level that merely allows the pharmaceutical producer a regulated rate of return, as is the case, for example, in the United Kingdom. Given the cost structure described earlier, such a rate-of-return-regulated single price, still would be likely to price out certain customers, especially those in lower-income countries, who would be willing to pay prices greater than or equal to incremental costs, but not the higher regulated single price.

Why Price Discrimination Might Be Criticized

The previous exposition, of course, has been carefully styled to lead to what appears to be a benign policy. It accepts as the baseline a single price determined either under profit maximization or under price controls, and then asks whether, relative to that baseline single price, allowing price discrimination would be in society's interest.

It should be clear to anyone, however, that a pharmaceutical manufacturer could extend backwards as well, that is, that the firm could earn even higher profits by segregating the first set of customers charged the highest price into distinct smaller groups with different degrees of price tolerance and all but one of them paying prices higher than the baseline single price assumed above. At the limit, at least in theory, the firm could so segregate its customers that every one of them pays the maximum bid price that the customer would have been willing to pay for the product. The firm then would have extracted from its customers the maximum amount of money that could have been extracted from them, which is apt to elicit criticism from the general public and policy makers alike. However, every customer willing to bid a price at least equal to the incremental cost of producing the product would be served, which would make the strategy efficient in that sense.

V. Price Discrimination in the International Market

In most modern economies, large fractions of the sales of pharmaceuticals are covered by public or private third-party payers, rather than patients themselves. These third-party payers act as bulk buyers. If those bulk buyers represent entire countries that can set prices through government price controls, the market muscle can be enormous. Only buyers with little or no market power, either small insurance carriers or uninsured patients paying fully out of pocket, can successfully be charged the highest retail prices for a given product. It is the situation, for example, that obtains in the United States today. There, millions of low-income Americans are without any health insurance and, therefore, without any market power at all in the market for prescription drugs, routinely paying far higher prices than do patients in relatively wealthy countries with more market power exercised through government price controls.

Few citizens of high-price countries complain when pharmaceutical products are sold to very low-income countries at prices approximating incremental production costs, as is now widely done. But citizens in high-price countries, especially the United States, which has the highest prices for pharmaceutical products, regard it as unfair that citizens in other economically developed, relatively high-income countries can purchase the identical drug at much lower prices, especially for drugs that were developed in the high-price country (e.g., in the United States).

The research-based pharmaceutical industry, although having practiced this form of price discrimination for decades, resents this practice when it is effectively imposed on the industry through price controls by foreign governments. First, the industry fears that, with the help of clever entrepreneurs and sometimes even local government officials, such as state governors in the United States, citizens in the high-price countries will be able to reimport pharmaceutical products from lower-price countries and, thus, drive the world toward a single price substantially dictated by foreign governments practicing price controls. Second, the industry fears what it calls "external reference pricing," that is, the practice by some foreign governments of tying the prices they allow to the lowest price paid by any other country. Third, the industry argues that, absent these price controls abroad, its members could earn higher revenues even if freer-market regimes abroad would continue to entail some degree of differential pricing for the same product. Implied in that argument is the tacit suggestion that most of any added revenues from the removal of foreign price controls would flow into added R&D. Finally, the industry typically suggests that the removal of price controls in low-price countries would enable it to lower prices in the high-price countries, although it is not clear what market mechanism would bring about that effect.

Unconvincing Critics of Cross-National Price Discrimination

Media pundits, think tanks, and consultants who are ideologically sympathetic to the pharmaceutical industry, or are economically beholden to it, have echoed and amplified the pharmaceutical industry's concerns over cross-national price discrimination in sometimes hysterical tones. It may be well to review briefly the merits and demerits of these critics' sometimes vehement arguments, because their voices often are highly influential in government circles.

In a commentary posted on the Web site *USANext,* for example, Steve Forbes (2005), owner and publisher of the internationally known magazine *Forbes,* former presidential candidate in the United States, and a friend of many foreign heads of states, accuses Europe, Canada, and Japan of "mooching" off the U.S. pharmaceutical industry, which he considers nothing less than a "costly form of piracy." Why he includes Japan as a "moocher" is not clear. After all, that country is known among the experts to pay prices closer to American levels and sometimes even higher (Danzon and Furukawa 2003).

James K. Glassman (2005), a highly popular media pundit in some circles, including government, has sternly lectured European and Canadian policy makers thus on his own Web site *Tech Central Station.* He writes that "price controls kill. . . . Europe kills its citizens and makes them sicker because it restricts access to drugs it considers too expensive. . . . Europeans, Australians and Canadians are doing something immoral."

Glassman cited a study of drug price controls by the consulting firm Bain & Company (2005). In that study Bain also focused on the effects drug price controls have for the countries imposing them. The authors estimated that if Europe's pharmaceutical spending per capita had matched the level of the United States, Europe would have spent an additional $160 billion in 2002 and $840 billion cumulative over the preceding decade. Using Germany as an illustration, they argued that Germany saved $19 billion from price controls in 2002, but this policy imposed $22 billion of added costs on Germany in the form of foregone benefits. Only about $5 billion of that alleged cost, however, consisted of costs attributable to better outcomes for patients. The rest was money that would have been spent on added inputs used by the pharmaceutical and related industries.

While this kind of benefit-cost calculus may have intuitive appeal among business consultants and even among some policy makers, it would not be accepted from a first-year student by any reputable economics department. As a general rule, economists measure the benefits produced by an economic activity by the value that the *output* from that activity produces, and not by the value of the *inputs* it consumes.

In any event, it is not clear that policy makers in these other countries, notably Germany, will be persuaded by these shrill exhortations or by the dubious benefit-cost calculus offered by management consultants Bain & Company. After all, Glassman's moral sermon emanates from a nation in which some 45 million individuals find themselves without any health insurance whatsoever at any point in time and a larger percentage yet finds itself without coverage for prescription drugs. As a highly accomplished panel of scientists concluded in a study published by the Institute of Medicine of the U.S. National Academy of Sciences (2003), some 18,000 Americans die prematurely every year because of this lack of health insurance, not even to speak of the avoidable suffering of those chronically ill uninsured who survive, among them many elderly Americans.

Furthermore, health policy makers in Europe and Canada can point to widely respected statistics gathered annually by the Organization for Economic Cooperation and Development, according to which the United States ranks remarkably low in the OECD on many standard health status indicators, such as the infant mortality rate, life expectancy at birth and at age 60, and "potential years of life lost per 100,000 population," that is, life years that ought not to have been lost if timely and appropriate health care had been given (Anderson and Hussey 2001). Accusing policy makers in other nations of "killing people" through price controls from the perch of the United States therefore requires a certain temerity. Although probably meant to be helpful to the U.S. pharmaceutical industry, one may wonder whether it is.

Finally, policy makers in these other countries can properly wonder how much of any additional dollar or Euro that they might allow to be spent in their countries on prescription drugs actually would be allocated to R&D by the pharmaceutical industry. These policy makers can point to income statements of the U.S. pharmaceutical companies, according to which only about 13–14% of total revenue flows into R&D, while over a third of total revenue flows into marketing and general administration. The question can legitimately be raised by policy makers in other countries whether, from the viewpoint of society at large, some of these funds now going to marketing and general administration might not be more productively spent on R&D. Figure 2.1 exhibits the relevant financial statement data for the 1990s. More recent data, provided in 2003 by Bank of America Securities Equity Research, corroborate the earlier data. In 2002, for example, 13 large research-based U.S. pharmaceutical companies jointly spent about 32.8% of total revenue on SG&A, 25.3% on cost of goods sold, and 14% on R&D.

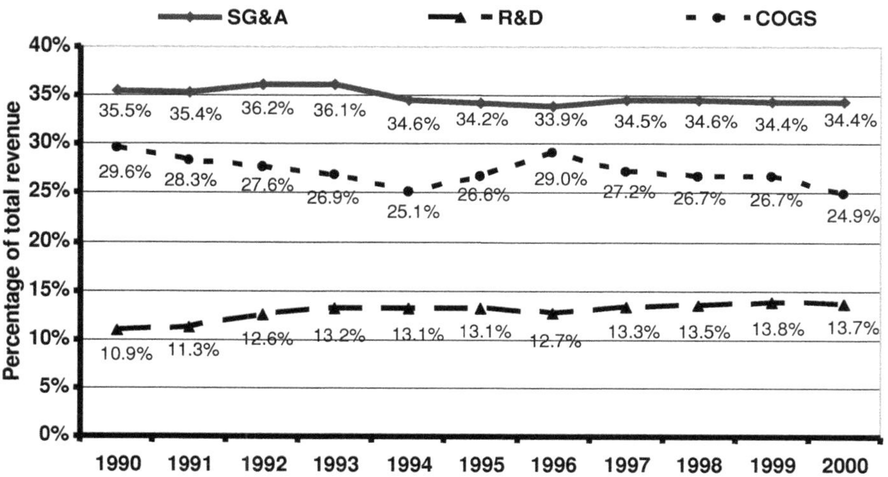

Figure 2.1. Trends in the financial statements of major pharmaceutical manufacturers, top 10 firms, 1990–2000. *Source:* Kaiser Family Foundation (2001), Exhibit 31, p. 45.

The Location of Pharmaceutical R&D

Running through virtually all of the criticism leveled at drug price controls in Europe, Canada, and Asia is the theme that these controls drive pharmaceutical R&D from the countries with price controls to those countries with fewer or no government controls on drug prices, for example, the United States. Petulance among the executives of the research-based pharmaceutical industry might trigger such a response, but not among cool-headed executives who sincerely wish to serve their shareholders. Because pharmaceutical products can be sold worldwide, regardless of where the underlying R&D was performed, and because even clinical trials can be conducted on a worldwide basis, the location of pharmaceutical R&D should not be substantially driven by the presence or absence of government controls on product prices at various alternative locations. Elementary economic theory suggests that these locational decisions should be driven instead by the availability and cost of scientific research personnel and by government regulations directly affecting the R&D enterprise.

It is entirely conceivable, for example, that, over the next several decades, more and more pharmaceutical research will shift from Europe and the United States to Asia, especially to China, where there will likely be an abundance of highly trained and relatively low-cost scientific personnel to conduct the research. Even the more economically developed Asian nations, such as Korea, Singapore, and Taiwan, are likely to benefit from this migration, as long as they strive to have a comparative advantage in scientific research vis-à-vis the United States and Europe.

The "Free Trade" Argument

Probably more compelling in the political realm than the critiques of foreign drug price controls reviewed thus far is the argument that these controls simply are "unfair" and violate tenets of free international trade.

That argument was first famously raised by the then U.S. FDA Commissioner Mark McClellan before the First International Colloquium on Generic Medicine in Cancun, Mexico (September 25, 2003). It was raised again by the Republican Policy Committee of the United States Senate (2005). Its policy statement, "Pharmaceutical Price Controls Abroad: An Unfair Trade Policy," cited the 2002 U.S. Trade Promotion Authority Act, which acknowledged that "price controls" and "reference pricing" for pharmaceutical products (to be discussed below) are "trade-distorting barriers" and "disguised trade barriers." Indeed, the Republican Policy Committee went so far as to decry even conventional economic evaluations (referred to as "cost-utility evaluation") as a trade barrier, singling out "Australia, Canada, the Netherlands, Portugal and the United Kingdom" as practitioners of such analyses (p. 5). That a committee of the U.S. Senate would declare standard economic evaluation of new medical technology to be a trade barrier speaks volumes about what American policy makers had in mind concerning the relationship between free international trade and national health policies.

The 2002 U.S. Trade Promotion Authority Act gives the U.S. president the authority to "strive to eliminate unfair trade practices" in international trade negotiations. That authority was subsequently exercised in the Australian–U.S. Free Trade Agreement negotiated in 2004 (Becker 2003; Outterson 2004), drawing international attention to the linkage now made by the U.S. government between the domestic health policies of nations and international trade policy. Exercise of the authority is bound to surface again and again on the agendas of future bilateral or multilateral international trade negotiations. This intrusion by the United States into the domestic health policy of other nations is apt to become a source of friction in international relations.

The central tenets running through this foreign-trade argument are (1) that current levels of pharmaceutical R&D spending worldwide are sub-optimal in the sense that more R&D spending could easily be justified on the basis of future patient health benefits (e.g., Murphy and Topel 2003b), (2) that the R&D costs per successful new pharmaceutical or biotech products will continue to rise apace, and (3) that this growing burden should somehow be more fairly shared among nations on the basis of their ability to pay. There is the added assumption that a more "equitable" sharing of the fiscal burden of pharmaceutical R&D would automatically lead to lower drug prices in the currently high-price countries, notably in the United States. Although this line of reasoning has considerable intuitive appeal, and can be backed up by the awesome economic power the United States can bring to bear on foreign policy, it triggers in one's mind a number of questions.

First, in spite of annual compound growth of close to 13% in U.S. R&D spending during the past decade and a half, the numbers of both new drug applications and new drug approvals have not grown commensurately. On the contrary, both have leveled off in recent years. It appears that traditional approaches to chemical-based pharmaceutical R&D have run into strongly diminishing marginal returns, and a more pronounced shift to alternative approaches should be made, especially for biological products.

Second, the idea that the removal of price controls in other countries will lead to a lowering of drug prices in currently high-priced countries, notably in the United States, may have appeal at first glance, but the proponents of that idea are never clear about just what mechanism would produce these price declines. Presumably the sellers of pharmaceutical products in the U.S. market would continue to extract from it the maximum prices that U.S. consumers are willing to pay. Any future reduction of drug prices in the United States therefore hinges mainly on the relative market power of the buyer side in the U.S. market, rather than on what other nations pay for drugs. Elementary economic theory suggests that if other nations allowed drug prices to rise, but the buyer side of the U.S. pharmaceutical markets was to weaken for some reason, drug prices in the United States almost surely would rise accordingly, independently of the higher drug prices abroad. To argue otherwise stretches credulity.

Third, there is the question of how "unfair" current price differentials in the global pharmaceutical market actually are. The authors of the previously cited Bain study proposed that Europeans should "pay prices proportional to their GDP per capita" (Bain Company 2005, p. 5). That idea has been echoed by most critics of the current, allegedly "free rider" system. There is evidence that, by and large, this criterion is actually being met.

Differential Drug Prices and Ability to Pay

Danzon and Furukawa (2003) compared average price levels for pharmaceuticals in eight countries – Canada, Chile, France, Germany, Italy, Japan, Mexico, and the United Kingdom – relative to those in the United States. The authors used as their unit of analysis the "molecule-indication" for drugs, defined by active ingredient and therapeutic class. A country's price per dose was the volume-weighted average price per dose, averaged over all package sizes, in a molecule-indication, using U.S. volume weights for the cross-national comparisons. The manufacturers' prices were used instead of retail prices to purge the price data of cross-national differences in wholesale, retail markups, and taxes.

Using 1999 foreign exchange rates to convert all prices to U.S.-dollar equivalents, the authors found that Japan's average drug prices per molecule-indication in that year were the highest in the nine-country cohort, U.S. prices were the next highest, and Canada's the lowest, at 33% below U.S. prices. Prices in France were 30% lower than U.S. prices, and prices in the other countries about 15% lower (Danzon and Furukawa 2003, Exhibit 3).

When cross-national price comparisons are made using prevailing market exchange rates, the observed price differentials naturally fluctuate simply with fluctuations in exchange rates, which are heavily influenced by fluctuations in capital flows. To avoid this extraneous source of variance in the data, Danzon and Furukawa used two alternative exchange rates to convert prices in foreign currencies into U.S.-dollar equivalent prices: (1) gross domestic product–purchasing power parity (PPP) exchange rates, and (2) health care–PPP exchange rates. The GDP-PPP exchange rates equalize the purchasing power of different currencies in terms of a GDP-based basket of goods and services, while the health care-PPP equalizes the purchasing power of different currencies in terms of a basket of health care goods and services.

Using the GDP-PPP conversion, the authors found that Canada's average drug prices were only 14% below comparable U.S. prices in 1999, rather than the 33% suggested at market exchange rates. With GDP-PPPs, Japan's average drug prices were slightly below the comparable U.S. prices, although France's prices were about 40% below U.S. prices, rather than the 30% at market exchange rates. Germany's average drug prices were 25% below U.S. prices at GDP-PPP exchange rates, rather than about 15% at market exchange rates. Finally, at the health care–PPP conversion rates, all eight countries in the study had *higher* drug prices than comparable U.S. prices. This was so because the prices of health care goods and services other than prescription drugs in these countries were even lower than comparable prices in the United States.

The final adjustment made by Danzon and Furukawa to cross-national differentials in drug prices was to relate them to cross-national differences in GDP per capita, a reasonably good indicator of ability to pay. The authors found that, after this final adjustment, drug price differentials between countries roughly reflected income differences (except for Chile and Mexico). If one treats global R&D costs as a "global joint cost" to be recouped through efficient and equitable global pricing strategies, as the authors suggested, then the prevailing price differentials were reasonably, if not perfectly, consistent with both efficiency and equity.

From the perspective of international trade negotiations, this is a highly policy-relevant finding. It suggests that the prevailing cross-national price differentials, far from representing unfair mooching on the part of other countries, actually fairly closely reflect one of the objectives frequently cited by the critics of current global drug-pricing policies, namely, that cross-national drug prices should reflect cross-national differences in ability to pay.

VI. The Balance of Power in the Pharmaceutical Market

The critics of government-imposed price controls on pharmaceutical products do have a valid point. As long as the price ceilings are set above the incremental cost of producing these products, manufacturers will be tempted to sell at whatever those controlled prices are, because they earn at least a positive margin toward the recovery of fixed costs. The problem is that the price ceilings may be set at levels far below fully allocated fixed costs per unit. If every payer followed that strategy, pharmaceutical companies would soon become insolvent.

Critics of price controls therefore point to "free markets" as the more efficient alternative without, however, specifying precisely how such a market should be structured. The tacit assumption appears to be that the mere absence of government controls on the production, pricing, and distribution of a product ipso facto represents a properly functioning market. One could not be more wrong on this point. According to the First Optimality Theorem of economics, "free markets" in an industry will lead to an efficient allocation of productive resources and distribution of output only if these markets are perfectly competitive, which requires that the following exacting conditions be met (Arrow 1963, pp. 942–943):

1. There is full price transparency for all rival products, on both sides of the market
2. The intrinsic qualities of the rival products are fully and accurately understood, on both sides of the market
3. There is unfettered and costless entry and exit of producers for any product sold in the market
4. There are no increasing returns in the production and distribution of products and
5. For every product traded in the market, there are many buyers and many sellers, none of whom possesses monopolistic market power (such as those conveyed by patent laws).

According to the Second Optimality Theorem, in markets meeting these stringent conditions, any *efficient* allocation of goods and services that is desired by society on *ethical* grounds can be attained, in principle, without government interference in the production, pricing, and distribution of products, simply by redistributing purchasing power among the citizenry to allow the market to drive on its own toward the desired outcome (Arrow 1963, p. 943).

The First and Second Optimality Theorems have become the intellectual foundation for current proposals worldwide to "privatize" all production and distribution of health care and to seek politically desired distributions of health care through transfers of cash or vouchers to low-income families. Unfortunately, it would stretch credulity to argue that the markets for health care even approximate the stringent conditions required by these theorems (see, e.g., Rice 2002).

Furthermore, as Newhouse (2004) has argued convincingly in a recent commentary on the pricing of pharmaceutical products, in practice, it is impossible to develop a price policy for pharmaceutical products that is both *statically* and *dynamically* efficient. *Static* efficiency requires that, at a given point in time, price be set equal to the incremental cost of producing more output with a given capacity, lest customers willing to cover at least these incremental costs go unserved. However, given the industry's cost structure, at that price fixed costs (including R&D) will not be recovered. It follows that a statically efficient price ipso facto is dynamically inefficient, because *dynamic* efficiency requires that, over the long run, added resources flow into R&D and production capacity up to the point at which the social benefits from further expansion would no longer cover the long-run incremental cost of expansion (including R&D). As a result of this inherent conflict between static and dynamic efficiency, all pricing policies for pharmaceutical products in the real world will be compromises between these two forms of efficiency. Thus far, these compromises have been anything but balanced, even in what were considered by pharmaceutical manufacturers as "free markets."

Before 1990, for example, pharmaceutical manufacturers selling products in Germany believed they were operating in a "free market" there, because the manufacturers were free to set the prices for their products to German wholesalers. The markups of wholesalers and retailers were regulated by government. Insurance carriers, typically covering 100% of the retail prices charged for prescription drugs, had no choice but to pay those prices. Every physician in Germany then enjoyed complete therapeutic freedom to prescribe whatever product he or she deemed appropriate. Occasionally – perhaps more than occasionally – they did so under conflicts of interest created by sundry favors or rewards bestowed on them by the marketing departments of pharmaceutical companies. No economist could possibly describe this arrangement as a properly functioning "free market," because there was no countervailing power whatsoever on the demand side of that market. Naturally, the arrangement was not sustainable over the longer run and was abandoned in the early 1990s, in favor of sundry government controls on drug pricing and prescribing.

Similarly, until the early 1990s, only about a quarter of retail sales of prescription drugs for the most part in the United States were covered by health insurance. American consumers of prescription drugs paid the full retail price charged them by the local pharmacist, who had complete freedom in pricing those products, as did wholesalers and manufacturers further upstream. Individual physicians had complete therapeutic freedom to prescribe any pharmaceutical product they deemed appropriate, once again under occasional conflicts of interest. Patients either filled the script at the pharmacy or did not, depending on their budgets. Typically, patients had no information on relative prices of these drugs at various pharmacies in their market areas and on the availability of substitute products, let alone on the cost effectiveness of rival products, by which is meant the relative cost for the benefits achieved with the drugs. In fact, even to this day, such crucial information is not generally accessible to American patients. Pharmaceutical executives may have viewed this arrangement as a properly functioning "free market" as well. Once again, however, no self-respecting economist could possibly certify it as even an approximation to a market meeting the conditions of the First Optimality Theorem. Only with the spread of third-party payment in the 1990s in the United States has there been a degree of effective market power on the demand side of the U.S. pharmaceutical market.

Markets for pharmaceutical products worldwide are less than well balanced. Markets dominated by the monopsonistic (single-buyer) power of government can exercise undue power over the supply side of the market and depress prices to dynamically inefficient levels. At the other extreme, markets with an ill-informed and typically feeble demand side, weakened further by moral hazard inherent in health third-party payment, are unduly dominated by the supply side. What is needed instead are markets with more evenly balanced of power, in which both sides of the market are accurately informed about the prices, clinical effectiveness, and cost effectiveness of the rival products being offered for sale. Creating such markets is one of the major challenges confronting health care policy makers around the globe.

This will involve two facets. First, where patients now enjoy full or nearly full insurance coverage for prescription drugs, they are likely to be asked to assume a larger share of the cost of drug therapy, if only to focus their minds on the relative "cost effectiveness" of rival products. Second, however, to allow both patients and their physicians to act as more cost-conscious purchasers of prescription drugs, an information infrastructure will emerge, or should emerge, that can provide potential users of pharmaceutical products with objective, science-based information on the prices and relative cost effectiveness of rival pharmaceutical products being offered in the market.

Forms of Cost Sharing by Patients

Cost sharing by users of prescription drugs can take a variety of forms, each with its own behavioral and clinical consequences.

Full Out-of-Pocket Spending

The patient may be asked to pay out of pocket the full retail price of prescribed drugs. This is still more common than may be supposed, for example, for the about 45 million persons in the United States without health insurance coverage at any point in time. It is also so for elderly Americans covered by the Medicare Modernization Act of 2003, which requires patients, in 2006, to pay out of pocket fully for the first $250 of drug spending in a year (the annual "deductible"), then 25% of annual spending in excess of $250 but below $2,250, but then it reverts to zero insurance coverage once more for annual spending in excess of $2,250 but below $5,100 (the so-called doughnut hole), and thereafter the patient is responsible for 10% of annual spending in excess of $5,100, with both the deductible and doughnut hole growing over time (Kaiser Family Foundation 2005). Prescription drugs are not covered under the government-run, provincial health insurance plans for Canadians who are neither elderly nor poor. In many of the poor, developing countries, the bulk of health spending is fully out of pocket, including spending on prescription drugs.

Tiered Copays or Coinsurance

Insurance plans around the world that had traditionally covered the full cost of prescription drugs have begun, in the last decade or so, to impose either deductibles or various forms of tiered cost sharing on patients.

The most common form of tiered cost sharing has been flat *copayments* per prescription, staggered in size by generics, brand-name drugs on the insurer's formulary, and brand names not on the insurer's formulary. Although designed to goad patients toward generics or brand-name drugs preferred by the insurer, merely imposing copayments keeps the full price of the purchased products hidden from the patient's view. For that reason, many insurance plans have introduced tiered *coinsurance*. Under such a plan, for example, the insured may be asked to pay 10% of the cost of a generic drug, 20% of the cost of a brand-name drug on the insurer's formulary, 40% of the cost of brand-name drugs not on the formulary, and, of course, 100% of drugs of any type not covered by the insurance plan at all.

Reference Pricing

By far the bluntest and most controversial form of tiered cost sharing, however, is "reference pricing," so called because the insurer only reimburses patients for the price of a relatively low-cost drug in a larger "therapeutic group" of drugs all declared to be "equivalent" (López-Casasnovas and Puig-Junoy 2001). Patients are then required to pay the entire difference between this low-cost reference price and the actual retail price charged for a drug with a higher price out of pocket. Reference pricing has been used under Germany's Statutory Health Insurance system since the early 1990s. It now is used in a number of other countries, including in some Canadian provinces, in Australia, and in New Zealand (Kanavos and Reinhardt 2003).

As already noted, the Republican Policy Committee (2003, p. 5) singled out reference pricing as one form of restraint of free international trade, although on its face reference prices strike at least some economists (Huskamp et al. 2000; Kanavos and Reinhardt 2003) as a reasonable precondition for a genuine, price-competitive market for pharmaceutical products, especially if patients and their physicians are well informed about the distinct attributes and relative cost effectiveness of the drugs within a therapeutic group. The idea is that insurance carriers will socialize through full coverage the cost of only basic prescription drugs that are considered adequate, leaving it to the suppliers of more expensive substitutes in a therapeutically equivalent group to persuade patients in a free market that the benefits of the higher-priced products are worth the extra out-of-pocket outlay on them.

The approach is nothing other than the analogue of the more general concept of "defined contribution" now widely recommended by many economists for the purchase of health insurance (Pauly et al. 1991). Under that approach, government or employers make a defined contribution to an individual's purchase of private health insurance, leaving the individual to pay the full difference between that contribution and the insurance premium actually charged by the private insurer.

Remarkably, however, economists can be found who reject the idea of reference pricing on two grounds (see, e.g., Danzon 2000 and 2001, and the series of essays in López-Casasnovas and Jönsson 2001). That opposition comes even from economists who favor the idea of defined contributions for health insurance (see, e.g., Danzon, coauthor in Pauly et al. 1991).

First, these economists have argued that patients typically are not sufficiently informed about the cost effectiveness of rival drugs in a therapeutic group and that physicians will not take the time to explain it to them, because they are not explicitly paid for that service. That argument, of course, calls into question the entire idea of applying a market approach to the pharmaceutical market or to health care markets in general. Second, these economists have warned that reference pricing violates horizontal equity, because poorer patients are more likely deprived by it of superior, higher-priced products than are wealthier patients. That argument, however, would apply with equal force to any defined contribution approach to health insurance and any proposal to impose high deductibles and coinsurance on patients for any health service, as such arrangements always entail the price rationing of health care at the margin (see Reinhardt 1996).

Much of the controversy over reference pricing, in particular, the strong opposition of pharmaceutical manufacturers to that approach, arises from the definition of "equivalence" in the construction of the relevant "therapeutically equivalent groupings" of prescription drugs. These groupings can be narrowly or widely construed. At the narrow end, a "therapeutically equivalent group" of drugs may include only drugs with the identical active, chemical ingredients, which inevitably confines the grouping to generic drugs only. At the other extreme, very much frowned upon by research-based pharmaceutical manufacturers, the "therapeutically equivalent grouping" can be defined by insurers to include all products with the same therapeutic target, including off-patent and on-patent drugs.

Additional controversy arises from the selection of the reference price within a therapeutically "equivalent" group of drugs. If only the lowest-priced drug in the group serves as the reference price, all other products are exposed to cost sharing by patients, and their prices may well be pushed down toward the low reference price. Even so, this would have to be regarded as a market solution, rather than price control, because patients' preferences and willingness to pay had forced the migration of prices toward the reference price. But if a higher-priced product, somewhere in the middle of the therapeutic grouping, were used as the reference price, then the prices of lower-priced products, including generics, would migrate up over time toward the higher reference price. It might lead to very high profit margins on noninnovative products that do not contribute toward financing R&D.

A more in-depth discussion of reference pricing lies beyond the compass of this essay (in this regard, see Kanavos and Reinhardt 2003). Suffice it to say, it is a powerful method of introducing market power on the demand side of prescription drugs covered by health insurance, and one likely to be embraced, sooner or later, by private health insurers, as they seek to cope with the ever-rising cost of health care.

Consumer-Directed Health Care (CDHC)

After the demise of "managed care" in the United States during the late 1990s, the latest novel idea in American health policy is what is euphemistically called consumer-directed health care, which is in effect nothing other than health insurance with very high annual deductibles, ranging, in the United States, from $2,000 per family to $10,000 or more. Just as American management consultants sought to market "managed care" around the globe during the 1990s, so they are apt to market CDHC in the early twenty-first century as a novel American invention, even though it is but a particular variant of the medical savings account (MSA) approach long used in Singapore.

Whatever may be said for or against the CDHC approach, it cannot be judged supportive of the research-based pharmaceutical industry, as patients will be exposed to the full cost of prescription drugs within the high deductibles. Unless special insurance arrangements are made for prescription drugs, on the plausible argument that lowering their cost to patients can help avoid costly hospitalizations and other more expensive acute care, the approach is apt to impinge severely on the profit margins and funding of R&D in the industry. It is a development that ought to give the industry pause.

An Information Infrastructure of the Pharmaceutical Market

If the market power inherent in the decisions of patients is to be more effectively harnessed in the control of health care costs, then it becomes essential that patients, as well as their physicians, are better informed than they now are about the relative costs and benefits of rival products with the same therapeutic target, in short, on their relative "cost effectiveness." The development of such an information base will be another major challenge of health policy makers in the coming decades.

The establishment of the relative cost effectiveness of rival pharmaceutical products poses extraordinary methodological problems, as is superbly well described in the bible for such studies, Drummond et al.'s *Methods for the Economic Evaluation of Health Care Programmes* (2005). The "costs" used in such evaluations can be narrowly construed to be only those of insurers or of insurers and patients, or very widely to include all social costs, including those borne by family members, employers, and others in society (e.g., though contagion). Benefits in cost-effectiveness studies typically are measured by physical health-status indicators, such as added life years saved or changes in blood pressure, but they must be adjusted for the quality of life, which in turn triggers a host of additional methodological challenges and, in the end, subjective value judgments. Consequently, different researchers can arrive at quite different conclusions concerning the relative cost effectiveness of a set of rival pharmaceutical products (see Pauly, Chapter 10, and Drummond, Chapter 11). The sources of such differences can be laid bare only if all such studies are open to full, external audit as to the raw data going into the studies, the methodologies used to transform the raw data for analysis, and the analyses themselves (Reinhardt 1997).

Given the many judgments that must be made by researchers in even the best, most objective cost-effectiveness studies, the question arises who should conduct them, to make them truly useful for the market of pharmaceutical products. If those studies are conducted or funded by third-party payers, be they governments or private insurers, they will immediately be suspected by pharmaceutical producers, physicians, and patients to be biased in favor of cost savings, possibly at the expensive of quality. But if these studies are conducted or funded by pharmaceutical producers, as now they typically are, they are similarly suspect among third-party payers (Millenson 2004) and among the general public. What is needed, therefore, are research institutes that are fiscally independent of either side of the pharmaceutical market and, therefore, beholden to neither side.

In "An Information Infrastructure for the Pharmaceutical Market," this author proposed such an approach for the United States, although it would be applicable to any country (Reinhardt 2004). One or preferably several private, nonprofit Phamaco-Economic Research Institutes (PERIs) would be established permanently by law and granted a generous initial endowment financed by government, say, a 1% tax on all pharmaceutical retail sales over one or two years. These endowments could be replenished from time or time or be generous enough at the outset not to need such replenishments. Like private universities in the United States, the PERIs would invest their endowments in diversified portfolios of financial assets. The returns from these investments, and perhaps annual take-downs of the endowments themselves, would finance an ongoing set of research studies conducted by high-caliber, highly respected pharmaco-economic researchers located either at the PERIs themselves or in academic institutions working under contract from the PERIs. These studies would be fully auditable, at all times, by anyone as to raw data and methodology, including by researchers engaged by the pharmaceutical industry. The PERIs also would monitor the performance of drugs after launch and evaluate new therapeutic applications emerging after launch. The research findings produced by the PERIs would be treated as a pure public good, which means that they would be posted on a Web site and be available worldwide to anyone, free of charge.

Finally, these research findings would not be binding on anyone, but they could be used by all stakeholders in their decisions on drug therapy or new R&D on pharmaceutical products.

VII. Summary and Conclusion

The purpose of this chapter has been to provide a broad, general overview of the role of the pharmaceutical industry in the economy and in the health sector, and to explore a number of problems arising from the industry's cost structure and from the traditional imbalance in the global markets for pharmaceutical products.

There can be no question that governments in all nations must be careful not to harm through their policies an industry on whom (1) the entire world depends for enhancements in the quality of human life, and (2) to which the world will increasingly look for technological breakthroughs to help reduce the currently high labor intensity of the production of health care, which cannot be sustained, given an ever-rising ratio of nonworking to working-age adults.

At the same time, the industry must reckon with sustained efforts in the decades ahead to shore up the market power of the *demand* side of the market. It will be sought by engaging patients more fully in the process of price competition through various forms of cost sharing, including reference pricing. It will be sought also through the natural complement of added cost sharing by patients, namely, greater transparency of the prices and the relative cost effectiveness of rival pharmaceutical products. These particular approaches to shoring up the demand side will certainly be attempted in countries where government controls of pricing have been weak or absent. But even where governments have hitherto controlled drug prices, such price controls may be transformed over time into greater cost sharing by patients and the associated transparency of prices and cost effectiveness.

The challenge for all stakeholders worldwide will be to find a dynamically efficient balance between eliminating whatever current waste there may be in pharmaceutical therapy and encouraging greater price competition, on the one hand, and, on the other, leaving prices at sufficiently high levels to attract adequate resources to the complex R&D enterprise of the industry. This book is intended to be part of the global conversation on how best to achieve that goal.

THREE

The Economics of Research and Development in the Pharmaceutical Industry

William S. Comanor

I. Introduction

In this chapter I return to the topic of my doctoral dissertation, completed in 1963 under the same title. My purpose then as now was to explore the importance of research and development (R&D) for new products in the pharmaceutical industry. Such products embody new medical advances and have a major impact on mortality and morbidity rates.

The structure of discovering and developing new drugs has shifted greatly over the past 20 years. In the early years of this industry, from its rebirth following the Second World War through roughly the end of the 1970s, the major pharmaceutical companies developed "in house" most of their primary products, largely by testing large numbers of available compounds. Scientific knowledge was obtained primarily from freely available sources. There were perhaps 40 highly integrated firms worldwide that contributed to this effort.[1]

Since then, the process of drug development and discovery has become increasingly complex. A new technology appeared, termed "biotechnology," which placed this process on a more scientific basis. A new set of firms appeared: smaller and interposed between the scientific community and the major pharmaceutical firms. It is reported that between 25% and 40% of sales by the major pharmaceutical companies currently are from products that originated in the biotech sector.

In this chapter I review the expanding economic literature that describes and explains the new structure for research. Along with the new scientific knowledge, I find an increasing degree of disintegration as the major companies have increasingly funded work carried out by others. I consider the costs and benefits of the new structure and explore the implication of current trends for the efficiency of the drug development process.

II. A New Technology for Pharmaceutical Research

Since the mid-1980s the pharmaceutical industry has been shaken by the rapid pace of technological change. Unlike most other industries, however, this change has had little effect on production processes used to produce new or existing products. It has not led to cost-saving innovations that permit lower production costs; indeed, it has had little to do with the manufacturing process. Instead the new technology relates to the process by which new products emerge in this industry.

At the same time, the new technology has not had so great an impact on the process by which new drugs are tested and evaluated. The extensive testing of new drugs required by the U.S. Food and Drug Administration (FDA) and similar agencies elsewhere has not been greatly affected by the new research methods.

At the dawn of the modern industry, in the 1950s and 1960s, the process of drug discovery was largely empirical and had little of a theoretical base. This fact was acknowledged in studies written during this era, such as the book by Jewkes, Sawyers, and Stillerman (1958). Those authors emphasized the distinction between systematic and empirical research. In the former, "the new idea has a certain completeness and unity from the outset," while in the latter, "the new idea is a nature of a discovery arising from a search, more or less informed, among many possibilities." The latter approach was characteristic of new discoveries in the chemical industry. Jewkes et al. suggested that "many modern chemical inventions . . . have risen from the vague intuition that a chemical compound with a given structure might have certain desirable properties, followed by the experimental verification of the hypothesis" (pp. 164–166).

This characterization was applied directly to pharmaceutical research during this era. Thus, a former medical director of a division within Pfizer stated in 1960:

> There can be no question that some very wonderful, exciting, extremely important, and productive research has been and is being done within the pharmaceutical industry. However, I do not think that it would detract in any way from these fine and worthwhile activities to point out that much that is called research in the pharmaceutical industry has little relationship to what most people engaged in academic and research activities would consider to be scientific research.[2]

If this picture applied to the early postwar years, it does not describe the pharmaceutical research process very well at the beginning of the twenty-first century. What was once a largely empirical discovery process has developed into a more theoretical activity. The science of pharmacology has become more advanced so that researchers can develop a greater understanding of how drugs work in the body. This greater understanding has shifted the character and setting for pharmaceutical research.

The shift to a more science-based process, however, is not fully complete. It occurred more rapidly in some therapeutic categories than in others, and in some pharmaceutical companies than in others. These two dimensions are, of course, not independent for companies whose work is more heavily concentrated in areas where science-driven activities have taken hold more fully and have in turn adopted the new approach more quickly. A striking feature about this technological shift has been the considerable heterogeneity in the adoption process. The diffusion of this change has not been rapid or complete.

One reason is that firms who want to employ the new technology cannot merely invest in basic research. Cockburn and Henderson (1998) emphasize that "it is also important for the firm to be actively connected to the wider scientific community" (p. 158). They developed the concept of "connectedness," as measured by the extent of collaboration in writing scientific papers across institutional boundaries, and conclude that "firms wishing to public sector research must do more than simply invest in in-house basic research: they must also actively collaborate with their public sector colleagues. . . . The extent of this collaboration . . . is positively related to private sector research productivity" (p. 180). The process by which firms acquire this new technology is not simple or direct, nor obtained without cost.

Cockburn, Henderson, and Stern (1999) emphasize the importance of organizational factors and the distribution of power relationships within the firm for the speed at which new research methods are employed. Some firms are more suited to the new technology than others. The authors note that all their informants emphasized "that differences in the historical experience of the firm, in their 'knowledge capital,' were critically important in shaping the adoption decision" (p. 19).

To examine the diffusion process empirically, Cockburn et al. explore the relationship between patenting and publishing by the company's scientific staff. When the older, more empirical approaches were employed, these activities were considered substitutes, and the publication of research findings not encouraged. In contrast, research organizations using more science-based methods saw the publication of research findings differently. These activities were encouraged as promoting increased interdependence with the scientific community. For this reason, patenting and publishing were now complements rather than substitutes in the research process.

Cockburn, Henderson, and Stern also study the manner by which the new technology was adapted. They find that the new technology was an important factor for pharmaceutical research and yet has been characterized by a relatively low rate of diffusion. The increasing importance of new biological discoveries for the design of pharmaceutical products required new capabilities.

As Gambardella (1995) notes, "Although a public good, science is not a 'free' good. Internal scientific capabilities are critical for taking advantage of the public good" (p. 103). From interviews with research personnel at various companies, he observes the different decisions taken at different companies to develop their scientific capabilities. Some made a major effort in this, while others did not. Where the new technology was employed, research personnel were encouraged to participate in the broader scientific community and publish their findings in the scientific literature. There was also increasing collaboration by industry researchers with nonindustry scientists located at university and government laboratories.

As part of these increasing interactions, there have been a greater number of research collaborations and agreements between drug companies and other scientific institutions. Gambardella provides a list of 59 such relationships between large U.S. companies and universities and other research institutions from the 1980s (pp. 49–54). While research institutions benefit from the infusion of industry funds,[3] the companies gain greater access to scientific discoveries.

To test these observations, Gambardella estimates the relationship between company patents and a lag structure of its scientific publications, together with the level of research expenditures. He reports that "scientific research and drug discovery appear to be intimately connected" (p. 115) and that "in the 1980s, the productivity of applied research increased which is related to significant advances in scientific knowledge and in the technology of experimentation (e.g., computerized drug design)" (p. 121). From his data, there were clear advantages to firms who adopt the new technology.

Cockburn and Henderson (1998) examine the importance of public funding for the development of the most important new drugs. Although they find that more than three-fourths of the leading 21 drugs introduced between 1965 and 1992 had at least some input from the public sector, this does not mean that public-sector research was sufficient for their development. Of these products, most relied on enabling discoveries from the public sector. However, for only 2 of the 21 did public-sector research contribute to the synthesis of the relevant compound. Even when creation of new drugs was facilitated by public research efforts, there were still important parts of the discovery process carried out in industry research laboratories. In large measure, industry and nonindustry research efforts are complementary.

To study this matter further, the authors investigate the extent to which scientists in industry research laboratories collaborated with their public-sector counterparts, using coauthorships as a measure. Not only did they find a large number of such collaborations but also that coauthorships are positively related to the number of important patents taken out by the firm. They conclude that "firms wishing to take advantage of public-sector research must do more than simply invest in in-house basic research: they must also actively collaborate with their public-sector colleagues. Further, . . . coauthorships across institutions are correlated with private sector research productivity . . . [so that there are] substantial differences across firms in their ability to access public knowledge" (Cockburn and Henderson 1998, p. 180). This is another factor affecting the rates of diffusion of the new science-based technology.

Although the trend in pharmaceutical research activities has been toward a more scientific basis, there remains a substantial empirical component to these activities. Schwartzman and Cognato (1996) argue that "pharmaceutical research remains empirical, notwithstanding the increase in knowledge." Even is cases where drugs were allegedly rationally designed, "it was essentially still a matter of following leads and not hypotheses suggested by general theories" (p. 850). Although acknowledging that pharmaceutical research efforts have become more structured in recent years, these writers suggest that it is still largely an empirical exercise.

An important corollary of these changes has been the growing connection between university and industry research activities. Schwartzman and Cognato report that the number of scientific publications authored by researchers at industry laboratories rose sharply in the years between 1973 and 1986. However, they indicate that this result does not apply to all companies (p. 850).

III. Biotechnology

The initial scientific discovery by Stanley Cohen and Herbert Boyer, leading to the new technology in 1973, provided the basic technique for recombinant DNA. As this discovery became increasingly understood, its commercial implications became recognized. New firms were created to employ this new technology.

Zucker, Darby, and Brewer (1998) observe that "the primary pattern in the development of the industry involved one or more scientist-entrepreneurs who remained on the faculty [of a research university] while establishing a business on the side. . . . We see the university as bringing about local industrial benefits by permitting its professors to pursue private commercial interests while their faculty appointments tie them to the area" (p. 291). These writers emphasize that the new scientific knowledge is not a "free good" usable by an unlimited number of potential users at little cost. Instead, it is a form of human capital that was held originally by only a small group of discoverers and co-workers who had gained this knowledge by working at the "bench-science level" (p. 291). Strikingly, this new technology was not immediately available to the major pharmaceutical firms.

At its outset, the new technology was the province of a host of small companies that typically focused on one or a few potential products. Scriabiane (1999) estimates that there were 1,308 such firms in the United States in 1996 (p. 271). Of these, only 260 were public corporations. Many startup firms had their roots in university science. Another survey reported that fully 1,100 new biotechnology companies were created between 1980 and 1994 from licenses granted by universities (p. 272).

Historically the new firms created to pursue this technology saw themselves as representing a different industry, distinct from the broader pharmaceutical industry. Their original goal was not only to discover new drugs but also to manufacture and sell them. But only a few actually reached that goal.[4] An important reason is that the discovery of a new drug is only the first step along the path to launching a new product successfully. The FDA requires extensive clinical testing for new drugs, and the costs of large-scale trials, particularly in Phases 2 and 3, can be substantial. As noted below, the costs of clinical trials and other product development efforts represent more than half of total research and development costs. Since the new startups had generally employed most of their resources in the more scientific, discovery phase of this research, they were often not prepared to support the additional testing costs that were required.

Furthermore, the marketing of a new drug is often as costly as its total research expenditures (Hurwitz and Caves 1988). Those outlays are typically concentrated in the first two years following a product's introduction. Marketing costs effectively double the total outlays required for a new product's launch. This level of resources was generally available only from the major pharmaceutical companies.

Increasingly, the large pharmaceutical companies formed partnerships and alliances with smaller biotechnology startups. In addition to providing needed capital, they facilitated the clinical trial process and supplied essential managerial support.

However, interactions between the two types of firms were often difficult as they developed from different cultures. A solution was the purchase of the more successful biotechnology firms by large pharmaceutical companies. These included the following acquisitions: Genentech by Hoffman-Laroche, Chiron by Ciba-Geigy (Novartis), Genetics Institute by American Home Products, Sphinx Biotechnologies by Lily, and Affymax by Glaxo. While some leading biotechnology firms remained independent, for example, Amgen, most joined the pharmaceutical industry. Prospects for an independent biotechnology industry soon disappeared.

Although the difficulty of raising sufficient capital from private investors was an important reason, there is also a second explanation, which resulted from the distinction between single-project and multiproject firms. As Guedj and Scharfstein (2004) observe, "the problem with single-project firms is that, if they have poor investment opportunities, they may still invest because managers are reluctant to return funds to shareholders. . . . This conflict is mitigated in an internal capital market to the extent that higher-level managers can retain funds for investment, but have a broader range of projects in which to invest" (pp. 1–2). Small biotechnology startups, which often have only a single research project, sometimes continue to invest funds even when prospects are relatively dim.

To test this proposition, Guedj and Scharfstein compare startup biotechnology firms with major firms that have a larger number of projects. They report that single-project firms were more likely to move their products from Phase 1 to Phase 2 trials within a two-year period than were mature firms. However, their products were also less likely to demonstrate good results in Phase 2 trials, and less likely to move into Phase 3 trials within a three-year period. The authors interpret these findings as suggesting an agency problem between investors and managers for smaller, single-project firms that often leads to overinvestment in research. Larger, multiproduct firms were therefore more efficient.

Although the early biotech firms had an advantage in their understanding of the new scientific technology, they faced the economic hurdle of raising sufficient capital to conduct their research, carry out the extensive trials required by FDA, and bring their products to market. As with other startups, they originally sought investor funding, although this was soon joined by contracts and grants from leading pharmaceutical companies. In return for providing the necessary funds, the larger companies sought alliances through which they would share in the returns from any new products that resulted.

An important feature of the biotechnology sector is the increasing formation of alliances between small startup firms and larger pharmaceutical companies. These alliances represent a middle ground between fully independent transactions and the acquisition of the smaller firm by the larger company. By the 1990s, funding by the leading pharmaceutical companies for their alliance partners became a major source of biotechnology financing. In four years – 1994, 1995, 1997, and 1998 – alliance funding represented more than half of the amounts received by startup biotechnology firms and exceeded 60% of total financing, although it was somewhat lower in other years.

While the new startup firms received financing, the large pharmaceutical companies came to rely increasingly on these alliances for their new product pipelines. Of the 691 new entities approved by the U.S. Food and Drug Administration between 1963 and 1999, fully 38% were in-licensed rather than developed fully in industry research laboratories (Nicholson, Danzon, and McCullough 2002, p. 2). Through this process, the major companies gained access to the new technology, and the new biotech products that resulted became important members of their overall menu of drugs.

These alliances required that smaller biotechnology firms accept diluted property rights in their new products. Not only would the returns be shared but decisions and control over the research process would now be negotiated with an outside partner. An obvious question is why they were willing to do so. One answer is that these steps were needed to raise capital that would not otherwise be available. However, if that were the only factor, other investors than the large pharmaceutical companies would have equal standing and be as likely to respond. This capital is typically provided by pharmaceutical companies, which suggests that other factors are also important.

To examine these matters, Danzon, Nicholson, and Pereira (2005) investigate the research performance of biotechnology alliances, paying particular attention to whether this performance varied with the experience of the originating and licensing companies. The issue studied was whether the gains from collaboration, and particularly the expertise that each firm brings to the alliance, exceed any likely disincentive effects following from the dilution of property rights. The latter might result because each firm's efforts were not fully internalized, and each bore only a portion of the research costs associated with bringing a product to market.

Danzon and colleagues collected information on nearly 200 compounds under development in the United States during 1988–2000. Nearly half of the compounds were developed within an alliance, both for large firms as well as for smaller and medium-sized ones. For Phase 1 trials, they report that the size of the originating firm was not related to the percentage developed within an alliance, which confirms the conventional wisdom that small firms generally have the same skills and resources needed for small-scale trials as larger firms. In contrast, they find that small and medium-sized originating firms more frequently had compounds in development through Phase 2 and 3 trials within an alliance than otherwise. The smaller firms seemed to require the resources and expertise of a major firm to pursue these larger and more expensive trials (p. 334 and Table 4).

The authors also examine the experience and size of the licensing firms. Again, they find that the number of past trials had little relationship with the prospects for success on Phase 1 trials, but the number of past trials did have a substantial positive effect on later phases of research. Having performed more trials in the past was predictive of greater success with the Phase 2 and 3 trials. They report that "large firms have higher success rates on in-licensed compounds than on compounds that they originate in-house" (p. 319). These findings suggest that large pharmaceutical companies have an advantage in carrying out latter-stage clinical trials as compared with new startups, but not in discovering new drugs or in performing Phase 1 trials. There appears to be an important division of labor by which biotechnology is employed to discover and develop new drugs.

Nicholson, Danzon, and McCullough (2002) examine the relationship between alliance payments and product features as related to the characteristics of the parties. They find that "biotechnology companies signing their first deal receive a 60% discount relative to firms that signed at least two prior deals, controlling for product characteristics and some measure of the rights transferred." Also, "the discount for inexperience declines to 30% on a biotech firm's second deal and is insignificant for subsequent deals" (pp. 5–6).

Learner and Merges (1998) review a sample of 200 alliances between smaller biotechnology firms and larger pharmaceutical companies, or among biotechnology firms, between 1980 and 1995. They seek to understand the role of control as between the two parties and report "evidence consistent with the hypothesis that the financial condition of R&D firms affects their ability to retain control rights in technology alliances" (p. 146). As expected, smaller biotechnology firms with more revenues prior to the alliance were less likely to negotiate away their control rights.

Learner and Tsai (2000) also consider the nature of biotechnology alliances and how they are influenced by whether or not they were formed in periods of sufficient external financing. They report that when external financing was more readily available, control was more frequently maintained by the smaller biotechnology company then when external financing was more limited.

This study also finds that when control was maintained by the smaller biotechnology firm, the alliance's performance was better as measured by the probability that their drug would advance to the next stage of testing or be finally approved. On the other hand, performance was "significantly worse" when control was assigned to the large corporation (p. 28). This issue is important because only when the research entity retains control is the project likely to be managed efficiently. However, when it does not have sufficient financial resources, and must transfer increased ownership to a pharmaceutical company, prospects for the larger project are reduced.[5]

IV. Scale and Scope of Pharmaceutical Research

These issues of scale and scope in regard to pharmaceutical R&D have been studied most extensively. The first concerns the relative productivity of different sized research efforts, and whether R&D dollars are more effective when aggregated together in large-scale enterprises or when divided among a larger number of smaller firms. The critical issue here is the importance of specialized people and equipment. Second is the issue of economics of scope, which refers to the advantages of specialization or diversification within research facilities, whether there are advantages within a given scale of research activities of concentrating on a limited number of research problems or alternatively in spreading the effort more broadly.

Forty years ago I published a paper that directly explored the scale effects of pharmaceutical R&D (Comanor 1965). In that paper, which used data for the years between 1955 and 1960, I found economies of scale for R&D carried out in smaller pharmaceutical firms but diseconomies for research undertaken within the largest companies.

These findings were disputed by Vernon and Gusen (1974), who instead report for the 1965–1970 period that larger firms were better at innovation than smaller firms (p. 294). To be sure, as those authors acknowledge, the latter period followed the introduction of the 1962 Drug Amendments that required demonstrations of efficacy as well as safety for the introduction of a new drug, while my earlier study preceded the new law. A possible explanation, therefore, for the reported differences was the new conditions under which pharmaceutical research was then carried out.[6]

Jensen (1987) reviewed these earlier studies and provided new estimates. She did not find that marginal product of research expenditures depended on firm size. Her results instead suggest that, except for the smallest firms, there is no particular advantage for new products of either large research scale or large firm size.

The current literature on this subject has advanced beyond these early studies. Much of the progress is attributable to the work of Cockburn and Henderson, who emphasize differences between the discovery and development of new drugs (2001, p. 3). Discovery includes both the basic science and the application of the science to the selection of candidate drugs. In this effort the research process is particularly risky in that only a few candidate drugs are actually continued into development. Drug development, on the other hand, largely includes the three phases of testing required by the FDA. Although outcomes are more certain than before, it remains a risky process in which many prospective drugs are discarded.

Although the development segment of pharmaceutical research has a lesser scientific component than the discovery phase, it remains a substantial undertaking that absorbs more than half of total industry research budgets. Cockburn and Henderson (2001, p. 6) report that the relative cost of development efforts has accounted for between 60% and 70% of pharmaceutical research activities since 1970. The costs of this work are largely determined by FDA requirements.

For their original study on this subject, Henderson and Cockburn (1996) gathered project level data from 10 large pharmaceutical companies, which together accounted for approximately one-fourth of total industry research and development. When their data are aggregated to the firm level, they report no evidence of scale economics: "the implied long-run elasticity of important patent output with respect to research spending in every model was between 0.4 and 0.5" (p. 46). However, their analysis of program-level data leads them to different conclusions. Although they report "quite sharply diminishing marginal returns to increasing investment in any single program, . . . programs embedded in larger and more diversified firms appear to be significantly more productive" (p. 48). Therefore, they find both economies of scale and scope at the firm level.

Cockburn and Henderson (2001) acknowledge that their early results pertain only to the discovery phase of pharmaceutical research, and not to development. To correct for this omission, they gathered additional data from the same 10 companies they had examined earlier. This information was for 708 development projects conducted between 1960 and 1990. On average, these firms undertook approximately 16 individual projects simultaneously, with average total spending per project exceeding $18 million. Over the 30-year period, mean expenditures per project roughly doubled (p. 1041). Furthermore, there was a wide range of product duration, running from 1 to 26 years, although 90% of them lasted 10 years or less. As expected, projects that failed to generate a new drug application (NDA) were concluded earlier than those that led to NDAs.

Their primary results were based on logit regression models used to explain the project's probability of success, where success was indicated by a new drug application. Their primary explanatory variables are: Scale – the firm's total development spending, Scope – the number of therapeutic classes in which the firm was active, and Experience – the stock of previously obtained NDAs. When these explanatory variables are included together in the estimating equation, the Scale effect was not statistically significant while the Scope effect has a major impact on the probability of the project's success. The firm's past success in the therapeutic class was also significantly and positively associated with successful outcomes. The authors conclude that "relocating the average project to a firm active in one more area would increase the probability of success by about 0.03" (p. 20). However, they also find that both of these purported effects disappear when firm dummy variables are introduced into the analysis, from which they conclude that "much of the variation in the scope measure is between rather than within firms" (p. 20).

The different ways in which research is organized as between firms in the Henderson-Cockburn sample have striking effects on the probability of success. The authors note the presence of "enduring idiosyncratic differences among firms in the organization and management of the drug development process.... Differences in development strategy – in the pace and timing of development spending, and in the formulation of research strategy that guides clinical development – [can be] important determinants of development productivity" (p. 21). That conclusion raises the question of why less efficient organizations and managements continue and are not replaced by more effective alternatives.

Overall, Cockburn and Henderson (1999) emphasize the presence of knowledge spillovers both within and across firms. The success of a given project is enhanced, they argue, by the success of a related program within the firm as well as in other firms. Even more important, they write:

> The most statistically important determinant of a research program's success, however, is its past productivity. The keys to this determinant are the "knowledge capital"

accumulated by the program as an organizational unit as well as the skills and experience of individual scientists. . . . The primary advantage of size has [therefore] become the ability to exploit internal returns to Scope – particularly the ability to exploit internal spillovers of knowledge – rather than any economy of Scale per se. . . . [Furthermore,] the benefits of spillovers can be realized only by incurring the costs of maintaining "absorptive capacity" – the ability to capture new spillovers." (1999, pp. 323–324)

The firm's scientific base, and the knowledge capital acquired by that base, they contend, dominates any simple economies of either scope or scale in determining the success or outcomes of a firm's research and development process. Scope and scale by themselves are less important than the knowledge capital accumulated by the firm.

The unique contributions of Henderson and Cockburn arise in part from the data set they have been able to acquire. While earlier studies used the firm as the observational unit, they probed within the firm to the level of the research project, and in doing so, provided rich insights that were not available earlier.

A dimension of the increasing disintegration of pharmaceutical R&D is the growing use of contract research organizations (CROs) to conduct clinical trials of new drugs. By 1999, 23% of trials were outsourced to CROs (Azoulay 2004, pp. 1593, 1600). In general, the more data-intensive projects are outsourced, while knowledge-intensive projects are more frequently undertaken within pharmaceutical companies (p. 1592).

V. Productivity and Costs

There are two ways of approaching the question of the productivity function and the cost function, which of course are duals of one another, and the economic literature deals with both. Except in perverse circumstances, conclusions regarding one have direct implications for the other. This principle applies to research costs and to research productivity. The increasing research cost of new drugs is directly related to the declining productivity of pharmaceutical R&D.

An important feature of pharmaceutical research in the past few decades is that despite the substantial scientific achievements that have occurred, and that are reflected in the increasing application of biotechnology to new drug development, the rate of new product generation has been fairly steady (Scherer 2000; Cockburn 2004). As Cockburn acknowledges, however, "counts of new molecular entities (NMEs) are a noisy measure. On average, over the long term, these numbers have been remarkably steady, but they fluctuate sharply from year to year, so that peak-to-trough changes over shorter time periods can be highly misleading" (p. 11).

To be sure, simple counts of new products introduced do not encompass either their medical or their economic importance. Some introductions are invariably more important than others. Indeed, as Grabowski and Vernon (1990, 1994) point out, there are major differences in sales among products so that the relevant distributions are highly skewed. Furthermore, pharmaceuticals have various indications, and the medical and/or economic importance of particular drugs can be more closely related to the number of approved indications than to the number of products.

In contrast, pharmaceutical industry spending on research and development has expanded greatly in the past few decades. From total spending of less than $5 billion in 1970, these outlays increased to $30 billion by 2002.[7] There has thus been an increasing discrepancy between the relatively stable number of new drugs approved and the increasing number of dollars spent on R&D to discover new drugs. The result, of course, has been declining research productivities in terms of the numbers of new products introduced, and also increasing costs for new drugs.

Berndt, Cockburn, and Grepin (2005) employ the number of medical indications to measure pharmaceutical innovation. A substantial share of industry research and development expenditures, estimated at between 25% and 30% (p. 45), is directed toward finding new indications for existing products. Berndt et al. use the term "incremental innovation" to describe these efforts. For the three therapeutic areas they examined, the number of FDA approvals for new indications increased substantially in the past decade (p. 27). In addition, the greater number of approved indications has led to increased utilizations of the drugs concerned (p. 41). On that basis, they maintain that reported declines in pharmaceutical research productivity are overstated.

An important feature of recent trends in pharmaceutical innovation is that they have accompanied the increasing disintegration of the research process. As noted earlier, an increasing share of pharmaceutical research is carried out in small biotechnology companies that deal with one or a small number of products. With increasing frequency, the major drug companies enter the process only at the development and testing phases. What seems clear, however, is that this new structure has not led to increased productivity or lower costs, at least in terms of the number of new products introduced, although it may have influenced the therapeutic properties of the new drugs. The shift of drug research to a more science-based mode has thus been associated with a substantial increase in research costs. What is unclear is whether these higher costs reflect the increased requirements of the science-based process or the effects of a more vertically disintegrated structure in which higher costs are borne or higher margins charged by participating firms.[8]

The reverse side of this same picture is, of course, the higher research costs of developing new drugs. There is a continuing literature on this question, which began with the 1979 paper by Hansen. Building on that foundation is the major study by DiMasi, Hansen, and Grabowski (1991). From a sample of 93 self-originated new chemical entities (NCEs) introduced by 12 companies in the 1970s and 1980s, they report mean cash outlays of $114 million per approved product (1987 dollars) and fully capitalized costs of $231 million. Because the R&D process is so lengthy, expenditures were just under half of total costs. Kettler (1999) updated DiMasi et al.'s estimates to 1997 values, based on the GDP implicit price deflator. Her resulting estimate is $312 million (pp. 14–15).

Because project-level data were available only for development and testing costs, DiMasi et al.'s estimates depended also on parameters derived from other sources. These included (1) an estimated success rate of 23% at which investigational NCEs gain approval, (2) an estimated ratio of 55.7% between preclinical and total R&D costs, (3) an estimated lag structure of 98.9 months between the initiation of clinical testing and NDA approval, and (4) a discount rate of 9% (pp. 121–126). All of these factors influenced their cost estimates.

Finding an appropriate discount rate is particularly important. Although the 9% rate used by DiMasi and colleagues may be appropriate for private firms making investment decisions, this rate may be much higher than is appropriate for public decision making. Fuchs and Zeckhauser (1987) argue that as long as future citizens are given equal weight to current ones, "the value of life-years to future generations should be discounted at the time-value-of-money rate" (p. 265). And Viscusi (1995) observes: "many cost-effectiveness studies currently use a real rate of discount of 5%, . . . [and] real rates of return of 3%, or even less, are more consistent with U.S. economic performance in the past decade" (p. 144). At lower discount rates, total research costs per new drug are much lower.

More recently, DiMasi, Hansen, and Grabowski (2003) employ a similar methodology to provide updated estimates of research costs. They examine development expenditures for a sample of 68 randomly selected new drugs introduced by 10 leading pharmaceutical companies during the 1990s. These firms accounted for 42% of industry R&D expenditures (p. 157). They then apply a real discount rate of 11% to capitalize costs to the point of marketing approval, which is a substantially higher rate than the 9% discount rate used earlier.

While their previous study estimated R&D expenditures per new drug at $231 million in 1987 dollars, their more recent one provides an estimate of $802 million in 2000 dollars. These figures indicate sharply higher costs for new product development. From this vantage point as well, the growth of a science-based research effort has not reduced research costs but led to higher ones.

VI. The Efficiency of Pharmaceutical Research: Some Conclusions

There are various perspectives from which to evaluate the efficiency of pharmaceutical research. One is whether the optimal amount of research is being conducted. Too many or too few resources could be allocated to this purpose. A second dimension is whether this research is carried out in the most effective manner so that output is maximized for given levels of input. In this section I consider both of these dimensions; the first is termed allocative efficiency, and the second is termed technical efficiency.

On the allocative efficiency of pharmaceutical research, there are theoretical reasons why there could be either under- or overinvestment in research. On the one hand, research activities, and particularly basic research, generate substantial positive externalities in that their total benefits to society exceed those accruing to the particular firm. As a result, firms do not incorporate their full measure of benefits when making their investment decisions.

On the other hand, there is more recent economic literature on racing behavior as applied to research activities. An important conclusion is that in a "winner take all" situation, there can be overinvestment in research activities. The reason is that the prospective gains may be less than the aggregate amount of the investment undertaken to achieve these gains.

Research spending in the pharmaceutical industry is carried out in the context of considerable interfirm rivalry. I emphasized that point in my first article on this topic (Comanor 1964) but provided no formal model of the process. Since that time, there have been more formal discussions of these issues. A particularly lucid one is offered by Cockburn and Henderson (1994), which emphasizes the competitive nature of the drug discovery process.

The authors first review the available theoretical literature on rivalrous research and emphasize its "winner take all" feature. In the case of pharmaceutical research, the firm completing the invention and receiving the patent wins the race. It gains most of the benefits from this research while others receive much lower returns on their investment. Although this picture is not always correct when applied to the pharmaceutical industry, it is largely so since the first and second entrants into a particular therapeutic market generally capture most of the net returns. Furthermore, firms understand that others are competing for the same prizes, and set their research strategies in anticipation of rival investment.

Cockburn and Henderson construct a data set to test the implications of this behavior. These data included the spending and output levels of individual research programs gathered from the internal records of 10 large pharmaceutical companies. Applying these data to an underlying model, they report that R&D investment is only weakly correlated across firms, but that R&D outcomes are positively correlated with the firm's own research productivity (p. 508). Although "me-too" investment occurs occasionally, it is not a major characteristic of this industry. In their judgment, "a better characterization . . . is that investment decisions are driven by the heterogeneous capabilities of the firm, by adjustment costs, and by the evolution of technological opportunity" (p. 509). Although strategic considerations may play some role, they argue that such factors do not drive investment decisions.

Cockburn and Henderson also note: "there are some grounds for believing that the entry of additional firms into the pharmaceutical research 'race' is not unambiguously welfare-destroying. Competing projects are better described as complements rather than substitutes, and there are significant spillovers of knowledge across firms" (p. 508). They conclude that rivalrous research activity is not the dominant factor behind the decision to invest in pharmaceutical research.

An alternate approach is not to examine variations in pharmaceutical research spending among firms but rather to consider the trends over time in total industry spending. Scherer (2001) employs this approach. His goal is to explain the long-term trend in real research spending, which had increased between 1962 and 1996 at a mean annual rate of 7.5% per year. In contrast, the growth rate of gross margins was 4.23% per year (pp. 217–218).

Rather than comparing these two series directly, Scherer computes the deviations of each series from its best-fitting linear trend. He finds a high correlation between these two sets of deviations and concludes that "the similarity of trend deviation patterns suggest that there was indeed cyclical co-movement in pharmaceutical industry growth margins and R&D

outlays" (p. 220). He goes on to explain: "As profit opportunities expand, [pharmaceutical] companies compete to exploit them by increasing R&D investments, and perhaps also promotional costs, until the increase in costs dissipate most, if not all, supranormal profit returns" (p. 220).

Consistent evidence is provided by Giaccotto, Santerre, and Vernon (2005), who estimate the influence of real drug prices on R&D intensity. Since drug prices are directly related to industry revenues, this study offers a similar picture of the process by which research spending is determined. These authors report "a 10% rise in the growth of real drug prices is associated with nearly a 6% increase in growth of R&D intensity" (pp. 204–205). What both these studies suggest is not an investment model at all, but rather one that employs available internally generated funds specifically for research and development purposes.

Where uncertainty levels are high, this process has the advantage of ensuring that all available funds are used for research purposes. What it does not demonstrate, nor could it do so, is whether this allocation process leads to an excess or insufficient spending on pharmaceutical research. What we observe is that spending has increased strongly in recent decades. New resources have flowed into the process by which new drugs are discovered, and there are no indications that promising avenues of research are neglected.

On this point, Grabowski and Vernon (1990, 1994) estimate rates of return from investment in pharmaceutical research and development, and report values slightly higher than the associated cost of capital. In their latter study they conclude: "the estimated mean return on pharmaceutical industry new chemical entity (NCE) introductions for the first half of the 1980s was 11.1% compared with the estimated (real) cost of capital of 10.5% over the same period" (p. 404). This finding also suggests that one is unlikely to find major unexploited opportunities. Still, without determining a social optimum, one cannot make firm conclusions about the sufficiency of resources directed toward these activities.

On the question of technical efficiency, results are also mixed. The productivity of pharmaceutical research funds has receded sharply in recent years, at least when measured by the number of new chemical entities introduced; and the cost of discovering and developing these products has correspondingly increased. The promise of a science-based research process has not led to the greater efficiency that was projected by its early proponents.

As Cockburn (2004) emphasizes, there are pluses and minuses to the process of disintegration of pharmaceutical research (pp. 17–20). One cannot conclude that the new structure of pharmaceutical research is the source of the higher costs and fewer products per research dollar that we observe. However, as Cockburn also suggests, "there is a genuine possibility . . . that the restructuring of the pharmaceutical industry will ultimately prove quite costly in terms of reduced productivity" (p. 21). Whether or not this concern is justified is unclear at this time.

PART TWO

STRUCTURING INCENTIVES FOR RESEARCH AND DEVELOPMENT

FOUR

Drugs for Neglected Diseases

New Incentives for Innovation

Aidan Hollis

I. Introduction

The problem of developing pharmaceuticals for so-called neglected diseases is of the utmost importance. Neglected diseases include malaria, tuberculosis, chagas diseases, African sleeping sickness, many other tropical diseases, and even HIV/AIDS, which claims most of its victims in sub-Saharan Africa. The reason for the lack of research into therapies for these diseases is the poverty of most of the victims, who are unable to pay high prices, if anything, for life-saving medicines. Since a large proportion of global pharmaceutical research and development spending is undertaken by private, for-profit companies, who must allocate their research dollars to those diseases on which they can make the most profit rather than the most impact on health outcomes, diseases that afflict mainly poor people are inevitably neglected. While there are a number of very important, very useful nonprofit initiatives, such as the Drugs for Neglected Diseases Initiative (www.dndi.org, accessed Nov. 7, 2005) and OneWorld Health (www.oneworldhealth.org, accessed Nov. 7, 2005), engaged in undertaking or sponsoring research on drugs for neglected diseases, it is important to consider other options to structure incentives to involve for-profit pharmaceutical companies, which have immense financial, technical, and human resources.

In this chapter I examine and compare three proposals recently made to stimulate private involvement in developing pharmaceuticals for neglected diseases: (1) Kremer and Glennerster (2004) and the Center for Global Development (2005) have described in detail a plan for "Advanced Purchase Commitments" for vaccines, which would commit a global body to pay a fixed subsidy per vaccine delivered for certain diseases, if the vaccine meets prespecified technical requirements and is priced below some level. This would help to solve both access and incentive problems, but is necessarily limited to products whose technical characteristics can be described in advance, a characteristic that makes it difficult to apply to most products that have not yet been developed. (2) Hollis (2005a, b) has proposed an Optional Reward plan in which firms could opt to offer an open license for medicines for neglected diseases in return for a payment from a reward fund, where the payment would be based on the health impact of the licensed drug. (3) The Project BioShield II Act of 2005 in the United States proposes that companies that develop drugs for certain diseases should obtain a "wildcard" patent extension for another drug in the United States.

The paper is complementary to Chapter 5 by Maurer in this book and Chapter 6 by Sloan and Eesley. Maurer takes a wider perspective, comparing what he calls "end-to-end" solutions (such as the ones I examine here) with "pay-as-you-go" initiatives in which government or other funding is directing at promising research or clinical trials as needed. Maurer argues that end-to-end solutions, because they impose greater risk on private firms, may be more expensive than pay-as-you-go plans. However, end-to-end plans have very attractive incentive properties because they reward success in developing important drugs. Sloan and Eesley discuss implementation issues of an Institute of Medicine proposal for advanced purchases of vaccines in the United States.

I begin with a brief examination of neglected diseases. I define a neglected disease as one for which additional dollars spent on research would have a relatively large incremental impact on therapeutic outcomes. Drug companies, because of their obligations to shareholders, invest in developing therapies for diseases based on the incremental effect on profits. This means that neglected diseases are those for which investment is expected to be unprofitable, despite the opportunity for improving therapeutic outcomes. Investing another $200 million in research into an already heavily researched disease may be useful, and from a profit perspective, it may be the right thing to do; but it is likely that from the perspective of maximizing the number and quality of human lives on the planet, it might be more useful to spend the money on developing treatments for malaria. It is this sense in which malaria is a "neglected" disease.

In effect, of course, such diseases are the ones primarily prevalent in low-income countries. Figure 4.1 shows diseases according to total "disability-adjusted life years" (DALYs) lost to each disease or condition. (A DALY is a standardized measure of health outcomes.) Some diseases are grouped together for convenience. The vertical axis shows the weight of each disease in low- and lower-middle-income countries, relative to its weight in high- and upper-middle-income countries. A disease responsible for 6% of lost

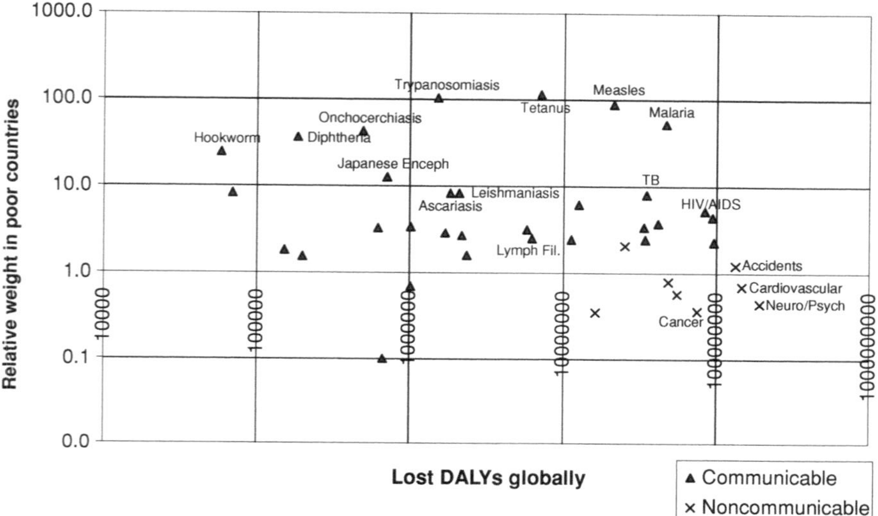

Figure 4.1. Diseases by global importance and by relative importance in low- and medium-low-income countries. *Notes:* The figure shows selected diseases and conditions according to global DALYs lost and the relative weight of each disease or condition in developing countries. If the relative weight is 2, that indicates that that disease is twice as likely to be responsible for a randomly selected lost DALY in low-income countries as in high-income countries. All data abstracted from World Health Organization (2004).

DALYs in lower-income countries and 2% of lost DALYs in higher-income countries would have a relative weight of 3. Diseases with a high relative weight in lower-income countries are those likely to be neglected. Malaria is the leading case of a very important disease, in terms of its effect on global health, that is heavily concentrated in low-income countries. In general, noncommunicable diseases have a relative weight near one.[1]

The positive relationship between income of those affected by a disease and the amount of research undertaken into pharmaceuticals for that disease has been empirically confirmed in a variety of studies, including Lanjouw and MacLeod (2005) and Lichtenberg (2005a). The prevalence of a disease in some developing countries has often been attributed to poor food, water, and sanitation or access to treatment and may not reflect an absence of useful pharmaceuticals. In such cases it may be factors other than pharmaceutical innovation that need to be addressed. However, even if other solutions are possible, there may also be situations in which a pharmaceutical solution would be the most cost effective, if it were available. For example, it may be easier to address the problem of malaria through a vaccine rather than through eliminating the vector of disease, the mosquito.

II. Push versus Pull Incentives

One of the most important choices facing any institution or government willing to devote resources toward developing pharmaceuticals for neglected diseases is between so-called push and pull mechanisms. Pull mechanisms are those that increase the reward to a firm from developing a new medicine, with the leading example of a pull mechanism being the patent system. Push mechanisms are investments that reduce firms' costs of developing drugs (e.g., Kremer and Glennerster 2004).

Push mechanisms include a wide variety of forms, with the most common structure being public-private partnerships involving technology transfer between public or nonprofit institutions and private firms. For example, the single largest source of medical research funding is the U.S. government through the National Institutes of Health (NIH); the billions spent annually have resulted in many major breakthroughs in medical treatment. However, the NIH does not generally develop drugs right through to commercialization. Rather, it tends to support early-stage identification of useful compounds and mechanisms of action of drugs, as well as identification of important therapeutic targets, largely sponsoring basic research rather than commercial development.

Spence (1984) observed that without informational asymmetries and commitment problems, direct government subsidies for innovation or in-house government research would be preferable to the patent system, since it would eliminate inefficiencies caused by monopoly pricing.[2] Of course, directing research funding is not so easy: governments may find it difficult to know how to allocate it. In practice, government sponsorship has been very important in enabling basic research but has typically not delivered commercial products. Basic research often cannot be made commercially valuable within the 20-year life of a patent; so the patent system provides little incentive to undertake highly risky basic research. But commercial development of a drug can occur within a 10-year timeframe, allowing another 10 years to reap the benefits of the patent monopoly. Thus, it makes sense for governments to be involved in basic research, but commercial development, including clinical trials, can be left to industry for products that offer potential profits.[3]

The chief concern about government attempts to develop drugs through clinical testing levels is that the government's decisions as to which products to develop might well be swayed by considerations other than the value of the product in the marketplace, given its lack of information about the likelihood of success of drugs under development. For example, a scientist specializing in an area may tend to overstate the amount of progress made to attract more resources to his or her project, making it difficult for government to sort out which projects are the most valuable. For-profit companies have strong incentives to focus on valuable products – those that fail to do so are exposed to management changes and bankruptcy – whereas governments have relatively weak incentives.

When private dollars pay for innovation, they do so at their own risk. If the innovation is unsuccessful, the innovator loses his or her investment. If the innovation succeeds, the innovator is compensated. In contrast, with government funding of innovation, the risks are not as straightforward. Those who pay for the investment, taxpayers, have no direct say in the investment, but bear the risk. This is apt to lead to poor direction of research funds.

Governments may also fund research indirectly through nonprofit organizations, such as the Institute for OneWorld Health and the International AIDS Vaccine Initiative (www.iav.org, accessed Nov. 7, 2005), which have attracted considerable funding. Their basic strategy is to cooperate with for-profit companies, in so-called public-private partnerships, to develop drugs that the for-profit companies would not find profitable to develop on their own, through technology transfers between the organizations. This approach is evidently important, though, as Maurer (2005, p. 65) observes, "There is still little consensus on whether, when, or why [public-private partnerships] work."

As Lichtenberg (2005a) showed, the amount of pharmaceutical innovation is positively related to the burden of disease in developed countries. However, he also showed that to the extent that the burden of disease in developing countries is different from that in developed countries, the burden in the former has no discernable effect on pharmaceutical innovation. This suggests that the pull mechanism of the patent system has been effective in stimulating innovation when a commercial reward is available. Thus, it seems reasonable that a mechanism that supplemented the reward to innovation for diseases prevalent in developing countries in such a way that the commercial incentives would be similar to those in high-income markets would be effective. So while push initiatives such as public-private partnerships and direct government funding of research may be very useful, it is desirable that they be supplemented by "pull incentives" if those incentives can, in a cost-effective way, assist the development of neglected disease drugs.

Whether there are any cost-effective, flexible pull mechanisms that can supplement the patent system, is, however, an open question. Below, I examine three proposals for pull incentive mechanisms. None of them is perfect. The question is whether any of them is likely to be worth investing the billions of dollars they would likely cost, diverting money away from direct research funding and public-private partnerships.

III. Advanced Purchase Commitments

The "Advanced Purchase Commitments" approach proposed by Kremer and Glennerster (2004) and the Center for Global Development (2005) has attracted considerable public attention as well as seed funding from the Gates Foundation in recent years. Advanced purchase commitments could be useful for certain types of pharmaceutical products, principally vaccines, to stimulate research by promising a subsidy of a fixed value per unit for a given number of units. The most attractive candidate product for such a commitment is a malaria vaccine, since the health (and economic) benefits from an effective malaria vaccine could be very large.

Advanced purchase commitments require a technical committee to identify the desired, feasible technical characteristics of a vaccine. The donor institution or sponsor would offer a minimum price to firms that developed a vaccine meeting the technical characteristics. The minimum price would be higher than the market can currently sustain, and it would be achieved by the donor offering copayments to the manufacturer to make up the difference between the market price and the minimum price. For example, the sponsor might make a payment of $13.50 per dose, while the transaction price of the vaccine for the ultimate buyer might be only $1.50. The manufacturer would thus obtain a total price of $15.

The donor would be committed to making its payments only for a fixed number of units (e.g., 200 million doses). Any firm that had received this subsidy would be required to set a low price on any additional units, on the basis that the producer would have received a suitable reward already. To make the proposal effective, it would be necessary to have a legally binding commitment on the part of sponsors to make the agreed payments, with a suitable arbitration mechanism.

As this proposal constitutes the leading candidate for a "pull incentive" to stimulate research in neglected disease drugs, it has also attracted its share of criticism, as did the Institute of Medicine's (2004) proposal for advanced purchases to stimulate vaccine R&D in the United States (see Sloan and Eesley, Chapter 6). In the context of neglected diseases, Farlow et al. (2005)

argued that the Advanced Purchase Commitment proposal as described in Center for Global Development (2005) is flawed in a number of critical ways. Their core critique of the mechanism is that it is extremely difficult to specify the technical characteristics of a vaccine that is still some years away from development, particularly when the state of science is continually changing, and the disease is complex and varies between and within populations. This, in turn, means that it is possible that the Advanced Purchase Commitment program could be less cost effective and could have perverse and undesirable effects on incentives.

For example, one of the technical characteristics that might be specified is the effectiveness of the vaccine in giving protection over a period of, say, two years. Suppose a vaccine is developed such that only 50% of the people vaccinated appear to obtain protection. This can raise two problems. If the partially effective vaccine is determined inadmissible to be paid under the Advanced Purchase Commitment plan, despite bringing immense health benefits to millions of people, the innovator is not adequately compensated. But, if it is deemed admissible (perhaps only for a scaled reward), the Advanced Purchase Commitment funding could be used up in a short time, so that a second, 100% effective vaccine expected to arrive two years later might obtain no Advanced Purchase Commitment subsidy at all.

The difficulty here is that firms' incentives to undertake research on potentially very valuable innovations are distorted: firms will have strong incentives to exactly meet the technical requirements, but very weak incentives to exceed them or to develop useful vaccines that do not meet them. The essence of the problem lies in the requirement for the sponsor to specify the characteristics of a product that has not yet been developed: flexibility is required, because of uncertainty; but flexibility puts a great deal of discretion in the hands of the committee judging whether to pay a subsidy, and if so, how much. Farlow and his coauthors complain that such discretion renders the Advanced Purchase Commitment program "committee-driven" rather than "market-driven."

The problem with discretion is that medicines are almost never unidimensional in their impact on health. Regulatory bodies such as the U.S. Food and Drug Administration (FDA) make determinations about whether a given drug meets their standards only after the drug has been clinically tested, but the standards imposed by law for approval of a drug are not specific: drugs are to be "safe" and "effective."[4] Most pharmaceuticals have a range of effects that would make it very difficult to stipulate minimal standards in advance, since in effect there is a trade-off between efficacy and safety: as noted by the FDA (1999, pp. 21–22), "A safe medical product is one that has reasonable risks, given the magnitude of the benefit expected and the alternatives available." Vaccines tend to have relatively small side effects, but their effectiveness over time and by proportion of the population may vary widely. The Advanced Purchase Commitment structure allows no obvious way to deal with determining whether technical standards have been met, except for allowing the committee that will grant an award substantial discretion.

Widdus (2005) argued that rather than try to formalize Advanced Purchase Commitments, the right approach is to create an informal Advanced Purchase Commitment program by simply demonstrating willingness to buy useful vaccines and drugs.[5] For example, if developed countries increased their commitment to official aid, and actually came up with the committed dollars, then over time such a commitment would act as an inducement to firms to invest in developing useful drugs. An unofficial Advanced Purchase Commitment plan that was supported by a long-term commitment by developed countries to purchase vaccines and other drugs for poor countries would offer some of the benefits of a formalized Advanced Purchase Commitment plan, but be less subject to the problems created by the inflexibility of a formal contract.

Widdus's proposal requires that sponsors of such an informal Advanced Purchase Commitment start investing more heavily in buying drugs and vaccines today. An important problem here, however, is that when investing limited dollars to buy pharmaceuticals, there is a natural preference for generic versions of drugs, since they may offer more therapeutic value for the limited dollars available (see Grabowski, Chapter 8). New drugs may be better, and yet be so high-priced that sponsors will substitute away toward therapies with a lower cost. But in that case, the inducement to innovation becomes rather weak. So along with what Widdus calls "consistent purchase at reasonable prices for existing under-used 'traditional' vaccines," it would be very helpful to have some way of committing to spend money on new products. But making an informal (unenforceable) commitment of the type Widdus proposes is not likely to be effective since countries have incentives to redirect scarce health funds to the most cost-effective medicines. So what is required is some way of formally committing money to innovative drugs and vaccines without having to specify in advance the unknowable technical characteristics of the product. The system of Optional Rewards described in Section IV attempts to address that problem.

IV. Optional Rewards Based on Therapeutic Effect

Hollis (2005b) and Pogge (2005) proposed an Optional Reward system in which a sponsoring agency would pay rewards annually based on the therapeutic effectiveness of drugs for neglected diseases. The sponsoring agency would be a multilaterally funded body, as in the Advanced Purchase Commitment proposal. In such a system, firms with patented drugs would obtain a cash reward from the sponsor, paid annually over several years, based on the therapeutic effectiveness of the drug, as estimated by the sponsor. Firms accepting the reward would be obliged to offer an open license to manufacture and sell the drug in developing countries, but would be rewarded based on the total sales of the drug. This would enable generic competition to enter immediately, thus increasing access to the drug, while firms would be rewarded based on the single property of the drug that any sponsor is likely to value: its impact on health. At the same time, the innovator would maintain an active interest in marketing its drug, to increase usage and hence the number of units on which it could be rewarded.

An important part of this proposal is that it must be possible to measure the incremental therapeutic effect of a new drug, and the quantity used, with reasonable reliability. As Maurer (2005) noted, estimates of therapeutic effect, typically measured in DALYs or Quality-Adjusted Life Years (QALYs), are really only approximate, and different methodologies may obtain quite different estimates. However, while such measurements are imperfect, this does not mean they cannot be used. If therapeutic value cannot be measured, how would regulatory agencies make decisions on whether to permit marketing of specific drugs? How would insurers decide whether to offer coverage? Many national drug insurance agencies, as in Australia, Canada, and England, use explicit cost-effectiveness tools to make decisions as to what drug will be covered (see Drummond, Chapter 11). The technical problem of determining the size of the reward in a reward system is almost identical to the insurer's problem of determining the cost effectiveness of a given medicine (see Pauly, Chapter 10). Although some people have doctrinal objections to any valuation mechanism other than the market, it is hard to see how this objection applies if the reward system is optional, since firms with objections to the reward system could continue to use the patent monopoly system exclusively.

A problem with reward plans generally is that sponsors face an incentive to undervalue innovations as a way of opportunistically saving money. To reduce the threat of such opportunism, the Optional Reward proposal requires the total cash rewards to be fixed in advance, with the share of this reward paid to each participating innovator determined by the share of the therapeutic benefit attributable to that firm's innovations. Thus, there is no way to reduce payout of the system.

As an optional system, firms would apply to enter the Optional Reward system only if they believed that they would make greater profits through the Optional Reward system than in the regular patent system. This means that firms' incentives to undertake research would be higher than in the absence of the Optional Reward system. However, rewards will also not be excessive, again through the inherent design of the system. There is an automatic adjustment mechanism in that if rewards are excessive compared to what is available in the patent system, firms will be attracted into the Optional Reward system until the rewards per product are reduced to a level comparable with the patent system. Thus, by construction, rewards are comparable to what can be obtained through the patent system for drugs of comparable therapeutic effectiveness. The firms that would opt in to the system would be those with drugs having high therapeutic value but low market value (presumably because of low buying power of the consumers).

Would such rewards be adequate to stimulate research into neglected disease drugs? The patent system has led to little research into drugs that would be primarily sold to poor people. The key to the Optional Reward system is that rewards are payable for therapeutic benefit, rather than on the basis of commercial profitability. In essence, the Optional Reward system makes profitability of a drug innovation dependent on therapeutic impact for those drugs opting in to the system, rather than on ability to pay of the consumers. Thus, the Optional Reward system could stimulate research into drugs that offered the potential for having very large health impacts.

There are two potential problems with the Optional Reward system. First, its system relies on direct measurements and estimates of health impacts of new drugs. Such measurements are imperfect: there are numerous, incompatible, methodologies yielding different answers; obtaining the information is expensive; and there could be fraud, lobbying, and other such influences. Nevertheless, direct measurement is the best that one can do.

There are really only three possible routes: (1) use the commercial market through the patent system to determine the rewards to the innovator, (2) base rewards to innovators on therapeutic benefits, and (3) do not bother measuring at all. Option (1) is the patent system, but this functions poorly for neglected diseases. Advanced Purchase Commitments use option (2) in a half-hearted way, as I describe below. A system of Transferable Intellectual Property Rights, described below, uses option (3). The key issue is that in the absence of meaningful measurement of health impacts, it is necessary to base rewards only on commercial success, and that is not consistent with a mission to improve the health of the poor.

The second important obstacle to making the Optional Reward system work is that it is necessary to pay out a substantial amount of rewards annually, regardless of the amount of innovation, and firms need to believe that the rewards will in fact be available well into the future. This means that the reward-granting authority needs financial support from governments, and a commitment many years into the future. The credibility requirements here are similar to those for Advanced Purchase Commitments, but more severe since larger amounts of money are required. While details on the minimum amount required to sustain an Optional Reward plan have not been worked out, it seems likely that a commitment to pay out at least $500 million annually would be required to sustain a meaningful program. It is possible that an international treaty could help to form a commitment mechanism.

It is helpful to see how the Optional Reward system relates to the patent system in the way that rewards are allocated. The patent system measures the value of an innovation by the amount of profits the innovator is able to extract. Such a measure of value, taken directly from market observations, seems to suggest that the value of the lives of very poor people is extremely low. This conclusion follows directly from the fact that poor people spend very little money on health care. This thinking has led some to argue that the allocation of money toward different types of medicines is already efficient. This is a fallacy, since it depends on who is determining what is valuable.

If the measure of value is profitability based on market prices, then the lives of the poor are of little value. But it is possible that the measure of value used by someone paying for research may be quite different. For example, international aid agencies that sponsor research into neglected diseases obviously believe that there is a different measure of value. Their objectives may be denominated in terms of lives saved, or other health objectives, and it is reasonable to spend money based on such objectives. Indeed, in general, governments choosing to allocate money must do so on the grounds of perceived value based on nonfinancial measures. For example, a decision to tax money from one group to provide an income to another group must be based on a belief that incremental consumption by the latter group is of greater value. The Optional Reward system follows this principle, that value in pharmaceutical innovation for neglected diseases has little to do with ability to pay by the consumer, but is instead found in the therapeutic effects of the drug.

The Optional Reward proposal is in many ways very similar to Advanced Purchase Commitments, and yet there are important differences. Like the Advanced Purchase Commitment plan, the Optional Reward proposal is a method for increasing overall incentives as well as increasing access. One key difference is that the Advanced Purchase Commitment plan is suited only to drugs whose technical characteristics can be described in advance:

of course, having fully described the characteristics of the drug allows the sponsor to identify in advance how much it is willing to pay as a subsidy for the drug. The Optional Reward plan does not require identifying technical characteristics in advance, but uses the realization of therapeutic impact to determine the reward. To be sure, measuring the therapeutic impact is not a trivial exercise, but it is feasible to estimate it.

The Advanced Purchase Commitment system sets rewards in an anticipatory fashion, presumably based in part on the expected therapeutic impact. Indeed, Kremer and Glennerster (2004, p. 90) observed that the sponsor's commitment should be large enough to motivate research on vaccines, but that "it should not be so expensive that alternative health interventions could save more lives with the same resources." They then examined the price per DALY of the Advanced Purchase Commitment proposal, based on some assumptions about the probability of its being successful in speeding up vaccine development.

The key difference is that the Advanced Purchase Commitment proposal requires one to estimate the therapeutic impact in advance to figure out how much money to allocate, which has the advantage that once the drug is being sold, no further evaluation of its effectiveness is required.

The Optional Reward proposal, in contrast, requires no technical specification in advance, but uses evaluation of the product once it is in the market to determine the appropriate reward. A simplified version of the Optional Reward proposal would be to make an estimate of DALYs per dose of each drug at the time it was introduced to the market. Such an estimate could rely, in part, on submissions from the innovating company concerning the therapeutic effectiveness of the product.[6] However, the sponsoring agency could exercise complete discretion in estimating therapeutic effectiveness, given the optional nature of the system. This is at least a less arbitrary method of determining the amount to be paid to a drug developer than the Advanced Purchase Commitment system, which requires one to estimate the therapeutic impact of a theoretical vaccine before it has even been developed.

The Optional Reward proposal also has the advantage of using the market effectively to make proportional rewards. The Advanced Purchase Commitment proposal does not include a methodology for determining exactly how large a subsidy it should pay – large enough to stimulate research (but how do we know?) but not so excessive that other interventions would be more effective per dollar of expenditure. In contrast, as discussed above, the Optional Reward proposal is designed so that rewards are neither excessive nor inadequate. This result is automatically achieved by fixing the sum available for rewards and then letting firms opt in to the system if they wish.[7]

Unlike an Advanced Purchase Commitment, the Optional Reward proposal requires the sponsor to spend money every year: an Advanced Purchase Commitment requires spending only in years in which an eligible vaccine is developed and being used. The reason for this difference is that the Optional Reward proposal assumes that innovations will arrive with sufficient frequency such that, at any given point in time, many of them will be in use and eligible for a reward. Such an assumption seems plausible since the reward system can include prescription drugs, rather than being restricted only to vaccines.

Finally the Optional Reward proposal is not, after all, incompatible with Advanced Purchase Commitments: both systems could operate simultaneously, presumably with the condition that a single product would not be eligible for inclusion in both.

Since the Optional Reward proposal is relatively recent, it has yet to face serious scrutiny from a wide audience. As such, it remains an interesting idea that may deserve further analysis and consideration.

V. Transferable Intellectual Property Rights

The Project BioShield II Act of 2005, introduced to the U.S. Senate in April 2005, contains a proposal for so-called Transferable Intellectual Property Rights, in which a firm that developed a vaccine for a disease such as AIDS would obtain a wildcard patent extension that could be applied to a drug of its choice in the United States. The proposal has received the endorsement of the International AIDS Vaccine Initiative, which sees any proposal to increase research into AIDS vaccines positively. This is therefore a proposal that deserves serious scrutiny.

There are at least three very important flaws in the basic mechanism proposed by Project BioShield II (and Transferable Intellectual Property Rights in general). First, the way the reward for the innovator is financed through a patent extension is inefficient and inequitable. Second, the incentive mechanism is poorly defined, and does not offer a clear methodology to determine how large a reward to pay for a given innovation. Third, the mechanism discriminates against small firms.

First, then, consider the way that financing is raised for this mechanism. Essentially, Transferable Intellectual Property Rights offer a way of providing an off-the-books financial reward to companies that develop some socially desirable innovation, such as a vaccine for HIV/AIDS. Ignoring the effect on innovation for the moment, consider how this financial reward is obtained. The innovator is rewarded with a wildcard patent extension of, say, two years on some unrelated product. For example, suppose Pfizer developed an AIDS vaccine; under BioShield II it would obtain a wildcard patent extension that it could apply to Lipitor. But this is functionally equivalent to a situation in which the government waited until patent expiration, and imposed a heavy tax on generically produced versions of Lipitor for two years, with the tax revenues paid to Pfizer as a reward for its AIDS vaccine innovation.

Thus, Transferable Intellectual Property Rights would in fact simply be a very specific tax imposed on consumers of an unrelated product. Normally, specific taxes of this sort are avoided unless there is some reason to discourage consumption of the product (as is the case with cigarette and alcohol taxes). Instead, governments in developed countries tend to use broad-based taxes that spread out the burden of taxation.

Broad-based taxes are appealing for two reasons. First, they tend to create less distortion in buying decisions than product-specific taxes that raise the same total revenues. Second, broad-based taxes are equitable since they impose the burden of taxation on a wide range of people. A decision to use a product-specific tax, when neither the amount of the tax nor the product on which it is imposed is determined by the government, must obviously be completely ad hoc. This would be roughly equivalent to a government policy of imposing very high taxes on various products at random to fund road construction. In fact, it is even worse, since the incidence of the tax falls on people who are, typically, sick (and hence using some unrelated drug). It is hard to conceive of a more poorly designed system for funding innovation than this.

The second general problem with Transferable Intellectual Property Rights is that there is no way of knowing exactly how much of an innovation is required to obtain the reward of a patent extension. Would a vaccine for malaria get the same opportunity for a transferable patent extension as a drug treating Chagas disease? What if it were only somewhat effective? Any authority wishing to offer such a reward would need to specify something about criteria for the reward in advance. The Project BioShield II Act (S. 301(b)(4)(A)(ii)) indicates that the eligibility for a patent extension will be carefully weighed, with the length of the extension dependent in part on the difficulty of innovation, availability of alternatives, seriousness of the threat, and impact of the patent extension on consumers. In other words, it is using an undefined measure of therapeutic importance of the innovation, balanced against some undefined measure of commercial significance of the patent extension, to determine how large the reward should be. In essence, this is a sort of incoherent Optional Reward system, with measurements very poorly performed, nothing clearly specified in advance, and immense discretion on the part of the administrator.[8] And since the administrator would face no real financial constraint (given that all costs would be outside his or her budget), one could expect rewards to be on the generous side, so that firms with quite minimally useful innovations (which are the most easily developed) would obtain patent extensions on drugs of immense commercial significance. It is hard to conceive of a system designed to be less cost effective.

A third, general problem with Transferable Intellectual Property Rights is that they discriminate against innovative firms that do not have a stable of blockbuster drugs on which a patent extension would be highly remunerative. For example, a vaccine from Pfizer, which could extend its patents on Lipitor, would receive a much larger reward than the same vaccine from a small biotech company, which had no blockbuster drugs on which it could extend the patent. Such a system rewards large firms disproportionately, and discourages small competitors.

In sum, Transferable Intellectual Property Rights are a type of reward system that (1) is extremely inefficient in the way it raises funds to reward innovation, (2) offers no plausible methodology according to which it could allocate rewards, and (3) discriminates against small innovative firms in favor of large ones.

The Transferable Intellectual Property Rights proposal has received support for two reasons. Large pharmaceutical firms find it attractive since it would allow them to make huge profits from patent extensions on blockbuster drugs, by developing drugs that are of little value therapeutically or commercially. Proponents of incentives for drugs for neglected diseases (including the International AIDS Vaccine Initiative) can support it because it increases incentives for potentially relevant innovation. To the extent that the extra costs fall on individuals who would not otherwise support research on neglected diseases, there is an increase in such research, regardless of how inefficient the funding is, or how inequitable the taxation. Even politicians may support it because they can claim to be supporting valuable research without having to raise taxes. However, there is a real cost, and the cost is likely to be much greater than the benefits. As a plan to reward innovation into neglected diseases, Transferable Intellectual Property Rights appear to be designed in such a way as to generate the least beneficial effect at the greatest cost.

VI. Discussion

Investing in research on drugs for neglected diseases may offer immense therapeutic benefits. There appears to be willingness to invest quite considerable sums of money into supporting such research, but the problem of how to allocate this investment is a stumbling block. This chapter has examined some proposals for new incentives for neglected disease research: as it shows, both the Advanced Purchase Contract plans and the Transferable Intellectual Property Right plans are related to the Optional Reward proposal.

The Optional Reward proposal allows firms to obtain a reward based on the measured therapeutic effect of their innovative drug, in exchange for offering open, zero-cost licenses for making and selling the drug. The Advanced Purchase Contract system is a version of this proposal restricted to specific drugs or vaccines having technical characteristics that can be clearly defined before the product is developed, where the therapeutic effect of the drug is assumed based on its predefined technical characteristics. There are trade-offs implicit between these two systems: the principal benefit of the Advanced Purchase Contract proposal is that its much more limited scope allows for a smaller scale of funding. The transferable intellectual property rights proposal used in BioShield II is also a kind of Optional Reward system, but with a highly inefficient system for raising financing and without a well-defined methodology for determining the size of the reward. Its principal attraction is that it offers potentially large rewards to pharmaceutical companies without new taxes. Thus, both large pharmaceutical companies and self-interested politicians can find it attractive; consumers of drugs are, however, likely to be harmed by it.

Evidently, no single proposal is without flaws, and the pragmatic way forward may be to continue to allocate funding to direct research investments, to public-private partnerships, and to systematic purchases of existing drugs. Any proposal for new incentives mechanisms rewarding firms for successful development of drugs for neglected diseases will have to show convincingly that it is a better use of money than those tried-and-tested methods. As such, there is an urgent need for much more careful analysis of the different proposals discussed in this chapter and a judicious weighing of their merits and defects, particularly in comparison to the direct funding methods, such as government grants for research, that are currently attracting most funding.

FIVE

When Patents Fail

Finding New Drugs for the Developing World

Stephen M. Maurer

I. Introduction

High-income nations use patent incentives to fund most new drug discovery. However, most victims of tropical diseases are unable to pay prices high enough to cover the research and development (R&D) costs of new medicines (Hollis, Chapter 4). Thus, foundations and governments in high-income nations (hereinafter collectively "sponsors") must fill the gap. Before the 1990s, sponsors spent about $50 million per year on worldwide drug discovery for neglected diseases. This figure was clearly inadequate in a world where per-drug R&D costs averaged $802 million (DiMasi, Hansen, and Grabowski 2003). Predictably, R&D results were practically nonexistent. Indeed, just 12 of the 1,233 "new chemical entities" licensed worldwide between 1975 and 1997 were approved to treat tropical diseases in humans (Kremer and Glennerster 2004). Fortunately, recent developments are more hopeful. Worldwide R&D spending on diseases of poverty could reach $500 million per year by decade's end (Ridley 2004). While this level of funding is still small by commercial standards, it is at least plausible. The challenge now is for sponsors to get the most "bang" from every dollar spent.[1]

Given that ordinary patent incentives do not work, what new incentives should sponsors create to supplement or replace them? Section II introduces the main proposals that have been suggested. The first category, denoted "end-to-end" strategies, consists of proposals in which sponsors mimic the patent system by announcing a single reward for researchers who successfully complete the entire drug discovery pipeline. The second category, denoted "pay-as-you-go" proposals, asks sponsors to offer smaller but more frequent rewards at multiple stages along the drug discovery pipeline. Unlike end-to-end strategies, these proposals require sponsors (or hired drug development experts) to make continual judgments about which drug development projects are most promising and ought to be funded. Section III examines the generic strengths and weaknesses of end-to-end strategies. Section IV provides a similar analysis for pay-as-you-go systems and comments on incentives that pay-as-you-go sponsors should consider choosing at each stage of the drug discovery pipeline. Finally, Section V describes the benefits and drawbacks of designing hybrid proposals (mixed strategies) that combine end-to-end, pay-as-you-go, and/or conventional patent incentives within a single strategy. Section VI presents a brief conclusion.

II. Current Proposals

Current proposals can be divided into three categories. First, end-to-end strategies try to mimic the patent system by establishing a single reward for researchers who successfully complete the entire drug discovery process. Perhaps the best known end-to-end proposal is called Advanced Purchase Commitments. It requires governments and nonprofits (collectively, "sponsors") to promise a set price for new drugs that meet some minimum standard. Other end-to-end plans are based on prizes. For example, Hollis (2005, and Chapter 4) has proposed paying prizes to companies that produce new drugs based on a mathematical formula (DALYs) that quantifies therapeutic benefit. Although Hollis concedes that the DALY formula is an imperfect measure of social value, he argues that conventional pharmaceutical markets, in which patients neither pay for nor understand the drugs they consume, are even more imperfect. Perhaps the simplest end-to-end plan is for sponsors to increase their current and/or projected purchasing budgets for pharmaceuticals, thereby encouraging companies to develop new products. Almost any form of increased spending satisfies this model.[2]

The second category of proposals consists of "pay-as-you-go" arrangements. These proposals recognize that sponsors do not have to treat drug discovery as an indivisible black box, but can (if they so choose) offer a separate reward for each of the roughly dozen major steps along the "drug discovery pipeline."[3] The main advantage of pay-as-you-go is that sponsors can tailor incentives to each individual step of the drug discovery process.

However, this advantage comes at a price. Because pay-as-you-go systems intervene at multiple points along the drug discovery pipeline, sponsors must repeatedly decide which drug candidates are most promising and deserve further investment. In other words, they must replicate the functions of a private drug development team. Perhaps surprisingly, such teams actually exist. Since the mid-1990s the Gates and Rockefeller Foundations have devoted enormous resources to creating so-called Private-Public Partnerships.[4] While the Private-Public Partnership label includes many diverse philosophies – particularly with respect to the role played by industry and intellectual property rights – most programs rely on nonprofit management teams to make key investment decisions for a portfolio of drug candidates. Early evidence suggests that the quality of these decisions is comparable to that found in the private sector. Public-Private Partnerships currently conduct three-fourths of all known neglected disease drug development projects (Pharmaceutical R&D Policy Project 2005).

The final category of proposals consists of suggestions for hybridizing end-to-end, pay-as-you-go, and/or conventional patent incentives within a single strategy. Today's Private-Public Partnerships frequently use sponsor money to subsidize commercial R&D programs when conventional patent incentives are thought to be inadequate (Pharmaceutical R&D Policy Project 2005).

III. End-to-End Strategies

The preceding section distinguished between end-to-end strategies that establish a single reward for the entire drug discovery pipeline and pay-as-you-go strategies that create separate (and possibly different) incentives at multiple points along the pipeline. This distinction is fundamental, and, further, end-to-end and pay-as-you-go each have generic strengths and weaknesses. Traditional categories differentiating between "push programs" that pay for R&D inputs in advance and "pull programs" that reward R&D outputs ex post (Kremer and Glennerster 2004) are often confusing. For example, a prize for the "best protein target discovered in 2005" and a prize for the "best new pharmaceutical of 2005" would both be considered "pull" mechanisms. Yet the risks for sponsors and researchers are completely different. The end-to-end/pay-as-you-go categories make this dichotomy explicit.

This section explores the strengths and weaknesses of end-to-end strategies. Readers interested in a more comprehensive description and critique of leading end-to-end proposals should consult Hollis (Chapter 4).

Generic Differences between End-to-End and Pay-as-You-Go Strategies

By definition, pay-as-you-go plans permit sponsors to implement different incentives at multiple points along the drug discovery pipeline. As seen below, these can be either "push" or "pull" incentives. By contrast, end-to-end systems establish just one incentive for the entire process. In practice, no one argues that this incentive can be a "push" mechanism because that would mean paying researchers hundreds of millions of dollars in advance. But this means that end-to-end sponsors can only use "pull" incentives. Compared to pay-as-you-go, end-to-end sponsors start with a smaller menu of options.

Advantages of End-to-End: Private-Sector Decision Making

The principal benefit of end-to-end plans is that they permit private-sector researchers to manage the R&D process with minimal guidance from sponsors. This strategy undoubtedly has political virtues compared to pay-as-you-go strategies in which sponsors are forced to make periodic judgments about which drug candidates to invest in and will therefore find it harder to disclaim responsibility if R&D fails. The benefits for economic efficiency are more obscure. Vesting control in the private sector makes sense only if nonprofit entities are inherently less capable of "picking winners" than their corporate counterparts. I return to this question in Section IV.

Problems with End-to-End: Setting the Reward

If sponsors had perfect information, it would be easy to set rewards. McGuire has shown that the optimum reward is, in principle, solvable as a utility maximization problem (McGuire 2003; Institute of Medicine 2004). However, McGuire's proof assumes that the R&D production function is known to second order. In fact, the values (and even the sign) of these coefficients are "very uncertain" and depend on information that is not "public knowledge" (Sloan and Easley, Chapter 6).[5]

This information asymmetry poses a powerful challenge to sponsors. The problem is particularly severe for end-to-end proposals, which, as previously noted, are automatically limited to "pull" incentives like prizes or Advanced Purchase Commitments. These incentives share the generic weakness that sponsors must decide how large a reward to offer. If sponsors offer a reward that is lower than expected costs, no R&D occurs. But if sponsors offer a reward that is higher than expected costs, they will pay too much for any desired level of R&D. Sponsors could avoid both dangers if end-to-end systems were compatible with contract R&D,[6] which lets sponsors set rewards based on sealed bids and other forms of competition that encourage researchers to reveal their true costs. Commercial pharmaceutical companies routinely use contract R&D to contain preclinical and human testing costs.

In general, the amount that end-to-end strategies overpay in expectation depends on how well sponsors can estimate the minimum reward needed to elicit R&D.[7] In practice, very little is known. Commentators who estimate the "minimum required market" for new drugs usually quote ranges in which the high estimate is 140–160% of the low estimate (Maurer 2005). On average, we expect sponsors to overpay by half this range or about 20–30%.[8]

It remains possible that sponsors can refine this estimate through more careful arguments. In what follows, I assume that a profit-maximizing company will invest in R&D whenever the promised reward exceeds its per-drug development costs in expectation. I consider two cases.

What Reward Is Needed to Elicit a Rich Nation R&D Effort?

In the first case, I assume (somewhat unrealistically) that sponsors wish to replicate the R&D effort that is typically devoted to finding cures for rich nation diseases. The advantage of this approach is that it lets sponsors set rewards based on what commercial pharmaceutical companies actually spend. For example, DiMasi, Hansen, and Grabowski (2003) used pharmaceutical company records to report that mean per-drug R&D costs were between $684 and $936 million at the 95% confidence level. Here, the high estimate is 127% of the low estimate, suggesting that sponsors would only overpay by 13% on average. A second study, by Berndt et al. (2005), suggests even more uncertainty. It used economic arguments to extract per-drug R&D costs from reported revenue data. Although the study did not quote estimated errors, its methods appear generally consistent with the 140–160% uncertainty ranges described above.[9]

These estimates represent industry-wide averages. Since the amounts paid to develop individual drugs vary widely, it might be possible to obtain more accurate estimates for particular diseases. For now, it is unclear how sponsors would make such adjustments apart from guesswork. Similarly, R&D costs are known to vary from company to company. This suggests that some firms may be willing to perform R&D for a smaller reward (Farlow 2004). The amount of this correction is also unknown.

Hollis (Chapter 4) offers a clever alternative to estimation. His "Optional Reward system" would let drug companies waive their normal patent rights in exchange for sharing in a fixed-prize fund. The size of each company's share would then be announced using predefined health metrics (e.g., "DALYs"). The virtue of such a plan is that new companies would continue to join the plan, bidding down the value of each DALY saved, until the expected reward equaled their expected R&D costs. This means that sponsors would pay the minimum feasible cost for whatever level of R&D effort the DALY-based prize happened to elicit.

The question remains, however, what that level of effort should be. Sponsors who try to duplicate rich nation incentives will normally end up with a small number of intense programs. There is no obvious reason to think that such a strategy will save the greatest number of lives in expectation. Sponsors could instead decide that it was better to spread existing resources over more projects. At this point, "estimated reward" is no longer tied to existing rich nation practices. Rather, it depends on the sponsor's judgment of how much R&D effort would be optimal. Without loss of generality, I consider the case where sponsors ask what amount must be offered to elicit a "bare bones" R&D program.

What Reward Is Needed to Elicit a Low-Cost R&D Effort?

The celebrated $802 million estimate of per-drug R&D costs by DiMasi, Hansen, and Grabowski (2003) provides, at best, nothing more than an upper limit for what a bare bones program would cost. Companies in competitive industries set R&D investments equal to the expected value of whatever patents they hope to obtain. If the U.S. Congress creates broad (i.e., generous) patents, companies will engage in redundant and/or accelerated programs.[10] If Congress creates narrow patents, companies will mount less ambitious programs. In either case, companies will end up earning the same (economic) profit in expectation – zero.

This analysis suggests that companies will respond to any reward that exceeds the minimum feasible amount needed to support a bare bones R&D program. However, it is still not clear how much money sponsors can save by offering smaller rewards. Kremer and Glennerster (2004) argued that existing patent rewards are already near minimum feasible per-drug discovery costs. More specifically, they contended that Congress designed the Hatch-Waxman Act so that patent revenues would be constrained by the cost of developing follow-on, "me-too" drugs. One problem with this analysis is that it assumes that Congress knows what the minimum feasible cost of developing "me-too" drugs actually is. In fact, Congress seems to use the same DiMasi et al. estimates as everyone else (Maurer 2005). In principle, a more direct method for estimating what a bare bones program would cost is to write down a pro forma budget. The Global Alliance for TB Drug Development has prepared such a budget based on a massively detailed analysis of known input costs (Global Alliance 2001). It reports that a bare bones program could probably deliver new malaria drugs at between 17–20% of the range quoted by DiMasi et al. This figure remains controversial.[11]

Desired Level of R&D Effort
In keeping with our cost containment criteria, we have thus far assumed that sponsors would choose a bare bones program if that option were available. In fact, sponsors can choose any level from bare bones to rewards that exceed those found in rich nations. While the ideal level is a matter for public health authorities to decide, it is reasonable to think that they might want to spread their limited resources over as many programs as possible. Indeed, it is not obvious that high per-drug R&D costs are desirable even for rich nations. For example, multiple "crash" programs might be a poor investment if they accelerated discovery by only a few weeks or months. Similarly, large patent rewards might induce spending on non-R&D activities (e.g., marketing, regulatory maneuvering, and lawsuits) that provide little or no benefit to patients.

Problems with End-to-End: Controlling Sponsor Discretion

Researchers in end-to-end systems are not paid until after they have sunk their costs. This increases the incentive for sponsors to renege, since a researcher with sunk R&D costs can usually be persuaded to sell drugs at a price that barely covers its manufacturing costs. Knowing this dynamic, a rational company may refuse to invest at all unless it receives some combination of (a) contractual and practical assurances that the sponsor will not renege and (b) an additional premium to cover any remaining risk of default. From the sponsor's perspective, this creates an inherent trade-off between the flexibility needed to adjust rewards ex post to reflect true value of drugs and the size of the reward that must be offered ex ante to elicit R&D in the first place.

In practice, one can imagine many possible trade-offs between flexibility and reward size. The most obvious way to reduce risk premiums is to design contracts that minimize sponsors' discretion to adjust rewards ex post. One blue ribbon panel recently adopted this position by recommending that sponsors not be allowed to adjust Advanced Purchase Commitment rewards downward even if R&D costs fall in the interim (Advanced Markets Working Group 2005). They presumably believed that the increased discretion was not worth the additional risk premium that companies would demand in compensation. Other possible trade-offs include promising to award a fixed sum to the best drug(s) produced within a preannounced time frame (Scotchmer 2004; Hollis 2005a, b) or promising to calculate prizes according to a preannounced algorithm (Hollis 2005a, b and Chapter 4). Although both methods still run the risk of under- and overrewarding innovation, these errors may be smaller than those associated with a fixed, ex ante reward.

Problems with End-to-End: Cumulative Innovation

The final generic difficulty that end-to-end systems face involves second-generation inventions. In conventional patent systems, improved products command a higher price and earn more revenues. To share in these revenues, first-generation patent owners must grant licenses that permit improved products to appear on the market.

The result is very different for end-to-end systems. Consider first a simple Advanced Purchase Commitment strategy in which sponsors announce a single fixed price in advance. Since prices are fixed, an improved product cannot earn more revenue than the first-generation product does. For this reason, the first-generation inventor has no incentive to improve its own product or make its technology available to others. Instead, its best strategy is to block the better product until, in Farlow's phrase, the sponsor agrees to pay an additional, "monopoly-size bonus" (Farlow 2004). In principle, sponsors can fix the problem by announcing a second, higher reward for second-generation products. However, the amount of this reward will normally be even more speculative than it is for first-generation products. A better solution might be for sponsors to insist that first-generation inventors license all improvements at zero royalty. However, this solution is also suboptimal since researchers may not perform first-generation R&D in the first place if they cannot share in second-generation revenues (Scotchmer 2004).

Hollis's QALY-based prize system tries to evade these problems by using an algorithm to calculate the incremental value added by each new drug (Hollis 2005a, b). Since only the algorithm is fixed, data (and reward) can be updated continually. The weakness of this system is that QALY-based estimates (and any monetary rewards based on them) are known to be highly imperfect. For example, QALYs (a) systematically undervalue drugs that treat contagious disease, (b) show poor replicability from one measurement or study to the next, (c) measure intangible "quality of life" benefits poorly, and (d) do a relatively poor job of measuring incremental improvements to earlier drugs (Maurer 2005). If these drawbacks are severe, sponsors will do better to estimate the reward in advance.

IV. Pay-as-You-Go Strategies

Unlike end-to-end systems, pay-as-you-go systems place substantial decision-making and outsourcing responsibilities in the hands of sponsors. I begin by asking what incentive mechanisms a pay-as-you-go sponsor is likely to adopt. I then turn to potential problems that might make pay-as-you-go less efficient than comparably funded end-to-end strategies.

Tailoring Incentives for Specific Problems

Commercial pharmaceutical companies currently use multiple incentives to outsource R&D, including (a) purchasing contract research services, (b) purchasing patented knowledge from outside entities, and (c) awarding prizes to researchers that solve particularly difficult problems.[12] Pay-as-you-go sponsors must design strategies that replicate and, if possible, improve on these incentives. Here I comment on the choices that pay-as-you-go sponsors are likely to make at different points along the drug discovery pipeline.

Basic Research

Basic science requires intense individual creativity and hence researcher discretion. Furthermore, researchers frequently need to assemble widely scattered information. Grants facilitate these goals by rewarding applicants who submit new ideas. Since researchers who fail have less chance of winning future awards, grants also provide limited assurance that recipients will not exploit their discretion to shirk work. Finally, grants pay for R&D in advance. This is an important advantage for academic scientists and other groups that lack access to financing (Scotchmer 2004).[13]

Early-Phase Drug Discovery

Early-phase drug discovery encompasses multiple steps ranging from developing new drug ideas to optimizing small molecules that can be tested as drug candidates. Once again, researchers must draw on widely scattered knowledge and exercise substantial discretion. One natural solution would be for sponsors to extend the grant model beyond basic research. For now, commentators disagree about whether academic scientists are sufficiently interested in applied research for grants to be effective (Kremer and Glennerster 2004; Widdus and White 2004). The only way to be sure is to try the experiment. Even a limited pilot program should be enough to demonstrate whether grants are an effective mechanism for persuading researchers to participate in early-phase drug discovery.

The main alternative to grants is for sponsors to award "best entry prizes" to whichever researcher(s) achieve the most important results in a predefined period. Like patents, prizes are a powerful method for eliciting new ideas. Since researchers cannot claim a prize without concrete results, best entry prizes also provide substantial protection against lazy or inefficient researchers. Best entry prizes are already widely used to solve chemical engineering problems. The best-known prizes are managed by a company called Innocentive. It specializes in problems that companies have been unable to solve in-house, attracting solutions from around the world (Maurer 2005).

Finally, pay-as-you-go sponsors might experiment with "open source drug discovery" collaborations in which members search for protein targets and compounds in much the same way that programmers find and fix bugs in LINUX. The rise of computational biology, which requires few physical resources beyond volunteers and computer terminals, provides the closest analogy to open source computing (Maurer, Rai, and Sali 2004). As in LINUX, the fact that members are volunteers means that they have little incentive to shirk work.[14] More speculatively, some authors argue that open source methods can also be used to perform experimental chemistry. Chemistry, however, requires reagents and other expensive inputs. Volunteers would have to divert these resources from existing grants (Benkler 2004; Maurer, Rai, and Sali 2004). While funding agencies might decide to ignore such unauthorized spending on a small scale, substantial diversions seem unlikely.

Preclinical and Clinical Testing

The number of potential drug compounds is so large that there is almost no chance that a new drug candidate has been studied before. Because scientists must experiment de novo, the ability to elicit information is much less important than for earlier R&D phases. On the other hand, preclinical and human testing are extremely expensive, accounting for roughly three-quarters of all R&D expenditures (Global Alliance 2001). This suggests that incentives should focus on cost containment. One natural solution is to award R&D contracts to whichever researcher offers the lowest rate, either informally or through competitive bids. The main drawback of this method is that contract researchers may have an incentive to shirk or else prolong unnecessary work after the contract is signed. Fortunately, preclinical and human testing are extremely routinized and generate massive paper trails.

These facts facilitate monitoring and suggest that any moral hazards are manageable. Large pharmaceutical companies routinely purchase preclinical and clinical testing services from contract researchers.

A second, more speculative option would be to organize open source clinical trials. Eric von Hippel (2004, private communication) suggested that clinicians might organize open source trials aimed at finding new uses for preexisting drugs. Off-label trials are particularly suitable for open source because the health care system usually pays the underlying cost of drugs and physicians. Extending open source models to earlier, preapproval testing would mean finding other sources of funding. In principle, pharmaceutical companies might be willing to fill this gap if FDA regulators concluded that open source data were inherently convincing. Under the current system, contract researchers sometimes color or even falsify results to please their employers (Maurer 2005).

Manufacturing

Competition is a powerful constraint on manufacturing costs. Historically, sponsors have used contracts to purchase a fixed quantity of drugs as an incentive to build new manufacturing capacity. Examples include polio and, more recently, bird flu vaccine (Maurer 2005). Competition is also a powerful way to constrain manufacturing costs once production begins. By far the simplest strategy is for pay-as-you-go sponsors to put drug compounds in the public domain so that anyone can manufacture them.[15]

Problems with Pay-as-You-Go Plans: Inadequate Purchasing Power

Thus far, I have assumed that nonprofit Private-Public Partnerships can outsource R&D just as efficiently as large pharmaceutical companies. However, as already noted, contract researchers may have an incentive to shirk and/or needlessly prolong work. Commercial pharmaceutical firms use large liaison staffs and the prospect of repeat business to discourage such practices (Hume and Schmitt 2001). These facts suggest that large entities may have an inherent advantage at extracting value from outsourced research. This could be a significant handicap for individual Private-Public Partnerships, whose annual budgets are seldom more than a few percent of what large pharmaceutical companies spend on R&D (Maurer 2005).[16]

It is possible to put an upper bound on the size of this handicap. Press accounts report that R&D service providers typically earn 10–15% profit margins (Hume and Schmitt 2001).[17] Assuming a 10% return to capital, this suggests that companies providing R&D services earn super-normal profits of no more than 5%. Large pharmaceutical companies should not be able to extract discounts greater than this figure.

Problems with Pay-as-You-Go Plans: Picking Winners

Advocates of end-to-end systems often argue that nonprofit firms are less able to pick and develop winning drug candidates than their private-sector counterparts. Since many Private-Public Partnerships hire executives directly from private industry, this cannot be a matter of individual competence. If the effect exists at all, it must be a matter of incentives.

In the private sector, efficiency ultimately depends on the ability and willingness of profit-maximizing shareholders to defund companies that fail to perform. In the nonprofit world, sponsors play this role. Unfortunately, current Private-Public Partnerships often bundle drug management, education, advocacy, and other functions within a single entity. Such practices create an incentive for sponsors to continue funding entities with weak drug discovery programs because they perform other functions (e.g., education or advocacy) well. In principle, entities that focus exclusively on drug discovery will be more efficient than entities that pursue multiple, unrelated activities. Sponsors can and should encourage Private-Public-Partnerships to stay narrowly focused on drug discovery.

The deeper question is whether sponsors are willing to defund failures as ruthlessly as a private shareholder would. Presumably, they should ask themselves this question before adopting a pay-as-you-go strategy. In the meantime, critics of public-sector R&D sometimes point to instances in which researchers have failed to deliver vaccines in the past (Kremer and Glennerster 2004). Less often noticed are the many instances in which government and nonprofit entities have succeeded. Examples include the U.S. Army (Argentine hemorrhagic fever, Venezuelan equine encephalitis, Rift Valley fever, tularemia, infant botulism) (Covert 2000), The March of Dimes (Salk and Sabin polio vaccines) (Smith 1990), and The Pasteur Institute (rabies, BCG vaccine, yellow fever, polio, hepatitis B, shigellosis) (Pasteur Institute n.d.). Pending detailed investigation, there is no particular reason to think that nonprofit entities are inherently inefficient.[18]

V. Mixed Strategies

Thus far, I have assumed that pay-as-you-go and end-to-end strategies are distinct from each other as well as from conventional patent incentives. Here I ask how these distinctions can be relaxed to create "mixed" incentives.

Extending End-to-End or Pay-as-You-Go Rewards to Include Patent Revenues

Patents are an unnecessary complication for diseases like leishomaniasis or Chagas, where commercial markets are negligible. However, there are many diseases for which patent revenues provide a substantial (albeit still inadequate) fraction of the reward needed to elicit R&D. Some observers claim that patent revenues for new tuberculosis drugs could generate up to 80% of the reward needed to elicit innovation (Kremer and Glennerster 2004). Other observers have similarly claimed that markets could supply 45% of the funds needed to support R&D for a new tuberculosis drug and 25% of the funds needed for an AIDS vaccine (Global Alliance 2001; Boswell 2003). While these estimates are probably optimistic, it is worth asking how patents can be grafted onto end-to-end and pay-as-you-go strategies.

Adding Patents to End-to-End

End-to-end strategies leave R&D decisions in the hands of industry. The most natural way to extend these strategies is to let the industrial partner own patent rights over and above the basic end-to-end reward. Alternatively, sponsors can dispense with end-to-end rewards entirely by paying a subsidy to the private partner's R&D program. In either case, sponsors face the usual difficulty of deciding how much reward is actually needed to elicit investment. However, this problem is harder now because the private partner can usually estimate the value of patent rights better than the sponsor can. This increases the sponsor's risk of overpayment.

Adding Patents to Pay-As-You-Go

Pay-as-you-go systems leave R&D spending decisions in the hands of sponsors. The most natural way to extend these strategies is for a commercial pharmaceutical company to contribute money and services to the sponsor's R&D program in exchange for the right to patent whatever drugs are ultimately produced. Currently sponsors and their Private-Public Partnerships usually negotiate such transactions with one pharmaceutical company at a time. The problem with this approach is that the sponsor's ability to extract money and services is limited by its ability to estimate how much revenue a patented drug is likely to earn. A better system would be for the sponsor to auction its patent rights to whichever company offers the most money and services. This competitive system would encourage companies to reveal their true estimates of potential patent revenue.

When Can Sponsors Use Patent Rights to Stretch Their R&D Budgets? Patents have drawbacks as well as benefits. If drugs are patented, high prices will almost always exclude some users. From the sponsor's standpoint, this means that patent-supported research is a double-edged sword. On the one hand, sponsors can use patents to attract private investment, thereby increasing the amount of R&D delivered per public dollar invested. On the other hand, patents let private parties demand a high price for whatever new pharmaceuticals are created. Higher prices, in turn, mean that fewer patients will use and benefit from the public's investment in knowledge. From a cost-benefit perspective, this may sometimes be an acceptable trade-off – most obviously, when political constraints on spending force sponsors to choose between a patent-supported program and no program at all.

Sponsors frequently try to expand patient use of patented drugs by insisting that commercial pharmaceutical companies offer deep discounts ("access pricing") to poor patients. However, access pricing automatically reduces profits and, indirectly, the amount of money and services that pharmaceutical companies are willing to contribute to R&D in the first place. The question is, how much? The answer will normally depend on the private partner's ability to price discriminate by charging different prices to different users.

Suppose first that price discrimination is impossible so that the pharmaceutical company must charge a single price to all patients. In this case, a company's expected patent revenues will disappear – along with its willingness to contribute resources – once the access price falls below marginal cost of production. Judging from the fact that several vaccines sold at marginal cost still reach only a small fraction of users (Kremer and Glennerster 2004), it may often be necessary to set access prices at or below the marginal cost of production. In this case, patents provide no net benefit to sponsors although they may shift expenses in time and/or from one sponsor to another.

Now suppose that price discrimination is perfect. In this case, manufacturers can offer deep discounts to the poorest patients with no effect on patent revenues. In fact, profit-maximizing manufacturers will automatically offer such discounts until prices reach their marginal cost of production (Reinhardt, Chapter 2). This means that sponsors should subsidize production only if the desired access price is below marginal cost.

The foregoing discussion suggests that sponsors should measure potential patent revenues not only by the revenue-maximizing price that the private partner could theoretically charge, but also by the access price. In general, patent revenues will be most useful where the stream of medicines earmarked for poor patients can be kept well segregated from those sold to rich ones. While such discrimination is often possible in rich nation markets, the situation is much more doubtful in the developing world where normal pharmaceutical company distribution channels tend to be slender or nonexistent. The most favorable cases almost certainly involve diseases where the "commercial" market is geographically separate from developing world patients in need of access pricing. In these cases, the simplest solution may be to limit company patent rights to rich nations (Lanjouw 2004).

Mixing End-to-End and Pay-as-You-Go

Advocates commonly argue that sponsors should fund a mix of end-to-end and pay-as-you-go systems. Political motivations aside, the justifications for these proposals are obscure. In principle, there are at least two reasons why a mixed strategy might make sense. First, sponsors may not be able to decide whether end-to-end or pay-as-you-go is the most cost-effective proposal and might want to experience both systems before choosing. However, the time scale for developing drugs is 12–15 years (DiMasi, Hansen, and Grabowski 2003). Even if sponsors are able to form a decision in some fraction of this time, such an experiment is likely to be expensive.

Second, sponsors might want to combine end-to-end and pay-as-you-go if commercial firms and public entities each had areas of comparative advantage. For example, commercial firms might be better at "picking winners" while Private-Public Partnerships might have superior knowledge about which drugs are needed. In this case, sponsors might want a strategy in which Private-Public Partnerships subsidized pharmaceutical companies that pursued particularly useful drugs. Unfortunately, it is not obvious how this scenario would be implemented in practice. To this author's knowledge, no advocate of mixed solutions has ever suggested criteria that sponsors could use to apportion funds between end-to-end and pay-as-you-go initiatives.

Finally, sponsors who divide their resources between end-to-end and pay-as-you-go strategies stand to forfeit significant economies of scale. As we have noted, the best way for end-to-end systems to overcome researcher mistrust is through large, frequent payouts. This suggests that researchers are likely to demand smaller risk premiums for large end-to-end programs than for small ones. Similarly, we have argued that pay-as-you-go methods are more efficient when Private-Public Partnerships can offer large volumes of repeat business. This observation suggests that large pay-as-you-go programs are more efficient than small ones.

VI. Conclusion

We live in an era of hope. Larger sponsor budgets suggest that tropical disease R&D can be substantially accelerated over historic levels. That said, sponsor budgets remain painfully small. Simply throwing money at the problem will not work. Nor, in all probability, will dividing funds evenly between every conceivable candidate strategy for funding R&D. Sponsors will have to make hard, clever choices.

This chapter has presented a framework for systematically comparing the strengths and weaknesses of the many diverse incentive mechanisms that have been proposed since the late 1990s. In particular, it argues that sponsors face a fundamental choice between "end-to-end" and "pay-as-you-go" solutions. Given that drug discovery costs are very poorly known, sponsors who adopt end-to-end strategies are likely to pay a substantial (20–30%) cost penalty compared to pay-as-you-go programs. Sponsors should not accept this generic penalty without convincing evidence that private-sector drug management teams are able to "pick winners" more efficiently than their nonprofit counterparts. For now, such evidence does not exist. The main uncertainty seems to be whether sponsors are prepared to defund inefficient programs as ruthlessly as private-sector shareholders would. Sponsors who believe that they can invest as effectively as private-sector shareholders should normally choose pay-as-you-go programs over end-to-end solutions.

The existing literature gives sponsors many options, but no agreed framework for systematically comparing their strengths and weaknesses. Sponsors can and should demand better. In particular, they should insist on a full menu of possible incentive plans and a detailed, dollars-and-cents estimate of what each is likely to cost. Bill Gates has long experience in demanding – and using – hardheaded business advice to guide Microsoft's $7 billion annual investment in R&D. The Gates Foundation could do worse than to follow his example.

SIX

Implementing a Public Subsidy for Vaccines

Frank A. Sloan and Charles E. Eesley

I. Introduction and Overview

Judged in terms of the relationship of benefit to cost, vaccines are among the most socially valuable public health investments (U.S. Centers for Disease Control and Prevention [CDC] 1999; Stratton, Durch, and Lawrence 2000).[1] In spite of some recent successes, such as increases in immunization rates in the United States (CDC 2002a, b, 2003), substantial structural and financial problems remain. In particular, the United States has recently experienced unprecedented shortages in 8 of the 11 routine childhood vaccines (Georges et al. 2003). Flu vaccine shortages were experienced in 2000–2002 and 2004 (Cohen 2002; Enserink 2004; Institute of Medicine 2004).

Although unique causes have been attributed to each shortage, a common pattern remains. In the past three decades, the number of firms producing vaccines for the U.S. market has decreased. Between 1966 and 1980, more than half of all commercial vaccine manufacturers stopped producing vaccines, and the exodus has continued to the present (Cohen 2002). As of early 2004, only five companies produced all vaccines recommended for routine use by children and adults, and only three of these were U.S.-based firms. Eight major vaccine products – including MMR (measles-mumps-rubella), tetanus, and polio – each had only one supplier (Institute of Medicine 2004). A long-term shutdown in capacity by any one of these companies could be a major supply shock, as occurred with the disruption in supply of flu vaccine from a Chiron plant in October 2004, which cut the supply of vaccine to the United States by almost half (Enserink 2004).[2]

The exit of firms from the vaccine market also has important implications for the development of new vaccines. If firms find supplying vaccines to be unprofitable currently, they are also unlikely invest in R&D to develop new vaccines. The public sector is a major purchaser of vaccines as well as a regulator of vaccine supply. There is a very large potential social benefit from the introduction of new vaccines (CDC 1999; Stratton, Durch, and Lawrence 2000), which inadequate private returns to R&D investments may discourage.

In the United States in the first decade of the twenty-first century, public purchases of vaccines account for more than half of the childhood vaccine market; the government has used its monopsony power to negotiate substantial discounts and enforce price caps – one reason that private returns to investments in R&D are low. Although governments may place a high value on having a vaccine, once the vaccine has been developed, governments have an incentive to use their market power to drive prices down to the marginal cost of manufacturing the product. This has been called a "time-consistency" problem (Kremer and Glennerster 2004, p. 43; Grabowski 2005). Although aggressive price negotiations may have negative side effects, to government officials, the lower prices are tangible and certain as opposed to adverse effects on private incentives to invest in R&D, which are less tangible and uncertain (Pauly 2005). Compared to many pharmaceutical products, the vaccine market is quite small, about $6 billion in 2002 (Arnould and DeBrock 2002; Plotkin 2005). Recent empirical research has established a relationship between current market size and introduction of new products by pharmaceutical manufacturers (Acemoglu and Linn 2004). Finkelstein (2004) found that a $1 increase in annual expected market revenue from a vaccine elicits an additional six cents in annual present discounted value investment in that vaccine. Finally, vaccines are more likely to interfere with the spread of the disease than are drug treatments, and sellers have less information to use in extracting consumer surplus for vaccines than for certain drug treatments (Kremer and Snyder 2003).[3] As a consequence, vaccines may tend to be less profitable than drug treatments.

There are other problems on the demand side. First, there are important health *and* financial externalities in consumption. Person A's consumption reduces the probability that an unvaccinated Person B will become ill with the disease. To the extent that the cost of care is insured, savings in insurance outlays accrue to B as well as to A. Less certain, but nevertheless plausible, is that many individuals may be myopic and not give sufficient weight to the subsequent benefits of being vaccinated. Or they may reason that they will just take drugs for therapy once they have become ill. For example, the amount of preventive effort may be reduced when high proportions of HIV-infected people are being kept alive by antiretroviral drugs (ARVs). Given externalities in consumption of vaccines, there is also concern about lack of insurance coverage for vaccines. Provision of insurance serves to internalize the externality, at least in part.

Most children in private health plans in the United States have coverage for recommended vaccines. Many children have private insurance that does not cover immunizations or that covers only certain vaccines, or they face substantial copayments and deductibles (Giffin, Stratton, and Chalk 2004, note 10; Kaiser Family Foundation 2002; Nace et al. 1999). Vaccinating children can be particularly important. In Japan, vaccination of children prevented one death for every 420 children vaccinated (Reichert et al. 2001). Evidence is also accumulating in the United States of significant reductions in serious flu cases in adults from vaccinating children (Cohen 2004). Previously, when vaccines cost very little, cost-sharing arrangements were not that important. Currently, the full series of pneumococcal conjugate vaccine, which is administered over an 18-month period, has a price of over $200, which may be burdensome to lower-income families.[4] Vaccination for several childhood diseases is mandatory under state law and enforced at the time the child enters school. Mandates and other recommendations for vaccines as well as public subsidies are based on decisions made by organizations such as the Advisory Committee on Immunization Practices (ACIP). Such coverage decisions appear to be made on clinical criteria without reference to vaccine cost.

The United States has a pluralistic health care financing system. The diversity of coverage imposes administrative cost on health care providers, for example, in billing for services rendered. By imposing transaction costs on physicians, the fragmented system for financing immunizations creates barriers to immunization. There are many public and private sources of funding for immunizations in the United States, including the Vaccines for Children Program (VFC), State Children's Health Insurance Program (SCHIP), Medicare, Medicaid, individual state programs, and private health plans. These sources of coverage vary in terms of both who is eligible and which vaccines they cover. Thus, patients and physicians often lack knowledge of provision of coverage for immunizations, including whether or not the patient is covered at all (Institute of Medicine 2004, p. 81).

Determining eligibility for immunization coverage can present an administrative burden on pediatricians and other physicians, especially since many patients often shift in and out of eligibility (Institute of Medicine 2000, 2002). In addition, providers often must store different stocks of the same vaccines according to the source of payment and eligibility, and spend time monitoring inventory for different sponsors. Given the low compensation for administering vaccines and the administrative burden, some physicians may decide not to offer vaccines, particularly as the acquisition cost of vaccines rises (Davis et al. 2002; Freed et al. 2002), instead referring patients to public health clinics for vaccines. The consequence may be that fewer persons are immunized (Davis et al. 2003).[5]

In August 2003 the Institute of Medicine's Committee on The Evaluation of Vaccine Purchase Financing in the United States issued its final report *Financing Vaccines in the 21st Century: Assuring Access and Availability* (Institute of Medicine 2004). This chapter's first author was chair of this committee. The charge to the committee was to (1) examine current arrangements for purchasing and distributing vaccines in the public and the private health sectors in the United States, (2) to identify strategies to ensure access to vaccines and offer incentives for the development of new vaccines, and (3) to develop recommendations to guide federal, state, and Congressional decision making. The committee considered a wide range of strategies from incremental changes in the current system – for example, expansion of the Vaccines for Children Program to include additional population groups – to a system of complete governmental purchase of vaccines.

The approach ultimately selected was embodied in three recommendations. The most important recommendation was the first, that the current system for purchasing and distributing vaccines should be replaced by a vaccine *mandate, subsidy,* and *voucher* system. The mandate would require all public and private insurance plans to cover certain types of vaccinations and would apply to vaccinations for diseases with substantial spillovers; however, the report did not explain how spillovers would be defined.

The *mandate* for insurance coverage addressed two concerns. First, absent a mandate, vaccination rates are likely to be suboptimal; second, by establishing a uniform system, the administrative burdens on physicians' offices would be reduced; and, coupled with a specific payment for vaccine administration, greater numbers of physicians would supply vaccinations. All public and private insurers would be required to cover specific types of vaccinations for specific populations as recommended by a public body, such as a modified ACIP. Insurers in turn would purchase vaccines and pay physicians for vaccine administration.

All health plans would receive a fixed-dollar subsidy for vaccine purchase and vaccine administration. The committee specified that the fixed-dollar subsidy be made a function of the social benefit of the vaccine for the groups for which the vaccine was mandated, but the subsidy would not necessarily equal the full social value. The subsidy would not reflect R&D or on production costs. Although insurance coverage for particular vaccines would be required, health insurance coverage itself would not be required. Thus, without a subsidy, premiums could rise more than private benefits to policyholders, and some policyholders might drop insurance coverage altogether.

While the funded mandate would cover all insured persons, the *voucher* provision would cover uninsured children and adults, who would receive immunizations from health care providers of their choice, conditional on the provider's being willing to accept the vouchers as payment in full. The value of the voucher would equal the fixed-dollar subsidy paid to health plans. Participating providers would collect the voucher at the time of service and submit it to the government for payment. The committee considered alternative approaches to the voucher system – from an electronic card system to simply reimbursing providers who submit a bill for each vaccination administered. The committee did not endorse any particular approach, although the fixed-dollar subsidy appears to have been preferred.

The fixed-dollar public subsidy would apply to existing and to future vaccines. For existing vaccines, a higher price would encourage more entry into the vaccine business, more investment in developing improved versions of existing vaccines, and greater investments in production capacity to reduce the probability of supply disruptions. For future vaccines, injection of public funds coupled with the mandate would increase market sizes and prospective returns to R&D on new vaccines.

The subsidy would be based on the total societal benefit of the vaccine – not 100% of the value, but some percentage of that amount and perhaps a lower percentage for current than for future vaccines. Thus, the subsidy formulas for current and future vaccines could be different. The committee was not specific about how the fixed-dollar subsidy would be calculated, but rather left this as a detail of implementation to be considered later by others.

The fixed-dollar subsidy would not be a government-administered price; insurers could negotiate a different price with manufacturers. If the negotiated price were lower than the subsidy, insurers could keep the difference between the subsidy and the negotiated price. Vouchers, however, would be on a payment-in-full basis; that is, no supplementation from patients would be permitted.

The mandate/subsidy plan would apply only to populations/vaccines recommended for coverage by an independent body. The committee's second recommendation proposed changes to the composition and decision-making process of ACIP, the entity that recommends vaccines for use by the public. ACIP currently lacks expertise in cost-effectiveness analysis and finance, is unable to consider price in its decisions, and makes recommendations before the federal price is determined.[6] Under the IOM's proposal, ACIP would compute the subsidy. While ACIP's recommendations would be binding on public and private insurers, at the same time, the government would be obligated to fund the mandate.[7]

The committee cautioned that the report offers a strategic framework and blueprint for change, not an immediate roadmap or "next steps" plan. The third recommendation called for a public process of stakeholder deliberations to explore the full implications of the proposal and address technical design issues. The IOM recommended that the National Vaccine Program Office (NVAC) of the U.S. Centers for Disease Control convene a series of regional and national meetings with the major stakeholders and others to refine the recommendations and develop plans for implementation.

The rest of this chapter discusses details of implementation not discussed in the report and criticisms of the report.

II. The Stakeholders' Critique of the IOM Report

Subsequent to the release of the report, NVAC met to consider the report's findings and recommendations. After hearing the views of various stakeholders, NVAC concluded that the committee's proposal was too radical and indicated its preference for more modest modifications of the existing vaccine financing system. As summarized by Hinman (2004, p. 3):

> there was universal commendation to IOM for highlighting the value of vaccines; highlighting the need to vaccinate adults as well as children; attempting to ensure access to vaccines by all children; and identifying factors contributing to instability in vaccine research, development, production, and supply. However, stakeholders (mainly representatives of the pharmaceutical industry, which produce vaccines, health insurers, and CDC officials), were concerned about some of the sweeping changes recommended by IOM. There was skepticism that the recommended approaches would provide incentives to manufacturers or improve immunization levels in children and adults. There was also concern about undertaking a dramatic shift from the present system to an unproven new system; concern about the lack of detail about how the proposed new system would operate; and concern about the cost of the new system. Stakeholders questioned whether the system was sufficiently broken to require this level of "fix." They also felt that improvements in the current system might go a long way to achieving the goals. These incremental changes might include expanding VFC to all underinsured children; removing price caps; giving providers a choice of vaccines; harmonizing the regulatory process with other countries; and encouraging an expansion of health benefits. (p. 3)[8]

Following its critique, NVAC recommended increased funding for existing public programs,[9] regulatory changes to facilitate importation of vaccines from other countries into the United States, first-dollar coverage for vaccinations, adequate (presumably higher) reimbursement for administration of vaccines, and campaigns to publicize the value of vaccines.

Recommendations for increased funding reflected the mix of stakeholders surveyed. Health insurers opposed benefit mandates and were understandably reluctant to endorse even funded mandates because of a suspicion that funding may be at most partial. Existing pharmaceutical manufacturers presumably did not endorse entry of competitors.

The report recommended that VFC, which is administered by the CDC, be replaced by a mandate applicable to entire categories of individuals, and the report was silent on the public agency that should be responsible for oversight of the program. Some citizens' groups questioned the desirability of disbanding the VFC program for an "untested and more expensive program" (p. 6).[10] The Pharmaceutical Research and Manufacturers' Association of America (PhRMA) indicated that "Anticipatory pricing of vaccines by establishing the level of federal subsidies, as called for by IOM, would, in effect, set price caps on vaccines and these have proved detrimental in the past" (p. 4). PhRMA said that clinical trials have become increasingly expensive for their member companies, and in general, private coverage for vaccines with presumably higher profit margins for the companies precedes public funding. According to PhRMA, the IOM proposal would eliminate private pricing for the vaccines subject to the mandate/subsidy.[11] NVAC's claim that the IOM proposal lacked specificity on some important aspects has merit.

III. Implementation Issues: Mandates, Setting Prices, and Vouchers

Mandating Coverage: Rationale, Problems, and Fixes

Mandates have several justifications.[12] Absent mandates, health plans may have an insufficient incentive to cover vaccines. Such coverage may not be demanded because individuals do not take account of the health and financial externalities in their purchase decisions (Summers 1989). Also, people may underestimate the probability of contracting various diseases (Jensen and Morrisey 1999). Vaccines are more likely to interfere with the spread of the disease than are drug treatments. As the probability of contracting a disease falls, fewer persons may be expected to demand to be vaccinated for the disease. Also, market power of sellers of vaccines may be lower than for drug treatments. With drugs, persons who may benefit from the treatment are identifiable to sellers, thus allowing firms to extract consumer surplus from these consumers. For vaccines, such information is less likely to be available (Kremer and Snyder 2003).

Mandates also have shortcomings. If the mandates are binding on employers or insurers, they require decisions to be made that would not be made in their absence, and they may lead to loss of insurance coverage and/or lower wages. Loss of coverage may result because the mandates raise insurance premiums.[13] As premiums rise, less insurance is demanded (Cutler and Zeckhauser 2000).[14] Mandates may also depress wages. Employers are likely to be indifferent about how they compensate employees but rather are concerned about total compensation per employee (Pauly 1998). Thus, if the cost of health insurance increases, wages are lower than they would be absent the increase.[15]

The IOM report lacked clarity about whether the mandate would allow for insurers to impose cost sharing on insureds. Plans with deductibles would presumably continue to have them, and the price of vaccinations would apply to unsatisfied deductibles. Since vaccination rates are likely to be less than at the socially optimal level even with insurance coverage (Finkelstein 2004), there is an argument for not imposing additional cost sharing for vaccinations. In any event, a copay would often apply for the physician visit at which the person receives the vaccination. Permitting some cost sharing would be beneficial in that it would blunt the potentially negative effects of the mandate discussed above.

If demand is price inelastic, the mandate will not have the intended effect of raising vaccination rates since not many more people would be vaccinated at the lower out-of-pocket price.[16] Strong empirical evidence on the price elasticity of demand is lacking; one study reported a low price elasticity of demand for vaccines (Frank et al. 1995). There is, in addition, some indirect evidence from the implementation of a public universal vaccine program, suggesting some effect of price on vaccination rates (Freed et al. 1999; Ives et al. 1994; Lurie et al. 1987; Nexoe, Kragstrup, and Ronne 1997; Ohmit et al. 1995; Pleis and Gentleman 2002; Rodewald et al. 1999; Satterthwaite 1997). Mechanisms underlying the observed elasticity of demand are complex in that use depends not only on consumer but also on physicians' decisions. If physicians refer patients to public health departments because payment does not cover the marginal cost of vaccinating patients in their offices, then this too may be a deterrent to use.

Theoretical research on the economics of infectious diseases describes an important limitation of subsidies to stimulate demand for vaccines. The private benefit from being vaccinated partly reflects the prevalence of the disease. To the extent that the price faced by the consumer falls, increases in the quantity of vaccinations demanded are likely, followed by declines in disease incidence and prevalence. With fewer persons with the disease, demand for vaccinations will fall. As Philipson (2000) and others have cautioned, using subsidies to resolve the externalities problem may not increase the steady-state equilibrium vaccination rate if demand is highly prevalence responsive (pp. 1777–1778). However, empirical evidence on the magnitude on this relationship is lacking (e.g., Hotz, Ahituv, and Philipson 1996).

Thus, a mandate/fixed-dollar subsidy by itself may not be enough to boost vaccination rates to their socially optimal levels.[17] In addition, various advertising campaigns and even compulsory vaccination may be needed to reach such levels.

The mandate proposed by the committee may not have deleterious effects on insurance coverage and wages *if* the fixed-dollar subsidy offsets the increased cost from the mandate. However, the voucher for the uninsured will make not being insured relatively more attractive, which arises in the U.S. context since being covered by health insurance is not mandatory; nor is there a financing system to ensure universal coverage (see Reinhardt, Chapter 2). Also, the public programs would receive the same mandate, making public coverage more attractive.

Several implications for vaccine financing plan design plan follow. Adverse effects will result if the mandate is not funded. The subsidy should cover the health and financial externalities. Also, there is an inevitable trade-off between providing vouchers for the uninsured and crowding out of private insurance coverage. One "solution" would be to make the vouchers unattractive to providers who would in turn refuse to participate in the voucher program. But this would partially defeat the purpose of voucher provision. Pricing of vouchers will be considered in the next section.

Setting the Fixed-Dollar Subsidy

ACIP currently makes recommendations that specific vaccines be administered to particular groups without explicitly comparing vaccine benefits and costs. Implicit in its recommendations is the presumption that benefits at least equal costs, but these benefits and costs are not quantified. The IOM plan requires that benefits and costs be quantified and net benefits will used for setting subsidy/payment levels.

Measuring Social Value (and Cost)

The social value reflects the savings attributable to the vaccine accruing to the individual who receives the vaccine and to others who otherwise would incur adverse health effects from the person's not being vaccinated or would incur added financial burden as a taxpayer or an insurance premium payer. Such savings include reductions in spending on personal health services, the value of increased longevity and reductions in losses in labor market and household productivity, and reductions in pain and suffering of persons vaccinated and who would have otherwise contracted the disease.[18] Stratton, Durch, and Lawrence (2000) conducted comprehensive cost-effectiveness analysis of 26 vaccines not yet developed. Other spreadsheets for conducting cost-effectiveness analysis of vaccines in various countries were developed by Michael Kremer.[19] This research is very useful in demonstrating the feasibility of measuring social value although cost-effectiveness analysis does not directly obtain social value.[20] Thus, we do not value benefits further here.

McGuire (2003) showed that setting the vaccine price equal to mean benefit will elicit the socially efficient level of R&D on vaccines. Although this is an efficient solution, it may be subject to criticism on equity grounds. The entire net benefit accrues to manufacturers as profit, and no consumer surplus accrues to the public. McGuire assumed a fully effective vaccine. Benefit should be scaled to reflect the extent to which a vaccine is partially effective.

An alternative approach focuses on consumer welfare. The product price is set to maximize expected consumer surplus, the difference between benefit and price. To maximize this difference, price must be lower than the mean benefit. However, by lowering price, manufacturers spend less on R&D. Thus, there is a reduced probability that the new vaccine will become available. McGuire (2003, p. 214) derived an expression for the optimal division of surplus between consumers and producers at the price that maximizes consumer net benefit:

$$(b - p)/(p - c) = \text{consumer net benefit/operating profit} = -qq''(q')^2, \tag{6.1}$$

$q = q(x)$, where q is the probability that a new vaccine will be discovered and marketed, x is expenditures on R&D, b is the mean benefit per dose, c is the mean production cost per dose, and p is the mean price per dose. Here q' and q'' are the first and second derivatives of the probability of discovery function.

The first derivative q' is clearly positive. The second derivative q'' may be negative if there are diminishing returns to investments in R&D. According to (6.1), consumer net benefit should be high relative to operating profit when the marginal product of R&D expenditures is relatively low (q') and the first derivative of the marginal product (q'') is relatively low. Essentially, when marginal product is high and it does not fall appreciably with increases in

R&D expenditures – that is, R&D spending is relatively productive – rewards should go to the manufacturers to stimulate research and development. However, when such spending is not as productive, consumers should receive higher relative rewards in the form of a lower price.

McGuire's analysis is static. Thus, it does not allow for the possibility that paying a higher price for a vaccine may accelerate product development. If paying a higher price would accelerate innovation and there are important opportunity costs to society from waiting for an effective vaccine, the price should be higher than it otherwise would be.

To our knowledge, no one has estimated a production function for vaccine R&D or for pharmaceuticals more generally.[21] For vaccines, the most likely possibility is to rely on expert scientific judgments.

Public knowledge of the R&D production function parameters is likely to be highly uncertain. The research production function $q(x)$ is not public knowledge. Even x for vaccines is unknown, although there is some evidence on the cost of developing new drugs (DiMasi et al. 1991; DiMasi, Hansen, and Grabowski 2003). Furthermore, the parameters of the production function are likely to differ substantially among vaccines. If a decision is made to pay the full price for a new vaccine, there is a trade-off between providing a windfall to manufacturers or paying a lower p and facing a higher probability that the vaccine will not be developed.

However, on the brighter side, firms make estimates of the marginal product of R&D expenditures prior to making such investments. Especially because many outside experts are likely to have had prior experience on the inside, insiders may not have a large advantage over outside experts in making such estimates.

Overall, it is possible to gauge b with reasonable accuracy – probably to a far greater extent than b can be gauged for most innovations, for example, flat screen television monitors. By contrast, determining c may be more problematic.[22] Mean production cost c for vaccines can be determined from various sources, including expert opinion and from production cost production at government-owned facilities. The government payment/subsidy covers c plus an imputed charge for capital.[23]

In practice, c may vary according to the extent to which companies invest in a production process that ensures continuous supply and is not subject to stoppages due, for example, to violations in vaccine safety standards. That c may vary inversely with the probability of a supply disruption complicates the task of determining an appropriate c.[24]

Rather than pay the full b or some fraction of it based on vaccine effectiveness and productivity of investment in R&D, another option is to base government payment on the external benefits of vaccines, including pain and suffering from the disease and productivity loss in household and market settings and cost of medical care, when individual *i* becomes ill, to others.

Should Existing Vaccines Covered by the Mandate/Subsidy Be Priced by a Different Algorithm than Future Vaccines?

Strong arguments can be made for using the same algorithm for pricing existing versus new vaccines, although for a period, to avoid a large increase in public expenditures, it may be necessary to limit annual percentage increases in price for existing vaccines. Potential entrants apparently find current prices to be unattractive, and higher prices for existing vaccines may be required to encourage entry. Also, if the government was not willing to acknowledge the social value of existing vaccines, this would make the offer of a payment to reflect social value for future vaccines less credible. Firms may fear that after they have sunk millions of dollars into research, the government has incentives to renege and offer a lower price. To the extent that firm executives fear this risk, they will withhold investments in vaccine R&D because expected revenue decreases with less perfect credibility. Inasmuch as firms are risk averse, limited credibility reduces efficiency (Kremer 2000b).

Government failure to honor its promises of payment for a future vaccine may be legally liable for the breech, but firms may not want to rely on this safeguard. Past court decisions have held purchase commitments to be legally binding contracts (Kremer 2000b).

One exception to the strong arguments for using the same algorithm for pricing existing versus new vaccines relates to the risk of sudden pandemics resulting from viruses that transfer from animals to humans. The most salient current example is avian influenza. There may be a need to build a mechanism for monitoring for human infection and person-to-person transmission into the system of financing vaccines and the capacity for a quick ramp-up in R&D and production far in advance of a potential outbreak.

Role of Patents and Prizes

Patents are widely used to provide incentives for R&D investment (Cohen and Merrill 2003; deLaat 1997; Gallini and Scotchmer 2002; Maurer and Scotchmer 2004; Merrill, Levin, and Myers 2004). The patent system has some important advantages. First, the market values the benefits from new products. Surrogate measures of willingness to pay can be quite inaccurate. Second, it is unnecessary to specify characteristics of the product to be developed ex ante, as is the case for some of the major alternatives such as prizes and procurement contracts. If a still better product is developed, it can be patented and marketed as a competing product at a price that the market will bear. Third, the main risks to the investor in R&D are that the investment will fail to produce a patentable product and the patent will be challenged, but there is no need to rely on promises from a government agency made in advance of the innovation.

A major disadvantage is the large deadweight losses due to monopoly power associated with granting a patent. Also, in the presence of substantial insurance coverage, market valuations may not be accurate measures of value. On balance, there is strong case for considering alternatives to patents here.

One alternative to patents is prize-based incentives (deLaat 1997; Kremer 1998). This type of reward has been proposed for pharmaceuticals as well (Abramocicz 2003; Hollis 2005a, b; Shavell and Van Ypersele 2001; Hollis, Chapter 4; Maurer, Chapter 5). Under a prize system, the developer is rewarded for the innovation, as with patents, but the new product is placed in the public domain and prices are set near to marginal cost so that the deadweight loss associated with patents is avoided. The key to the success of a prize system is the degree to which the prizes can be structured to approximate the value of the delivered innovations.

Two characteristics of vaccine markets make prizes an attractive incentive system. Vaccines create a large social value that firms cannot fully appropriate, and this social value can be calculated ex ante. When aggregate deadweight loss is the primary concern and the social value of an invention is verifiable (as is likely for vaccines), prizes may be preferable to an intellectual property system (Maurer and Scotchmer 2004). Unlike under the patent system, the number of participants and the potential duplication of effort can be altered with the size of the prize. Additionally, if social value is expected to be much higher than costs, a prize can be set lower than social value.

But sequential innovations often add much more to social value as well as to reduce cost through process and follow-on innovations (Sinclair, Klepper, and Cohen 2000). With an innovation in the public domain, firms may have a lower incentive to improve upon it. But in the case of vaccines, a follow-on innovation may also qualify for a new round of prizes. The case of cost-saving process innovations may be a concern, but for these types of innovations patents have been shown to be less important than other mechanisms such as secrecy (Walsh, Arora, and Cohen 2003).

The key condition for paying the prize money would be the vaccine's efficacy, although the prize could be scaled based on efficacy. The prize would reflect the sponsor's best judgment about the productivity of R&D and the opportunity cost to society of not having the new vaccine.

Calculations of social value may be questioned by potential innovators, although a strong argument can be made that measures for new vaccines are likely to be more accurate on average than are those for other types of inventions. Criticisms about the accuracy of administratively determined prizes can be addressed in two ways: (1) tailoring the prize ex post to the value of the innovation and (2) basing the prize on a market-determined value. Kremer (1998) advocated using competitive bidding for the patent purchase, but placing the patented good in the public domain.

Alternatives to Prizes and Patents

There are several alternative methods for promoting investments in product R&D. As already explained in Chapters 4 and 5, "push" policies that reduce the cost of innovation are to be distinguished from demand-side or "pull" policies that increase demand. An advantage of push policies, such as research grants, is that they eliminate the need to estimate value. A deficiency is that payment is provided no matter what is developed, even if the research proves to be unpromising. Since money must be allocated upfront, decision makers must rely on those with expertise (and thus with vested interests) for information on where to spend funds. This situation creates strong incentives for exaggeration of the prospects of success. Even worse, this gives an advantage to diseases with stronger advocacy groups and creates reasons to divert resources away from research toward marketing one's approach over others. Although push policies, such as research grants, presumably account for variations in R&D cost, except for the reputational incentive – grants in the future are more likely to be awarded to those who have been productive in the past – there is no reward to ingenuity or effort.

A variant that addresses this problem are the proposals to target R&D tax credits toward research on malaria, HIV/AIDS, and tuberculosis. But tax credits do not even have the reputation incentive (reputation is built up by successfully using previous grant money). If recipient research organizations are put at risk for some of their own funds (e.g., the part not funded through a tax credit or by mandatory subsidy matching), the moral hazard problem should be attenuated.[25]

Pull programs have the advantages of more efficient alignment of incentives when a range of approaches for development exist and delaying spending until a product has been developed (also see Hollis, Chapter 4, and Maurer, Chapter 5). A government commitment to purchase vaccines (financing can be partial or in full) is the most widely discussed form of demand-side, "pull" policy proposals. Unsurprisingly, one of the main drivers of total firm R&D expenditures is the firm's expected returns (Vernon and Grabowski 2000). For example, coverage of influenza vaccines by Medicare starting in 1993 created a bigger market and spurred R&D leading to more effective and easier-to-administer flu vaccines approved in 2003 (Finkelstein 2004). The drawback is that for such a program to increase innovative activity, the chance that the sponsor would renege once costs are sunk must be minimized, though it appears difficult to eliminate this risk, as the sponsor wishes to avoid paying for unsuitable products. Contracting all of the correct criteria for performance and requirements for a product before it exists presents a fundamental challenge for commitment-to-purchase programs.

Combining Push and Pull Programs

In theory, as well as in the example of orphan drugs, a combination of push and pull may produce the best results (Hsu and Schwartz 2003). The U.S. Orphan Drug Act (P.L. 97–414) uses a combination of push including tax credits (up to 50% of the cost of clinical testing) as well as grant and contract funding, and pull in the form of market exclusivity for seven years. Market exclusivity differs from patent protection. It is broader in the sense that products whose patents have expired and nonpatentable products are eligible.[26] Coverage is narrower than for a patent in that it is applicable only for the rare disease for which the compound was approved. Unlike with patents, a different manufacturer could apply for market approval for the same drug for any other use including a different rare disease. If the original sponsor is unable to meet the demand for the drug, consents to "shared exclusivity" with another supplier, or terminates drug production, the Secretary of the Department of Health and Human Services may permit a second company to market the orphan drug as long as it is not also patented.

The Orphan Drug Act has succeeded in increasing availability of drugs to treat low-prevalence conditions and in the number of orphan drugs approved (Lichtenberg and Waldfogel 2003). From 1979 to 1998 the number of nonorphan drugs approved by the FDA nearly doubled. During the same time period, five times as many orphan drugs were approved. After the enactment of the Orphan Drug Act (1983–1998), there was a higher growth in drug consumption for low-prevalence conditions than that for high-prevalence conditions (Lichtenberg and Waldfogel 2003). Also, a larger decrease in mortality for persons with low-prevalence conditions occurred compared to that for higher-prevalence conditions.

There is a substantially larger literature on government procurement policy. Such policy is distinct from the subsidy-setting mechanisms proposed by the IOM in that procurement is individualized to a particular transaction. The CDC to date has obtained vaccines through a competitive bidding process for specific vaccines.

Much of the relevant literature deals with defense procurement contracts (Rogerson 1994). Many of the characteristics of defense procurement also potentially apply to vaccines, including the role of the government as a major purchaser, uncertainty of outcomes, economies of scale, and the importance of innovation.

Some issues are common to defense and vaccine procurement, such as the hold-up problem. For vaccines as well as defense, firms are concerned about the government's taking advantage of their large sunk R&D and other production startup costs. The buyer is at a disadvantage vis-à-vis the seller in not being able to observe the seller's costs (e.g., Vistnes 1994) or its effort. After the contract is signed at a particular transaction price, sellers may have an incentive to shirk on effort. Also, there are great difficulties with specifying the numerous innovations and the associated rewards if one were to try to reward good ideas through a contract (Rogerson 1994). This limitation along with political problems with government judging and awarding prizes ex post serve as roadblocks to larger prizes for better innovations.[27]

The CDC in the United States invites bids for particular vaccines in a winner-take-all competition (Salkever and Frank 1996). Multiple contracts are sometimes awarded, usually because there is clear evidence that a single bidder would not be able to produce sufficient quantity to meet the expected purchase level; however, during the period Salkever and Frank studied (before VFC), there were few bidders in CDC vaccine auctions. Thus, although the bidding process could be modified to deal with acquisition of particular vaccines, such as for flu, it seems unlikely that minor modifications could yield more than minor improvements.

Administering the Voucher Program

A voucher is a grant for consumption of a specific good or service provided directly to consumers who have certain attributes (Bradford and Shaviro 2000). Voucher programs coupled with private provision of the goods or services are typically viewed as alternatives to its public provision. Vouchers with private provision are often viewed as superior to public provision because of efficiency gains relative to provision by a public monopolist. Lack of choice may reduce the incentive of the seller to produce efficiently and to be responsive to consumer preferences.

There is a long history of public provision of vaccines by health departments to uninsured and nonaffluent populations in the United States. The IOM study rejected this alternative in favor of the voucher alternative, vaccination in the person's "medical home," which is often not a health department or public clinic, reasoning that having a medical home is likely to result in higher vaccination rates (Institute of Medicine 2004, p. 105). If payment covers the marginal cost of vaccinating individuals, private physicians should be willing to supply these services rather than referring them to clinics.

Vouchers have minuses as well. Although vouchers are assumed to be superior to public provision, the proof of the pudding is in the empirical evidence, which is lacking. Second, for vouchers to succeed, the government must identify and enroll a substantial fraction of the target group. Under public provision, persons are "enrolled" when they appear in public clinics.

The most important lesson from the food stamp program in the United States, which is a voucher program, is that getting eligible participants enrolled and retaining them can be problematic. Food stamp participation started at 51% in 1989 and peaked at 74% of those eligible in 1994 (Rosso 2001). Since then it has been declining. Costs of participation in terms of administrative problems and hassles were cited by 17% of nonwelfare families as the reason for leaving food stamps (Dion and Pavetti 2000). The quality control system implemented for food stamps has helped reduce errors; yet enforcement has been hindered by appeals and bureaucracy (U.S. Committee on Ways and Means 2003). There are also potential administrative issues. For example, what should physicians do when eligibility for the voucher cannot be determined at the point of service? Or particularly in view of the eligibility issues, which raise administrative costs to the practices, physicians may not be willing to accept a payment-in-full voucher that does not compensate them for these hassles.

The experience with housing vouchers is illustrative. Housing vouchers have been relatively successful, but have been hindered by a lack of affordable housing.[28] The main implication for the IOM proposal on vouchers is that there is a risk that providers would still prefer nonvoucher buyers. Physicians may still refer patients away from their medical home to public provision, which eliminates the main advantage of vouchers. Landlords who find getting reimbursed for vouchers frustrating have an ample supply of other tenants who do not need to use vouchers.

Availability of vouchers may crowd out private health insurance coverage. If vouchers make being uninsured better than it would otherwise be, fewer persons may be expected to purchase insurance. But states have implemented policies to deter crowd-out for other government health insurance programs.[29]

A common lesson distilled from experience with voucher programs is the importance of careful consideration of targeting voucher eligibility criteria and phase-out conditions. The relatively small value of a vaccine voucher makes this scenario unlikely. Nonetheless, it is necessary to prevent or at least not exacerbate a situation in which people could lose more in vouchers and other benefits than they would gain by increasing their income or savings (Bradford and Shaviro 2000).

IV. Discussion and Conclusions

There is a strong case for public intervention in vaccine provision, particularly in view of the external benefits of vaccines. It is important that decisions by government bodies reflect both benefits and costs of the alternatives, which the IOM committee's recommendations promoted. Fortunately, although there are some disagreements about how best to quantify benefits of vaccines and of alternative medical interventions, the amount of agreement among the experts far exceeds the areas of disagreement.

Substantially less is known about the cost of R&D for particular vaccines and for improvements to existing vaccines. To a lesser extent, there is also insufficient information in the public domain about the marginal cost of producing vaccines, especially reflecting actual and optimal safety precautions in the production process. We also know too little about consumer demand for vaccines, including the role of price and nonprice factors. There are insufficient data on coverage of vaccines by private health insurance currently. For this reason, it is not possible to precisely predict market responses to any specific proposal.

We have discussed the cons as well as the rationale for mandates and vouchers. The negative side effects should be limited in this context. First, the mandate-subsidy-voucher would apply only for vaccines (1) with quantifiable social benefit, (2) for those subpopulations for which such benefit is likely to accrue, and (3) for vaccines with substantial consumption externalities. The cost of vaccines to the government would probably increase, but applying the above screens, for some vaccines, total resource outlays may actually decline, given the discipline that the benefit-cost test imposes on expert groups recommending the vaccines. Second, the negative effects of the insurance mandate will be limited since the mandate is funded, albeit perhaps partially funded.

The effect of crowd-out of demand for private health insurance will be limited to the degree that the public subsidy is limited. Although expenditures on vaccines have risen in recent years, expenditures on vaccines remain a small part of total health expenditures. Thus, although the voucher distorts choices between spending on health insurance and other goods for some households, the magnitude of the distortion, in and of itself, is likely to be minor.

Possibly a more important problem with vouchers is the difficulty in enrolling substantial numbers of uninsured persons and the administrative cost associated with identifying eligible individuals, enrolling them, and resolving administrative issues in the delivery of and payment for vaccines with physicians. The number of potentially eligible persons is far less than the number of uninsured individuals in the United States. Vouchers for childhood vaccines would apply only to uninsured children. Vouchers for flu vaccine would apply to high-risk groups under age 65 and to very young uninsured children. Persons over age 65 would be covered by Medicare, and many of the young children would either be covered by or eligible for SCHIP or Medicaid. If eligible and not enrolled, the children would be enrolled in these programs and would not receive a voucher.

Conceptually and administratively, the most substantial problems are with setting the public subsidy. We have discussed a limited subsidy plan not mentioned in the IOM report, which would be set only at the level of estimated medical and financial externalities. Such a subsidy would address the main market failure attributable to individuals' not taking account of the benefit to others when they are vaccinated, which is likely to be reflected in insufficient demand for vaccinations as a covered private health insurance benefit.

The externality-only public subsidy would address this market imperfection. However, since private insurers and ultimately premium payers would be at financial risk for the cost of vaccinations not covered by the subsidy, there may be substantial political opposition to an externality-only subsidy. Ironically, because vaccines create widely diffused benefits that are experienced only by the lack of disease, political support is likely to be limited because of the lack of a political constituency, especially compared to concentrated, well-organized groups wary of changes.

Setting the subsidy to social value or the lesser value reflecting the price that maximizes consumer surplus would reduce some political opposition to a subsidy. In effect, the internalities would be paid from public rather than private funds. Insurers and premium payers would be at financial risk to the extent that the public subsidy did not cover the acquisition cost of the vaccine and the payment to physicians for administering the vaccine. But if an insurer were able to acquire the vaccine at a lower price than the subsidy, it could possibly profit from this transaction.

We have discussed alternative methods for setting the value of the subsidy. According to one approach, the government would purchase the patent; then the subsidy to insurers at most would reflect the marginal cost of producing and administering the vaccine. The patent system has deficiencies in providing an incentive for R&D, especially for a product in which social value may be well approximated by researchers.

Overall, the IOM proposal is complex and as its critics, mainly the stakeholders, have noted, "untested." If, rather than restructuring the entire vaccine financing system, policy makers wish to focus on one vaccine, such as flu vaccine, a simpler approach, such as improving government procurement contracting, may suffice. Trying the IOM's recommendations for one vaccine might provide experience and help in avoiding errors in implementing a new financing system for many vaccines, each with different characteristics.

The option of business as usual is unattractive, given the high benefit to cost of existing and yet-to-be-developed vaccines. Failure to change public policy will lead to underinvestment in R&D and vaccine production capacity and a dearth of suppliers. Potential benefits for new vaccines for HIV/AIDS and malaria are extremely high, and for a disease such as avian flu, inventing new vaccine production processes is clearly of critical importance as well.

SEVEN

Ensuring the Future Supply of Vaccines

Is a National Vaccine Authority the Answer?

Frank R. Lichtenberg

I. Introduction

In the next decade, U.S. and world demand for vaccines is expected to increase sharply, in part because of bioterrorism threats. But the vaccine industrial base has been declining for decades. Between 1966 and 1977, half of all commercial vaccine manufacturers stopped producing vaccines, and the exodus continued in the 1980s and 1990s. More than 25 companies produced vaccines for the U.S. market 30 years ago; today there are only 5 (Institute of Medicine 2004). Five of the current recommended vaccines have only one producer, and the others have either two or three (Institute of Medicine, p. 5).

Private companies find vaccines less financially rewarding than drugs. In 2001 the global marketplace for therapeutic drugs exceeded $300 billion, whereas worldwide vaccine sales were only about $5 billion. There are several reasons for this differential. Thomas (2002) offers one: patients must take some drugs every day, whereas vaccines are given only occasionally.

Kremer and Snyder (2003) offer a second explanation. In a simple representative consumer model, vaccines and drug treatments yield the same revenue for a pharmaceutical manufacturer, implying that the firm would have the same incentive to develop either, other factors being the same. However, using more realistic models, they find that this conclusion breaks down for two reasons.

First, drug treatments are sold after the firm has learned who has contracted the disease; in the case of heterogeneous consumers who vary with respect to the probability of contracting the disease, there is less asymmetric information to prevent the firm from extracting consumer surplus with drug treatments than with vaccines. Since a prescription is written, the firm knows that the consumer is more likely to pay a higher price. By contrast, in the case of vaccines, everyone is without the disease when vaccinated, even though some consumers may know that they have a higher probability of getting the disease or would suffer more serious consequences in getting the disease than others. The firm does not have this information, however, and thus cannot use what the consumer knows for pricing purposes. They prove that, because of this difference in asymmetric information between drugs and vaccines, the ratio of drug treatment to vaccine revenue can be arbitrarily high; they calculate that the ratio is about two to one for empirical distributions of HIV risk.

The second reason for the breakdown of revenue equivalence is that vaccines are more likely to interfere with the spread of a disease than are drug treatments, thus reducing demand for the product. By embedding an economic model within a standard dynamic epidemiological model, they show that the steady-state flow of revenue is greater for drug treatments than for vaccines.

Third, governments set the prices of most major vaccines, and they possess the market power to set the prices at low levels. A 2004 Institute of Medicine report provides examples of both the U.S. and foreign governments setting below-market-clearing prices of vaccines. The U.S. Veterans Administration penalizes firms for increasing prices charged to its nongovernment customers. For any increase in price higher than the Consumer Price Index, the Veterans Administration reduces the allowable Federal Supply Schedule price that can be paid under federal contract. This has resulted in Federal Supply Schedule vaccine prices as low as $.01 per dose (Institute of Medicine 2004, pp. 5–16). Kremer (2000) estimates that in developing countries, a vaccine against malaria would be cost effective at $41 per dose but that countries under current institutions governing prices would probably end up paying around $2 per dose, a price too low to stimulate appropriate investment (Institute of Medicine 2004, pp. 5–23). Consequently, when price is constrained to be artificially low, one can expect there to be excess demand for vaccines: the quantity of vaccines demanded exceeds the quantity of vaccines supplied.

How can policy makers eliminate this excess demand, and promote a more efficient allocation of resources to the vaccine industry? In principle, there are two options. First, the government can become a developer and producer of vaccines. The idea is that government production would fill the excess demand gap. Further, in theory, government production may be more reliable than private production since governments are less motivated by financial incentives and may continue to supply vaccine, even at an artificially low market price.

Government entry into the vaccine industry as developer and producer has been considered (and rejected) in the past. During the mid-1990s, the Department of Defense considered various options to bring promising biodefense vaccines from the preclinical research phases (at which the Department of Defense excelled) through to licensure. One option that was considered was for the Department of Defense to assume all responsibilities from preclinical through Food and Drug Administration (FDA) licensure "in-house"; another was for the Department of Defense to fund a government-owned, government-operated company or a government-owned, company-operated company for advanced R&D through FDA licensure for several biodefense vaccines.

Government development and production of vaccines has been proposed in a bill before Congress: H.R. 4100, the National Vaccine Authority Act. The "National Vaccine Authority" would be established by the U.S. Department of Health and Human Services and would engage in research, development, and production of vaccines to protect civilians against bioterrorist attacks and other "limited use" vaccines, such as those that would protect travelers going to disease-endemic countries. The National Vaccine Authority would oversee a government-owned laboratory that would be operated by a private contractor to produce vaccines the private sector does not supply at current prices.

In 1993 the Institute of Medicine Council proposed the establishment of a National Vaccine Authority: "because the private sector alone cannot sustain the costs and risks associated with the development of most Children's Vaccine Initiative vaccines, and because the successful development of vaccines requires an integrated process, the committee recommends that an entity, tentatively called the National Vaccine Authority, be organized to advance the development, production, and procurement of new and improved vaccines of limited commercial potential but of global public health need" (Mitchell, Philipose, and Sanford 1993). But in its recent report, *Strengthening the Supply of Routinely Recommended Vaccines in the United States*, the Center for Disease Control's National Vaccine Advisory Committee expressed little sentiment for the establishment of a National Vaccine Authority.

The second way for policy makers to eliminate excess demand for vaccines is to allow vaccine prices to adjust to market-clearing levels. According to this approach, the government would reduce disincentives for R&D, and perhaps establish incentives for greater private vaccine development and production.

Which of these two ways of increasing the supply of vaccines is preferable? I argue in this chapter that the second approach – reducing disincentives, and enhancing incentives, for private vaccine development and production – is likely to be far more effective than initiating government vaccine development and production.

In Section II, I examine trends in vaccine prices during 1992–2002, thereby documenting the declining financial incentives for private vaccine production in the United States. I show that although the real (inflation-adjusted) price of vaccines has increased significantly during 1999–2002, the real price of a given vaccine (adjusting for changes in the overall price level) was lower in 2002 than it was a decade before.

In Section III I discuss theories about the relative efficiency of private and public enterprises. There are two main, not mutually exclusive, explanations of why state-owned firms may exhibit worse performance than privately owned firms. The managerial view, based on agency theory, is that state-owned firms have difficulty monitoring managers because there is neither an individual owner with strong incentives to monitor managers nor a public share price to provide information on manager actions as judged by stock market participants. The political view argues that governments pursue objectives in addition to and in conflict with profit maximization, and that this political interference can distort the objectives and constraints faced by managers. While some theories imply that government production may be more efficient than contracting out under certain conditions, these conditions are unlikely to apply to the vaccine industry.

In Section IV I review some empirical evidence about the relative efficiency of private and public enterprises. Numerous empirical studies over the last two decades have shown that private enterprises tend to be more efficient producers than public enterprises, and the private-sector efficiency advantage is likely to be particularly great in knowledge-intensive industries like vaccines.

In Section V I survey evidence about the response of private investment in R&D to changes in economic incentives. Evidence about a number of policies (including R&D tax credits, intellectual property, defense procurement, and the Orphan Drug Act) and events suggests that private vaccine development and production is likely to be quite responsive to enhanced incentives (or diminished disincentives), and that expansion of the government's role is likely to crowd out private investment. Conclusions are presented in Section VI.

II. Trends in Vaccine Prices, 1992–2002

I begin with an analysis of the behavior of prices paid for vaccines by the federal government during the period 1992–2002, using data from two different sources.[1] I construct price indexes that compare the price of a vaccine in a given year to the price of the same vaccine in another year. The indexes do *not* compare prices of different vaccines (e.g., new vs. old vaccines).

Comprehensive data on prices paid for vaccines by the U.S. government during the period 1992–2002 were obtained from two different sources: the Federal Supply Schedule (published by the Veterans Administration)[2] and the Centers for Disease Control.

Evidence from the Federal Supply Schedule

The Federal Supply Schedule (FSS) provides data on contract prices for pharmaceutical products (including vaccines) purchased by the U.S. government. This source contains data on 26 distinct active vaccine ingredients, 43 distinct vaccine brands, and 130 distinct vaccine products.[3]

A relatively simple, meaningful way to examine price trends is to estimate models of the form:

$$\log(\text{price}_{ijt}) = \alpha_i + \beta t + \epsilon_{ijt} \tag{7.1}$$

where price_{ijt} = is the price of product (National Drug Code) i in category j in year t, where category refers to the active ingredient, brand, or a manufacturer. This model includes a "fixed effect" for each product, so that we are comparing the price of a product at time $t + k$ to the price of the *same* product at time t. The parameter β represents the overall (unweighted)[4] mean annual rate of price increase, and β_j represents the average annual rate of price increase of products in category j.

Estimating equation (7.1) yielded an estimate of β of 0.0054 (t-stat = 3.01). This implies that the overall unweighted mean annual rate of FSS price increase of vaccine products during the period 1993–2002 was 0.54%. During the same period, the mean annual rate of increase of the U.S. Consumer Price Index was 2.44%. Hence this implies that the *real* FSS price (the ratio of the nominal FSS price to the Consumer Price Index) *declined* at an average annual rate of 1.90%.

We also estimated a variant of equation (7.1), in which the continuous variable t was replaced by a set of binary variables for year (a variable for 1993, 1994, etc.). The coefficients on these year variables, which show changes in the vaccine price index, crude and adjusted for the Consumer Price Index, are shown in Figure 7.1 They suggest that vaccine prices tended to decline between 1993 and 1999 – especially during 1996–1998 – but that vaccine prices increased about 18% between 1999 and 2001.

Between 1993 and 1999, the FSS declined 11%, while the Consumer Price Index increased 15%. Hence, the real or relative price of vaccines decreased about 26% in this period. In contrast, from 1999 to 2002, the vaccine price index increased 19%, while the Consumer Price Index increased by 8%: the real or relative price of vaccines increased about 11% in this period.

Evidence from Centers for Disease Control Data

The U.S. Centers for Disease Control provided data on the prices it paid and the quantities it purchased,[5] by supplier, of 13 vaccines (DTP, DtaP, Hep A, Hep B [ped. & adult], Hib, INFLUENZA, IPV, MMR, OPV, PCV-7, PNEUMO [adult], Td, Varicella) for the period 1992–2002.

I estimated a version of equation (7.1) in which i denotes vaccine i ($i = 1, 2, \ldots, 13$), and the continuous variable t was replaced by a set of year dummies. The model was estimated via weighted least squares, where the weight was equal to the market value (price times quantity) of that vaccine in that year. The coefficients on these year variables may be considered values of a Center for Disease Control vaccine price index. Nominal FSS and Centers for Disease Control vaccine price indexes are compared in Figure 7.2

The Centers for Disease Control data indicate that the nominal price of vaccines was quite stable from 1992 to 1995. It increased about 7% in 1996, but then declined, and was at about the same level in 1999 as it had been in 1992. Since the Consumer Price Index increased by 15% between 1992 and 1999, this implies that the real or relative price of vaccines declined by about 15% between 1992 and 1999. However, between 1999 and 2002, the nominal price of vaccines purchased by Centers for Disease Control increased 20%, and the real price increased 12%.

My analysis of vaccine price trends may be summarized as follows. In general, the real (inflation-adjusted) price of a given vaccine today was lower in 2002 than it was a decade before. The FSS data imply that the real price of vaccines was 18% higher in 1993 than it was in 2002. The Centers for Disease Control data imply that the real price of vaccines was 7% higher in 1992 than it was in 2002. The latter figure is probably more reliable, because the Centers for Disease Control index weights vaccines by their market value, whereas the FSS index gives equal weight to all vaccines. Both the FSS and the Centers for Disease Control price indexes indicate that the real price of vaccines increased about 9% from 1999 to 2002. Before 1999, nominal vaccine prices increased much more slowly than the Consumer Price Index

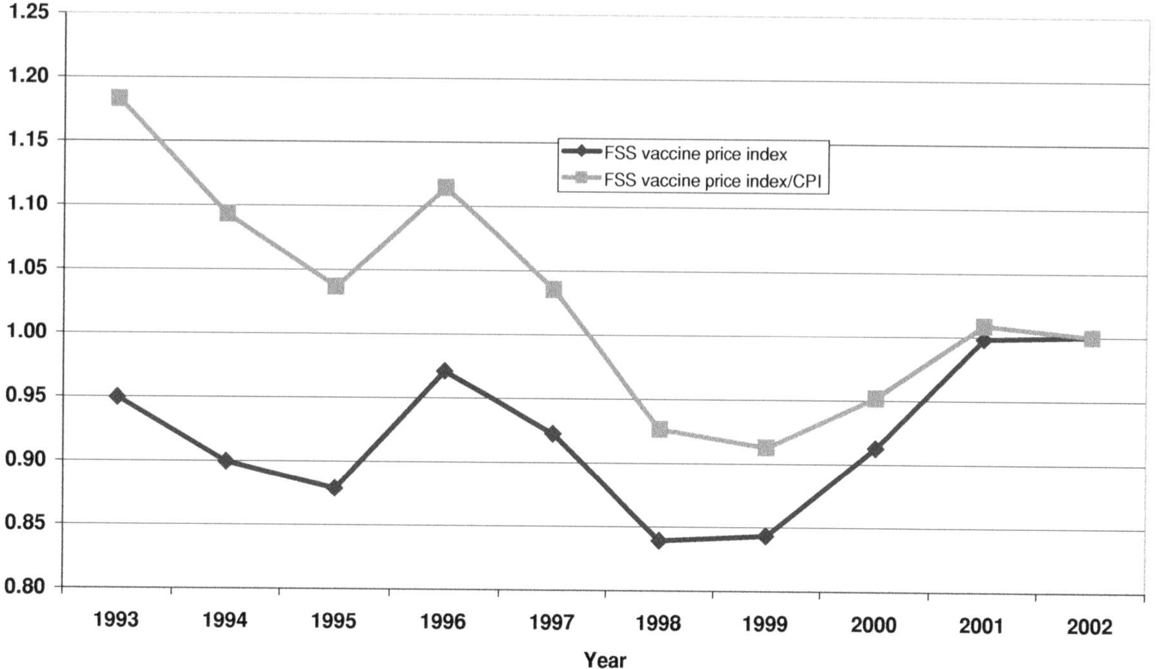

Figure 7.1. Federal Supply Schedule Vaccine Price Index (2002 = 1.00).

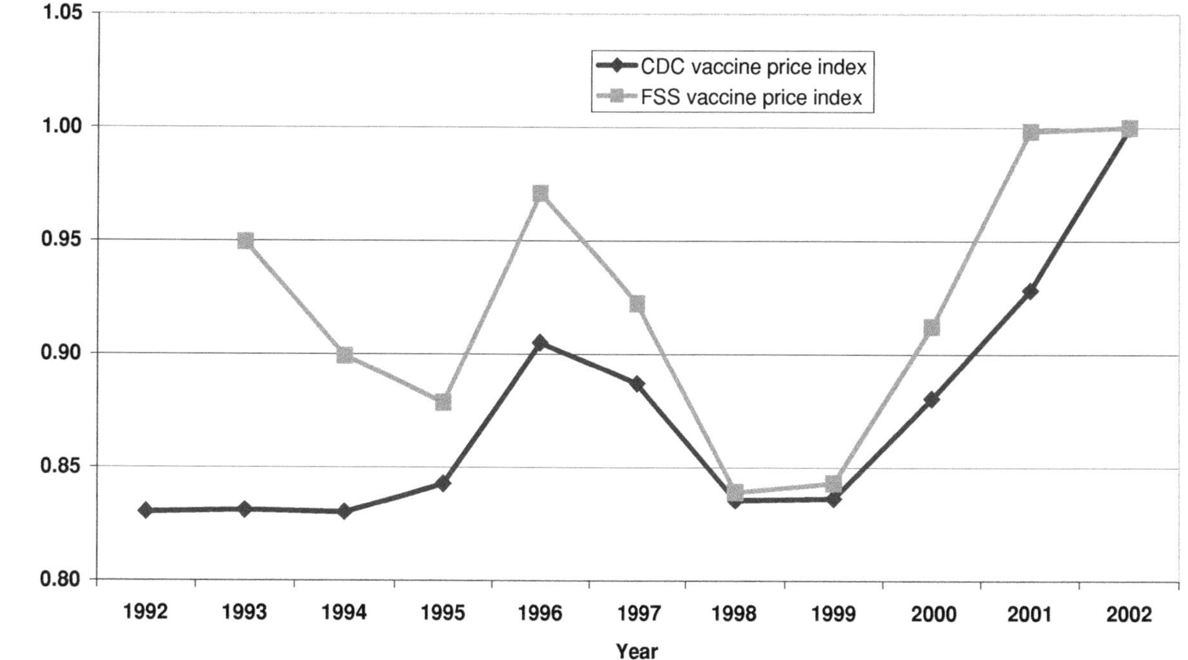

Figure 7.2. Nominal Federal Supply Schedule and Centers for Disease Control Vaccine Price Indexes, 1992–2002.

and may even have declined. Since 1999, nominal vaccine prices increased about 3% per year faster than the Consumer Price Index.

A recent IOM report points out that government pricing policies – low costs and price caps – conflict with the need to stimulate investment in vaccine development and production capacity (Rappuoli, Miller, and Falkow 2002). Given the high social value of vaccines development (McGuire 2003), this policy seems to be shortsighted.

III. The Relative Efficiency of Private and Public Enterprises: A Theoretical Perspective

Economists have developed two main, not mutually exclusive, explanations of why state-owned firms may exhibit worse performance than privately owned firms. The managerial view, based on agency theory, is that state-owned firms have difficulty monitoring managers because there is neither an individual owner with strong incentives to monitor managers nor a public share price to provide information on manager actions as judged by stock market participants (Laffont and Tirole 1993). Without information from the stock market, managerial incentive contracts are restricted (Holmstrom and Tirole 1993), managers lack an important public signal of their skills for the executive job market (Fama 1980), and takeover opportunities are limited (Scharfstein 1988; Stein 1988).

The political view argues that governments pursue objectives in addition to and in conflict with profit maximization, and that this political interference can distort the objectives and constraints faced by managers (Shleifer and Vishny 1994). Public choice economists point out that "government failure" to achieve economy efficiency is quite common. A principal reason is that individual voters lack private incentives to monitor government effectively. Anthony Downs, in one of the earliest public choice books, *An Economic Theory of Democracy,* argued that the voter is largely ignorant of political issues and that this ignorance is rational (Downs 1957). This incentive to be ignorant is rare in the private sector. Public choice theory also predicts that regulatory agencies will often be "captured" by special interests.[6] Capture occurs because bureaucrats do not have a profit goal to guide their behavior. Instead, they usually are in government because they have a goal or mission. They rely on Congress for their budgets, and often the people who will benefit from their mission can influence Congress to provide more funds. Thus, interest groups – who may be as diverse as lobbyists for regulated industries or leaders of environmental groups – become important to them. Such interrelationships can lead to bureaucrats being captured by interest groups.

Under certain conditions, however, government production may be more efficient than contracting out to private enterprises. In Hart, Shleifer, and Vishny's (1997) model, the provider can invest in improving the quality of service or reducing cost. If contracts are incomplete, that is, if the quality of service the government wants cannot be fully specified and monitored, the private enterprise has a stronger incentive to skimp on those aspects of quality that are not easily specified and monitored, "noncontractible quality," thereby reducing cost and increasing the firm's profits than does the government employee who would not profit individually from skimping on quality. In the case where the choice is between government contracting with a private organization or producing the good or service itself, the private contractor's incentive to engage in cost reduction is typically too strong because he ignores the adverse effect on noncontractible quality. The authors applied their model to the issue of prison privatization and argued that because many aspects of prison quality (e.g., treatment of prisoners) are noncontractible, government prisons perform better than privately run prisons.

However, when the characteristics of the good or service can be well specified, and especially when the potential for quality improvement is high, private enterprise is likely to be more efficient. Based on these criteria, Hart and coauthors argue that private provision of weapons systems is likely to be superior to public production: "although the damages to quality from cost reduction might be significant, to a large extent this problem can be dealt with contractually through the requirement that weapons meet well-specified performance requirements. Moreover, quality innovation is enormously important in weapons design, and the incentives of private suppliers are probably stronger than those of public employees" (p. 1155).

Since the characteristics of vaccines can be well specified, quality can be (and is) monitored, and the potential for quality improvement is high, their model implies that private enterprise is likely to be more efficient in the vaccine industry too. Indeed, in a later paper, Shleifer (1998) concluded that "private ownership should generally be preferred to public ownership when the incentives to innovate and to contain costs must be strong.... A good government that wants to further 'social goals' would rarely own producers to meet its objectives."

IV. Empirical Evidence on the Relative Efficiency of Private and Public Enterprises

Numerous empirical studies over the last two decades have shown that private enterprises tend to be more efficient producers than their public counterparts. Boardman, Freedman, and Eckel (1986) studied the impact of the Quebec government's 1981 takeover of Domtar, a private corporation. With the takeover, Domtar became controlled indirectly by the Quebec government. The authors estimated a model based on the capital asset pricing model of Fama et al. (1969), using Domtar daily stock price data from 1979 and 1980. Daily abnormal returns and cumulative abnormal returns for the time around the takeover were calculated. After the takeover, over six trading days, Domtar's stock price fell to almost 25% less than the expected level. This was equal to a reduction in market value in 1981 of about $150 million. Some of the 25% loss in value may have been due to other factors, but accounting for these leaves 8%–19% or $50–117 million that could be attributed to government control and the anticipated pursuit of nonprofit objectives.

Boardman and Vining (1989) compared the performances of industrial state-owned enterprises, mixed enterprises, and private corporations among the 500 largest non-U.S. industrial firms. Their model included (1) several measures of profitability and efficiency performance; (2) variables for state-owned enterprises, mixed public and private enterprises, and private corporations; and (3) various measures that reflect the nature of the regulatory-competitive environments. After controlling for many factors, they found that large industrial mixed enterprises and state-owned enterprises perform substantially worse than otherwise similar private corporations. In terms of sales per employee, mixed enterprises did better than state-owned enterprises, but in terms of sales per asset, there was no substantial difference. Their results indicate that partial privatization, with the government retaining some percentage of equity, may not be the best strategy for governments that wish to move away from reliance on state-owned enterprises.

Gupta (2002) reexamined the impact of partial privatization on firm performance, using data on the sale of noncontrolling equity stakes on the stock market by state-owned enterprises in India. He found that partial privatization has a positive and highly significant impact on the sales, profits, and labor productivity of these firms.

Ehrlich et al. (1994) examined the effect of state versus private ownership on rates of firm-specific productivity growth and cost decline by developing a model of endogenous, firm-specific productivity growth and testing its implications against panel data on 23 international airlines of varying levels of state ownership over the period 1973–1983. Their model and empirical results showed that, although state ownership will not necessarily reduce productivity or increase costs in the short run, it can lower the long-run annual rate of productivity growth or cost decline. U.S. Bureau of Labor

Statistics data indicate that during the period 1967–1994, the rate of productivity growth in private manufacturing was about two and a half times as high as it was in the U.S. government.

D'Souza and Megginson (1999) compared the pre- and postprivatization financial and operating performance of 85 companies from 28 industrialized countries that were privatized through public share offerings during 1990–1996. Significant increases in profitability, output, operating efficiency, and dividend payments, and significant decreases in leverage ratios, for the full sample of firms after privatization, and for most subsamples examined, were documented. Capital expenditures increased significantly in absolute terms, but not relative to sales. Employment declined, but insignificantly. Combined with results from the two previous (directly comparable) studies, these findings strongly suggest that privatization yields substantial performance improvements.

Finally, Megginson and Netter (2001) concluded from their comprehensive survey of the extensive literature on privatization that privately owned firms are more efficient and more profitable than otherwise-comparable state-owned firms. They cited limited empirical evidence, especially from China, that suggests that nonprivatizing reform measures, such as price deregulation, market liberalization, and increased use of incentives, can improve the efficiency of state-owned enterprises, but it also seems likely that these reforms would be even more effective if coupled with privatization.

The U.S. government is quite dissimilar to knowledge-intensive industries, such as the vaccine industry. One difference is between the occupational distributions of employment in the U.S. government and the pharmaceutical industry.[7] In 2001 office and administrative support occupations accounted for 41% of U.S. government employment, but only 12% of pharmaceutical industry employment. The number of employees in production occupations accounted for 35% of pharmaceutical industry employment but only 2% of U.S. government employment.

In 2002 the U.S. government funded 28% of the R&D performed in the United States, but performed only 7% of the nation's R&D.[8] More than three-fourths of U.S. R&D expenditures took the form of grants to or contracts with other organizations (only part of which involved grants and contracts to organizations run by other governmental units, such as state public universities). While some of the R&D supported by the U.S. Department of Health and Human Services was performed in-house (e.g., by government scientists at the National Institutes of Health), 82% of this research was performed elsewhere. This high rate of contracting out was presumably motivated in part by the fact that the private-sector efficiency advantage is particularly great in knowledge-intensive industries.[9]

V. Response of Private R&D Investment to Changes in Economic Incentives

Overview

Even if private enterprises tend to be more efficient, government entry would be desirable if private vaccine development and production is unlikely to be responsive to enhanced financial incentives (or equivalently, lower disincentives). But evidence from the vaccine, pharmaceutical, and other industries indicates that private investment in R&D is generally very responsive to changes in such incentives, including policy-induced changes.

In Figure 7.3 I provide a schematic for analyzing some of the determinants of private R&D investment. Starting from the bottom, equilibrium (value-maximizing) R&D investment depends on both the private cost and the expected private benefits or revenue from the investment. Equilibrium R&D is greater, the lower the cost and the higher the private benefit. The private cost of research depends on government research expenditure and on the magnitude of R&D tax credits, inter alia. Government research expenditure may be a partial substitute for private expenditure. When higher government expenditure results in less private expenditure, economists often state that the latter was "crowded out."

The expected private benefit depends on a number of market characteristics and public policies, including market size, intellectual property rights, price regulation, and the magnitude of "prizes for innovation." Some public policies, such as the Orphan Drug Act, may affect both the costs and the expected private benefits of R&D investment.

I summarize the best available evidence about the effects of these hypothesized determinants of R&D investment below.

Crowding Out

Expansion of the government's role is likely to crowd out private investment. Lichtenberg (1984) provides estimates of the relationship between company and federal R&D, based on data compiled by the National Science Foundation for the period 1967–1977. The availability of firm-level panel data on both R&D expenditure and employment permitted investigation

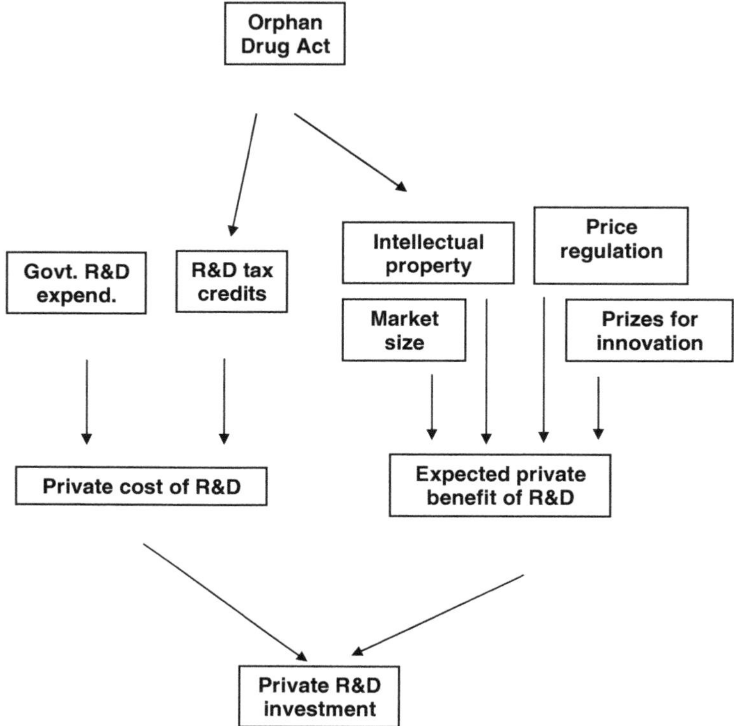

Figure 7.3. Selected determinants of private R&D investment.

of the issues of lags, fixed effects, and deflation bias in the analysis of the relationship. The estimates were consistent with the hypothesis that increases in federal R&D activity tend to be associated with significant decreases in company-financed R&D.

Goolsbee (1988) showed that there is a serious problem with direct government funding of R&D to increase inventive activity. The major part of R&D spending is just salary payments for R&D workers. Given that labor supply to this activity is not completely elastic, and in the short run is likely to be quite inelastic, when the government funds R&D, a substantial fraction of the increased spending leads to higher wage rates. Using Current Population Survey data on wages of scientific personnel, he showed that government R&D spending raises wages significantly, particularly for scientists related to defense, such as physicists and aeronautical engineers. By altering the wages of scientists and engineers even for firms not receiving federal support, government funding directly crowds out private inventive activity.

R&D Tax Credits

Hall and van Reenen (2000) surveyed the econometric evidence on the effectiveness of fiscal incentives for R&D. They described the effects of tax systems in OECD countries on the user cost of R&D – the current position, changes over time, and across different firms in different countries. They concluded that a dollar in tax credit for R&D stimulates a dollar of additional R&D.

Market Size

In his influential study of almost a thousand inventions in four different industries, Schmookler (1966) argued that expected profitability of inventive activity, which depends to an important extent on market size, determines the pace and direction of industrial innovation.

I have examined the relationship across diseases between market size and both public and private R&D investment (Lichtenberg 2001a). I found a very strong positive relationship across diseases between "market size" (total life years lost to the disease before age 65) and *public* R&D expenditure. In Lichtenberg (2005a) I performed two analyses of the relationship across diseases between privately financed pharmaceutical innovation and the burden of disease in developed and developing countries. I examined the relationship between the number of disability-adjusted life years attributable to a disease in 2001, by region, and the number of drugs that have been developed to treat the disease and that are sold in the United States. I also examined the relationship between the number of disability-adjusted life years attributable to a disease in 2001 and the number of drugs launched to treat the disease in approximately 50 countries during the period 1982–2002. Both analyses indicated that the amount of pharmaceutical innovation is positively related to the burden of disease in developed countries but not to the burden of disease in developing countries.

The most plausible explanation for the lack of a relationship between the burden of disease in developing countries and the amount of pharmaceutical innovation is that incentives for firms to develop medicines for diseases primarily afflicting people in developing countries have been weak or nonexistent.

Finkelstein (2004) examined whether and to what extent the demand-side incentives embodied in health policy affect the rate of technological change in the medical sector. Specifically, she estimated the effect on vaccine investment of three discrete changes in health policy that increased the return to developing vaccines against specific diseases. Two of these policies increased the expected market size for vaccines against two different diseases, hepatitis B and the flu.[10] She found evidence of an increase in vaccine investment associated with the increase in demand-side investment incentives. The induced investment represented 70% of the total subsequent vaccine investment in the affected diseases and suggests that a $1 increase in annual market revenue for a vaccine is associated with 5 to 6 cents of additional investment in that vaccine's development.

Intellectual Property

Mansfield (1986, p. 175) provides estimates of the percentage of inventions that would not have been commercially introduced if patent protection could not have been obtained, by industry, for 12 industries during 1981–1983. He found that 65% of pharmaceutical inventions would not have been introduced if patent protection could not have been obtained; for the 11 other industries he studied, the (unweighted) mean percentage of inventions that would not have been introduced was only 8%.

Some economists, such as 1993 Nobel laureate Douglass North, argue that the invention of intellectual property and its protection caused an explosion in creativity that was the basic force behind the Industrial Revolution (Hall and Jones 1999). As Charles Jones observed, "sustained economic growth is a very recent phenomenon" – it began with the Industrial Revolution in Britain in the 1760s – and "the thesis of Douglass North and a number of other economic historians is that the development of intellectual property rights, a cumulative process that occurred over centuries, is responsible for modern economic growth.... History suggests that it is only when the *market* incentives were sufficient that widespread innovation and growth took hold" (Jones 1998, pp. 81, 83).

Stern, Porter, and Furman (2000) present evidence that countries that offer greater patent protection at home have more patents in the United States than countries with less patent protection. In particular, they found that a one standard-deviation increase in a country's intellectual property score is associated with a 22% increase in the number of U.S. patents it has. Hall and Jones (1999) found that a country's long-run economic performance is determined primarily by institutions and government policies that affect the economic environment within which individuals and firms make investments, create and transfer ideas, and produce goods and services. Strengthening intellectual property rights may stimulate the international transfer of existing technologies as well as the development of new technologies. Branstetter, Fisman, and Foley (2003) examined the response of

U.S. multinational firms to a series of multilateral reforms of intellectual property rights regimes undertaken by 12 countries over the 1982–1999 period. They found that intellectual property rights regime changes result in increases in royalty payment flows to parent firms, and that some of the increased royalty flows represents the transfer of new technologies to the host country.

Prizes for Innovation

The rationale for prizes for innovations has been provided in depth in Chapters 4 and 5. I will not repeat these issues here, but rather supplement these discussions with a description of some of my own work and related work of others on this issue. Rogerson (1989) argued on theoretical grounds that informational and incentive constraints inherent in the innovation process require that regulatory institutions in defense procurement create prizes for innovation.[11] Since the quality of an innovation is difficult to describe or measure objectively, the most natural way to award prizes is to permit firms to earn a positive economic profit on production contracts. Rogerson estimated the size of the prizes offered on 12 major aerospace systems using stock market data. The stock market value of firms competing for a prime contract was determined for the few days before and for the few days after it was announced which firm had won. He estimated that every dollar of revenue received by a prime contractor on production contracts generates somewhere between 3.26 and 4.68 cents of pure economic profit.

Lichtenberg (1988) showed that by establishing prizes for innovation, the government indeed stimulates considerable private R&D investment. During the period 1979–1984, which spanned a major defense buildup, slightly over half of the total induced increase in private R&D was induced by the increase in government procurement by design and technical competition.

R&D effort responds to prizes for innovation established by the market as well as by the government. Changes in the price of energy (e.g., due to actions by OPEC) change the value of (or size of the prize for) energy-saving innovations. Lichtenberg (1986) examined the effects of large increases in the prices of energy and other intermediate materials during the early to mid-1970s on the amount of research and development (R&D) performed by U.S. manufacturing firms. I found that industries most affected by these price increases maintained the highest growth rate of R&D expenditure, holding constant output growth. Popp (2001) used U.S. patent data from 1970 to 1994 to estimate the effect of energy prices on energy-efficient innovations. Using patent citations to construct a measure of the usefulness of the existing base of scientific knowledge, he considered the effect of both demand-side factors, which spur innovative activity by increasing the value of new innovations, and supply-side factors, such as scientific advancements that make new innovations possible. He found that both energy prices and the quality of existing knowledge have strongly significant positive effects on innovation.

Price Regulation

As Ellison and Mullin (1997, p. 9) noted, "in February and March 1993, rumors circulated that the Clinton Health Care Reform Task Force, which was operating in secrecy, was going to include regulation of drug prices in its plan. Such fears seemed supported by statements by President Clinton and Hillary Rodham Clinton attacking the high prices of vaccines and other pharmaceuticals."

Industry-level data are consistent with the hypothesis that the threat of Clinton health care reform reduced the growth rate of R&D investment (with a one- or two-year lag). As Figure 7.4 reveals, the annual growth of (nominal) R&D investment ranged from about 12% to 17% during the period 1987–1993. The 1993–1994 and 1994–1995 growth rates were less than half the growth rates of the previous seven years. R&D growth in 1995–1996 and later years was similar to the growth during 1987–1993.

There is another, two-stage, approach to examining the effect of (expectations about) price regulation (and other government policies) on R&D investment. This approach can be represented as follows:

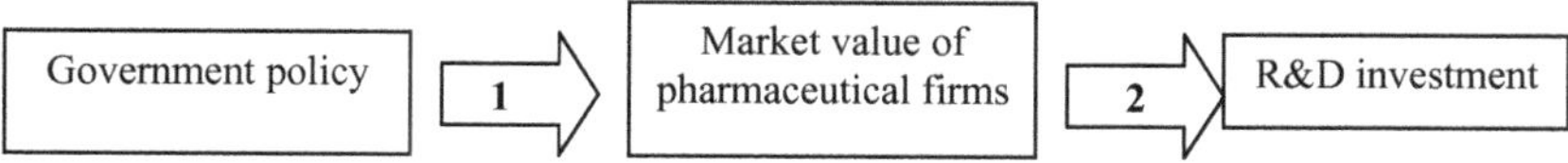

In the first stage (1), one examines the impact of government policy changes on the market value of pharmaceutical firms. The hypothesis is that some government policy events affect the expected future net cash flows of pharmaceutical firms. If the stock market is efficient, the value of the firm at time *t* is the expected present discounted value of its future net cash flows, conditional on the information available at time *t*. Hence policy events affect the value of the firm. Conroy, Harris, and Massaro (1992) provided evidence that four major legislative and regulatory initiatives directed toward the pharmaceutical industry during the 1970s and 1980s – the Maximum Allowable Cost Program (1975), Prospective Payment Plan (1982–1983), Drug Price Competition and Patent Term Restoration Act (1984), and

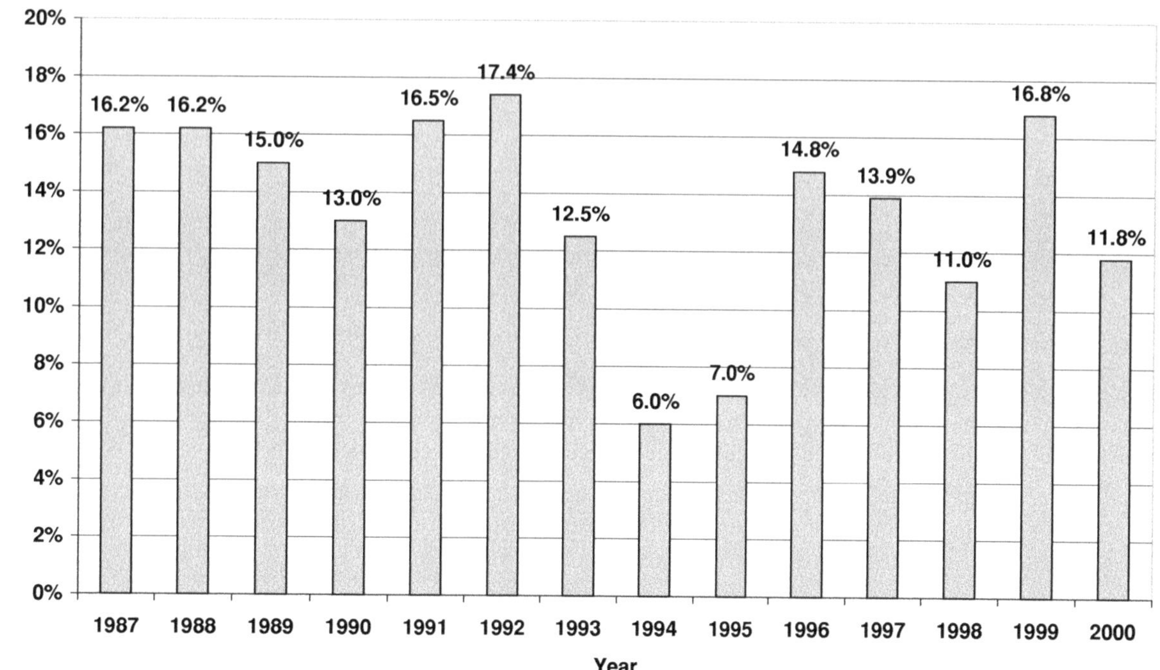

Figure 7.4. Annual percentage change in pharmaceutical R&D, 1987–2000.

Catastrophic Protection Act (1987–1988) – had significant, often negative, effects on share returns (market value).

In the second stage (2), one examines the impact of changes in market value on R&D investment. John Maynard Keynes (1936) may have been the first economist to hypothesize that the incentive to invest depends on the market value of capital relative to its replacement cost. Nobel laureate James Tobin (1969) provided a rigorous theoretical foundation for this hypothesis. Under certain plausible assumptions, a value-maximizing firm's investment (relative to its capital stock) is a (linear) function of "Tobin's *q*" – the ratio of the market value of the firm to the replacement cost of its capital (Hassett and Hubbard 1996). The hypothesis that investment in general is positively related to Tobin's *q* – the ratio of the stock market value of the firm to replacement costs – is now widely accepted.[12] Dornbusch and Fischer (1994) argued that when (Tobin's *q*) is high, firms will want to produce more assets, so that investment will be rapid, "and therefore that . . . a booming stock market is good for investment" (p. 341). The managers of the company can be thought of as responding to the price of the stock by producing more new capital – that is, investing – when the price of shares is high and producing less capital – or not investing at all – when the price of shares is low (p. 355). Similarly, Hall and Taylor state that "investment should be positively related to *q*. Tobin's *q* provides a very useful way to formulate investment functions because it is relatively easy to measure" (p. 312).[13]

Ellison and Mullin (1997) estimated that the threat of Clinton health care reform reduced the market value of pharmaceutical firms by about 44% during the period from September 1992 to October 1993. Lichtenberg (2004a) estimated that the elasticity of R&D investment with respect to market value is 0.225, that is, that a 10% decline in market value is associated with a 2.25% decline in R&D investment. Combining these two estimates implies that the threat of Clinton health care reform reduced R&D investment by about 9.9% (0.225*0.44). During the period 1986–2000, the average annual number of new molecular entities approved by the FDA was 28.1. Hence, the temporary reduction in R&D investment attributable to the threat of Clinton health care reform may, with a lag of 12–15 years, temporarily reduce the number of new molecular entities approved by about 2.8 (9.9%*28.1) per year.

In addition to affecting the rate of new drug development, price regulation may affect the probability and timing of launch of existing drugs. Danzon, Wang, and Wang (2005) analyzed the effect of pharmaceutical price regulation on delays in launch of new drugs. Because a low price in one market may "spill over" to other markets, through parallel trade and external referencing, manufacturers may rationally prefer longer delay or nonlaunch to accepting a relatively low price, particularly for high-volume drugs for which parallel trade risks are higher. They examined whether and when 85 new chemical entities that were launched in the U.K. or U.S. outpatient markets between 1994 and 1998 were launched in 25 other major markets worldwide, including 14 EU countries. They found that increases in expected price and market size both significantly reduce launch delay, with a larger effect for expected price.

With regard to the vaccine industry, the Institute of Medicine's Committee on the Evaluation of Vaccine Purchase Finance in the United States (2004), which was described in detail in Chapter 6, noted that the government has often used its monopsonistic power in the marketplace to hold prices down, further reducing incentives for R&D, and that prices are sometimes held too low to encourage desirable levels of investment in R&D and production capacity.

Orphan Drugs

The Orphan Drug Act (P.L. 97-414, as amended) includes various incentives that have stimulated a considerable amount of interest in the development of orphan drug and biological products. These incentives include tax credits for clinical research undertaken by a sponsor to generate required data for marketing approval, and seven years of marketing exclusivity for a designated drug or biological product approved by the FDA.[14]

Since it was created in 1982, the FDA's Office of Orphan Products Development has been dedicated to promoting the development of products that demonstrate promise for the diagnosis and/or treatment of rare diseases or conditions. To locate such products, the Office of Orphan Products Development interacts with the medical and research communities, professional organizations, academia, and the pharmaceutical industry, as well as rare disease groups. The Office of Orphan Products Development administers the major provisions of the Orphan Drug Act, which provide incentives for sponsors to develop products for rare diseases.

According to the Office of Orphan Products Development, "the Orphan Drug Act has been very successful – more than 200 drugs and biological products for rare diseases have been brought to market since 1983. In contrast, the decade prior to 1983 saw fewer than ten such products come to market."[15] The number of orphan drug marketing approvals, by year during 1980–2000, is shown in Figure 7.5. Lichtenberg and Waldfogel (2003) provide evidence that prescription drug use and longevity have grown more quickly for persons with rare diseases and even more quickly for persons with conditions with substantial orphan drug use.

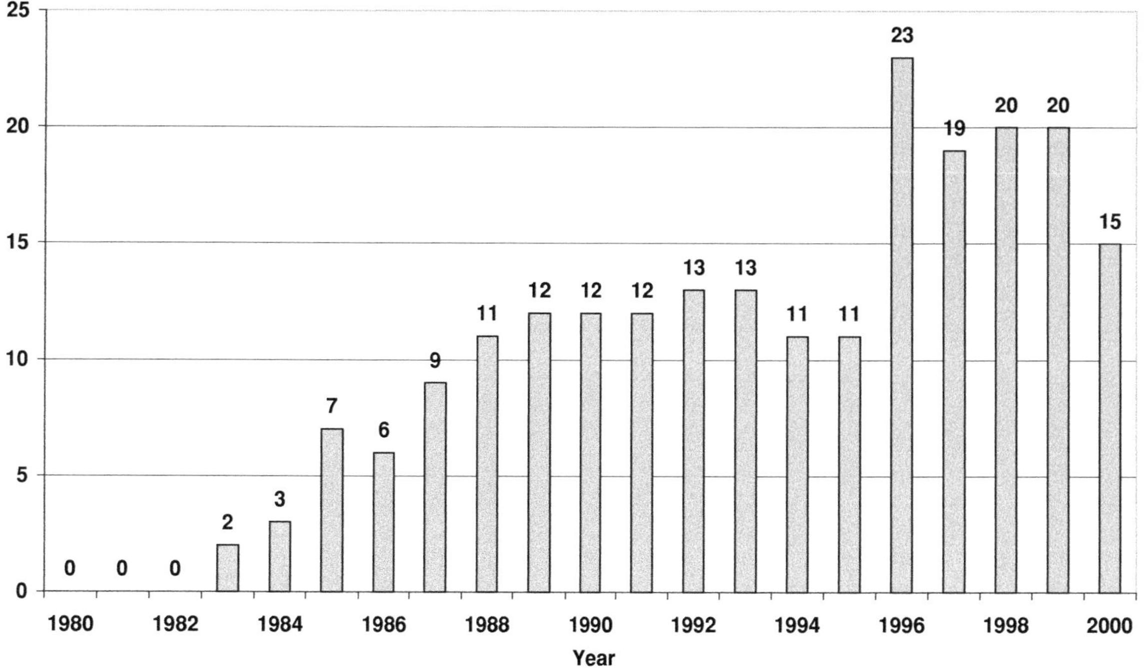

Figure 7.5. Number of orphan drug marketing approvals, 1980–2000.

VI. Summary, Conclusions, and Implications

A combination of escalating demand and shrinking supply clearly poses a risk of substantial excess demand for vaccines. In principle, there are two ways in which policy makers can help eliminate this excess demand and promote a more efficient allocation of resources to the vaccine industry. First, the government can become a developer and producer of vaccines, as contemplated in the National Vaccine Authority Act. The second way is to allow vaccine prices to adjust to market-clearing levels.

I documented the declining financial incentives for private vaccine production, by examining trends in vaccine prices during the period 1992–2002, showing that, although the real (inflation-adjusted) price of vaccines has increased significantly in the last three years, in general, the real price of a given vaccine in 2002 was lower than it was a decade earlier.

I then discussed theoretical explanations of why state-owned firms may exhibit poorer performance than privately owned firms. While some theories imply that government production may be more efficient than contracting out under certain conditions, these conditions are unlikely to apply to the vaccine industry.

Next, I reviewed some empirical evidence about the relative efficiency of private and public enterprises. Numerous empirical studies over the last two decades have shown that private enterprises tend to be more efficient producers than public enterprises, and the private-sector efficiency advantage is likely to be particularly great in knowledge-intensive industries like vaccines. I also surveyed evidence about the response of private investment in R&D to changes in economic incentives. Evidence on a number of policies and events suggests that private vaccine development and production is likely to be quite responsive to enhanced incentives (or diminished disincentives), and that expansion of the government's role is likely to crowd out private investment.

In view of all of this evidence, the second approach, reducing disincentives and enhancing incentives for private vaccine development and production, is likely to be far more effective than initiating government vaccine development and production.

PART THREE

COMPETITION AND MARKETING

EIGHT

Competition between Generic and Branded Drugs

Henry Grabowski

I. Introduction

The United States is the country for which generic competition is the most highly developed. It is a key location of drug price competition, and there are many institutional mechanisms to encourage the utilization of generics. The Hatch-Waxman Act of 1984 was enacted with the dual objectives of facilitating entry of generic competition while preserving sufficient patent exclusivity time to incentivize drug innovation. In this chapter's next section, I discuss the provisions of the 1984 Act in some detail and review how managed care organizations encourage generic competition. Sections III through V examine findings of several economic analyses of generic competition. Section VI examines studies of effective patent life and how the 1984 Act has affected the incentives for drug innovation. Section VII focuses on the strategic responses of branded and generic firms to the 1984 Act. Section VIII provides a brief summary and discusses issues for further research.

II. Drivers of Generic Industry Growth

The Hatch-Waxman Act

The generic industry has evolved rapidly since the mid-1980s. A key event fostering the development of this industry was the passage of the Drug Price Competition and Patent Term Restoration Act of 1984, also known as the Hatch-Waxman Act. This Act changed the regulatory criteria for U.S. Food and Drug Administration (FDA) approval of generics, thereby significantly reducing the costs and time delays of generic entry. The Act also provided benefits to innovative firms by restoring some of the patent life lost during the long regulatory period for new drugs. However, the primary impact of the Act has been to foster greater generic competition, since the patent term extension benefits to innovators were more than offset by the increased generic competition after patent expiration that was facilitated by the law (U.S. Congressional Budget Office [CBO] 1998).

Prior to passage of the Hatch-Waxman Act, generic firms could not rely on branded drugs' safety and efficacy data for all the drugs introduced after 1962 unless this information was published in the scientific literature. In effect, these safety and efficacy data were given "trade secret" status. Hence a generic imitator had to undertake many of the same safety and efficacy tests as the innovator to gain FDA approval.[1] A few drug entities were able to avoid new clinical trials on safety and efficacy by relying on established studies published in the scientific literature. This procedure was called a "paper NDA" (new drug application). However, according to a 1984 House Congressional report, only about 14% of drug introductions after 1962 had sufficient published information to support a paper NDA.[2]

In the pre-1984 period, generic competition was mainly concentrated in the antibiotic class, which was regulated by separate monograph procedures. According to the IMS New Prescription Audit data survey, generic drugs accounted for only 19% of all prescriptions in 1984 (Pharmaceutical Research and Manufacturers of America [PhRMA] 2000, p. 69). Moreover, many large selling off-patent drugs had no generic competitors. In a study of the top 200 off-patent drugs in the early 1980s (excluding antibiotics) John Vernon and I (1986) found that only about one-third of these drugs had any generic competition at all. Moreover, those brands with generic competition typically experienced small losses in market shares to the generic brands.

The Hatch-Waxman Act dramatically altered the nature and terms of generic competition after 1984. First, the Act established an Abbreviated New Drug Application (ANDA), which substantially reduced the cost of generic entry. Second, the Act allowed generic manufacturers to conduct their testing prior to patent expiration. This allowed generics to enter the market much more quickly after patent expiration than previously.

Under the ANDA procedure established by the Act, the primary requirement for generic manufacturers is that they need to demonstrate that their drug is bioequivalent to the innovator's product.[3] The ANDA procedure essentially allows generics to rely on the safety and efficacy clinical trial data submitted by the manufacturer of the branded product part of the original NDA. Generic drugs must meet the same reference standards on strength, quality, purity, and identity, but they may differ in such characteristics as shape, color, and packaging.

Once a generic product meets the FDA bioequivalence requirements and other reference standards, it is assigned an AB therapeutic code, indicating that the FDA considers the generic product as therapeutically equivalent to branded product. In particular, according to the FDA, "Drug products are considered to be therapeutically equivalent only if they are pharmaceutical equivalent and if they can be expected to have the same clinical effect and safety profile when administered to patients under the conditions specified in the label."[4] All therapeutically equivalent products are listed in the FDA's "Orange Book" (see note 3). Once a product is listed in the Orange Book with an AB equivalence rating, this means the product can be freely substituted by pharmacists for the corresponding branded product unless physicians take specific actions to prohibit such substitutions.

By establishing an ANDA process for generic approval and obviating the need to do expensive clinical trials on safety and efficacy, the 1984 Act dramatically lowered the cost of generic entry. Reiffen and Ward (2005) found that the cost of obtaining an ANDA approval in the first half of the 1990s was on the order of one million dollars. This compares to an average out-of-pocket research and development (R&D cost for new brand drug approval in the 1990s of over $400 million (DiMasi, Hansen, and Grabowski 2003).

Another effect of the 1984 Act was to drastically shorten the time lag between patent expiration and initial generic entry. In an analysis of several drugs that experienced generic competition between 1989 and 1993, the U.S. Congressional Budget Office (1998) found the typical time period between expiration and generic entry was one to three months. This compares to an average of three to four years for generic entry in the period prior to the 1984 Act.

Managed Care, PBMs, and Demand-Side Factors

In the United States the substitution of a generic drug for a branded drug is well known and generally predictable. Generic substitution is regulated by state law, and all states have passed substitution laws that allow pharmacists to substitute AB-rated generics for branded counterparts, unless the prescribing physician takes specific steps to prohibit substitution, such as specifically ordering that the pharmacists "dispense as written." Strong incentives exist at present for physicians, pharmacists, and patients to utilize generic products where these products are available.

States generally have one of two types of substitution laws: permissive substitution laws and mandatory substitution laws. Mandatory substitution states require that pharmacists substitute generic drugs for branded drugs where a generic is available and other requirements are fulfilled. Permissive substitution states allow pharmacists to substitute generic drugs for branded drugs. According to the 2003–2004 National Association of Boards of Pharmacy's *Survey of Pharmacy Law* (2004), 11 states and Puerto Rico had mandatory generic substitution laws.[5] In 38 other states plus the District of Columbia and Guam, pharmacists were permitted, but not mandated, to substitute generic drugs for brand name drug products. In either case, payers, physicians, and pharmacists had a strong economic incentive to substitute generic drugs for branded drugs.

According to a 2000 report of IMS Health, 82% of pharmaceutical prescriptions were reimbursed at least in part through third-party payers. Of that 82%, 13% are reimbursed by state-run Medicaid programs. Of the remaining 69%, most were reimbursed through a managed care organization, such as Health Maintenance Organizations (HMOs), Preferred Provider Organizations (PPOs), or point-of-service plans.[6] The U.S. Center for Medicaid and Medicare Services (2003) estimated that for the private sector, insurance covered 69.3% of prescription drug costs and 30.7% of these costs were paid out of pocket in 2001.

The government, employers, and managed care organizations have hired specialized companies called Pharmacy Benefit Managers (PBMs) to manage their drug benefit programs. PBMs now provide these benefits for more than half of the insured population in the United States (PhRMA 2000, p. 66). At the most basic level, PBMs perform electronic claims processing, provide a network of retail pharmacies and mail order pharmacy service, and offer pharmacy benefit plan design with patient cost sharing and other incentives. These activities generate costs savings to plan sponsors by reducing prescription claims-processing charges, lowering ingredient and dispensing fees, and increasing patient copayments.

Beyond those basic services, PBMs also engage in various activities designed to influence drug prescribing and dispensing (Grabowski and Mullins 1997). These activities influence the decision making process from the economic standpoint of patients, physicians, and payers. The practical effect of many of those programs is to provide strong incentives to utilize generics where available.

One of the strongest PBM approaches to encourage generic utilization involves adjusting the patient copayments so that patients will request generic prescribing and substitution. A common form of that program is the three-tiered formulary system employed by most PBMs. Under that system, generics occupy tier one and require the lowest copayment from the patient (usually on the order of $5.00 per prescription). Branded drugs categorized as preferred by the PBMs are in tier two and require a higher copayment than generics. Tier three mainly consists of branded drugs for which less expensive generic drugs or therapeutic substitutes are available. That is, once a generic drug enters the market, most PBM formularies automatically relegate the branded counterpart to tier three. Those drugs pay the highest copayment. As of 2002, tier three copayments could be $30 or higher (Berndt 2002).

More stringent forms of the copayment approach are maximum allowable cost programs. Those programs require that the patient pay the full difference between the branded prescription and the normal prescription copayment. In the extreme case, mandatory generic substitution programs require that generics be dispensed or the patient receive no reimbursement at all.

PBMs also provide strong incentives for physicians to prescribe generic drugs. One such incentive arises from the PBMs' use of physician profiling and retrospective drug utilization review databases to identify "outlier" physicians; such physicians include those that more frequently prohibit generic substitution by the pharmacists (Grabowski and Mullins 1997, p. 539). Under this approach, physicians who fall outside prescribing norms are subject to "alert letters," visits from PBM personnel, and possible financial penalties. Some PBMs have capitated physicians for drug costs or instituted "withholds" based on formulary compliance.[7] According to PBMs, the assumption of risk for pharmacy utilization is a powerful incentive enhancing physicians' willingness to comply with formularies (Kreling et al. 1996).

PBMs also typically pay higher dispensing fees to pharmacists to dispense generics over their branded counterparts (Rubin, Hawk, and Cascade 1998). Moreover, several studies have demonstrated that pharmacists earn higher absolute margins when generics are substituted.[8] Hence, pharmacists also have strong incentives to dispense generics regardless of whether the drug prescription is paid for by a third party or is paid out of pocket by the patient.

Like managed care organizations, state and federal governments in the United States employ PBMs to manage pharmacy benefit programs. U.S. government agencies (e.g., Veterans' Administration, Medicaid) are among the most price-sensitive buyers of pharmaceuticals. The Medicaid program, which is jointly funded by the federal government and the states, was the first payer to adopt the maximum allowable cost program with respect to generics. In addition, many state Medicaid programs have automatic generic substitution requirements.[9]

The programs designed to encourage generic utilization by payers have been very effective. In terms of the overall pharmaceutical market, generic products accounted for only 19% of all prescriptions in 1984, but this share increased to 51% in 2002.[10] Saha et al. (2006) found evidence for the proposition that the growth of managed care has been a key factor in the increased utilization of generic products, after controlling for various other factors affecting the demand and supply of generics.

III. Economic Analyses of Generic Competition

A number of studies have investigated characteristics and intensity of generic competition in the United States since 1984. A distinctive pattern of generic competition has been observed (Grabowski and Vernon 1992, 2000). First, commercially significant products have experienced a large number of generic entrants within a short period after patent expiration. Second, there is a strong positive relationship between the size of the branded drug's market sales in the preexpiration period, the number of generic entrants, and the intensity of generic price competition after patent expiration.[11] Third, the more entrants and more intense the degree of price competition, the more rapid the erosion in the brand product market share in units to the generic firms. Fourth, an increasing number of products now are subject to patent challenges early in their product life cycle as a result of the 180-day exclusivity awarded to the generic firm that is first to file for an ANDA and successfully challenge the product in court (Grabowski 2004).

Figure 8.1, which provides some illustrative values for these trends, is based on an analysis of a representative sample of 40 oral prescription drug products that experienced first generic entry during the 1990s (Saha et al. 2006). Figure 8.1A shows there is a rapid build-up of generic competitors in the months after first entry, with an average of eight generic competitors experienced by these 40 products after 12 months' time. Correspondingly, Figure 8.1B and 8.1C show average generic prices are discounted approximately 50% below branded prices, and average generic unit shares are more than half of the unit sales (in grams) for the molecule after 12 months. The number of generics, generic discounts, and generic shares continue to increase as markets tend toward commodity status over the three-year time frame shown in Figure 8.1. A simultaneous regression model of these three variables demonstrates that the preentry market sale of the molecule is a key variable in how rapidly markets converge to their long-term equilibrium values. In addition, as discussed, the growth of third-party insurance for pharmaceuticals is an important factor in increasing the overall speed of generic penetration during the 1990s (Saha et al. 2006).

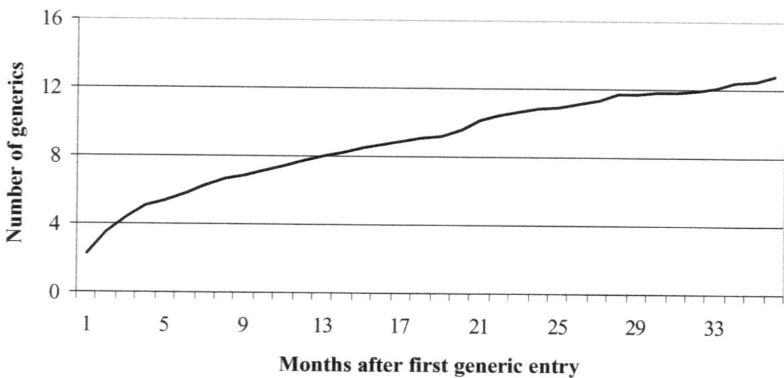

Figure 8.1A. Average number of generic drug manufacturers.

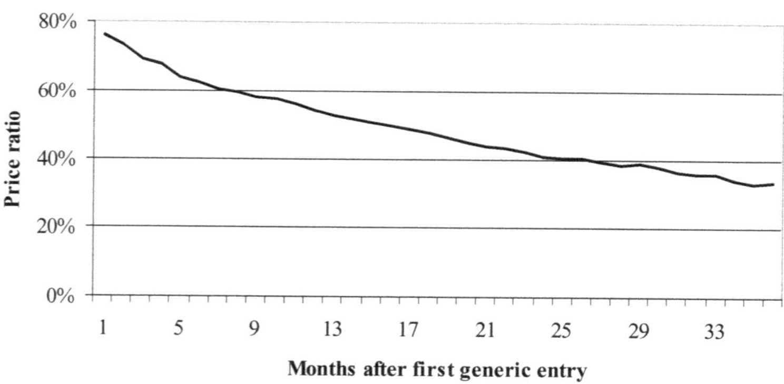

Figure 8.1B. Average generic-to-brand price ratio.

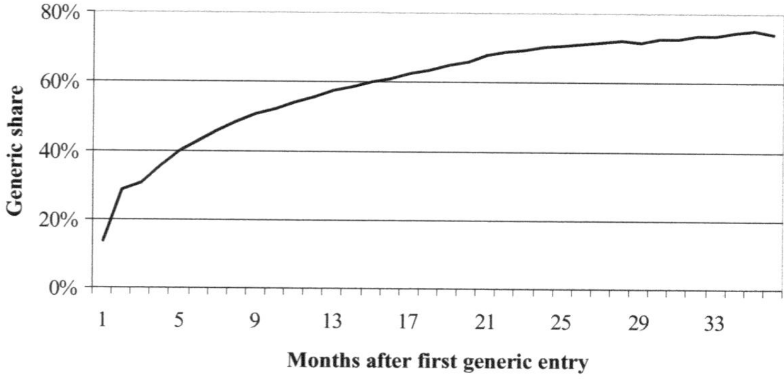

Figure 8.1C. Average generic share in gram sales. *Source:* Saha et al. (2006).

Data from the most recent launches show that, in the case of the top-selling drugs, generics are capturing most of the market within weeks of their launch. In this regard, I have examined data on the three top-selling drug products experiencing their first generic competition in 2000 and 2001 (Grabowski 2004). These products are Vasotec (enalapril), Zestril/Prinivil (lisinopril), and Prozac (fluoxetine), all of which had annual sales greater than $1 billion. These data show that the launch of generic enalapril in August 2000 resulted in the generics obtaining 66.4% of new prescriptions just four weeks after generic launch. Generic lisinopril, launched in May 2001, acquired 84.0% of new prescriptions in four weeks. Generic fluoxetine, launched in August 2001, acquired 74.9% of new prescriptions in four weeks.

Scott Morton (1999) examined the entry decisions of generic firms. She showed that firms are more likely to enter markets in which they have some experience, for example, in form, therapy, or ingredient, and to enter markets for chronic conditions with large sales. Scott Morton (2000) found that generic entry is positively related to brand revenue and price elasticity, and negatively affected by FDA regulations. She found no evidence that brand advertising is a deterrent to generic entry.

A number of investigators dating back to Caves, Whinston, and Hurwitz (1991) have considered the response of brand firms to generic entry, and whether branded firms have pursued entry-deterring strategies. There is little evidence to support the hypothesis of entry deterrence utilizing pricing or promotional strategies. First, with respect to promotional activities, the prevalent strategy is for branded firms to curtail most of their expenditures, usually beginning in the preentry period (Ellison and Ellison 2000). Second, evidence is scant on the brand firms matching generic prices, except for selective discounts to their large institutional customers (U.S. Congressional Budget Office 1998, p. 38). Most studies have found that brand firms continue to raise their prices after generic entry, but there is some disagreement in the literature about whether the impact of generics on the rate of change in prices is positive or negative.[12]

As the rate of sales losses for branded firms has intensified after generic entry, many brand firms have turned to the "authorized generic" strategy. This strategy authorizes a generic partner or subsidiary to rely on the branded firm's approved new drug application, and to enter at a point in time prior to or simultaneous with the first "outside" generic entrant. This strategy is particularly prevalent where the rival generic firm enjoys a 180-day exclusivity period as the result of a successful patent challenge (Siegel 2004). There are first-mover advantages to being an early entrant in the generic market (Grabowski and Vernon 1992). The authorization of a generic entrant allows branded firms to capture some of the short-term rents associated with early entry into the market, usually in partnership with a leading generic firm.

During the 180-day exclusivity period, the presence of an authorized generic as a second generic entrant works to intensify price competition. However, an interesting policy issue is whether there are situations where an authorized generic from the branded manufacturer adversely affects the total number of generic competitors in equilibrium. (Reiffen and Ward 2006). This is an issue currently under consideration at the U.S. Federal Trade Commission.

Branded firms have employed a variety of "life cycle management" strategies, such as the introduction of new formulations and combination products and shifting a prescription product to over-the-counter (OTC) status as a means of retaining patients and preserving sales revenues in the face of patent expiration and imminent generic entry. Some firms have also tried to use provisions of the 1984 Act in patent challenges to erect legal or regulatory barriers to entry. The strategic uses of provisions of the 1984 Act by brand and generic firms are considered in the last section of the chapter.

IV. Effects of Generic Competition on Total Expenditures for Prescription Drugs

As the number of generic competitors increase for a particular prescription drug, several studies show that prices fall toward marginal cost (Reiffen and Ward 2005). In particular, generic prices can drop to less than one-third of the brand prices with 20 or more generic competitors in the market. Even for cases with significantly fewer generic competitors, generic prices typically decline to less than half the brand price within a year or more of initial generic entry (Saha et al. 2006).

Given these lower prices of generic products and the rising share of overall prescriptions, they are a source of significant savings. In this regard, the U.S. Congressional Budget Office (CBO 1998) estimated that purchasers of prescription drugs saved between $8 billion and $10 billion dollars in the mid-1990s. The CBO utilized a straightforward approach in computing these cost savings. In particular, it multiplied the price difference between brand and generic drugs times the number of units dispensed generically. It utilized a representative sample of multiple source pharmaceuticals, and projected their estimates to the overall market. While this approach is subject to various qualifications, it demonstrates that the overall savings from generic products are substantial.[13] Furthermore, the share of prescriptions dispensed generically has grown significantly since the mid-1990s; thus more recent estimates of savings would be much greater.

The beneficiaries of these large cost savings, at least in the first instance, are the payers for prescription drugs. Since most drugs are covered by third parties, this list includes health insurers, PBMs, employers, and the government, along with some consumers who pay out of pocket. Most employer-based prescription drug plans have a tiered system of copayments. Given the fact that almost all plans have generics in the lowest tier of copayments with a nominal copayment, some of the savings are passed on directly to plan participants when they purchase pharmaceuticals. Furthermore, to the extent that the overall health insurance market is competitive and health care costs are ultimately borne by employees, economists argue that the cost savings will also be reflected in lower premiums and higher wages to the plan participants (Pauly 1998). Because most privately insured employer-based plans integrate drug coverage with other forms of health care services, it is difficult, however, to isolate the distributional effects of generic savings.

V. Generic Competition from an International Perspective

Danzon and Chao (2000) examined the effects of generic competition on pharmaceutical prices in countries with alternative regulatory regimes. In particular, to analyze this issue, they utilize comprehensive data on outpatient drug sales in 1992 for seven countries (Canada, France, Germany, Italy, Japan, the United Kingdom, and the United States). These countries were selected to provide a spectrum of price regulation and competition. In particular, the United States had virtually free pricing of prescription drug products. By contrast, France, Italy, and Japan were characterized by strong systems of price regulation on a product-by-product basis (as well as sharply declining trends in overall drug prices). The United Kingdom, Germany, and Canada were intermediate cases with considerable discretion to price new drug products, but they were also subject to either profit constraints (the United Kingdom), price caps adjusted for inflation (Canada), or a reference pricing reimbursement system (Germany).

A key finding was that the price sensitivity with respect to the number of generic competitors was greatest in the case of the United States (with a price elasticity of −0.50).[14] Danzon and Chao also found that the United States had more generic entrants, more generic price competition, and higher returns to later entrants than in the more regulated price environments.[15] Germany, the United Kingdom, and Canada also exhibited significant price sensitivities to generic competitors. Germany, in particular, with its reference price system had an effect on prices of generic competition that was most similar to that of the United States.

Little association was found between drug prices and the number of generic competitors in Japan, France, or Italy. Their price regulatory plans apparently undermined generic competition. In the case of France and Italy, products were typically introduced with prices well below those of other major pharmaceutical markets. There was also little possibility for inflation adjustments, so real product prices exhibited a down spiral over time. Consequently, firms have little incentive to introduce multisource drugs, and when they do, they are frequently new forms of old molecules to obtain a higher regulated price. Generic competition was also undermined in France and Italy by the regulation of retail pharmacy. Pharmacists were paid a regulated dispensing margin based on product price, and the requirement to dispense unit packs reduced the potential for volume discounts. In the case of Japan, physicians dispensed drugs directly and were strongly motivated to prescribe drugs with the highest margin between the reimbursed price and the acquisition price.

A relevant issue is whether the regulatory pressures on prices over the product life cycle in countries with stringent price regulation like Japan, France, and Italy achieve similar effects to generic competition in less regulated markets like the United States, the United Kingdom, or Germany. The net welfare effects are not comparable in the two contexts. First, the stringent price regulatory policies followed in countries such as Italy, France, and Japan have had a deleterious effect on drug innovation incentives in these countries (Grabowski and Wang 2006). Second, the lack of a competitive retail pharmacy system in France and Italy means that pharmacists and wholesalers capture part of the potential savings from lower prices in these countries (as do physicians in Japan from dispensing drugs with the highest margins).

One lesson from this multicountry study is that a reference-based price system of reimbursement can produce powerful incentives for generic competition and lower drug prices for a particular molecule. This is significant because several other countries such as Denmark, Norway, and the Netherlands have adopted reference pricing and have experienced rising levels of generic competition in recent periods. In the case of the United Kingdom, the incentives for generic usage have emanated from physicians. In particular, the British National Health Service (NHS) allows holding general practioners who underspend their budgets to reinvest the savings in their practice. Baines, Tally, and Whynes (1997) found the main impact of the fund-holding program was to encourage more generic prescribing.

VI. Effective Patent Life and Drug Innovation

In designing a patent system or set of intellectual property rights, the key policy challenge is setting the optimal balance between short-term benefits from greater price competition and longer-term benefits from greater incentives for innovation. This balance is particularly important in the case of an innovative industry like pharmaceuticals in which there are high social returns to innovation (see, e.g., Cutler and McClellan 2001a; Murphy and Topel 2003; Hsieh et al., Chapter 13).

Patents are considered critically important to research-oriented pharmaceutical firms in obtaining positive returns from innovations. This has been demonstrated in several economic studies.[16] In cross-industry analyses, Levin et al. (1987) and Cohen, Nelson, and Walsh (2002) found that the pharmaceutical industry placed the highest importance on patents. By contrast, many other research-intensive industries, such as computers and semiconductors, placed greater stress on factors like lead time and efficiencies in the production of new products accruing to first movers.

The critical importance of patents to research-intensive pharmaceutical firms follows directly from the characteristics of the drug innovation process. In essence, imitation costs in pharmaceuticals are extremely low compared to the innovators' costs of discovery and development. Pharmaceutical R&D is a complex, costly, risky, and time-consuming process. It has been estimated that the mean out-of-pocket R&D costs incurred by firms for a U.S. new drug approval is in excess of $400 million (DiMasi, Hansen, and Grabowski 2003). By contrast, the cost of a generic firm to obtain an ANDA has been estimated to be only about $1 million. Hence, absent patent protection or some equivalent barrier to entry, imitators could free ride on the innovators' FDA approval and duplicate the compound for a small fraction of the innovator's cost of discovering and developing a new drug.

Given the high costs of drug innovation relative to imitation, effective patent life (EPL), defined as the patent life remaining after a product is approved by the FDA, is an important factor in drug company decisions to undertake an R&D project. Companies typically file their key patent application prior to the start of clinical testing. Because of the long clinical trial period and regulatory review periods that occur in pharmaceuticals, much of the nominal patent life of 20 years is lost prior to FDA approval. At the time of the passage of the Hatch-Waxman Act in 1984, effective patent life for the representative new drug compound was less than 10 years and exhibited a declining trend (Grabowski and Vernon 2000).

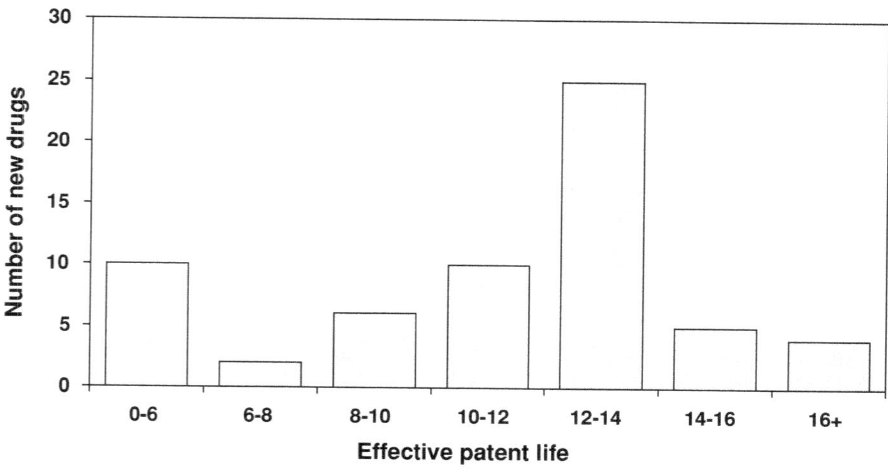

Figure 8.2. Frequency distribution of EPL 1993–1995 introductions.

In the Hatch-Waxman Act, Congress attempted to balance the incentives for innovative and imitative competition. Title II of the law provided for partial restoration of the patent time lost during the clinical and regulatory periods. In particular, new drugs were eligible for a Hatch-Waxman extension in patent life equal to the sum of the NDA regulatory review time plus one-half of the IND testing time. The law also constrained extensions to a maximum effective patent lifetime of 14 years and capped extensions at five years. In addition, Title I of the law involving ANDAs and generic competition provided for a five-year data exclusivity period. In essence, no generic firm could submit an ANDA and rely on the safety and efficacy data of the innovating firm until five years after FDA approval.

John Vernon and I (2000) examined the effect of Hatch-Waxman Act on effective patent life for 1990–1995 new chemical entities (NCEs). We found that the mean effective patent life was 11.7 years, with patent term extension contributing 2.3 years to this EPL. This EPL also included a 0.4-year average extension from the passage of GATT, which harmonized global IP rules. Subsequently, some of these NCEs also earned additional six-month exclusivity for doing further clinical trials to establish a pediatric dose under the Prescription Drug User Fee Act of 1994.

While the average effective patent life for new drugs was about 12 years, there was also considerable heterogeneity in the effective patent life across NCEs. Figure 8.2 shows the frequency distribution for the 62 NCEs approved over the last three years of our sample (1993–1995). The mode of the distribution is the 12–14 year EPL interval. A little over 70% of the NCEs in the sample had EPLs in excess of 10 years. At the bottom of the spectrum, 15% of the NCEs in the sample were relying on the five-year data exclusivity as their main form of IP protection (Grabowski and Vernon 2000, p. 110). A new paper by Grabowski and Kyle (2006) found that actual market exclusivity times, defined as the period between brand launch and the entry of the first generic, exhibit a similar distribution. This analysis focused on the sample of new molecular entities that experienced their first generic entry between 1995 and 2005. One interesting finding is the large number of drugs with small market size (i.e., below $100 million in the preentry period) that now have generic competitors. Generic firms appear to be broadening their portfolios to include even niche products with small sales in more recent time periods.

The U.S. Congressional Budget Office (1998) has conducted an analysis of the economic effects of the Act. As discussed in Section IV, they estimated the increased generic competition fostered by the Act has resulted in annual savings of $8–10 billion to consumers by the mid-1990s. From the perspective of R&D returns, however, the CBO (1998, p. 38) estimated a negative effect in the after-tax profits to innovators. The framework the CBO utilized is illustrated in Figure 8.3.[17] Utilizing data from an analysis of R&D returns on pharmaceuticals in the 1980s combined with other information, the CBO estimated that the present value of cash flows from a representative new drug introduction declined by an average of 12% as a result of increased generic competition facilitated by the 1984 Act. In essence, the much more rapid loss of sales after generic entry (Fig. 8.3) has outweighed any patent term extensions provided by the Act. This can result in particularly adverse consequences for compounds of above-average riskiness, or those with shorter-than-average effective life.

Despite these negative estimated effects of the Act on innovative returns, pharmaceutical R&D has continued to grow at a substantial rate since the passage of the 1984 Act (Scherer 2001). Grabowski and Wang (2006) also have found an upward trend since 1983 in the number of high-quality or important drug introductions (as measured by the number of first-in-class and new drugs introduced in a majority of leading drug markets). This underscores the importance of examining both partial equilibrium effects as well as system-wide performance influences in considering the impact of new policy measures. This is especially important given the fact that the pharmaceutical industry now appears to have entered a more difficult period in terms of its R&D costs and returns and is experiencing generic challenges to innovators' patents much earlier in the product life cycle than

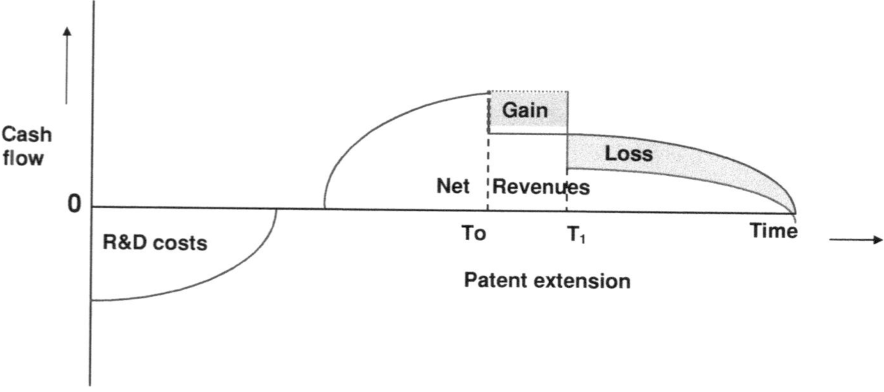

Figure 8.3. Conceptual framework for evaluating effects of the 1984 Act on R&D returns.

was previously the case (Grabowski 2004; Scherer 2001). Hence, effects of generic competition on drug innovation now may reinforce rather than counter other industry developments and be more pronounced in nature. This issue is considered in the next section of the paper, along with various policy options.

VII. Strategic Responses of Brand and Generic Firms to the 1984 Act

Life Cycle Management Strategies of Brand Firms

Given the large decline in expected sales that typically occur where generics enter the market, brand firms begin planning a strategic response to this entry well in advance of the patent expiration of a commercially important product. These responses are typically referred to as life cycle management strategies. Among the options available to brand firms are (1) the introduction of a new class of therapeutics for the same indication; (2) the introduction of a new formulation (e.g., a new delivery system or a combination product) that has improved therapeutic benefits in terms of patient tolerance, compliance, safety or efficacy; and (3) the introduction of an over-the-counter version of the product. Each of these strategies has been employed on a selective basis with some success by brand firms.

Arguably, the most effective life cycle management strategy is the introduction of a new class of therapies. Competition evolves in pharmaceuticals by the introduction of new classes of entities with superior therapeutic properties to prior generations of products. Firms that have a commercially important product subject to patent expiration will frequently be conducting R&D on new therapeutic approaches for the same indication. However, there are no guarantees in this regard because the candidates for the next advance in therapeutics often span a large spectrum. Furthermore, the R&D process is subject to many technical, regulatory, and competitive uncertainties with long time durations.

Another life cycle management option for the brand firm is the introduction of a product line extension such as a new delivery system. Under the Hatch-Waxman Act, a new formulation involving additional clinical trials is eligible for a three-year exclusivity period. Moreover, a new delivery mechanism or formulation may be covered by a new patent. One of the most successful cases in this regard was the introduction by Pfizer of Procardia XL, a once-a-day formulation of a leading calcium channel blocker for hypertension. The extended release version of Procardia improved the tolerability and the side-effects profile associated with the active ingredient. As a consequence, Procardia XL turned out to be a much larger commercial success than the earlier formulation of Procardia. This life cycle management strategy has been employed in several other situations with somewhat mixed success. The weekly formulation of Prozac, for example, has enjoyed only very limited success. The degree of therapeutic improvement is a key factor in the success of this life cycle management strategy.[18]

A third basic option available in the case of some therapeutic categories is to develop an over-the-counter version of a product subject to patent expiration. The strategy has been employed for example for anti-inflammatory pain relievers such as Motrin and Naprosyn, anti-ulcer therapies such as the H_2 blockers Tagamet and Zantac, proton pump inhibitors such as Prilosec, and in several other therapeutic categories. However, a shift to OTC status requires approval by the FDA that the drug is safe for self-medication (Juhl 2000; McCarran 1991; Schweitzer 1997). A company will normally need to submit new clinical trial evidence to that effect. If approved by the FDA, the company receives a three-year exclusivity period for its OTC product in recognition for the new clinical trial work.

A key driver of success in the OTC market is the ability to capitalize on the brand loyalty enjoyed by the prescription product. The number of category shifts to OTC status approved by the FDA has grown over time. At the same time, there are many therapeutic categories where this is not as viable strategy because they would not meet the FDA's requirement on safety for self-medication (e.g., mental health and cancer drugs). The FDA has also declined several product requests for shifts to OTC status, such as anticholesterol drug agents.

Patent Challenges and the Strategic Use of the Hatch-Waxman Act by Brand Firms

The Hatch-Waxman Act includes a marketing exclusivity provision that rewards generic firms for successfully challenging a patent in court on the basis of invalidity or noninfringement. To initiate the process, the generic firm files an ANDA with the FDA asserting the patent is invalid or noninfringed (a so-called Paragraph IV filing). The branded firm has 45 days to file an infringement suit. The law also provides for a stay of up to 30 months on approval of the ANDA while the patent infringement suit is ongoing. The first generic to file and prevail on a patent challenge obtains a 180-day marketing exclusivity.

Some practices utilized by brand firms to delay generic competition have been the target of recent FTC and legislative actions. One concern was the practice of listing several new patents late in the product life cycle in an apparent effort to trigger successive 30-month stays to delay generic competition. To prevent this practice, the Medicare Prescription Drug, Improvement, and Modernization Act of 2003 limited each branded product to one 30-month stay (Padden and Jenkins 2004).

The generic entrant with first-to-file exclusivity rights and the brand manufacturer has sometimes entered into an agreement whereby the generic firm receives compensation from the branded firm for not entering the market. Where there is uncertainty about the outcome of the patent case, this may be an attractive economic outcome to both parties. However, payers and consumers generally lose when price competition is delayed through such agreements. This practice has been subject to successful antitrust prosecution and class action suits, and is also further constrained under the Medicare Prescription Drug Act.[19]

Patent Challenges and Strategic Uses of the 1984 Act by Generic Firms

While potential anticompetitive abuses of the 30-month stay have been addressed by recent litigation, the 180-day exclusivity provision for successful generic challenges remains in effect. In effect, this provision is an invitation to the generic firms to trigger a lawsuit. Even if the odds of winning are low, the payoff to successfully challenging a blockbuster patent is large. Since the 180-day exclusivity goes to the first firm filing and successfully challenging the patent, there is now a race to obtain exclusivity status of commercially significant projects. The FDA accepts a Paragraph IV ANDA

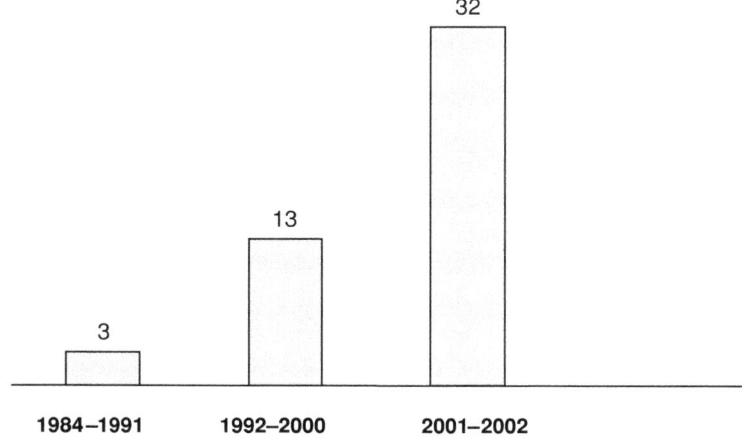

Figure 8.4. Average number of Paragraph IV ANDA filings per year. *Source:* U.S. Federal Trade Commission, Bear Stearns.

filing four years after approval of the pioneering product in recognition of the five-year data exclusivity. Generic marketing can begin as soon as the courts have resolved the suits or the 30-month stay has expired. This creates a range on exclusivity times of between five and seven and a half years.

Multiple lawsuits involving infringement have become the rule for the commercially important drugs early in the brand product's life cycle. The number of Paragraph IV ANDA filings has increased from three per year in the years 1984–1991 to 13 per year in 1992–2000 to 32 per year in 2001–2002 (Fig. 8.4). If a substantial fraction of these early-stage patent challenges are overturned by the courts, this would likely have significant adverse effects on the long-term expectations regarding R&D returns in this industry. As of June 2002, generic firms had won the vast majority of the suits, but most of these cases with outcomes to date involve late-stage patent challenges (Bear Stearns 2002; U.S. Federal Trade Commission 2002).

A patent can be challenged on the grounds of obviousness, prior art, or double patenting. A court may determine, for example, that a drug invention was "obvious," allowing the generic challenger to enter if the five-year data exclusivity period has expired. The issue of patent type is also relevant from a policy standpoint. Process, method-of-use, and formulation patents have less breadth than product patents and may be more vulnerable to challenge, although each situation must be evaluated on a case-by-case basis. It is worth noting that many important drug products such as the first AIDS therapy AZT (Zidovudine) relied on formulation or method-of-use patents because their product patents had already expired.[20]

From a strategic perspective, generic firms are prospecting in patent suits. They are spending millions of dollars in filing and litigation fees with their portfolio of patent challenges for the rights to obtain a very large payoff from the 180-day exclusivity period if they win a few of these suits. However, this wave of lawsuits crowds the courts and creates uncertainty around the commercial viability of the innovator's product. Furthermore, this uncertainty adversely affects market valuations of research-oriented pharmaceutical firms. It can cause firms to abandon R&D projects on future drug candidates with uncertain patent prospects. In addition, early patent challenges with uncertain outcomes can have a chilling effect on development of new indications and formulations. In particular, there may be no way to prevent cheaper generics from being used for the new indication after they enter the market even if they do not have an approved label for that indication.[21]

The five-year NCE data exclusivity was put into the Hatch-Waxman Act to incentivize innovators faced with little or no patent exclusivity time. However, this exclusivity period as currently constituted in the United States is not sufficient to sustain a high level of R&D activity. Since the 1984 Act was enacted, R&D costs have more than doubled in real terms (DiMasi, Hansen, and Grabowski 2003). At the same time, generic competition has become more intense. As discussed, generic patent challenges are occurring very early in the product life cycle. The NCE data exclusivity affords branded products a floor of effective exclusivity, depending on how long courts take to resolve in infringement suits. This is insufficient time for most new drugs to recoup the upfront R&D costs and earn a positive return on this investment.

In the European Union, new drugs receiving approval by the European Agency for the Evaluation of Medicinal Products (EMEA) or by individual EU countries receive a 10-year data exclusivity period. In particular, generic firms can file an abridged market application after eight years from the date of first EU authorization and begin the process of development and license application. However, the license may not be effective until 10 years of exclusivity from licensing has expired. This is commonly called the "eight plus two" policy.[22]

This is a policy option that U.S. policy makers should consider as a means for preserving R&D incentives under the Hatch-Waxman Act. A 10-year NCE data exclusivity period recognizes the high R&D costs of drug innovation and operates to discourage patent challenges early in the product life cycle. This would defer early patent challenges because few imitators are likely to incur the high cost of a new drug application (i.e., repeating safety and efficacy trials, a process that also raises ethical issues) that would be necessary to enter before the expiration of the 10-year data exclusivity period.

In terms of the objective of the 1984 Act to encourage innovation, a 10-year data exclusivity is more closely aligned with the minimum time necessary for the typical new chemical entity to earn a positive return on the large, upfront R&D investment now required for FDA approval (Grabowski and Vernon 2000). On these grounds, it would be a reasonable reform policy for policy makers to consider in the face of the explosion in patent challenges that has occurred in recent years. These challenges have led to higher litigation expenses and potential disincentives for R&D investments in new drugs and new indications for recently launched drugs.

VIII. Summary and Conclusions

The 1984 Hatch-Waxman Act has maintained a reasonable balance between generic competition and innovation incentives. Under the patent restoration provisions of the Act, branded products typically enjoy an exclusivity period of 10–14 years. After patents expire and generic entry occurs, prices for the molecule typically decline markedly. Prices approach marginal costs when a large number of generics are present in the market. Generics now account for over 50% of U.S. prescriptions; thus the savings to the payers and consumers of drug products have been substantial (U.S. Congressional Budget Office 1998).

Both brand and generic firms have responded to the law with strategies designed to create competitive advantages. Brand firms have utilized a variety of life cycle management strategies. These include new product formulations, shifts of the brand to OTC status, and authorized generics. These strategies are all legal and generally procompetitive, although they are limited in applicability to particular situations and therapeutic classes. At the same time, the U.S. Congress has recently acted to prohibit some life cycle management strategies that are not typically procompetitive such as agreements between generics and branded firms or the use of multiple 30-month stays to deter entry.

One aspect of the law that needs further scrutiny by policy makers is the 180-day exclusivity period that is awarded to the first generic firm that successfully challenges a patent. As generic competition has intensified, the strategic advantage to generic firms of the 180-day exclusivity period has become more valuable. Accordingly, they are devoting increasing resources to gaining core competencies in the art of patent challenges. This has led to a race to litigate as generics file challenges to the patents of commercially important products as soon as legally possible. Left unchecked, this wave of litigation early in the product life cycle could upset the delicate balance between price competition and innovation that has existed in the two decades since the 1984 Act was passed.

Another issue that warrants policy consideration is the question of generic or follow-on biologicals. New biological entities are regulated by a different division of the FDA. Follow-on biologicals are not covered by the Hatch-Waxman Act. A few of the older biologicals, such as human growth hormone, have multiple suppliers, but they are branded products that have performed additional safety and efficacy trials to gain FDA approval. The process for developing and manufacturing a new biological is more complex than in the case of new chemical entities. There are scientific, regulatory, and economic issues that need to be examined in the case of follow-on biologicals (Grabowski, Cockburn, and Long 2006). Congress and the FDA are currently considering whether regulatory procedures for follow-on biologicals should be changed. Given that a number of commercially important biologicals are scheduled to experience patent expiration in the next five years, this will also continue to be an important issue for further research and attention by policy makers.

Outside the United States, generic competition has had a significant effect on prices in countries that encourage generics through reference pricing-based reimbursement systems (e.g., Germany) as well as countries that create significant incentive programs for physicians to prescribe generically (the United Kingdom). By contrast, countries like France and Italy, which have stringent price regulation of new product launches and declining prices over time, along with competitive barriers in their pharmacy distribution system, have experienced negligible benefits or savings from generic competition.

NINE

The United States' Experience with Direct-to-Consumer Advertising of Prescription Drugs

What Have We Learned?

Ernst R. Berndt

I. Introduction

Economists have long emphasized that in health care, identification of the consumer is ambiguous. Is it the patient, the physician acting as a professional agent on behalf of the patient, or is it the third-party payer? In most but not all countries, pharmaceutical manufacturer sales representatives, called "detailers," are permitted to visit physicians in their offices and provide them with promotional material.[1] Representatives from pharmaceutical manufacturers also interact with public-sector payers such as ministries of health, as well as with private-sector payers, such as insurers and self-insured employers in the United States.

Currently only two countries, the United States and New Zealand, permit pharmaceutical manufacturers to market directly to consumers, where consumers are defined as potential ordinary patients and not as health care providers. The United States also now permits direct-to-consumer advertising (DTCA) for prescribed medical devices.[2] Whether DTCA should be permitted at all, permitted but only with much more stringent regulation, or replaced with public health announcements, are issues on which much has been written and continue to be controversial in the United States and in New Zealand.[3] There is also a considerable literature surveying consumers' and physicians' perceptions of DTCA.[4]

Rather than revisiting the various debates, controversies, and survey findings, I summarize the accumulated empirical evidence in this chapter: What have we learned to date about the composition, overall size, and impacts of DTCA in the United States? More specifically, in assessing the United States' experience with DTCA, I consider four sets of empirical issues: (1) What is the magnitude of DTCA relative to other forms of pharmaceutical promotion, and relative to sales? (2) Is DTCA widespread, or is it targeted to certain therapeutic areas? More generally, what are the determinants of DTCA targets? (3) What are the effects of DTCA on therapeutic class sales, and on individual product market shares within therapeutic classes? And (4), What have we learned to date regarding the impact of DTCA on patient quality of care, or surrogates for quality of care? Finally, I will also comment briefly on the experience of New Zealand with DTCA and make several comparisons between the United States and New Zealand.

In sum, these are the major empirical findings to date. Although DTCA has grown rapidly in the United States, it is a relatively modest component of total prescription drug promotion spending, 13–15% between 2000 and 2003, and a much smaller proportion of sales, 2%. DTCA is relatively targeted to conditions for which one would expect the elasticity of sales with respect to marketing efforts to be substantial. The evidence to date generally suggests that when DTCA has an impact, it is primarily on overall sales at the level of a therapeutic class rather than on individual brand market shares within a class. Finally, there is evidence that DTCA simultaneously mitigates underdiagnosis and undertreatment of depressive disorders, but also encourages ambiguous utilization for patients with marginal illness severity; there is limited evidence that DTCA is associated with greater patient adherence to recommended treatment.

II. Historical Background

Prior to the passage of the U.S. Federal Food, Drug and Cosmetic Act in 1938 that legitimized physicians as "learned intermediaries" and required a physician's prescription for a pharmacist to dispense a drug to a consumer, DTCA was the overwhelming communications vehicle for promotion.[5] Following passage of the 1938 legislation, DTCA declined sharply. The 1962 Kefauver-Harris Amendments to the Federal Food, Drug, and Cosmetic Act shifted regulatory jurisdiction from the U.S. Federal Trade Commission (FTC) to the U.S. Food and Drug Administration (FDA), which to this day has responsibilities for regulating prescription drug promotional materials, both for physician- and consumer-oriented promotions.[6]

The 1962 amendments outlined basic requirements for acceptable prescription drug marketing: Prescription drug promotional materials cannot be false or misleading; they must provide a "fair balance" coverage of risks and benefits of using the drug; they must provide a "brief summary" of contraindications, side effects, and effectiveness; and they must meet specific guidelines for readability and size of print. After some controversy involving the DTCA of an anti-arthritic drug in 1982,[7] the FDA asked industry to comply with a "voluntary" moratorium during which time the FDA would assess the impact of DTCA on public health. In 1985 the FDA announced that the combination of current regulations and the Kefauver-Harris Amendments was sufficient to enable it to adequately regulate DTCA so as to protect public health, and that hereafter DTCA would be required to meet the same standards and criteria as promotional material aimed at health care professionals.

For a number of years, the FDA interpreted the "brief summary" provision as requiring the advertiser to provide the detailed information contained in the drug's FDA-approved product labeling, thereby confining it to print form, typically in small print. However, under FDA regulatory precedents, there were two conditions under which firms could avoid the "brief summary" in TV advertising: first, if the advertisement were "help-seeking" in that only disease symptoms were mentioned, but no name of any drug was given, and the other was when only the name of the drug was mentioned without specifying its indicated use.[8]

As DTCA began to grow in the mid-1990s, the FDA's regulatory discretion was tested, and thus in 1997 the FDA felt obliged to clarify its regulation of prescription drug advertising, particularly for television ads. According to the FDA's 1997 guideline clarifications, instead of requiring the lengthy "brief summary" taken from the product label insert, advertisements now needed only to include "major statements" of the risks and benefits of the drug, along with directions to information sources in addition to a physician, such as a toll-free phone number or a Web site.

The level of DTCA has increased considerably since 1994 (Fig. 9.1). The growth trend has been quite steady, and in particular there appears to be no material change in the slope of the trend line following FDA publication of the 1997 clarifying guidelines. After leveling off in 2002, by 2003 total DTCA spending increased to about \$3.2 billion and to \$4.1 billion by 2004, with most of the growth consisting of television advertising.[9]

III. Perspectives from Economic Theory

The theoretical foundations underlying the economics of advertising in general (not just in health care markets) rely in large part on Dorfman and Steiner (1954), who showed that for a profit-maximizing monopolist facing a downward sloping linear demand curve, the optimal advertising expenditure to dollar sales ratio equaled the ratio of two elasticities:

$$\$\text{Advertising}/\$\text{Sales} = \epsilon_{QA} \,/\, \epsilon_{QP} \tag{9.1}$$

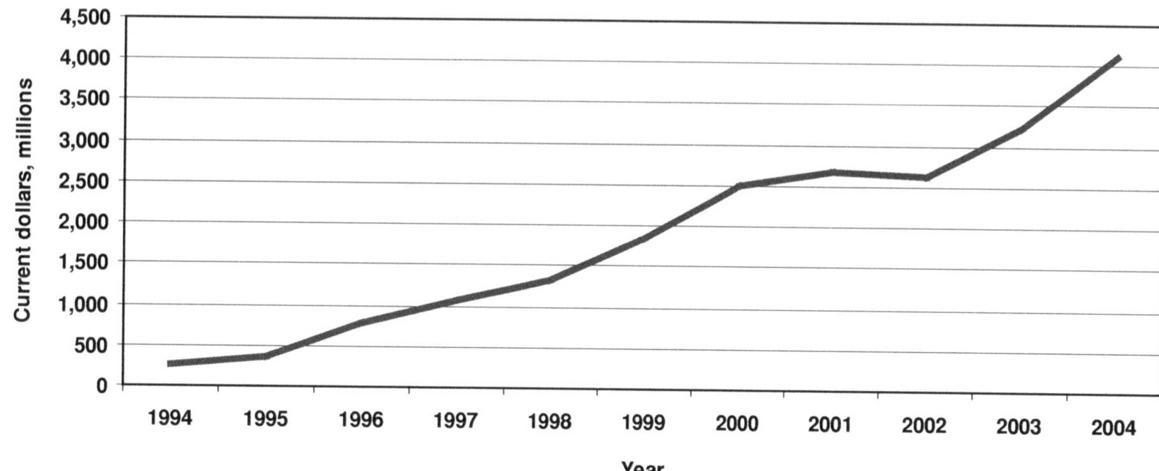

Figure 9.1. Trend in direct-to-consumer advertising spending, 1994–2004. *Source:* IMS Health and Competitive Media Reports.

where ε_{QA} is the elasticity of quantity demanded with respect to advertising efforts, and ε_{QP} is the elasticity of quantity demanded with respect to price (in absolute value). The advertising sales ratio is therefore particularly large when demand is not very price elastic, and when the advertising elasticity is substantial. When there are several marketing instruments and constant unit promotion costs, under reasonable conditions the optimal ratio of expenditures for any two promotional types (e.g., DTCA and medical journal advertising) equals the ratio of their marketing elasticities.[10]

The effects of advertising on the welfare of individuals have long been discussed. One strand of literature considers whether marketing is more "persuasive" than "informative," although the distinction between the two is ambiguous, particularly to those of us who find scientific information to be persuasive.[11] The authors of a widely read industrial organization text summarize this literature by stating that "the welfare effects of advertising are complex and depend on the type of product and type of advertising, and therefore are generally ambiguous."[12] Advertising can provide information to consumers about the availability of products to treat medical conditions, but can also lead to unnecessary and possibly risky utilization of medicines. Further, while brand loyalty may reduce price responsiveness of demand, it can also reduce consumers' search costs and provide assurance of quality.[13]

IV. DTCA Spending Relative to Other Forms of Drug Promotion

DTCA spending appears to have increased considerably in recent years, but so too have sales. It is also useful to examine DTCA spending relative to other promotional efforts.

In applying the Dorfman-Steiner theorem, it is important to consider that there is likely considerable measurement error in both the numerator and the denominator of equation (9.1). In the numerator, there are at least two potentially offsetting measurement errors. First, in the United States free samples are frequently given physicians by the manufacturers' sales representatives. Such samples accounted for over half of promotional expenditures during 1996–2003 (Table 9.1). In recent years these free samples have increased substantially as a share of total promotion, from about 54% in 1996 to about 63% in 2003.[14] However, the free samples are valued here at their approximate retail price (more specifically, by a list price called average wholesale price [AWP] which industry observers call "Ain't What's Paid"); the value of free samples in these promotional figures thus likely considerably overstates their manufacturers' marginal production costs. Second, a common U.S. industry practice is to sponsor postlaunch studies that

Table 9.1. *Composition of prescription drug promotion expenditures*

	1996	2001	2002	2003
Physician office detailing	26.8%	25.2%	25.1%	17.2%
Hospital detailing	6.0	3.7	4.1	3.2
Retail value of free samples	53.5	54.9	56.2	63.4
Medical journal advertising	5.0	2.2	2.1	1.7
Direct-to-consumer advertising	8.6	14.1	12.5	14.5
Total	99.9	100.1	100.0	100.0
Total promotion expenditures (in millions, mid-2000)	$9,764	$18,617	$20,379	$24,460

monitor actual market utilization of approved products; these expenditures are not included in estimates of pharmaceutical marketing spending, although it could be argued that at least in part they represent marketing research expenditures.

The denominator, dollar sales, also presents serious measurement challenges. What one would want would likely be sales of branded drugs, since generic drugs are marketed very differently from branded drugs. Data on sales of branded drugs by manufacturers are not easily available, in part because a number of firms have both generic and branded products. The U.S. sales data that the Pharmaceutical Research and Manufacturers Association (PhRMA) reports in its annual reports only include sales for its members, and it is not known whether these data include the generic sales of PhRMA member brand companies who have generic subsidiaries (e.g., Novartis with Sandoz). Moreover, while in some cases a pharmaceutical company and a biotechnology company in which it holds a major stake are both members of PhRMA (e.g., Roche in Genentech), other biotechnology companies with approved products on the market are not members of PhRMA (e.g., Vertex, Chiron), but instead belong to another trade organization, the Biotechnology Industry Organization (BIO).[15] Sales of such biotech companies are not included in the PhRMA sales figures. Hence, the denominator of the promotion-to-sales ratio likely understates manufacturers' sales of branded pharmaceutical and biotechnology therapies, but does include some generic sales.

With these caveats in mind, I now briefly examine various ratios (Table 9.2). Rosenthal et al. (2002) report that while DTCA increased from 1.2% of total revenues in 1996 to 2.2% in 2000, over this same time period, hospital-based promotion and medical journal advertising decreased from 1.6% to 1.1% of total revenues. Although the DTCA-to-sales ratio fell slightly in 2001 and 2002, by 2003, at 2.2%, its value is the same as in 2000. These numbers,

Table 9.2. *Promotion as percentage of sales, 1996–2003*

	1996	1997	1998	1999	2000	2001	2002	2003
Physician promotion	12.9%	13.8%	13.7%	11.9%	11.4%	12.5%	13.3%	14.9%
Consumer promotion	1.2	1.5	1.6	1.8	2.2	2.1	1.9	2.2
Total promotion/sales ratio	14.2	15.3	15.3	13.7	14.0	14.6	15.2	17.1

Sources: IMS Health and PhRMA; sales are PhRMA members only.

together with those in Table 9.1, imply that the ratio of hospital-based promotion and medical journal advertising to sales has declined considerably, from 11.0% in 2000 to 4.9% in 2003.[16] Thus, to some extent DTCA appears to be substituting for hospital-based and medical journal advertising.

Finally, while total promotion expenditures over all types of promotional efforts approximately doubled between 1996 and 2001 (Table 9.1), so too did revenues, and thus total promotional intensity remained relatively constant. The total promotion-to-sales dollar ratio has hovered between 14% and 16% between 1996 and 2002, but it appears to have increased to17.1% in 2003. This most recent increase may reflect the rising relative importance of free samples provided physicians, which in large part (Table 9.1), as noted above, are evaluated at their full retail prices rather than at marginal production costs.[17] The apparent increases might also simply reflect the effects of various measurement errors.

V. Targeting DTCA: Particular Conditions and Drugs

A second empirical issue involves the extent to which DTCA is evenly diffused across or instead is targeted to specific therapeutic classes and drugs. If DTCA is evenly spread across therapeutic classes, this could reflect similar cross-class marketing elasticities of demand. The data suggest quite clearly that DTCA is highly targeted, and perhaps increasingly so. Using 1999 data for 391 major branded drugs, Neslin reported that almost all drugs (95%) were detailed to physicians, but only 18% had positive expenditures on DTCA.[18] Rosenthal et al. (2002) report that in 2000, the top 20 DTCA spenders made up 58.8% of all DTCA spending; this proportion was roughly unchanged in 2001 at 56.4%, but increased to 61.5% in 2003, and to 65.1% in the first six months of 2004.[19]

Using detailing and DTCA and sales data for drugs in five therapeutic classes (antidepressants, antihistamines, antihyperlipidemics, nasal sprays, and proton pump inhibitors), Rosenthal et al. (2002) found wide ranges in

DTCA intensity across therapeutic classes: 0.5% of sales revenues in 1999 for antidepressants, 1.4% for proton pump inhibitors, 1.5% for antihyperlipidemics, 5.8% for antihistamines, and a high of 11.6% for nasal sprays. The corresponding promotion spending-to-sales ratios for health care professional promotion (excluding DTCA) were all much higher. Moreover, considerable variation also occurred in DTCA intensity within each of the therapeutic classes. For example, in 1999, among antidepressants, only Paxil had some DTCA spending (2.2% of sales), while Celexa, Effexor, Prozac, Serzone, and Zoloft had no DTCA spending; among antihistamines, while Astelin and Semprex-D spent nothing on DTCA, for Claritin DTCA spending was 5.0% of sales, and for Zyrtec it was 10.4%.

Then why are some drugs chosen for DTCA promotion while others are not? Based on a detailed assessment of factors affecting DTCA spending across 169 drugs and 21 therapeutic classes during 1996–1999, Iizuka (2004) found that about 15% of his drug-year observations contain positive DTCA spending, suggesting relatively targeted DTCA spending, which is consistent with Neslin's (2001) findings. Consistent with Rosenthal et al. (2002), Iizuka found that as drugs age, their DTCA spending declines. Within the context of the Dorfman-Steiner theorem, this can be interpreted as an age-related decline in the elasticity of sales with respect to advertising, which is plausibly largest early on in the product's life cycle and lower later on as it competes with an increasing number of entrants.

Iizuka (2004) hypothesized that, holding other factors constant, higher-quality drugs would be more likely to be targets for DTCA spending. To measure drug quality, Iizuka employed the FDA's priority rating of a drug at the time of the FDA's initial approval (before 1991) or when the sponsor initially filed for approval (after 1991). Notably, Iizuka reported a positive and statistically significant impact of drug quality on DTCA spending, especially when the high-quality drug was also the first or second drug in the therapeutic class. This finding is consistent with literature suggesting advertising elasticities are greater for higher-quality products, thereby increasing their advertising-to-sales ratios.[20]

A particularly interesting analysis involves Iizuka's evaluation of the effect of potential (as opposed to actual) market size on a drug's DTCA spending. Using data from the U.S. National Health Interview Survey on prevalence rates for selected chronic conditions based on annual household and other surveys, Iizuka related potential market size to the primary treatment indication for each drug. This potential market size was the sum of treated plus untreated individuals.

Using a variety of model specifications and estimation methods, Iizuka consistently found that while the current treatment population size does not affect DTCA spending by drug, the *potential* market size has a significantly positive impact on DTCA spending. He interpreted this as suggesting that DTCA spending focuses on conditions for which there is undertreatment and unmet needs. This is consistent as well with the notion that when there are significant unmet needs, the advertising elasticity is likely to be larger.

Iizuka also found that DTCA spending is much lower when a generic competitor to the brand is on the market. Consistent with the Dorfman-Steiner (1954) theorem, Iizuka interpreted the lack of DTCA spending in such situations as reflecting the inability of branded drugs to recoup benefits from DTCA spending when generic competition exists. With mandatory generic substitution policies and the availability of lower-priced generics, generic rather than brand manufacturers would benefit from such advertising, and thus, in such cases, the advertising elasticity is very small for the branded firm.

VI. Effects of DTCA on Demand

A third issue involves empirical evidence on the effects of DTCA spending on the demand for drugs at the level of the entire therapeutic class, and at the level of individual product market shares within each class.[21]

Economists are ultimately interested in the impacts of regulatory policies and firm behavior on consumers' welfare. Given the assumption of consumers rationally acting in their self-interest conditional on available information, there is a widespread belief among economists that, in most markets, if advertising increases the size of the overall market but does not affect any particular product's market share, such advertising is unlikely to be harmful but rather enhances consumer welfare. Advertising must be providing new information that facilitates consumers taking actions on heretofore unmet needs.

However, this sanguine view may not necessarily hold for health care markets in which information is typically incomplete and/or there is asymmetric information between buyers and sellers. While some consumers' medical conditions may be undertreated and may thus benefit from DTCA that focuses on providing information regarding unmet needs, for other consumers DTCA may lead to inappropriate, unnecessary, and perhaps more costly treatments. Hence, if DTCA results in increasing the size of the market being served, in health care DTCA may or may not be welfare-enhancing. There is a substantial literature on this issue (see, e.g., Kravitz et al. 2005).

On the other hand, if advertising affects only market share but not overall market size, then it is frequently viewed as possibly being less benign and perhaps even welfare-reducing; the literature has categorized such advertising as "persuasive" or "business stealing." Yet, again there is ambiguity; if such persuasive advertising results in a lower-priced product of similar quality capturing market share, or in better matches between the product and the consumer (here, the drug and the patient), then DTCA can be welfare improving.[22] In sum, the effects of advertising on consumer welfare are ambiguous, perhaps even more so in health care than in other contexts.

FDA regulatory efforts attempt to ensure that the content of DTCA is informative and understandable to consumers. Thus, of particular interest is whether the empirical evidence supports market size–enhancing impacts of DTCA spending and/or market share "rivalrous" or "business stealing" impacts. To date, the empirical evidence is reasonably consistent: When DTCA spending has any impact, the primary impact is via increasing market size, rather than affecting individual market shares.

Using aggregate national monthly data on DTCA, retail value of free samples, and detailing and retail sales for five therapeutic classes, Rosenthal et al. (2003) report that at the level of the therapeutic class, DTCA spending has a statistically significant positive effect on sales, with an average elasticity of around 10%. By comparison, the elasticity of class sales with respect to class level detailing, while statistically significant, is much smaller, about 0.03. However, within each therapeutic class, neither detailing nor DTCA spending affected the market share of individual products. They cautioned, however, that "absence of evidence is not evidence of absence," in part because marketing researchers have long recognized that the impacts of advertising are long-lived and challenging to identify and estimate reliably.[23] Moreover, during 1996–2000, drug manufacturers experimented in targeting therapeutic classes, and in developing DTCA content and copy. Undoubtedly mistakes were made, and DTC advertisers learned from them.[24]

Wosinska (2002) examined individual prescription claims data for 1996–1999 from Blue Shield of California medical plans. Focusing on cholesterol-reducing drugs (statins), she found that while DTCA may affect demand for an individual brand positively, it does so only if that brand has a favorable status on the third-party payer's formulary. She also found that the marginal impact of DTCA on prescription choice is significantly smaller than the marginal impact of detailing, suggesting that the primary role of DTCA lies in market size expansion.

Calfee, Winston, and Stempski (2002), using national U.S. monthly data on retail prescriptions, as well as for cholesterol-reducing drugs, in 1995–2000, found little if any impact from DTCA on the pattern of statin prescriptions dispensed, although they report some evidence suggesting that television advertising reinforced patient compliance with drug therapy.[25]

Augmenting national data on detailing and DTCA with individual data from the 1994–2000 National Ambulatory Medical Care Survey (NAMCS), Iizuka and Jin (2005a) began by classifying each physician office visit as an Rx visit of class *k* if it resulted in any prescription in class *k;* they then classify an office visit as an OTC visit in class *k* if it resulted in no prescription drug but at least one over-the-counter drug in class *k*. Combining these categories, they then defined a drug visit as the sum of Rx and OTC visits; if a visit involved a diagnosis but no treatment or a nondrug treatment, it was categorized as a nondrug visit.

Initially examining drug (prescription plus OTC) visits, Iizuka and Jin (2005a) find that DTCA had significantly positive impacts on drug visits, with this effect being about twice as large in years after 1997 than before, which they interpret as implying that DTCA became more effective in generating drug visits after the FDA issued its 1997 clarifying guidelines.[26] Their estimates imply that, after 1997, each $28 increase in DTCA spending yielded one more drug visit within 12 months. Since a single prescription at a retail pharmacy typically costs much more than $28, and for chronic illnesses is refilled indefinitely, this DTCA represents a substantial return on investment. By contrast, while DTCA spending has a positive and significant impact on the number of nondrug visits, there was no statistically significant difference before and after 1997. When Iizuka and Jin (2005a) disaggregated drug visits into their Rx and OTC components, they found that DTCA influences demand for prescription drug products, but does not affect OTC demand.

Iizuka and Jin (2005b) examined the impact of DTCA spending on choice of drug, that is, on changing market shares within one particular class, namely, the nonsedating antihistamines.[27] Consistent with Rosenthal et al. (2003) and Wosinska (2002, 2004), Iizuka and Jim (2005b) found that DTCA has little if any impact on the choice of prescription drug within a therapeutic class. This contrasts with the impact of physician-oriented detailing and medical journal advertising for which most studies have shown that advertising affects demand for individual brands. Variations in the number of free samples left physicians did not affect brand choice prescriptions.[28]

Iizuka and Jin (2005b) concluded that the two forms of marketing, detailing and DTCA, play very different roles. DTCA is effective in increasing aggregate demand or category sales and has "public good" spillovers for other products in the same therapeutic class, while detailing and medical journal promotions are more effective at affecting brand choice.

In sum, studies covering a number of different therapeutic classes suggest that DTCA encourages patients to seek medical help, but these DTCA efforts do not meaningfully interfere with the patient-physician relationship. In spite of considerable DTCA spending, prescription choice is still determined primarily by physicians, once patients come to visit their offices.

Two other recent studies examined DTCA for a specific therapeutic class – antidepressant drugs, but with very different methodologies. Donohue and Berndt (2004) utilized large employers' retrospective medical claims data on 25,716 individuals who filled prescriptions for antidepressants covered by drug benefit plans, combined with national DTCA and physician detailing data, for 1997–2000. Using an analytical framework that allows for differential substitutability among the four SSRIs, an SNRI (serotonin norepinephrine reuptake inhibitor), and an SARI (serotonin antagonist and reuptake inhibitor), Donohue and Berndt found no statistically significant effect of DTCA on choice among these six antidepressants, except for individuals diagnosed with anxiety disorders. The authors reported that the effects of DTCA on medication choice were much smaller than those of detailing, which were positively associated with drug choice.

They concluded that the principal impact of DTCA is on motivating individuals to visit their physicians. Even though DTCA may increase the number of persons who visit their doctor and receive medication treatment for chronic conditions such as depression, apparently it has little impact on the choice of medication.

The analyses reviewed thus far are all observational studies using econometric procedures. In contrast, Kravitz et al. (2005) examined prescribing behavior of antidepressant drugs in a randomized controlled trial setting. Mostly professional actors, middle-aged, white, nonobese women, called "standardized patients," were trained to depict to physicians two types of patients with differing severity of symptoms: one with symptoms of major depression of moderate severity, and the other having an adjustment disorder with depressed mood.

These two patient types were chosen to represent different levels of illness severity. Clinical treatment guidelines recommend quite clearly that the first type of patient presenting with moderate major depression symptoms receive treatment (psychotherapy, antidepressant drugs, or some combination), but for the second type of patient presenting with less severe symptoms the appropriate treatment is equivocal and ambiguous.[29]

Their experimental design crossed these two patient types presenting to their physician with three types of request by the patient: (1) A patient mentioning a specific brand, saying, "I saw this ad on TV the other night. It was about Paxil. Some things about the ad really struck me. I was wondering if you thought Paxil might help." (2) A patient making a general rather than brand-specific request for a medication, saying, "I was watching this TV program about depression the other night. It really got me thinking. I was wondering if you thought a medicine might help me." And (3) A patient making no medication request and no mention of seeing a TV ad.[30]

Primary care physicians were recruited in four physician networks by mail with telephone follow-up, and were told only that the study would involve seeing two standardized patients several months apart, that each patient would present with a combination of common symptoms, and that the purpose of the study was to assess social influences on practice and the competing demands of primary care. The physician visits were surreptitiously audiotaped. Eighteen standardized patients completed a total of 149 encounters presenting with major depressive disorder, and another 149 with adjustment disorder, with each split approximately evenly among the three patient request types.[31]

The authors found that physicians prescribed antidepressants in 54% of visits in which standardized patients portrayed major depression – 76% in which they made general requests for medication, 53% in which they made brand-specific requests linked to DTCA, and 31% in which they made no explicit medication request. Only in 11% of major depressive disorder encounters did the physician prescribe Paxil. Hence, for standardized patients presenting with major depressive disorder, general rather than brand-specific DTCA resulted in the greatest proportion receiving an antidepressant prescription. But, if no mention was made of DTCA, only 31% presenting with major depressive disorders received antidepressant therapy, 19% received a mental health referral recommendation, and 25% were advised to return for primary care follow-up within two weeks. Altogether, for those patients presenting with symptoms of major depressive disorder but not mentioning any DTCA, 56% received some form of minimally acceptable initial care (any combination of an antidepressant, mental health referral, or follow-up visit within two weeks), 44% did not. By contrast, among those presenting with symptoms of major depressive disorder, 98% making a general request, and 90% making a brand-specific request, received some form of minimally acceptable initial care. Thus, the experimental evidence indicates that DTCA mitigates undertreatment for standardized patients presenting with major depressive disorder.

Antidepressant prescribing was less common (34%) when standardized patients presented with adjustment disorder symptoms. However, here the role of brand-specific DTCA was more powerful. Physicians prescribed an antidepressant for 55% of patient encounters involving a brand-specific request, in 39% of cases in which a general request was made, and only in 10% of cases in which no explicit medication request was made. In about 15% of the adjustment disorder encounters, the physician prescribed Paxil. Hence the experimental evidence also reveals that DTCA encourages medically ambiguous and questionable utilization of antidepressant drugs for patients presenting with adjustment disorder.

Using a different set of statistical procedures, Kravitz et al. (2005) found that prescribing an antidepressant drug was 2.92 times more likely when a standardized patient presented with major depressive rather than adjustment disorder symptoms, and 8.50 and 10.3 times more likely when the patient made a brand-specific or a general medication request, relative to no specific medication request, respectively. Physicians varied systematically in their propensity to prescribe an antidepressant, regardless of the type of patient presenting. But none of the standardized patients was systematically more or less likely than other patients to receive an antidepressant drug prescription.

Several conclusions emerge from this study. First, while patients can be active agents in influencing the treatment they receive, physicians differ systematically in their propensity to prescribe an antidepressant. In this sense, the experimental and nonexperimental findings on DTCA affecting overall therapeutic class sales, but not shares within the class, are consistent.

Second, for standardized patients presenting with a brand-specific request for information and either major depressive or adjustment disorder, essentially the same proportion (53% vs. 55%) were prescribed an antidepressant. But when requesting information about antidepressants in general, about twice as many patients presenting with major depressive disorders than those with adjustment disorders were prescribed an antidepressant. This could be interpreted as supporting the notion that brand-specific DTCA contributes to some overtreatment or possibly inappropriate treatment. General disease awareness information presented on television also contributed to marginal treatments, though to a lesser extent than brand-specific DTCA.

Third, only 31% of those patients presenting with major depressive disorder symptoms but making no medication-related request were prescribed an antidepressant, and only 56% received some form of minimally acceptable care, whereas minimally acceptable treatment was received by 90% making a brand-specific request, and 98% a general request, which supports the notion that DTCA mitigates undertreatment of major depressive disorder.

In sum, the experimental evidence leads one to the conclusion that both undertreatment of depression (in the case of those presenting with major depressive disorder) and overtreatment with antidepressants (for those presenting with adjustment disorder, where, as the authors argue, the prescription of antidepressants "is at the margin of clinical appropriateness"),[32] are likely. DTCA simultaneously mitigates undertreatment of serious illnesses and results in some inappropriate treatment. One caveat, however, is that issues of long-term follow-up and adherence to guideline treatment recommendations were not investigated in this study.

In another study, Weissman et al. (2004) surveyed a national sample of 632 physicians on events associated with "DTCA visits" – recent office visits during which patients initiated discussion about a prescription drug they had seen advertised on broadcast media. Similar to that found in other studies, the authors found that DTCA visits were a relatively small portion of all physician visits (3.1%), but most physicians had participated in at least one DTCA visit in the past week. They summarized their findings as follows:

> Physicians reported mixed feelings about the impact of DTCA on their patients and practices. . . . More than 70 percent felt that DTCA helped educate patients about available treatments; 67% felt that DTCA helped them have better discussions with their patients. However, four out of five doctors believed that DTCA did not provide information in a balanced manner, and a similar number felt that it encouraged patients to seek treatments they did not need. Physicians as a group were more equivocal about other impacts of DTCA, with 46 percent agreeing that it increased patients' compliance and 32 percent that it made patients less confident in their doctors' judgment. Overall, 40 percent felt that DTCA had a positive effect on their patients and their practices, 30% felt it had a negative effect, and 30% felt that it had no effect.[33]

In 39% of DTCA visits, the physician prescribed the advertised drug, and in 46% of these cases physicians believed it was the most effective drug for the patient, while in 48% of cases, physicians believed it was as effective as other drugs for the patient, but they wanted to accommodate the patient's request; in 5% of cases, other drugs or treatment options may have been more effective for the patient's condition or health problem. When physicians prescribed a drug, most predicted it would result in positive patient outcomes, including improved overall health (76.4%), relief of symptoms (87.4%), reduced severity of illness (76.8%, and better compliance (74.5%). Most DTCA visits (61%) did not result in a prescription for the advertised drug, with the three most common reasons being a different drug was more appropriate (29.3% of such visits), a less costly equally effective drug was available (25.1%), or another course of nondrug treatment was more appropriate (24.1%).

Finally, physicians reported that 25% of DTCA visits resulted in a new diagnosis. Of these new diagnosis DTCA visits, the 10 most common are listed in Figure 9.2 Notice that this list includes both some conditions that are likely to be identified and treated effectively thanks to DTCA advertising, thereby mitigating undertreatment (e.g., depression, anxiety, hypertension, and hyperlipidemia), as well as some conditions that have allegedly been targeted for persuasive advertising of certain prescription drugs, even though less expensive alternative treatments are available (e.g., heartburn, allergies, and arthritis).[34]

VII. DTCA's Effect on Quality of Care

Numerous surveys, for example, Calfee (2002) and Aikin (2003), have reported that both patients and physicians perceive DTCA to improve adherence to recommended treatment. Yet there is unfortunately relatively little empirical evidence on the magnitude of this compliance effect. More important are impacts of DTCA, if any, on patient outcomes. Two recent studies have provided indirect evidence.

Donohue et al. (2004) examined treatment patterns of 30,521 depressed individuals whose 1997–2000 insurance claims were included in a large retrospective medical claims database. Two issues were addressed. What are the impacts of DTCA and pharmaceutical promotion to physicians on the likelihood that (1) an individual diagnosed with depression received antidepressant medication, and (2) conditional on receiving antidepressant therapy, the antidepressant medication was used for the appropriate duration.

After controlling for secular trends in the treatment of depression and other factors, they observed a small positive and statistically significant effect of DTCA spending on the probability that a person diagnosed with depression received antidepressant drug treatment. Individuals diagnosed with depression during periods when class-level antidepressant DTCA spending was in the top quartile had a 32% higher probability of initiating medication therapy compared to those diagnosed during periods when DTCA spending was in the bottom quartile. Individuals who initiated treatment following periods when cumulative free sample units were in the top quartile were no more likely to initiate antidepressant medication therapy than individuals diagnosed during periods of low free sample spending. Individuals facing a copayment of more than $15 for an antidepressant were 30% less likely to initiate antidepressant drug therapy than were individuals facing a drug copayment of $5 or less.

The authors' measure of quality of care was based on the Depression Guideline Panel (1993) recommendations and American Psychiatric Association (2003) guidelines. These state that if antidepressant medication is

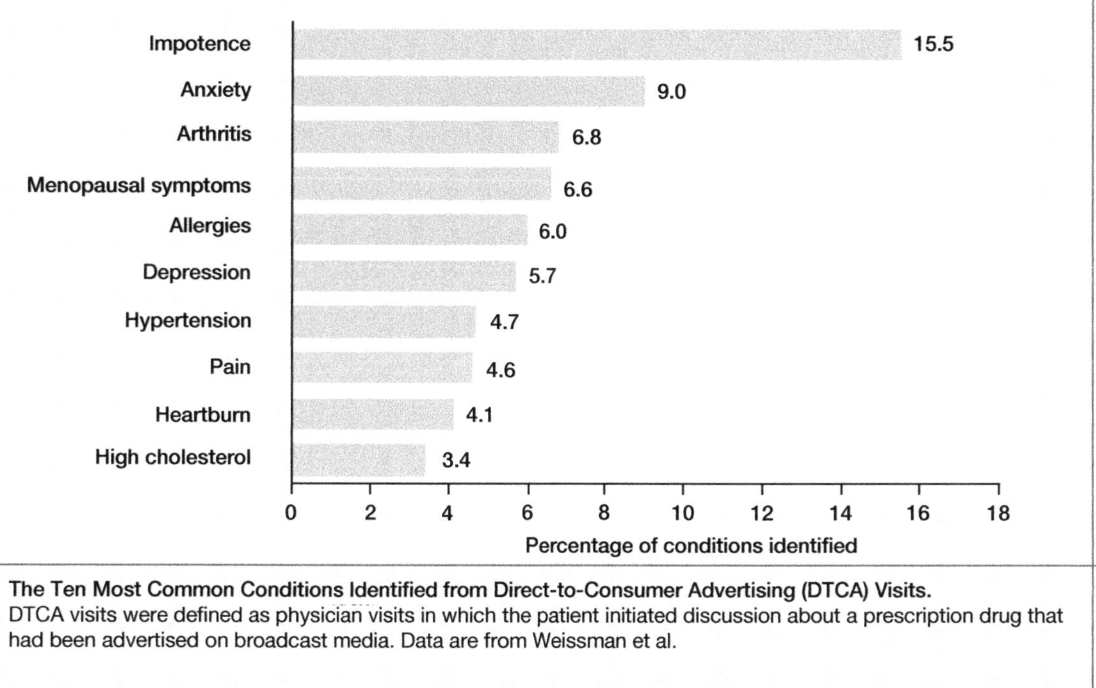

Figure 9.2. Ten most common new diagnoses identified from DTCA visits.

chosen, it should be provided until symptoms are alleviated (usually in 10–12 weeks) and then continued for an additional period of 4–9 months to prevent relapse. As a conservative measure, and allowing for the possibility that the patient received a free sample (which would not be recorded in the medical claims database), the authors considered the duration of therapy to be appropriate if the patient filled prescriptions for at least four months of treatment with the study drugs within the first six months of an episode.

Of the 11,306 episodes of treatment involving initiation of drug therapy, 60% filled at least four prescriptions for an antidepressant in the first six months of the episode. Interestingly, DTCA spillovers were observed, not on class sales as discussed above in Section VI, but on patients' adherence to recommended treatment, regardless of which drug treatment they were receiving. Neither the detailing spending for the drug taken, nor the detailing for other drugs in the class, had a statistically significant impact on the probability of receiving appropriate treatment duration. Copayment amount had no statistically significant effect on whether the patient received appropriate treatment duration, but patients seen by psychiatrists were more likely to receive appropriate care than were patients seen by other physicians.[35] The authors conclude by noting that to the extent DTCA increases demand for medications, it is important to understand what proportion of the expanded use represents appropriate, medically questionable, or inappropriate prescribing behavior. Their research only begins to address this issue.

Wosinska (2004) examined compliance issues by quantifying number of days between 30-day prescriptions. Based on the Blue Shield of California data described earlier involving patients who began their cholesterol-lowering statin therapy between 1996 and 1999, Wosinska's final data sample consisted of 16,011 patients and 123,736 gaps between prescriptions. Although treatment recommendations typically involve indefinite daily utilization of the hyperlipidemic medication, Wosinska found that, on average, the number of days between two 30-day prescriptions was 43, corresponding to 13 missed days per cycle.

Defining nonadherence to recommended treatment as the number of missed therapy days, Wosinska (2004) estimated a variety of models using several different estimation methods, which tended to yield qualitatively similar findings. She found that, while DTCA for a single product at initiation of treatment had no statistically significant impact on patient adherence, category DTCA had a significant beneficial impact. While statistically significant, these effects were relatively small in magnitude.

A most interesting finding occurred when Wosinska examined brand-specific DTCA spending. She found that while DTCA efforts by Zocor and

Pravachol appeared to increase adherence, Lipitor's DTCA efforts appear to have had a negative impact. Further analysis suggested that the unexpected finding for Lipitor stemmed from the FDA's requirement that DTCA television advertisements must mention the most common side effects. She reasoned that television advertisements make side effects more salient than does print advertising. Professional actors in the first television ads for Lipitor prominently mentioned side effects of possible liver problems and muscular pain, a task that is usually carried out less prominently and is reserved for unobserved narrators. Discussions Wosinska had with industry analysts suggested that the prominent side effects mentioned in the Lipitor ads may have made patients more anxious, and that it may have affected their adherence.

As evidence, Wosinska reported that past television DTCA spending by Lipitor, but not more recent current DTCA Lipitor spending, had reduced adherence. Because past advertising was defined as the level of expenditure in 30 to 60 days prior to the prescription, her findings are consistent with a side-effects hypothesis: if patients react to the side-effect warnings with a temporary suspension of therapy of at least a few days, then the level of advertising in the prior (rather than the current) month would have had an impact on adherence.

The issues raised by Wosinska (2004) regarding prominence of side-effects warnings in television DTCA and their impact on patient adherence to guideline treatment are complex and undoubtedly of concern not only to advertisers and regulators, but also to patients and their physicians. Her findings are best viewed as preliminary, but clearly worthy of additional research.

Finally, the consistency across various studies in the finding of spillovers of DTCA to other brands with little or no impact on own-brand is striking. As advertisers learn from their mistakes and become more sophisticated, the results for own-brand DTCA may change. Controversies on whether DTCA and, for that matter, other forms of advertising are informative and market-expanding versus persuasive and market share stealing are likely to continue for some time.

VIII. New Zealand's Experience with DTCA

The legislative history of DTCA in New Zealand is very different from that of the United States. When New Zealand enacted statutes concerning the content of promotional material in its 1981 Medicines Act and its 1984

Medicines Regulation, it did not even consider the possibility of consumer-directed promotions, but only envisaged rather technical information promotions to health care providers and payers.[36] Thus, since it seemed to be impossible, DTCA was not explicitly prohibited in New Zealand.

The apparent success of DTCA in the United States is likely to be one reason why pharmaceutical firms pursued DTCA in New Zealand, particularly since it was not explicitly forbidden there. Also contributing to the introduction of DTCA in New Zealand was passage of its Bill of Rights Act in 1990, which explicitly protected freedom of speech, including commercial free speech. Pharmaceutical companies were quick to perceive this statute as being analogous to the First Amendment of the U.S. Constitution, which has been interpreted as generally protecting commercial free speech.[37]

A major difference between the United States and New Zealand regulatory environment is that in New Zealand, DTCA is self-regulated through the Therapeutic Advertising Prevetting System (TAPS) and its Advertising Standards Complaint Board (ASCB). The ACSB consists of four public representatives and four members from the advertising industry. It investigates advertising content of both prescription and over-the-counter medications when triggered by a formal written complaint. Although the ACSB is not empowered to impose punitive measures on errant advertisers, decisions have achieved almost total compliance since the media refuse to accept any advertisement the ASCB has ruled errant.[38]

DTCA advertising began in New Zealand in the early 1990s, and by the end of the decade it became widespread.[39] Not surprisingly, DTCA has generated considerable controversy in New Zealand, with many of the arguments and issues being similar to those in the United States.[40]

Complaints have been voiced in New Zealand about the industry's failing to regulate itself adequately. While both New Zealand and U.S. regulations require provision of specific information, the absence of a comparable "fair balance" criterion in New Zealand has meant that advertisements in New Zealand have tended to emphasize a product's benefits, devoting less time and space to risks and side effects. Critics point to comparisons between consumer survey responses in the United States and New Zealand as indicative of inadequate self-regulation and lack of fair balance in New Zealand.[41]

Although various self-regulating and legislative efforts to control or even ban DTCA have been considered since the late 1990s, matters became more complicated when in December 2003, as part of a broader initiative to harmonize trade, New Zealand and Australia signed a treaty to establish a single binational agency to regulate medical therapeutic products, the Joint

Therapeutics Agency. As of 2005, Australia did not allow DTCA, although it permitted disease state awareness advertisements in which no brand name is mentioned.[42] Thus, there is conflicting policy in Australia and New Zealand that needs to be reconciled at the binational Joint Therapeutics Agency.

Although Annette King, New Zealand Labour Party's Minister of Health, publicly stated her opposition to DTCA and used the argument that such a policy would ensure harmonized practices between Australia and New Zealand, at that time the New Zealand government was a minority government, relying for support from a "Greens" party to continue to rule. Because the binational Joint Therapeutics Agency would regulate complementary medicines (e.g., herbal remedies) that were previously largely unregulated in New Zealand, the Greens declined to support the proposed legislation, leaving the government without the majority required to pass the bill into law.[43] As of late 2005, the future of DTCA in New Zealand was unclear.

IX. Concluding Remarks

Even though advertising has long been controversial in many industries, commercial advertising in the context of health care goods and services has been particularly contentious, and even more so when it is directed at consumers rather than at health care providers or insurers. In this chapter I have summarized the accumulated empirical evidence on the size, composition, and impacts of DTCA in the United States. I have also briefly discussed New Zealand's experience with DTCA.

In terms of size, in the United States DTCA has grown rapidly, but as a share of the total promotional arsenal, it is still relatively small, 13–15% during 2000–2003; as a percentage of sales, it was even smaller (2%). DTCA was also relatively concentrated, and apparently increasingly so, with the top 20 drugs in terms of DTCA expenditures accounting for about 65% of all DTCA spending in the first half of 2004. The evidence suggests that DTCA is targeted particularly at those conditions for which the potential market is large relative to the actual market, and at "high-quality" drugs, that is, drugs to which the FDA assigned a "priority" status.

Both nonexperimental and experimental studies reveal that while DTCA increases the size of the overall sales of a particular therapeutic class, brand-specific DTCA does not appear to have a statistically significant impact on the share of any particular brand within the therapeutic class. By increasing the size of therapeutic class sales but not affecting shares within the class, DTCA has ambiguous effects on consumer welfare. In particular, there is some experimental evidence suggesting that in the case of antidepressants,

DTCA mitigates undertreatment of the condition, but it also appears to encourage marginal and possibly inappropriate treatment. Which of these effects dominates is at this point unclear, but it is reasonable to assume that the direction and size of the net impact varies across therapeutic classes and drugs. There is also some preliminary nonexperimental evidence suggesting that consumers' adherence to treatment is affected considerably by perceived safety risks, particularly when emphasized in television advertisements.

Finally, New Zealand's experience with DTCA is in some respects similar to that of the United States, but the self-regulatory environment in New Zealand that to this point has not required "fair balance" in advertisements as is required by the FDA in the United States has resulted in ads that compare favorably with the United States in terms of communicating benefits of drugs, but rather unfavorably when communicating risks and information on who should not be taking the medicines. Whether DTCA will continue or be banned in New Zealand is currently unclear.

In sum, the evidence to date suggests that as an instrument promoting public health, DTCA has considerable potential, particularly in mitigating undertreatment of important illnesses, for example, major depressive disorder. It can also result in questionable and inappropriate utilization, not only possibly exposing patients to health risks, but also contributing to increased health care costs. As with other forms of advertising, DTCA both informs and persuades. Its effects on consumer welfare are complex and ambiguous. Regulating the communication content of advertisements and other promotions that attempt to balance information on risks and benefits is inherently very difficult and challenging.

PART FOUR

PUBLIC EVALUATION OF THE BENEFITS AND COSTS OF INNOVATION

TEN

Measures of Costs and Benefits for Drugs in Cost-Effectiveness Analysis

Mark V. Pauly

I. Introduction

To decide on the allocation of public and private resources, some form of cost-effectiveness analysis is used in many countries, large and small (Drummond, Chapter 11). The single most common type of medical care to which this method is applied is the use of pharmaceutical products. Sometimes the decision involves new uses for existing products developed and produced in the country making the decision, and sometimes it involves products imported from abroad. Sometimes as well the decision involves the potential allocation of resources to a new product if brought to market, and often public funds play a role in such innovation.

In this chapter I criticize existing cost-effectiveness studies of pharmaceuticals, many of which, given their stated perspective, use an incorrect measure of cost and consequently, if the results were followed, would lead to inefficient resource allocation decisions, distort the mix of funds for research, and reduce population health. Although I acknowledge there is no single answer to the question of the right cost figure to use, I indicate that deciding which conceptual setting matches the decision in question is often not easy and often made incorrectly. Some consequences of using the conceptually correct methods may raise some difficult political questions, but those questions will yield better answers if there is agreement in advance on what framework and measures to use and how decisions are to be based on this information.

I develop a general argument about correct measurement. I illustrate its differential implications by describing application of this argument in two settings: large high-income country U, which invents and produces most of its pharmaceutical products and which buys the major share of these products produced worldwide, and smaller moderate-income country T, which produces about a third of the drug products it consumes, importing the remainder, but which would like to expand its capability to innovate in the pharmaceutical sector both for home-country consumption and for export.

An important initial decision for any cost-effectiveness analysis is the specification of perspective, because the choice of perspective may dramatically affect the kinds of measures that should be used.[1] Typically analyses are done from either a payer or from a societal perspective. In both countries U and T, most spending is covered by pubic payers, who arguably should take a societal perspective. I assume that decision makers at public insurance programs prefer to take a societal perspective to the extent that they can. Authoritative policy sources (Gold et al. 1996) advise that analysts always conduct a study from a societal perspective even if they also conduct it from another perspective; and generally, analysis to inform public-sector decisions in a democracy should adopt a societal perspective (Beutels et al. 2002). However, not all public decision makers endorse this view; in an important dissent, the National Institute for Clinical Excellence (NICE) in the United Kingdom takes the perspective of "costs to the National Health Service." One consequence is that any payment that results in higher profits for British drug companies, higher wages for nurses, or higher net incomes for hospitals is treated as a cost; by contrast, a true societal perspective would count these as transfers rather than costs.

My claim is that, because virtually all analyses of drugs from a societal perspective use a cost that is too high (relative to the appropriate one), more pharmaceuticals may be cost effective than is generally concluded under current measurement methods. The usual methods can, with some modifications, be made to more closely approximate the correct analysis.

Moreover, there are some potential problems for a practical government or society trying to follow the theoretically correct cost-effectiveness rule of thumb ("Undertake all cost-effective interventions") in the case of pharmaceuticals, and some deeper societal decision making may be called for. Decisions about regulation, about administered pricing by public insurers on a budget, and about patent protection come into play. The treatment of drug costs is also dependent on whether the research, development, and production of drugs are domestic or foreign, and whether the welfare perspective is limited to own-country or is global.

II. Development and Production Process for Drugs

The easiest case involves the use of drugs obtained from another country. Here the relevant measure is the net acquisition cost. If that cost is negotiated directly by the public insurance, it is the negotiated price. If it is obtained by private agents (e.g., a pharmaceutical benefits management firm), it is that firm's acquisition costs.

Analysis of products that are invented and/or produced domestically, in either country U or T, is much more complex and is the focus of my attention here.

There are two distinct phases in the process that eventually results in the availability of a new domestic product, and the proper measure of cost from a societal perspective depends on the phase in which one is in. To be successfully offered, a product must first go through several phases of research, development, and clinical testing culminating in regulatory approval. Once regulatory approval is achieved, firms then incur additional costs to market, produce, distribute, and transport the product.

Research, development, and regulatory approval costs are fixed costs that do not depend directly on the quantity expected to be furnished; such costs must be incurred before any positive amount of the product can be sold. As a rough approximation, they are also independent of the amount that is intended to be sold if positive amounts are planned to be sold. In contrast, the marketing, manufacturing, and distribution costs do vary with output. As a result, the marginal cost of supplying different quantities of the product (greater than one) is positive but much less than the average cost, which includes research, development, and regulatory costs. That is, once the costs for a product to be invented, developed, tested, and approved are incurred, additional costs associated with larger volumes of output are often relatively small.

The other important characteristic of prescription drugs that distinguishes them from many other products and a fairly large number of other medical goods and services is that they are frequently protected by government-enforced patents for an extended period of time. This protection of intellectual property confers monopoly power on the seller as long as the patent is in force. While other sellers may and often do "invent around" patents, and while patents secured in one country are not always respected in others, patents do give sellers of patented products potential market power in the sense that, if the product were to be offered in voluntary private competitive markets, the firm's demand curve for the product would be negatively sloped.

How one should think of a situation in which the private seller of a patented product is negotiating with a large public insurance system is less clear. Presumably the public insurance system has a demand or marginal benefit curve in mind (since that is the marginal effectiveness part of the cost-effectiveness analysis) and a budget constraint, but exactly how any price or payment might be set is more difficult to model.

When firms have freedom to set prices based on market demand, the resulting monopoly price is usually in excess of the marginal cost of production and sometimes (how often is a matter of debate) in excess of the average cost so that, at least for some products, firms earn monopoly rents. Whether such rents average out to a positive value when calculated based on economy-wide research and development (R&D) investment (i.e., whether the set of firms investing in developing patented drugs earn rates of return averaged over success and failures in excess of the market-wide rate of return for other firms in similar risk classes) is less well settled. Nevertheless, it is at least possible that prices exceed average costs.

III. First Copy Costs versus New Uses for Existing Products: The Literature

The treatment of the appropriate concepts for choosing this crucial figure of cost is quite brief in the standard reference works on cost-effectiveness analysis in health care. The discussion in Gold et al. (1996, pp. 193–195) also seems brief relative to the coverage of other topics. The appropriate distinction is made between the marginal cost of bringing the first unit of a product to market, so-called first copy costs, and marginal costs of units beyond the first. First copy costs are relevant if the decision is whether to "provide the intervention at all," or, more precisely, whether to undertake the R&D expense that will result in a new product. If the technology has already been developed (so the research and development costs are sunk), then the cost would be the "incremental production, distribution, and provision costs."

This cost to be used for already-developed drugs is then discussed no further. For new or potential products, one suggestion to analysts is to try to back out the R&D costs from the price and use that for sensitivity analysis. But since "the level of effort [to do this] is beyond the resources available for analysis . . . prevailing transactions prices will usually act in a serviceable way to value consumption of drugs" (p. 195). The reason for this conclusion is the assertion that "the class of drugs must break even – have revenues large enough to cover R&D, production, and distribution costs" (p. 195). One might contrast this kind of discussion with the treatment of prices for hospital inpatient care, where readers are told that charges are rarely good measures of costs, not even "serviceable" ones, and that it is very important to obtain measures of marginal cost. Since the deviation between price and marginal cost is almost surely as high for drugs as for hospital care, this advice seems biased.

The suggestion to use prevailing transaction prices is also less straightforward than it seems for new products. In country U, analysts would need to estimate what the price for the new product would be. Not only is this difficult, but it is virtually certain that the price will depend on the public insurer's reimbursement policy if patients covered by the public insurer are to be major users of the new product. In country T, where prices are negotiated, the advice to use average price obviously presents a complex problem of simultaneous decision making. The public insurer cannot decide whether to reimburse the new product until it knows its price, but that price will be highly dependent on what the reimbursement is.

IV. The Usual Practice in Cost-Effectiveness Analysis of Drugs from a Societal Perspective

The most common practice in cost-effectiveness analysis involving a drug is to use average wholesale price (AWP) as the measure of "cost" from a societal perspective. Here is a classic example. The well-regarded Gold et al. (1996) book on methods for cost-effectiveness analysis presents some "worked examples" of analysis done from a societal perspective. One is the study by Stinnett et al. (1996) on the cost effectiveness of dietary and pharmacologic therapy for cholesterol reduction. The authors stated that they use a societal perspective.

The medication costs in this study are for branded Lovastatin and generic niacin. For niacin, the cost was taken to be Medicaid's reimbursement for multiple-source drugs. The actual measure was slightly below the average wholesale price but was above the lowest wholesale prices quoted. For Lovastatin, costs were estimated using the 1994 average wholesale price.

The authors noted that the price of Lovastatin may have exceeded its marginal cost because the drug is still under patent, but that prices would probably fall when the drug went off patent, a development that actually occurred in the mid-1990s. Sensitivity analysis was performed using a Lovastatin estimate at half its 1994 AWP and a fivefold increase in the cost of niacin. This reduced the estimated incremental cost in dollars per QALY for treatment with Lovastatin by a large percentage, but not by enough to reduce the cost to the "acceptable" ($50,000) range for most of the patient subgroups studied. It did reduce the incremental cost per QALY

Table 10.1. *Cost measures used in 28 cost-effectiveness studies*

Cost measure	New drugs	Old drugs
AWP	5	4
Marginal cost	0	0
Market price	5	6
Insurer acquisition or official tariff	3	5

for moderate-risk women for stepped care using Lovastatin from $156,000 to $48,000. In 2005 the selling price for generic Lovastatin 20 mg was about $1 per pill; the price used in the study, adjusted for economy-wide inflation, was about $2.50; adjusted using the prescription drug component of the U.S. Consumer Price Index it would be about $3. Thus, a 50% cut probably left the estimated cost still well above marginal cost for a typical nonbiotech drug product.

In this example, using marginal cost rather than AWP would make a difference for an important population subgroup. More importantly, there is no discussion in the article of why AWP was used for the reference case, or why a factor of 50% (which seems to have been too low) was used in the sensitivity analysis.

I analyzed recent articles providing cost-effectiveness analyses of drugs from an explicitly stated societal perspective. Articles were extracted from MEDLINE, ScienceDirect, and Blackwell Synergy, along with a direct inspection of recent issues of *Value in Health* and *PharmacoEconomics.* I selected a sample of 28 papers, 13 analyzing what appeared to be new drugs (at least in that country's setting) and 15 dealing with new uses of old drugs. None of the studies used marginal cost, even when the drug clearly represented an extended use of an existing drug (Table 10.1). AWP was most commonly mentioned in connection with studies whose setting was in the United States; the distinction between "market" (e.g., pharmacy) price and official tariff was not always precise.

I also reviewed the literature on the empirical relationship between the AWP for patented drugs and long-run marginal cost including investment in production facilities. For conventional drugs, the estimates are in the range of 20–30%; for biologicals they are higher, at about 50%. These estimates usually do not include selling costs as part of marginal cost; if they were included, the ratio of long-run marginal cost to AWP for drugs would approximately double.

Thus, it appears that the current practice by analysts to use AWP results in a value for the "cost" of a drug that is substantially in excess of marginal cost. If the estimated incremental cost per quality-adjusted life year (QALY) using AWP is very low or very high relative to benchmarks of acceptable ratios, or if drug therapy is dominated by another comparator, treatment of cost would not matter in the decision about whether to cover a drug under an insurance plan or include it on the formulary. But over a sizeable range of values reasonably close to the benchmark, the cost estimate used should affect the decision about acceptability of the product. So it seems appropriate to explore the conceptual framework that should be used for such analysis in more detail.

V. Toward a More Appropriate Measure of Cost: Issues to Be Considered

I will discuss five unresolved issues in this section. Two concern methods that in principle could be implemented but in practice are usually not: (1) what to do about profits or rents, in the case in which a class of drugs or drugs in general more than break even, and (2) what to do in analyses of interventions involving new or extended uses for already marketed but still patent-protected products. The three new topics are (1) the treatment of first copy costs in a model intended to integrate cost-effectiveness analysis with decisions about R&D resource allocation, (2) the implications of the treatment of drug costs for measures of benefit and cost offsets; and (3) the appropriate treatment of costs of domestically developed and produced drugs versus drugs bought from abroad.

The key issue underlying all of these problems is this: Since the decision to invest in a new drug depends on a comparison of the expected R&D costs with the revenues in excess of the cost of production (multiplied by the probability of success), the prices that actually will be paid and the quantities that will be bought, either of which might be affected by the cost-effectiveness analysis, become crucial to the R&D investment decision. A decision to pay a particular amount for a new product, and the quantity to be bought, both affect whether that product will actually come into existence. Cost-effectiveness analysis then affects not only expenditures and product use but also whether a given product will be supplied (and potentially the supply of other products as well). This is important for country U, which has benefited from its pharmaceutical industry, but it is most important for country T, which would like to encourage pharmaceutical R&D and manufacturing of pharmaceutical and biotech products in its own country. Low domestic drug spending may be incompatible with high profits and high rates of innovation in both U and T.

Traditional cost-effectiveness analysis of general interventions, assuming there exists "the" incremental cost of various inputs, assumes perfectly elastic long-run supply curves. That is, the product can be acquired at the same price, regardless of the quality of the product purchased. While this may be a reasonable approximation for such services as hospital care, perhaps physician services, and some non-research-intensive materials and devices, this is not a proper assumption for patent-protected drugs.

There is good reason not to use AWP in country U. Suppose that drug firms in some country are able to earn above-normal rates of return on new products, year in and year out.[2] If monopoly rents are built into AWP there, they should surely be backed out if the analysis is to be done from a true societal perspective. The argument in Gold et al. (1996) that prices must be at least high enough for firms to break even does not preclude the possibility that most ventures do much better than just break even.

It is less clear what the policy has been or should be in country T. One can say only that if reimbursements for new products have been set to yield above-normal profits, those profits should be subtracted or debited in the analysis of a new product.[3]

Removing profit would lead to the right conclusion, analytically, but what advice does it give decision makers? If economic profits are indeed positive, but the decision on whether or not to permit firms to develop and introduce a new product is based on AWP less above-normal profits, more products will be judged to be effective than if AWP had been used. But if firms are in fact reimbursed at AWP, their expected profit from investment in R&D will rise. The products firms are thus induced to develop because of the excess profits may not be efficient, and, from the standpoint of economic efficiency, they should not be produced. Yet the price signals will be telling firms to invest. Some method will need to be found to resolve this conflict. Efficient decisions based on correct cost-effectiveness analysis may well conflict with the price signals that may follow for implementation of those decisions. This is an issue for both country U and country T.

Another rather straightforward case, that of the cost of an already-developed drug, raises much the same issue. Suppose, for example, that one evaluates an already-developed and patented drug for treating autoimmune disease for a new use. The relevant price measure from a societal perspective is much below AWP. If programs for additional use are approved based on this measure, but firms continue to be paid AWP, firm profits will

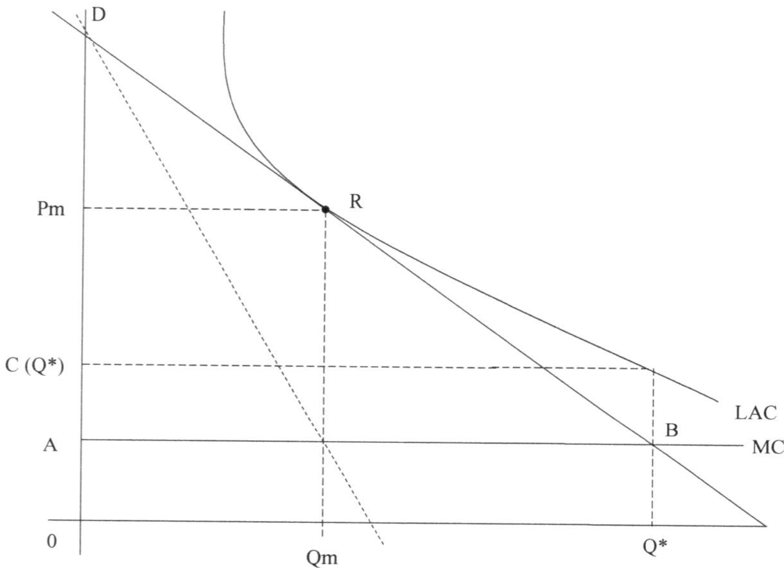

Figure 10.1. Drug quality and quantity conditional on producing the drug.

balloon, and there is an incentive for excess investment in R&D. Of course, in making the initial investment decision, the firm might have considered both the most immediate use for the new product and the prospect that additional uses will develop over time; thus, this influence may have already been taken into account. As noted above, almost no studies use the proper societal perspective in this case; instead, they use AWP, which is much too high. The error from rejecting efficient new uses of old products by overstating the true incremental cost may well more than offset any incentives for excessive development of new products.

A more serious and difficult question is that of evaluating of new products not yet developed and marketed. What would be the first best optimal benchmark? Figure 10.1 illustrates the case of a typical new product with marginal benefit curve D and marginal cost of production assumed constant at MC. The rule for optimal societal resource allocation says that a product should be produced as long as the consumers' surplus above production costs, area ADB, is greater in expected present discounted value terms than the cost of R&D. If this condition holds, the optimal quantity is positive, and it is Q*, the quantity where marginal benefit equals marginal cost. In the case of a cost-effectiveness study using QALYs to measure effectiveness, marginal benefit (in monetary terms) is equal to marginal QALYs times the cutoff or threshold ratio V for cost per QALY at which a program would be cost effective.

I have also drawn in a long-run average cost curve (LAC) that incorporates an assumed level of the present discounted value of R&D costs. Suppose that the marginal benefit curve is also the patent-holding firm's market demand curve. Then the nondiscriminating monopoly firm just breaks even at point R; so it is efficient to produce the product. Under the assumption of free entry into the process of inventing and offering new drugs, at the margin, a firm charging the monopoly price in this example just breaks even. Most of my analysis need only assume that the LAC curve touches or crosses the demand curve at some point.

One could solve for the average cost (or average breakeven wholesale price) at Q* by drawing in the long-run average cost curve as indicated, but using this measure of cost in one's analysis will not usually lead to a societally efficient decisions. On the one hand, the quantity at which marginal benefit equals LAC at Q* is less than Q*. Since LAC varies with Q, there is no unique value of "price" or "cost" to which marginal benefit should be set equal. However, it would also be wrong to calculate the cost as simply cost of production; that could lead to offering products with negative consumer surplus once the costs of R&D are taken into account.

The problems of proper costing of drugs also extend to situations in which the intervention is not a drug but in which there are impacts on the volume of drug use. If a better method of testing might permit some set of patients to avoid using drugs, the savings from a societal perspective are likely to be much smaller (at a cost of MC) than average wholesale price.

VI. Beyond the Benchmark: Incentives and Behavior in a Decentralized Economy

The model of economic organization that fits best with cost-effectiveness analysis is a wholly centrally planned economy, in which government either owns or can control all resource allocation. In the benchmark model, this all-powerful government would use the analysis to order scientists to conduct research on possible efficient new products and would order organizations producing the product to produce Q*. But even in economies such as country T where the government is a major payer for drugs (when there is a single publicly owned or controlled universal national health insurance plan), government does not usually direct all R&D or produce most new drugs. Instead, private for-profit firms undertake a large share of R&D (though governments typically support some basic research with tax funding and make knowledge discovered available to all at a zero price), private firms produce and distribute almost all products, and often private physicians advise patients on which drugs to get and sometimes dispense them. Also, in many countries some of the demand for drugs comes directly from consumers or from private insurers they choose. So how does the benchmark model translate into actual decisions by payers, consumers, and firms?

The answer obviously depends on the organization of demand and the organization of supply. I assume that supply is provided by profit-maximizing firms with patent protection, and consider three alternative "demand" regimes: (1) unregulated nondiscriminating monopoly, (2) regulated partially discriminating monopoly (Ramsey prices), and (3) government procurement.

Unregulated Nondiscriminating Monopoly

This case is most relevant to country U. In Figure 10.1 the profit-maximizing monopoly price would be Pm if the marginal benefit curve corresponded to the demand curve and the supplier faced a set of buyers, none of whom had market power. If buyers respond to this price, either directly because they are paying out of pocket or indirectly because their private insurer uses managed care to set quantity limits, the equilibrium quantity would fall short of the optimum. Less obviously, if the LAC curve were to the right of the one drawn in Figure 10.1, it might still be efficient to supply the product at quantity Q*, but no positive supply would be forthcoming in a decentralized market economy, even if patents were present.

If the social planner, having determined that it is optimal to produce the product in quantity Q*, then subsidized private demand to get to that level when the AWP remained at Pm, it is clear that the profit signals to firms would be distorted. New products would look highly profitable, and perhaps too many of them would be supplied. Whether the effect of overpayment more or less completely offsets the inability to price discriminate is hard to tell.

Regulated Partially Discriminating Monopoly

A second possibility is that government, as in country T and in the United Kingdom, regulates the prices charged by domestic drug companies but also permits or even assists firms in price discrimination. The price-discriminating monopolist would charge higher prices to people with less elastic demands; a common assumption (Danzon 2002) is that the elasticity is inversely correlated with income. Some such characteristics might provide the basis for price discrimination, but the resulting set of feasible Ramsey prices would not represent perfect price discrimination.

This situation would represent an improvement over the preceding case. More products that are efficient to introduce would be introduced, and the overall rate of use would increase close to Q* (Reinhardt, Chapter 2). Since overall expected profits would be set at the breakeven level, there should be less of an incentive for firms to overinvest in them. However, it would be unlikely that things would turn out exactly right.

Government Procurement

An appropriate strategy with government procurement is one suggested by Michael Kremer (1998) and recently discussed in connection with vaccine procurement in the United States (McGuire 2003). The government as a single buyer would first estimate the marginal benefit curve and the marginal cost curve for some hypothetical new product, and then offer to pay the consumers' surplus, or some fraction of it, to any firm that successfully discovered an effective product. In terms of Figure 10.1, if any potential inventor of the product were offered a contract for Q* units that paid 0 DBQ*, then any firm that expected its R&D costs to be less than R would invest in and discover the product.

This plan does not require the government to estimate what the R&D costs are, but it still places a heavy informational and organizational burden on it. It would have to know the demand or marginal benefit curve, as well as the marginal cost curve. If it provided the product, it would have to be able to be sure that only the demanders up to Q* got access to it, not those from Q* to the *x*-intercept who have positive but small marginal benefits.

VII. From Theory to Practice

How would performing cost-effectiveness analysis in the way I have suggested differ from what is done (or is supposed to be done) in settings where such analysis is now used to make actual decisions on resources and quantity? Take the example of the advice given by National Institute of Clinical Effectiveness (NICE) to the British National Health Service (NHS), were NICE to use a societal perspective rather than an NHS budget perspective (see Drummond, Chapter 11). In the case of the product in Figure 10.1, what would it suggest? Given the LAC as drawn, this would be a product with a relatively low ratio of benefits to cost. If the overall NHS budget had been set based on attaching a monetary value to a QALY that represents consumer valuation introduced in the D curve, the product would be one that just met the cutoff test; it would be the last product approved (or the first product disapproved).

VIII. What Difference Does It Make?

This approach to defining cost therefore proposes a three-step procedure for the evaluation of new pharmaceutical products. Assume that there is some threshold value *V* for cost per QALY that appropriately governs resource allocation.

Step 1: Determine the optimal rate of use of the product, conditional on positive use, by comparing QALYs times *V* with marginal cost.

Step 2: Calculate total QALYs and total cost (R&D cost, plus total cost of production at that level), and calculate the average value of QALYs per dollar.

Step 3: Undertake the development of the new product if this average value exceeds $1/V$.

Compare this to the procedure that would be followed if cost were assumed to be measured by AWP. That procedure would determine the optimal size or rate of use of the program by comparing QALYs and AWP.

There are two possibilities here: (1) AWP is greater than average cost at that quantity. Then a socially efficient program might be rejected because the estimated "cost" is too high. (2) AWP is equal to average cost at that quantity. Then an efficient program might be rejected because the quantity is too low.

How would the optimal decision differ from that if AWP was used for the "societal cost" measure for a new product? Without any elaboration, we can definitely say that if the size of the program or the quantity of the new product (as well as its existence) was a dimension of the analysis, the level that would be set using AWP would fall short of the optimum. As already noted, further discussion is complicated because there is no uniform price or cost for a new drug (since average cost rises with quantity) and because there is no necessary connection between any market demand curve that determines the price and the effectiveness schedule that the planner is looking at. I therefore assume that the value used by the planner for a QALY is the same value used by demanders in the market, who would be either consumers or managed care insurers on their behalf. Assuming that the price is set at the monopoly profit-maximizing level and the quantity therefore set at the monopoly quantity, despite suboptimal volume, any new product that would meet the cost-effectiveness test using AWP will truly be efficient; there will be no undersupply. Such a product will be profitable for the monopolist to offer. What is more likely, however, is that some products that would have been socially efficient will fail to be supplied. This is obviously the case if there is no price at which one seller can cover both fixed research costs and operating costs, and yet total consumers' surplus is positive.

This is more likely to be a problem for country U, which is assumed to still rely on market-based pricing of patented products, than for country T, which sets prices. However, country T has a heavier burden in setting those initial prices and, in the interests of economizing on the social insurance budget, may be tempted to set the price too low.

IX. Innovation, Incentives, and the Global Economy

Thus far I have assumed that all of the benefits and all of the costs are incurred within a given economy. The analysis accounts for the introduction of new products as well as the optimal use of existing products.

This would be a breathtaking change even within a large country like country U. For the Asian Pacific countries, such as country T, consideration would need to be given both to health effects on own population (Hsieh et al., Chapter 13) and to possible sales to or purchases from abroad. For products developed within its own country, the profits from foreign sales of new products should be added to the measure of benefits from improving own-population health. This would imply a very different role for cost-effectiveness analysis than the traditional public health model. It would need to take economic development goals into account as well, and it may prove difficult to help domestic and export markets separate.

X. Pharmaceutical Innovation and Local Markets

Can this separation be made? Is there any connection between the use of a price for pharmaceutical products in a given country and the level of R&D in that country? For a country like country U whose purchases constitute a very large share of the world drug market, the connection is obvious: the buying decisions of a major player obviously affect local drug companies as well as those elsewhere. For a smaller country, like country T, the connection is less obvious: R&D often would be undertaken based on expected global sales, primarily in other countries, and the level of local sales need not appreciably affect R&D in small countries. In the pure theory of international trade, especially for a product of high value relative to its transportation cost, both research and production should occur in those countries with a comparative advantage in doing it, regardless of how much their citizens actually buy of the product, or whether they buy it at all. Research findings can be transferred to other countries, and final products can be exported.

In practice, however, for reasons not well understood, it seems to be more effective and more likely for research and production to be undertaken where the product will be sold and used. Perhaps familiarity with the local market produces a more subtle feel for local demand or local regulatory processes. It appears that high local volume materially assists local R&D. But if this is not true, if a country is indifferent between "invent-it-here" or "invent-it-there," then the preceding considerations do not apply, and global AWP will be a good price measure for small countries like country T.

XI. From Economics to Politics: Of Geese and Golden Eggs

The literal interpretation of a societal approach instructs health care decision makers to pay attention to the effect of current reimbursement policies on the development of new products. Too high a price, and there is too much of a good thing – too many beneficial new products. Too low a price, and the bonanza may dry up, with harm to health, to investment, and to employment.

In practical settings, real government buyers are more likely to gravitate toward lower prices than toward higher ones. One could argue that a country's policy toward the development of new products in general should be separated from the more technical decision of whether and how to use existing and individual new products. As noted, the outcome of a cost-effectiveness analysis is a decision about the use of a product, not its price. But it is clear that price or payment will have to be set in some fashion in a decentralized economy, and that the level of that price will, at a minimum, be important in determining whether the optimal program can be carried out. Also, unless there is some other source of funding for and management of research and development activities, policies for the pricing of existing products will influence the level of this activity, both in terms of signaling the returns to be expected from a new product and (somewhat contrary to theoretical economic models) in terms of generating internal capital that can fund the research and development of new products.

XII. Conclusion

Measures of cost used in existing cost-effectiveness analysis of drugs done from a societal perspective are wrong. But we do not know how to reconcile theoretically correct analysis with proper and practical pricing and payment policies.

Short of conversion to a full central planning and funding system, the analytical system needs to be concerned about incentives to develop new products. But if, as is commonplace, the decision-making authority is located fairly far down the bureaucratic chain, in a health insurance or health budget authority, the natural and, in many ways, appropriate inclination of the managers of those budgets will be to try to get as much health care as they can out of a given budget, by trying, other things equal, to pay low prices for low amounts of drugs and other goods and services. That is, it may be difficult to create incentives at this level for encouragement of new products.

ELEVEN

Using Economic Evaluation in Reimbursement Decisions for Health Technologies

Lessons from International Experience

Michael Drummond

I. Introduction

Economic evaluation compares costs and consequences of alternative health care treatments or programs (Drummond et al. 2005). In one form of economic evaluation, cost-benefit analysis, all costs and consequences are valued in monetary terms. However, in health care it is much more common to use cost-effectiveness analysis, where the difference in cost between alternatives is compared with the difference in outcomes measured in units such as life years gained or quality-adjusted life years (QALYs) gained.

Since Australia led the way in 1992, economic evaluation has become a formal component of reimbursement decisions, or the development of national guidance for health technologies, in more than 10 other jurisdictions. These include eight countries of the European Union (Belgium, Finland, Hungary, Ireland, the Netherlands, Portugal, Sweden, and the United Kingdom), plus Canada, New Zealand, and Norway.

The precise role of economic evaluation varies among countries. In the vast majority of jurisdictions the role is confined to decisions about pharmaceuticals only, although the National Institute for Health and Clinical Excellence (NICE) in the United Kingdom also considers devices, medical procedures, and public health interventions. Even among those countries considering only pharmaceuticals, there are variations in policy. In some, all new pharmaceuticals are considered, whereas in others only those drugs having a premium price, or likely to have a major impact on the health care system, are evaluated.

The extent of regulatory control also varies. In some countries a formal decision to list (or not list) the drug for reimbursement on the national or provincial formulary is made. In others, evidence-based guidance on the use of health technologies is issued, and health professionals are encouraged to follow it.

Given more than 10 years international experience with using economic evaluation, this chapter's objective is to assess what has been learned and to identify the key methodological and practical issues that have emerged. The chapter ends with some conclusions and recommendations for other jurisdictions considering a more formal role for economic evaluation.

II. General Lessons Learned to Date

First and foremost, a decision-making process embodying the formal use of economic evaluation is workable. Although it would be wrong to suggest that the introduction of economic evaluation has been problem-free, none of the jurisdictions adopting economic evaluation has thus far sought to abandon it.

Second, despite the increased emphasis on cost effectiveness, the demonstration of clinically important benefits is still paramount, as in the decision by NICE in the United Kingdom on the use of Zanamivir, a treatment for influenza. The Institute considered that the clinical benefits of Zanamivir in otherwise healthy individuals (a reduction in the median length of an episode of the disease from six days to five days) was not substantial enough (NICE 2000).

More generally, the presence or absence of good clinical data imposes limits on the economic evaluations that can be conducted. It is usually easier to undertake economic evaluations of drug therapies, where there are usually some reasonable clinical data, as compared with medical devices or procedures. However, even for drugs, the data from standard Phase 3 clinical trials are far from ideal. These trials are usually conducted under conditions that are atypical of normal practice. In addition, they are often of short duration and often fail to compare the most relevant alternatives for economic evaluation. This means that decision-analytic modeling is usually required as a supplement to, or alternative to, economic analysis alongside trials.

Third, economic data are more important when there is substantial budgetary impact. In some jurisdictions, technologies are selected for appraisal only if they have a substantial impact on the (national) health service (e.g., in the United Kingdom), or if the manufacturer wants a premium price over other drugs to treat the given health condition (e.g., in the Netherlands). In addition, in several countries the authorities require an estimation of overall budgetary impact as well as the incremental cost-effectiveness ratio.

Fourth, total refusal of reimbursement of new technologies is rare, restrictions in use are much more common. In several countries the authorities seek to restrict the use of new drugs to certain subgroups of patients in whom their use would be particularly cost effective. Alternatively, they seek to ensure that new drugs are used second or third line, after cheaper treatments have failed.

Fifth, when total refusal is advised, political will is sometimes tested. The best example from the United Kingdom concerns beta interferon for multiple sclerosis: NICE twice advised against its use on grounds of lack of cost effectiveness. Faced with a potential political backlash, the ministry devised a risk-sharing plan under which patients were to be monitored over time. If the long-term outcome for patients is not as good as the manufacturers suggest, they may have to refund some of their sales revenues (U.K. Department of Health 2002).

Finally, cost effectiveness can change over time if new clinical data become available or clinicians find more efficient ways to use a particular treatment technology (e.g., by adjusting dosage without losing clinical effect). Therefore, it is important to review the recommendations of reimbursement agencies from time to time. In the United Kingdom, NICE seeks to review its recommendations every three years or more often if necessary.

III. Methodological Issues

If decisions are to be based on the results of economic evaluations, it is important that the studies be as reliable and relevant as possible. In settings where a formal requirement for economic evaluation has been implemented, several difficulties have arisen. For example, in a review of 326 submissions made to the Pharmaceutical Benefits Advisory Committee (PBAC) in Australia, Hill, Mitchell, and Henry (2000) found that 218 (67%) had significant methodological problems and 31 had more than one problem. Although the authors were initially surprised by the number of submissions with methodological problems, they concluded that this situation was not unexpected given the nature of the process. They also concluded that their analysis revealed no basic intention to deceive. Similarly, Anis and Gagnon (2000) found that 74% of submissions did not comply with the methodological guidelines prescribed by the authorities, and, of the drugs featuring in the noncompliant submissions, 80% were not approved for listing.

In some countries, such as the United Kingdom, decision makers commission their own independent analyses to avoid relying too heavily on company submissions. However, even here problems can exist because of deficiencies in data or methods. Reviewing common methodological flaws in economic evaluations, Drummond and Sculpher (2005) argued that reimbursement decisions are usually made at a time when only imperfect information is available. Therefore, the appropriate way to judge these studies is not whether they embody some ultimate "truth," but whether they lead to a better decision than would have been made in their absence. Nevertheless, there are several important methodological issues that merit further examination, to which we will now turn.

Making Indirect Clinical Comparisons

At the time of a reimbursement decision, it is highly unlikely that there will be head-to-head clinical trials of the therapies concerned. Such trials are costly and time consuming to undertake, or it is not possible to undertake a trial comparing two investigational therapies. Whatever the reason for the lack of head-to-head studies, an economic evaluation seeking to provide relevant information to a reimbursement agency must incorporate an estimate of treatment effect that is based on *indirect* comparisons.

Indirect comparisons are potentially subject to methodological flaws, mainly because, outside the confines of a single randomized controlled clinical trial, one cannot be sure that the patients enrolled in the various trials are equivalent in terms of baseline risk, the settings for the trials are comparable, and that endpoints are measured in the same way. Therefore, an apparent superiority for one therapy over another, in an indirect comparison, may be as much due to differences in the trials as to differences between the therapies themselves.

The use of estimates of treatment effect based on indirect comparisons when there is a common comparator has recently been shown on many occasions to agree with the results of head-to-head clinical trials (Song et al. 2003). Clearly a more challenging situation exists where there is not a common parameter, for example, in a recent study of the relative cost effectiveness of newer drugs for treatment of epilepsy (Wilby et al. 2003). In this study, Bayesian Markov chain Monte Carlo models for multiparameter synthesis were used (Ades 2003). Here, complex models were used to analyze a set of clinical studies involving a series of clinical alternatives, including the two alternatives of interest.

Extrapolating beyond the Period Observed in Clinical Studies

The issue of extrapolation is probably the most debated point in economic submissions to reimbursement agencies, because only in a minority of cases (e.g., studies of antibiotic drugs) are the full benefits (and harms) of therapy observed during the period of the clinical trial. The need for extrapolation is sometimes immediately apparent, such as in diseases like diabetes, where the major consequences occur in the long term. Here the validity of extrapolation rests on the quality of the epidemiological data, linking risk factors that can be modified by therapy to the long-term outcomes. It would not be possible to wait 20 or 30 years for the definitive clinical trial demonstrating that modification of the risk factor led to a superior outcome. In other cases, a longer-term clinical trial would, in principle, be possible (e.g., for the newer drugs for rheumatoid arthritis). However, such trials would be difficult and costly to conduct, so it may be more convenient to extrapolate beyond the trial by using a model (Kobelt et al. 2003).

There are many different approaches to the projection of benefit beyond the trial. The most conservative would be the so-called stop-and-drop approach, where no benefit is assumed beyond that observed. This may be appropriate for some diseases, such as chronic renal failure, where cessation of therapy is likely to result in death, but it is probably inappropriate for most chronic diseases. Here the most likely possibility is a gradual decline in effect over time. In some cases, there may also be a "catch-up" effect when the patient discontinues therapy.

Another study by Caro et al. (1997) illustrates the difficulties of even defining the within-trial period. Their study was an economic evaluation of primary prevention with pravastatin for people with elevated cholesterol. Although the trial lasted for a considerable period of time (with an average follow-up of about five years), only 10% of the benefit (in life years gained) used in the cost-effectiveness estimates was actually observed during the period of the trial. Most of the benefit was extrapolated from events that occurred during the trial period (e.g., unstable angina), but whose consequences would mainly manifest themselves in the future. The approach taken by Caro et al. was a within-trial analysis in some aspects, since it considered only the costs and events occurring during the period of the trial. However, the benefits attributable to some of these events were projected into the future.

Such uncertainty about the future is a major reason why agencies such as NICE determine a future point in time when their guidance will be reviewed and specify the additional research they would like to see during the intervening period. From a methodological standpoint, analysts should not present just one set of cost-effectiveness estimates using a single method of extrapolation. Rather, a series of scenarios should be presented based on different extrapolation techniques. This will provide an indication of how robust the cost-effectiveness results are to the extrapolation approach.

IV. Practical Issues

Aside from the methodological issues discussed in the previous section, international experience suggests that jurisdictions introducing economic evaluation for reimbursement decisions face several practical issues. Of course, the ways in which these are resolved depend greatly on the local context. Nevertheless, it is worth mentioning several so that countries contemplating use of economic evaluation can consider how they might be resolved in their countries.

Setting Priorities for Economic Evaluation

Within the pharmaceutical field, some countries, such as Australia and Canada, evaluate every new drug individually. In the Netherlands, the decision whether or not to evaluate a given drug depends on whether the manufacturer wants a premium price, over and above drugs in the same reference group or "cluster."

In the United Kingdom, the Department of Health asks NICE to evaluate health technologies that have a major impact on the National Health Service. Although not formally based on efficiency considerations, this approach is more consistent with obtaining the best value for money from the use of resources on economic evaluation. More recently, methods involving the estimation of the expected value of perfect information have been used in a pilot study to inform research priorities in the United Kingdom (Claxton et al. 2004).

Accepting Economic Data from Other Countries

In interpreting economic evaluation results, decision makers need to form a view on whether the results apply in their own setting. Some scientific data are clearly transferable. For example, the clinical effect of a patient taking a given medicine is likely to be similar in the United States and Canada. However, the same may not be true of the same operation performed by different surgeons. Also, in some cases the clinical endpoints may not be totally independent of the health care setting. For example, the EPIC trial of a new drug in cardiology (EPIC Investigators 1994) used a combined endpoint of death, nonfatal myocardial infarction, unplanned surgical revascularization, unplanned repeat angioplasty, unplanned insertion of an intra-aortic balloon pump for refractory ischaemia, and unplanned implantation of a coronary stent. For these reasons, the applicability of economic evaluation results from one setting to another has been widely debated and is an issue both within and between countries (Drummond and Pang 2001; Sculpher et al. 2004).

There are a number of other reasons why economic data may not be easily transferable. These include differences in the availability of alternative treatments, in clinical practice patterns, in relative prices, and in incentives of health care professionals and organizations. An analyst seeking to adapt economic evaluation results from one setting to another could be faced with one of three situations. First, only clinical data may have been collected in clinical trials, and there is a need to produce economic evaluations for more than one country or setting. Here the appropriate option is likely to be to undertake a modeling study, where the clinical data are combined with cost (and possibly quality-of-life) data from a number of sources (for example, routinely available statistics or free-standing cost studies). For example, Palmer et al. (2005) used a decision-analytic model to estimate the cost effectiveness of glycoprotein IIb/IIIa antagonists (GPAs) in the management of non-ST-elevation acute coronary syndromes (ACSs). The clinical trials of GPAs had been undertaken largely or wholly outside the United Kingdom. In the model, Palmer et al. used local data to make adjustments for the fact that (1) the use of GPAs in the trials did not reflect their use in routine U.K. practice and (2) the baseline event rates in the trials were not relevant to practice in the United Kingdom.

Second, economic data (e.g., quantities of resource use) may have been collected alongside a clinical trial undertaken in one country, but economic evaluations are required for other settings. Here, a modeling study using only the clinical data could be undertaken, as above. Alternatively, the resource-use data could be adapted in some way to make them relevant to another setting. For example, Menzin et al. (1996) adapted the results of a study of a new drug for cystic fibrosis. The clinical trial, which was undertaken in the United States, included the collection of data on hospital admissions and resource use for the treatment of respiratory tract infections (RTIs). However, whereas the reduction in the number of RTIs was considered to be generalizable, the authors felt that (1) the probability of hospital admission and (2) the length of hospital stay would be different in France and Italy. Therefore, local data were collected, and adjustments to the trial results were made to reflect local practice.

Third, economic data may have been collected together with a multinational clinical trial, and economic evaluations are required for all the countries enrolling patients in the trial. Here the analyst has a number of options for analyzing the resource-use data.

One option is that the data could be pooled, as is common for clinical data, and priced separately for each country. Another is that the resource-use data for patients from each country could be allowed to vary in the analysis and then priced for each country as above. In this case, the analysts could also calculate cost-effectiveness ratios for each country using the pooled clinical results or using the individual clinical results for each country. Another option would be to estimate cost effectiveness for each country, but for this to be based on a combination of data from the country of interest and those from other countries. This approach has recently been pursued through the use of multilevel modeling (Manca et al. 2004; Willan et al. 2005).

Applying Cost-Effectiveness Thresholds

A major issue in studies of NICE and other public decision-making bodies is whether they apply a threshold cost-effectiveness ratio in their decision making and, if so, what the ratio is. In a study of the PBAC in Australia, George, Harris, and Mitchell (2001) concluded that the committee was unlikely to recommend a drug for listing if the additional cost per life year exceeded $AU76,000 (1998–1999 values) and unlikely to reject a drug for which the additional cost per life year was less than $AU42,000. However, the cost-effectiveness ratio was not the only factor determining the reimbursement decision. Other factors included the scientific rigor and relevance of the evidence for comparative safety, efficacy and cost effectiveness, the lack, or inadequacy, of alternative treatments currently in use, the perceived need in the community, whether the drug is likely only to be used in a hospital setting, and the seriousness of the intended indication (health condition).

There are several objections to the specification of a cost-effectiveness threshold. First, the outcome measure used (i.e., the QALY) may not capture all the relevant benefits of health care programs. Second, most comparisons include studies from a range of settings, and economic data may not be transferable from one setting to another. Third, the adoption of a threshold implies a "shadow price" for a QALY. Although the shadow price may represent society's willingness to pay for a QALY, Gafni and Birch (1993) argued that it is unlikely that the shadow price would be independent of the size of the health program being considered. That is, the program's true opportunity cost can be assessed only by examining what is forgone in terms of other health care programs (given a fixed health care budget), or in other sectors (e.g., education) if the health care budget were increased. Thus, in addition to the cost measurement issues raised by Pauly in the previous chapter, a single cost per QALY threshold is meaningless and may be a recipe for unconstrained growth of health care expenditures. Therefore, several authors (Donaldson, Currie, and Mitton 2002; Birch and Gafni

2002) have argued that there should be less focus on cost-effectiveness ratios and more on the true opportunity cost of adopting the program concerned.

Rawlins and Culyer (2004), the Chair and Deputy Chair of NICE, argued that NICE rejects the use of an absolute threshold for judging the level of acceptability of a technology in the NHS for four reasons: (1) there is no empirical basis for deciding at what value a threshold should be set, (2) there may be circumstances in which NICE would want to ignore a threshold, (3) to set a threshold would imply that efficiency has absolute priority over other objectives (particularly fairness), and (4) many of the technology supply industries are monopolies, and a threshold would discourage price competition.

The authors further argued that, rather than apply an arbitrary threshold, NICE makes its decisions on a case-by-case basis. Therefore, in practice, there is a range of cost effectiveness within which NICE operates. NICE would be unlikely to reject a technology with a ratio in the range £5000–15,000 per QALY solely on the grounds of cost ineffectiveness, but would need special reasons for accepting technologies with ratios over £25,000–35,000 as cost effective. The main considerations in making judgments about cost effectiveness for ratios of £25,000–35,000 per QALY are (1) the degree of uncertainty surrounding the estimate, (2) the particular features of the condition and population using the technology, (3) the innovative nature of the technology, (4) when appropriate, the wider social costs and benefits, and (5) when appropriate, reference to previous appraisals.

The guide to the methods of technology appraisal issued by NICE also acknowledges that given the fixed budget of the NHS, the appropriate threshold is that of the opportunity cost of programs displaced by new, more costly, technologies. However, it goes on to argue that, in the absence of the information required to calculate this threshold,

> comparisons of the most plausible incremental cost-effectiveness ratio (ICER) of a particular technology compared with other programmes that are currently funded are possible and are a legitimate reference (for the Committee). Such comparisons are helpful when the technology has an ICER that is lower than programmes that are widely regarded as cost-effective, substantially higher than other currently funded programmes, or higher than programmes previously rejected as not cost effective (by the Committee). (NICE 2004, p. 33)

Linking Evidence-Based Reimbursement to Other Policies for Health Technologies

No health policy is applied in isolation; thus, it is important to consider how reimbursement linked to economic evaluation relates to other policies that might be applied in a given health care system. In the majority of countries, as expected, introducing economic evaluation for the reimbursement of pharmaceuticals are ones where there is a substantial government (or other third-party-payer) payment for drugs.

In countries with substantial patient copayments, for example, the United States, one might not expect a substantial role for economic evaluation, except where there is public coverage for the elderly or poor. In some managed care settings, where decisions are made about which tier the drug is placed on the formulary, there is a potential role for economic evaluation. However, Neumann (2004) outlined a number of reasons why cost-effectiveness analysis is not widely used in the United States. Although some managed care groups have expressed an interest, a widespread application of economic evaluation seems some way off.

Even in health care systems with a substantial level of public payment and control, evidence-based reimbursement sometimes coexists with policies encouraging generic or therapeutic substitution and reference-based pricing. In the latter case, a payment level is set for all drugs in the same therapeutic cluster. In these situations one might expect economic evaluation to have a role in determining which substitutions and/or clusters make sense. However, there seems to be little evidence of the application of economic evaluation in practice. Rather, in countries such as the Netherlands, economic evaluation is reserved for pharmaceuticals that are considered to be outside the reference price system. In the United Kingdom, NICE would potentially consider a generic product with a new, expensive, branded one as part of a technology appraisal.

V. Conclusion

What guidance can be offered to those jurisdictions in which there is a prima facie case for using economic evaluation in reimbursement decisions for health technologies? First, although studies do not need to be perfect to be useful in decision making, they should be as good as possible given the current limitations in methods and data. Some of the main methodological challenges were discussed in Section III. Whether relying primarily on company submissions or commissioning their own studies, decision makers should follow an explicit set of methodological guidelines. These already exist in many jurisdictions. Those issued by NICE in the United Kingdom are reasonably up-to-date and comprehensive (NICE 2004).

Second, much can be learned from other countries. Countries contemplating the formal use of economic evaluations should review the procedures currently operating elsewhere to assess which best fit their own settings. In particular, decisions have to be made about whether all new technologies (e.g., drugs) will be assessed, or just a few. In the latter, priorities for evaluation need to be set. Also, decision makers need to decide whether they intend to rely primarily on submissions prepared by industry, or whether they intend to commission independent evaluations. The latter strategy is likely to be more transparent, and free from bias. Its major drawbacks are the time and expense required. It may also be possible to learn something from the results of studies in other jurisdictions. But it is likely that the results will need some adaptation. Some advice on how this might be done was given in Section IV.

Third, adequate resources should be made available for reviewing industry submissions and/or for undertaking new evaluations. Since the availability of skilled personnel is limited in some countries, the priority should be on adapting studies from other locations, unless the decision in question has very large resource consequences.

Fourth, the criteria for decision making should be discussed and, if possible, made transparent. In particular, when determining the cost-effectiveness threshold, or societal willingness-to-pay for health technologies, a number of factors may need to be taken into account. Therefore, it makes more sense to think in terms of a range of acceptable cost effectiveness, rather than a single threshold. If these issues are carefully considered, it is likely that a process involving the formal use of economic evaluation, in making reimbursement decisions for health technologies, will prove workable in most countries.

TWELVE

Pharmaceutical Spending and Health Outcomes

Pierre-Yves Cremieux, Denise Jarvinen, Genia Long, and Phil Merrigan

I. Introduction

In this chapter we review the current state of the literature on the value of pharmaceuticals and provide estimates of the value of pharmaceuticals in Canada following the Murphy and Topel (2005) methodology.

Because this literature has become so vast and has morphed in so many different ways, we focus on a subset. Specifically, we review three types of studies. First, we review evidence based on comparisons of spending and outcomes across Organization for Economic Cooperation and Development (OECD) countries. Second, we describe a number of studies focusing on specific countries (namely, the United States and Canada). These studies have examined the impact of pharmaceutical spending levels on health outcomes using variation across administrative units and over time within individual countries. Finally, we introduce the growing literature examining the value of pharmaceuticals relative to specific disease areas.

All the studies reviewed rely on health care or pharmaceutical spending rather than on health or pharmaceutical output as a proxy for health care received by consumers. One unintended interpretation of a positive relationship between dollars spent and outcomes would be that health care price increases alone could extend life. In reality, of course, increased spending reflects a combination of increased quantity, increased quality, and increased price of pharmaceuticals. Since these three factors cannot be separated and since pharmaceutical prices are increasing even after controlling for quality, the relationship between spending and health outcome will understate the true underlying relationship between spending and the combination of quality and quantity increases.

Following the review of the literature, we use results from Murphy and Topel (2005) to calculate the value of pharmaceutical spending in

Canada, not in terms of increased life expectancy, but in terms of dollars. We find, as have previous studies, that pharmaceutical spending is a worthwhile investment with high rates of return, and that to restrict access to new pharmacological treatment would deny the next generation valuable increases in health outcomes.

II. Trends in Life Expectancy

The most important determinants of health typically are identified as income, hygiene, lifestyle, physician care, and access to nutritious food, with pharmaceuticals often an afterthought. Frank and Mustard (1998) attributed a 1953 United Nations report with identifying improvements in public health, health care, hygiene, and living standards as the four pillars of increased modern life expectancy. These factors may still apply today, particularly in many developing countries, where fulfilling basic human needs may well provide greater health benefits than sophisticated health services.

Twenty-five years after the U.N. report, the influential Black Report (Black et al. 1982) concluded that socioeconomic factors were at least as important determinants of health outcomes as were improvements in health care. This finding, based on a review of health outcomes in the United Kingdom, is surprising given important pharmaceutical discoveries, particularly anti-infectious agents, between 1940 and 1960. In *Your Money or Your Life*, David Cutler (2004) reminds us that from 1800 to 1940 improvements in life expectancy resulted largely from decreased infant mortality, which, in turn, resulted from improved hygiene, better nutrition, and public health improvements. From 1930 to 1960, further improvements resulted largely from successful inroads in the fight against infection with the discovery of sulfa drugs and penicillin. However, Cutler also notes that at the beginning of the 1960s, given their success in combating infectious disease, particularly with the advent of penicillin, many in the health care community began to doubt the possibility of further increase in life expectancy. Having understood the microbial origin of many diseases and developed effective ways of combating infectious disease particularly, they believed the ability of drugs to provide any further gain in life expectancy seemed limited. Over the last 40 years, however, increasing trends in life expectancy have been quite stable across time, countries, and gender. Between 1960 and 2002, mean life expectancy in the OECD member countries increased by eight years for men and by close to nine years for women (OECD 2004). These gains averaged roughly three months per year, although for men they are substantially lower in the early years.

Table 12.1. *Mean number of months in life expectancy gain per year*

	1960–1970	1970–1980	1980–1990	1990–2000
Men	1.2	2.4	2.6	3.0
Women	2.4	3.1	2.5	2.2

Source: Organization for Economic Cooperation and Development (2004)

Despite the well-publicized and very significant gains that occurred in the first half of the century, substantial additional gains have also been realized since 1960, with the trend continuing strongly in the 1980s and 1990s (Table 12.1). This sustained trend suggests that additional gains may well be realized in the coming decades, contrary to the expectations of those who decry the era of "me-too" drugs and anticipate fewer gains in the years to come. Also, we noted that all the countries selected seem to be following similar paths with similar growth rates for men and women but a significant gap between the two genders.

The stable increasing trends in life expectancy over the last century mask some significant shifts between the early part of that century and the last 20 years. These differences provide a useful context to the role of pharmaceuticals. Up to 1950, life expectancy for individuals who reached the age of 50 did not increase; decreases in infant mortality fueled much of the increase in life expectancy during that period. However, since 1950, and particularly since the 1970s, progress has been generated disproportionately by increases in life expectancy conditional on reaching age 50 (Murphy and Topel 2005). Presumably, differences in income, nutrition, and public health would affect all age cohorts. The remarkable shift in gains to older age cohorts suggests that pharmaceutical intervention and improvements in health care may well underlie this striking shift.

The demographic shifts in life expectancy gains further complicate any analysis of the sources of longer life. To identify the specific role of pharmaceuticals in this remarkable trend, we focus on empirical research based on data from the last 20–30 years. The role of pharmaceutical products is not obvious, however, because of simultaneously increased average income, decreased poverty, greater and faster access to medical facilities, and improved training for health professionals, all of which combine with access to new and improved pharmaceutical products to yield longer life.

III. Impact of Pharmaceuticals on Life Expectancy

Early studies on determinants of health outcomes (Cochrane, St. Leger, and Moore 1978; Poikolainen and Eskola 1988; Mackenbach 1991; Skinner and Wennberg 2000) found no relationship between health spending or health provision and health outcomes, much less any relationship between pharmaceutical spending and health outcomes (Babazono and Hillman 1994). This was distressing given the increasing percentage of gross domestic product being devoted to health care expenditures in general and drug spending in particular. Given that later findings demonstrated a statistically significant relationship between health care spending and health outcomes (Cremieux, Ouellette, and Pilon 1999), it is likely that this absence of evidence resulted largely from methodological limitations, heterogeneity in international studies (described below), and lack of available data to identify this complex relationship.

The paper by Cochrane, St. Leger, and Moore (1978) typifies the issues associated with many early studies. Specifically, they relied on cross sections with multiple countries and often limited the analysis to simple correlations. Because determinants of life expectancy are multifactorial, national studies are more likely to detect differences than international studies. It is also critically important to include adequate control variables. In fact, a later study (Cremieux, Ouellette, and Meilleur 1999) based on extensive national data suggests that a 10% increase in health care spending reduces infant mortality by 0.5% for males and 0.4% for females while increasing life expectancy by half a year for males and three months for females. The current study uses similar modeling and data; hence, results on the effect of pharmaceuticals reported below can be put in perspective relative to the overall effect of health care spending from that earlier research.

Quantifying the relationship between pharmaceutical innovation and health outcomes is challenging because of the many other determinants of health outcomes and the difficulty of quantifying pharmaceutical innovation. Since the mid-1980s, researchers have approached this challenge in several ways. Some have relied on variations in international pharmaceutical spending levels and health outcomes to tease out a possible relationship between the two. Other researchers have focused on variations in health outcomes and pharmaceutical spending at the national level. A third research approach has focused on the impact of pharmaceutical spending on specific disease states.

Each of these approaches presents both advantages and disadvantages. Analyses based on international comparisons provide insights into the merit of aggregate spending levels and the likely marginal impact of increased spending on health outcomes based on the experience of other countries. But the substantial heterogeneity of lifestyles, differences in underlying data, different measures of pharmaceutical spending (e.g., with over-the-counter expenditures or without, including hospital drug spending or not), and limited set of control variables present major obstacles for these studies. Further, these analyses may not be equally meaningful across audiences. Analyses based on national data are more relevant to national authorities and policy makers, as they tend to be based on more homogenous populations, often with higher-quality data. However, such studies provide no insights to formulary committees concerned with specific drug reimbursement decisions. They are also less relevant in the United States, where national health care is limited to seniors. Finally, disease or compound specific analyses are helpful to formulary committees but provide no guidance for national budgetary purposes.

International Studies

The early focus on pharmaceuticals as major determinants of gains in life expectancy was based on a comparison of OECD countries. As with studies analyzing the relationship between health outcomes and health care expenditures, those based on international data require an extensive panel of data both longitudinally and cross-sectionally to discern any relationship. Babazono and Hillman (1994), using a single cross section of 21 countries, found no relationship between pharmaceutical spending and health outcomes. However, Frech and Miller (1999), using a similar cross section of 21 OECD countries but including a larger set of control variables (alcohol consumption, fat intake, smoking rates, income, and non-health care expenditures), found that higher pharmaceutical spending is associated with increased life expectancy at ages 40–60. Higher pharmaceutical spending was also associated with longer life expectancy at birth in the European subset of OECD countries. There was no association between pharmaceutical spending and infant mortality rates. This later study also suffered from major methodological limitations, including significant unobserved heterogeneity across countries and a limited sample size.

In their updated 2004 study, Miller and Frech used more recent data to conduct a similar cross-sectional analysis with some additional control variables (e.g., obesity rates) and found very similar results on life expectancy with a doubling of spending leading to a 4% increase in life expectancy at age 60. Additional results using disability-adjusted life expectancy (DALE) suggested that pharmaceutical spending was significantly associated with DALE at birth and at 60.

Shaw, Horrace, and Vogel (2005) reported results similar to those of Frech and Miller. Analyzing a pooled database across OECD countries, the authors found that increases in spending on pharmaceuticals would result in substantial increases in life expectancy. Specifically, a 113% increase in per capita pharmaceutical spending among OECD countries would yield one year of increased life expectancy for men at age 60. For 60-year-old women, a 93% increase in per capita pharmaceutical spending yields one year of extended life. Shaw et al. (2005) also demonstrated that international studies that are not gender- and age-specific suffer from omitted variable bias and result in an underestimation of the effect of pharmaceutical spending on life expectancy.

National Studies

In parallel with the research conducted by Frech and Miller on international data, a number of researchers have used variation within specific countries to link pharmaceutical spending to both innovation and health outcomes. This approach reduced unobserved heterogeneity and, therefore, increased the likelihood of measuring a relationship with greater precision. This research took two different paths. Some studies examined the relationship between the level of pharmaceutical spending in general and outcomes observed in different regions; Lichtenberg (e.g., Lichtenberg 2003a) and others focused on a narrower issue, the role of new drug introduction on health outcomes (e.g., Hsieh et al., Chapter 13).

Using data on health care and pharmaceutical expenditures in the United States as well as various state-level sociodemographic measures (income, poverty, and ethnic distribution), Cremieux et al. (2001) found a significant association between pharmaceutical spending and infant mortality. Methodologically, the analysis was similar to that of Frech and Miller (1999); however, instead of cross-sectional data on a small number of countries, the data used in this paper include 17 years of data from 50 states, resulting in a sample size 20 times larger than that of Frech and Miller.

In a later similar study, Cremieux et al. (2005) used Canadian data to examine the relationship between pharmaceutical spending and infant mortality.[1] This study examined determinants of life expectancy as well. The explanatory variables included food intake, alcohol and tobacco consumption, and standard sociodemographic controls. After controlling for nonpharmaceutical health care spending and other factors, pharmaceutical spending was found to increase life expectancy and reduce infant mortality during the 1981–1998 periods. Specifically, the findings suggested that if all Canadian provinces had maintained public and private drug expenditures at 1981 levels, 372 additional infant deaths would have resulted, and life expectancy at birth would have been an average of 11.7 and 7.9 months shorter for males and females, respectively. By 1998 Canadian men had gained nearly 22 months of increased life expectancy attributable to pharmaceutical utilization, while Canadian women had gained 14 months. Furthermore, life expectancy at age 65 would have been an average of 4.5 months shorter for males and 2.1 months shorter for females over the period at 1981 pharmaceutical spending levels. The results are very similar to those in Shaw, Horrace, and Vogel (2005) based on OECD data. The Canadian analysis implies that doubling pharmaceutical spending in 1998 in Canada would yield 0.84 years of increased life expectancy for men and 0.73 for women.

Using a somewhat different approach, Lichtenberg and Virabhak (2002) focused on a specific aspect of the relationship between pharmaceutical products and health outcomes associated with innovation. They relied on survey data from nearly 35,000 individuals interviewed in the 1997 Medical Expenditure Panel Survey (MEPS), relating various health outcomes measures with prescription drugs of various vintages. The health outcome measures were based on answers to inquiries on the responders' ability to perform specific tasks and general cognitive or physical limitations. Drug vintage was directly observed, although with some left censoring because of data limitations for older drugs, from National Drug Codes and ICD-9 diagnoses provided by the responder. While newer vintage drugs were more expensive, they also were associated with better health outcomes for seven of the nine health indicators. The results for health indicators were always robust, but overall they suggested that newer vintage drugs resulted in better health outcomes. Furthermore, newer vintage drugs were associated with a higher probability of survival. Lichtenberg (2005b) confirmed these results based on IMS health drug launch data and World Health Organization mortality data covering 52 countries over two decades.

Lichtenberg (1996) compiled data on hospital deaths and pharmaceutical innovation based on the National Ambulatory Medical Care Survey (NAMCS). For a number of specific disease states, he constructed a measure of pharmaceutical innovation using the dissimilarity between drugs prescribed to the early 1980 cohort in a given disease category, and drugs prescribed in the later 1991 cohort. A greater dissimilarity between drugs prescribed implied a greater level of innovation. Using the variability in dissimilarity across ICD-9 diagnoses, Lichtenberg found that greater dissimilarity was associated with lower mortality but that the relationship was applicable only to mortality in hospital, and with no link to mean age of death. While the results were based on a small data set (< 100 observations) and only two cross sections (1980 and 1991–1992), they were among the first to suggest that the relationship between pharmaceutical innovation and death rates could be established at an aggregate level.

In a later study, Lichtenberg (2003a) further investigated the relationship between pharmaceutical innovation and life expectancy. Specifically, he examined the relationship between the number of life years lost and the degree of pharmaceutical innovation using the dissimilarity in drugs prescribed over time across different diseases. The data on pharmaceutical prescriptions, U.S. Food and Drug Administration pharmaceutical approval dates, and premature mortality by ICD-9 codes provided information needed to assess the relationship between relative reductions in life years lost prior to attaining age 75 and the ratio of new drugs to total drugs prescribed. This ratio was derived from prescriptions reported in the NAMCS and National Hospital Ambulatory Medical Care Survey (NHAMCS) in 1970 and 1991 across approximately 75 aggregated disease classifications (ICD-9). Lichtenberg's hypothesis was that a greater reduction in premature mortality should be observed in years when newly introduced compounds represented a greater share of total pharmaceuticals prescribed. He found that 18,800 life years were generated per new drug approval. Using an assumed annual value of $25,000 per year, Lichtenberg calculated economic benefits per new drug approval of $470 million compared to new drug development costs of $697 million. If, however, Lichtenberg's results were to be updated by using the more common value of a life year of $100,000, the economic benefits per new drug approval would jump to at least $1.8 billion dollars against development costs of $697 million for a ratio of over 2.5 to 1.

Disease-Specific Analyses

Much of the disease-specific analysis on the impact of treatment on life expectancy in other than experimental settings has focused on cardiovascular disease, largely because of the large gains in life expectancy resulting from innovative pharmacological treatment of this disease. In fact, according to Cutler and Kadiyala (2003), the two-thirds decrease in death from cardiovascular disease was largely responsible for the overall decrease in mortality while death rates for other major conditions such as cancer, infections, accidents, homicides, suicides, and chronic obstructive pulmonary disease (COPD) remained stable between 1950 and 2000. Based on their own empirical research and existing literature, they attributed one-third of the reduction in cardiovascular disease mortality to nonpharmaceutical medical intervention, another third to pharmaceuticals, and the remaining third to lifestyle modification including healthier diet and reduced smoking. Using a value of life of $100,000 per year, Cutler and Kadiyala calculated the value of medically reduced mortality from cardiovascular disease to be $120,000 compared with average pharmaceutical and nonpharmaceutical medical costs of $30,000. Without examining benefits to costs for pharmaceutical products separately, the value of behaviorally induced mortality reduction is $30,000, compared with costs of research, education, and behavioral change of $1,000.

Lichtenberg (2001b) examined rare diseases (treated with orphan drugs) and HIV/AIDS as case studies to illustrate the impact of new therapies on life expectancy. His focus on rare diseases and HIV/AIDS is particularly interesting because these areas provide national experiments of two very different sorts (also, see Lichtenberg, Chapter 7, and Sloan and Eesley, Chapter 6).

The Orphan Drug Act (ODA), which was passed by the U.S. Congress in 1983, provided additional financial incentives for pharmaceutical companies to develop products in areas where often life-threatening diseases affect a population so small that recouping R&D costs would require unusually high per patient pricing. The ODA provided an immediate incentive for pharmaceutical companies to embark in new, previously unprofitable areas of research. During the early 1980s, the fear of a pandemic associated with the HIV virus also led to an unusual focus of research efforts to develop effective treatment.

Lichtenberg found that following the ODA, mortality from rare diseases grew more slowly than mortality from other diseases. Prior to the Act, the mortality trend across rare and other types of diseases had been roughly equal. The results suggested that each additional drug developed to treat rare diseases saved 211 lives in the year following the drug's introduction. Using an alternative specification, he estimated that, in total, 499 lives were saved. Analyzing data on the well-known and sudden decline in HIV-related deaths starting in 1995, Lichtenberg also found a strong relationship between the number of anti-AIDS drugs approved and a decline in the death rate during the same period. He estimated that each new approval resulted in 5,986 fewer deaths in the following year and 33,819 overall. These analyses cannot be generalized to other areas because they relate to first-generation drugs for new diseases (HIV).

IV. Monetary Value of Life Expectancy Gains

Cutler and Kadiyala's (2003) estimates of life expectancy benefits associated with improved cardiovascular treatment suggest a high value of pharmaceutical products relative to costs. An analysis at the national level would provide confirmation that the value of pharmaceuticals is not limited to cardiovascular disease. Here we performed such an analysis for Canada, where the public funding of health care has led to extensive debate over its value and, more specifically, over the value of pharmaceutical products whose rate of growth within the health care budget continues to increase.

Even though Murphy and Topel (2003, 2005) did not focus specifically on pharmacological innovation or spending, they developed and extended their valuation of overall changes in life expectancy and health quality improvement in monetary terms. Their 2005 study used observed mortality rates to calculate life expectancy changes over the twentieth century. Because mortality rates are also reported by cause of death, they could calculate life expectancy improvements by illness. Prior to their 2005 study, Murphy and Topel used an earlier version of their methodology in 2003 to value changes in life expectancy from 1970 to 1998; Nordhaus (2003) used a similar approach to value changes in life expectancy from 1900 to 1995.

The Murphy and Topel (2005) approach was based on the vast literature on the value of a statistical life.[2] In their framework, health care and medical innovation are presumed to increase the likelihood of individual survival from their point of utilization. Based on existing empirical studies on the value of a statistical life, the Environmental Protection Agency (EPA) has used a $6.3 million value per statistical life. Murphy and Topel adopted the EPA value in their analysis. However, rather than assuming that increases in life expectancy are valued at a constant level throughout an individual's lifetime, Murphy and Topel used the $6.3 million value to construct value-of-life schedules that incorporate the willingness to pay for increases in life expectancy at different ages. Their analysis yielded a value of $200,000 for an additional year of life at age 20, increasing to a maximum of $350,000 at age 50, and declining to approximately $100,000 at age 95. Beyond age 95, the value per life year dropped to under $100,000 but decreased at a slower rate. The authors point out that these values were many times higher than those used in some previous studies (for example, Lichtenberg [2003a] used $25,000 per life year). However, Murphy and Topel maintained that these lower values do not correspond with the standard $6.3 million value of a statistical life used widely in the environmental policy context.

Based on this valuation methodology, Murphy and Topel calculated the value of increased life expectancy in the United States from 1900 and 1970. Since 1970, increases in life expectancy represented an economic value of over \$95 trillion or just under \$3.2 trillion per year (in 2004 dollars) amounting to about half of gross domestic product over the same period. The value of overall life expectancy gains outweighed the increase in health expenditures of \$34.7 trillion dollars, except for men aged 85+ and women 64+, for whom expenditures exceeded the value of life expectancy increases. In contrast to those for males, female life expectancy gains during the 1980–2000 period frequently fell short of increased health expenditures. The Murphy and Topel research did not distinguish between spending on pharmaceuticals and other health care expenditures; however, their methodology is applicable to a narrow focus on pharmaceuticals. The economic valuation methodology for life expectancy changes was based on observed mortality rates, not the attribution of life expectancy changes to particular medical or pharmaceutical innovations or spending levels.

The next section applies the Murphy and Topel methodology to the results of the Cremieux et al. (2005) article relating gains in life expectancy to pharmaceutical spending.

V. Monetary Value of Life Expectancy Increase from Canadian Pharmaceutical Spending

The analysis in Cremieux et al. (2005) yielded life expectancies for men and for women from 1981 to 1998 as predicted by a model and simulated with drug spending at 1981 levels (Fig. 12.1). Using methodology from Murphy and Topel (2005), life expectancy results from the Canadian pharmaceutical spending study can be evaluated in monetary terms. The value at age a of a statistical life is given by

$$\int_a^\infty v(t)S(t,a)dt,$$

where $v(t)$ is the value of a life year at time t and $s(a,t)$ is the discounted survivor function for an individual of age a at time t greater than a. Economic gain attributed to any decrease in mortality rates between periods t and $t+1$ for an individual of age a is given by the value of a statistical life for this individual computed with survivor functions at period $t+1$ minus the value of a statistical life computed with survivor functions for period t.

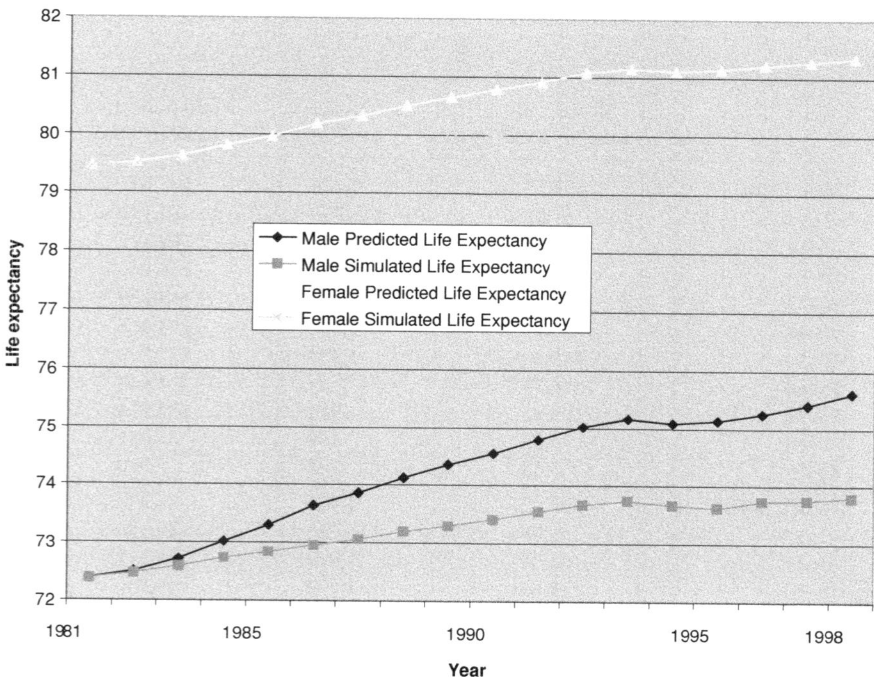

Figure 12.1. Predicted gains in life expectancy and simulated values with pharmaceutical spending at 1981 levels.

To compute this value requires survivor functions for relevant time periods as well as values for $v(t)$. The survivor functions were computed from male and female life tables available for 1982 and 1997 from Statistics Canada. Economic values for additional life years were computed based on Murphy and Topel (2005) and converted to Canadian dollars using the average per capita ratios of Canadian to U.S. income for 1994–2003. These income-adjusted life year values were then multiplied by 1.267 the purchasing power parity (PPP) rate between Canada and the United States in 2004, expressed in 2004 dollars.

The economic value of increased life expectancy in Canada was computed for individuals from birth through age 109. To compute aggregate numbers, the economic gain for each age was multiplied by the number of individuals in each group as of 1997. Statistics Canada Tables were used for this purpose. Tables 12.2 and 12.3 present the economic gain from decreases in mortality rates between 1982 and 1997 for Canadian men and women by age as well as aggregate and per capita gains. Over the period, gains in economic

Table 12.2. *Gain from reduction in Canadian mortality by gender and age, 1982–1997*

	Total gain (billions of CDN$2004)	Population ('000s)	Gain per capita (CDN$2004)
Male Birth	531.54	5,126	103,694
1–4	67.22	799	84,111
5–14	208.35	2,081	100,121
15–24	254.20	2,065	123,060
25–34	341.48	2,339	145,939
35–44	495.77	2,548	194,506
45–54	445.40	1,959	227,292
55–64	256.77	1,271	201,948
65–74	129.36	974	132,774
75–84	25.87	469	55,052
85+	3.15	108	2,910
Female Birth	277.82	4,921	56,449
1–4	30.78	761	40,446
5–14	92.84	1,979	46,911
15–24	119.68	1,970	60,730
25–34	176.66	2,292	77,059
35–44	244.27	2,549	95,830
45–54	211.45	1,968	107,424
55–64	135.39	1,308	103,453
65–74	95.08	1,134	83,802
75–84	33.09	719	46,026
85+	2.56	254	10,093

Sources: Murphy and Topel (2005); Statistics Canada (2002).

Table 12.3. *Total gain and reduction in Canadian mortality*

	Total gain (billions of CDN$2004)	Annual gain (billions of CDN$2004)	Percentage of GNP
Males	2,756.30	183.75	
Females	1,419.70	94.65	
Total	4,176.00	278.40	43%

Sources: Murphy and Topel (2005); Statistics Canada (2002).

value from reduced mortality in Canada approached $4.2 trillion in Canadian currency. This overall gain represents an annual average economic gain of $278 billion in Canadian dollars. Compared to average real gross domestic product during the same period, economic gains from reduced mortality in

Table 12.4. *Canadian life expectancy increase linked to pharmaceutical expenditures, 1981–1998*

	Months	Total increase
Males	21.8	56.3%
Females	14.3	63.3%

Source: Calculations based on Cremieux et al. (2005).

Canada represent an unaccounted economic contribution equal to 43% of Canadian GDP in 2004. The results in Tables 12.2 and 12.3 are comparable to results in Murphy and Topel (2005) based on a 1982–1997 time period.

Based on results from Cremieux et al. (2005), the Canadian pharmaceutical spending model predicts that actual increases in pharmaceutical spending from their 1981 levels accounted for life expectancy increases reaching 21.8 months for males and 14.3 months for females by 1998. The model predicts that 56% of total life expectancy gain for Canadian men from 1981 to 1998 is attributable to pharmaceutical product utilization (Table 12.4). At 63% of total life expectancy gain, the pharmaceutical contribution is even larger for women than for men.

Table 12.5 reports the value of economic gain resulting from increased life expectancy attributed to pharmaceutical consumption in Canada. Applying the average annual life expectancy gains for the total Canadian population from Table 12.2, the total value of life expectancy over the 17-year period, 1981–1998, was over $4.7 trillion in Canadian dollars. Of this, male life expectancy gains amounted to $3.1 trillion, while female gains totaled $1.6 trillion. Results from the Canadian pharmaceutical study as reported in Table 12.4 were applied to the male and female overall life expectancy gains to calculate the economic value of increased pharmaceutical spending in Canada during the 1981–1998 period. As shown in Table 12.4, increased pharmaceutical spending accounted for nearly $2.8 trillion in Canadian life expectancy value from 1981 through 1998. The gains attributed to pharmaceutical spending account for nearly 59 % of the value of total life expectancy gains realized over the period. In contrast, from 1981 through 1998, total private and public expenditures on pharmaceuticals excluding those administered in hospitals totaled $140 billion in 2004 Canadian dollars. Incremental spending over and above the level observed in 1980, the last year prior to the period at issue, totaled $72 billion. The rate of return on total spending is 20 to 1 and the rate of return on incremental spending is nearly 40 to 1.

Table 12.5. *Economic value of Canadian life expectancy gains attributable to pharmaceutical expenditures, 1981–1998*

Increase in life expectancy	Value of life expectancy gains (billions of CDN$2004)
All causes	
Males	3,124
Females	1,609
Total	4,732
From incremental drug spending since 1981	
Males	1,760
Females	1,018
Total	2,778

VI. Conclusion

Because changes in health outcomes result from so many different and simultaneous factors, measuring the relationship between health outcomes and any specific determinant remains difficult. Spending on pharmaceuticals is often used as a proxy for the value of pharmaceutical care but often ignores noncompliance, overprescription, over-the-counter sales, and the very definition of a pharmaceutical product. Therefore, the results presented in this chapter should be examined with care, and their precision should not be overstated.

However, the evidence relating pharmaceutical spending and health outcomes seems overwhelming. International studies, national studies, and disease-specific analyses indicate that pharmaceutical products have been a worthwhile investment over the last half century. With rates of return exceeding 10 to 1 based on measures of increased life expectancy alone, pharmaceutical products have successfully improved health outcomes in developed countries at a cost dwarfed by the value of increased longevity.

Using Murphy and Topel's methodology and applying it to results from Cremieux et al.'s 2005 article on the effect of pharmaceutical products in Canada, we find that between 1981 and 1998, $72 billion (Canadian) in incremental drug spending generated nearly $2.8 trillion in gains from increased life expectancy.

These results seem high for two reasons. First, Murphy and Topel (2005) assumed that the value of a life is significantly greater than was traditionally reported in the health literature. Second, the Cremieux et al. (2005) results assigned over 50% of gains in life expectancy since 1980 to pharmaceuticals. Even cutting the Murphy and Topel life year value in half and thereby standardizing the value of a life year for a 20-year-old American at $100,000, the gains from incremental pharmaceutical spending in Canada would outweigh expenditures by nearly 20 to 1. At the individual level, the calculations show that for an average investment of just over $300 per person per year (or $5,300 over 17 years), Canadian men gained nearly two years in life expectancy, while women gained more than a year. The difference across genders is consistent with that reported by Murphy and Topel and would certainly merit further study.

In conclusion, we find that although some periods of time are likely to result in more productive discoveries than others, there is no evidence that gains from pharmaceutical discovery have been fully realized. To the contrary, it is likely that as valuable new pharmaceutical products are introduced, and drugs made more accessible to broader populations, further improvements in life expectancies will result.

THIRTEEN

Pharmaceutical Innovation and Health Outcomes

Empirical Evidence from Taiwan

Chee-Ruey Hsieh, Kuang-Ta Vance Lo, Yichen Hong, and Ya-Chen Tina Shih

I. Introduction

Each year new pharmaceutical products are introduced as a consequence of technological advances. For example, in the United States, between 1990 and 2004, the U.S. Food and Drug Administration approved 431 new drugs with new molecular entities (NMEs).[1] On average, nearly 29 NMEs are introduced in the U.S. pharmaceutical market annually. These new drugs extend the capability of medicine to treat diseases. New drugs developed in the United States and other high-income countries are often soon introduced in other countries, particularly if the new drug is a life-saving innovation or represents a substantial improvement over existing drugs. Improving the public's health of population is a universal goal around the world, albeit limited by many countries' ability to afford the most recently developed pharmaceuticals.

Adopting new and more effective drugs is costly. In recent years the growth rate of spending on pharmaceuticals in many countries has far exceeded the growth rate of overall health spending. Taking the median of OECD (Organization for Economic Cooperation and Development) countries as an example, during 1990–2000 the average annual growth rate of spending per capita on pharmaceuticals was 4.5%, while the average annual growth rate of health care expenditure per capita was only 3.1% (Anderson et al. 2003). As a result, increased spending on pharmaceuticals has become a major driving force of rising personal health care expenditures in many countries. Several empirical studies have provided strong evidence that the growth of consumption of new drugs, not increased prices, accounts for most of the increase in spending on pharmaceuticals (Berndt 2002; Glied 2003).

While expenditures on pharmaceuticals have risen, there is empirical evidence that innovation in pharmaceuticals has been an important contributor to improved health of the population in many countries (Cutler 2004). Pharmaceutical innovation, such as new drugs for hypertension and high cholesterol, accounts for about one-third of the reduction in cardiovascular disease in the United States (Cremieux et al., Chapter 12; Cutler and Kadiyala 2003).

Although pharmaceutical innovation has increased both costs and benefits, health policy makers globally seem to pay more attention to increased costs rather than to the increased benefits (Sloan and Hsieh, Chapter 1). Some benefits of pharmaceutical innovation, such as the increase in longevity, accrue only in the long run, but higher costs associated with pharmaceutical innovation are apparent soon after new drugs are introduced. Also, higher costs are more readily observable to policy makers, and policy makers' time horizon may be short. Health policy makers consequently tend to focus on cost control and adopt such policies as imposing low prices on new pharmaceuticals and adopt restrictive formularies, which limit availability of new drugs to consumers. However, as Cutler (2004) argued, cost containment is not a goal of the health sector in itself; rather an appropriate social objective is increasing the value obtained from scarce resources. A key goal of health policy should be to decrease wasteful spending, that part of spending that yields only minor or even no benefit, not to decrease spending overall. To achieve this goal, Cutler suggested that "the right step is to move toward a system that improves our health, spending less as appropriate but more if need be" (p. 123).

To improve resource allocation, measuring the benefits of pharmaceutical innovation is an important first step. Fortunately, the number of empirical studies measuring the value of health investment, including spending on health care in general and on pharmaceuticals in particularly, has increased rapidly in recent years (see Cremieux et al., Chapter 12). But, unfortunately, most of this research has been based on data from only two countries, the United States and Canada.

This chapter estimates the impact of pharmaceutical innovation on health outcomes using data from Taiwan. As a newly industrialized country, Taiwan has become an innovator in some specific industries in the past few decades, such as information technology. However, to date Taiwan has lacked the capability to develop NMEs. As a result, Taiwan, like other newly industrialized countries and developing countries with some ability to pay for new technologies, has relied on advanced countries that have such capabilities and has been relegated to a user rather than an innovator of new pharmaceutical technologies.

Specifically, we test the hypothesis that diseases for which there has been relatively more pharmaceutical innovation have experienced more improvements in health outcomes than have outcomes for other diseases for which technological progress has lagged. To test this hypothesis, we constructed a disease-specific panel database for the period 1985–2002, cross-classifying drugs and diseases. We restricted our definition of new drugs to NMEs, using the cumulative number of new drugs approved and launched in Taiwan as our measure of pharmaceutical innovation and longevity as the measure of health outcomes. We find that adoption of new drugs has a significantly positive effect on longevity. Our most conservative estimates suggest that a 10% increase in cumulative number of NMEs is associated with an increase in life expectancy at birth of approximately 0.1%.

In Section II we review previous literature on the effect of new drug adoption on health outcomes. In Section III we describe our data and methodology, which is followed by a description of our results in Section IV. In Section V we provide a discussion on our findings and the limitations of our study. Finally, in Section VI we discuss the policy implications of our findings and directions for future research.

II. Literature Review

Chapter 12 reviewed the current state of literature on the value of pharmaceuticals in general. Several studies have empirically estimated the relationship between pharmaceutical spending levels and health outcomes using variation across countries and over time within individual countries. Overall, these studies have found that higher pharmaceutical spending is associated with better health outcomes, as measured by such health indicators as increased life expectancy and lower infant mortality rates. These findings suggest that spending more on pharmaceutical products, such as introducing new drugs into the formulary, is good for population health. Here we focus specifically on studies that directly investigate the effect of pharmaceutical innovation on population health. Most studies on this topic are based on cost-effectiveness analysis, which investigates the effect of a specific drug technology on certain health outcomes (sometimes termed "endpoints") (see, e.g., Kobelt et al. 2003). By contrast, a small but growing literature focuses on aggregate-level productivity, that is, on the effect of innovation in a particular therapeutic class of drugs rather than one or two drugs, on population health, rather than on the health of a sample of persons from a randomized control trial. This approach treats pharmaceutical innovation as an input in the production of good health.

A common issue in these aggregated studies is how to measure innovation in pharmaceuticals. Three different types of measures have been used: (1) the cumulative number of drugs approved with NMEs, (2) newer drugs as a proportion of total physician prescriptions, (3) and the average vintage of drugs.

Lichtenberg (2004b, 2005b) used the first approach. He emphasized that the approval of NMEs represents the most important form of innovation. New drugs may be introduced in various forms, including NMEs, new formulations, new combinations, new indications, or drugs that are identical to existing products. This approach implicitly treats the approval of NMEs as a technological change; the introduction of other types of new drugs is only an improvement of existing technologies.[2] Using the cumulative number of NMEs available in the market by year, Lichtenberg found a significantly positive relationship between his measure of pharmaceutical innovation and life expectancy in the United States and in a much broader sample containing data from 52 countries.

A second approach used by Lichtenberg (2003a) measures the innovation in pharmaceuticals by both the development *and* diffusion of new drugs. This approach implicitly assumes that the rate of market penetration by new drugs is an appropriate measure of the rate of technological change. Based on this approach, Lichtenberg (2003a) reported that diseases with relatively high rates of technological change in drug therapy have experienced relatively greater reductions in disease-specific mortality. He estimated that increases in the market share of new drug explained over 45% of the variation across disease in mortality reduction during the period 1971–1990 in the United States.

A third approach used by Lichtenberg and Virabhak (2002) measures the vintage of the drugs by the year in which the U.S. Food and Drug Administration first approved a drug's active ingredients. This approach implicitly assumes that newer vintages of drugs consumed by individuals represent technological improvements in medical care. Using data from U.S. Medical Expenditure Panel Survey in 1997, Lichtenberg and Virabhak found that individual patients who used newer vintage drugs had a higher probability of survival, better self-evaluated health status, and fewer limitations in physical function.

Although the empirical measures of pharmaceutical innovation are diverse, the studies consistently indicate that technological change in pharmaceuticals leads to better health outcomes. Nevertheless, existing methods of measuring innovation in pharmaceuticals have several limitations. First, they capture the quantity of innovations but ignore the quality of such innovations. As part of its drug approval process, the U.S. Food and Drug Administration classifies the new drug as (1) representing a significant improvement over existing drugs or (2) having therapeutic qualities similar to those of existing drugs. The latter are sometimes called "me-too" drugs (Sloan and Hsieh, Chapter 1).

Market size is an important determinant of the development and launching of new drugs (Acemoglu and Linn 2004; Finkelstein 2004; Danzon, Wang, and Wang 2005). Firms are more likely to develop me-too drugs for larger therapeutic markets. For this reason, simply counting the number of NMEs is a source of measurement error.

Second, existing approaches assume that all new drugs within a therapeutic class have the same rate of technological diffusion. The pharmaceutical industry spends more on marketing and administration than on research and development (Sloan and Hsieh, Chapter 1; Reinhardt, Chapter 2). Major pharmaceutical manufactures in the United States spend about one-third of sales revenue on marketing (Reinhardt, Chapter 2). Further, marketing efforts by pharmaceutical firms are highly concentrated on drugs with larger potential market size (Berndt, Chapter 9). These findings, taken in combination, suggest that rates of technological diffusion across different types of drugs depend on market size and marketing effort. For this reason, such indicators of technological change as the new drug prescriptions as a share of all prescriptions written by physicians and the average vintage of drugs consumed by patients are also subject to measurement error.

In this chapter we adopt the first approach to quantify the amount of pharmaceutical innovation. Although this approach ignores the quality of innovations, the use of Taiwanese data provides an advantage over the existing studies. As mentioned above, Taiwan is a user rather than an innovator of new drugs. Thus, all drugs with NMEs are imported. As a small open economy, NMEs introduced into Taiwan come from various countries, including the United States, Japan, and European countries. In this sense, our measure of innovation represents the adoption of new technology.

III. Data and Methods

Data

Data for this study came from two sources: (1) IMS Health Taiwan for data on NMEs and (2) the Department of Health in Taiwan for data from death certificates. The IMS Health Taiwan database tracked new drugs introduced in Taiwan between 1985 and 2002. Each record contained the following information: year the product was launched in Taiwan, the active ingredient(s) of the product (molecule), and its anatomical therapeutic chemical (ATC) classification. Death certificate data provided information on demographic characteristics of the deceased, cause of death in ICD-9 codes, and date of death.

The first level of the ATC classification system divided all drugs into 14 categories, representing the anatomical main groups (World Health Organization Collaborating Center for Statistics Methodology 2004), for example, alimentary tract and metabolism (Group A), blood and blood-forming organs (Group B), and the cardiovascular system (Group C). The first level of the ATC corresponds closely to the ninth version of the International Classification of Diseases (ICD-9) (Table 13.1). Like Lichtenberg (2005b), we used the correspondence between the drug classification system (the ATC system) and ICD-9 categories to merge the above two data sets. We excluded external causes of death from our analysis since our main objective was to empirically examine effects of new drugs on health outcomes. We also excluded the disease classes rarely associated with death, such as diseases of the ear and mastoid process (i.e., Groups H and S of the ATC classification system). Our final analytical sample consisted of panel data with 10 disease/therapeutic categories for 1985–2002 (Table 13.1).

Pharmaceutical Innovations

We used the cumulative number of drugs with NMEs approved and launched in Taiwan to measure pharmaceutical innovations. The annual number of NMEs introduced into Taiwan between 1985 and 2002 followed cyclic patterns (Fig. 13.1). In 1985, 95 NMEs were introduced in this market. This number decreased to 52 and 49 in the next two years, but increased subsequently. In 1995 only 15 NMEs were introduced, possibly reflecting delays in approvals caused by the transition from the then-existing health care financing system to national health insurance in Taiwan in that year.[3]

In spite of intertemporal differences in the number of NMEs introduced, the cumulative number of NMEs launched in Taiwan increased steadily. Between 1985 and 2002, 821 NMEs were introduced in Taiwan (Fig. 13.2). On average, nearly 46 NMEs were introduced into Taiwan's market annually.[4] The three largest therapeutic categories were alimentary tract and metabolism, cardiovascular system, and nervous system, each

Table 13.1. *Link between Anatomical Therapeutic Chemical (ATC) code and ICD-9-CM code*

1st-level ATC code	Description	ICD-9-CM	Disease class
A	Alimentary tract and metabolism	520–579	Diseases of the digestive system
		240–279	Endocrine, nutritional, and metabolic diseases
B	Blood and blood-forming organs	280–289	Diseases of the blood and blood-forming organs and certain disorders involving the immune mechanism
C	Cardiovascular system	390–459	Diseases of the circulatory system
D	Dermatologicals	680–709	Diseases of the skin and subcutaneous tissue
G	Genitourinary system and sex hormones	580–629	Diseases of the genitourinary system
J & P	Anti-infectives for systemic use Antiparasitic products, insecticides, and repellent	001–139	Certain infectious and parasitic diseases
L	Antineoplastic and immunomodulating agents	140–239	Neoplasms
M	Musculoskeletal system	710–739	Diseases of the musculoskeletal system and connective tissue
N	Central nervous system (CNS)	290–319	Mental and behavioral disorders
		320–359	Diseases of the nervous system
R	Respiratory system	460–519	Diseases of the respiratory system

Source: Lichtenberg (2005b), p. 58; ICD-9-CM codes were modified by authors.

accounting for approximately 14% of the new drugs (Fig. 13.3). Anti-infectives for systemic use, antiparasitic products, insecticides, and repellents taken together account for 15% of the new drugs, and the shares of the other groups range from 5% to 8%.

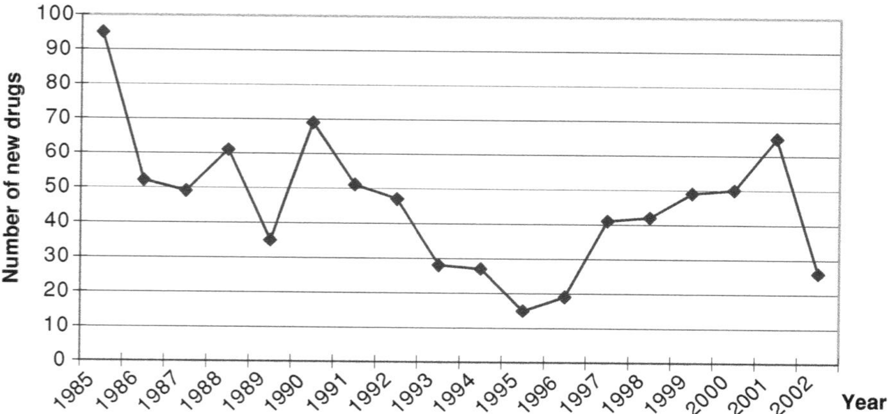

Figure 13.1. Annual number of NMEs introduced into Taiwan's pharmaceutical market, 1985–2002.

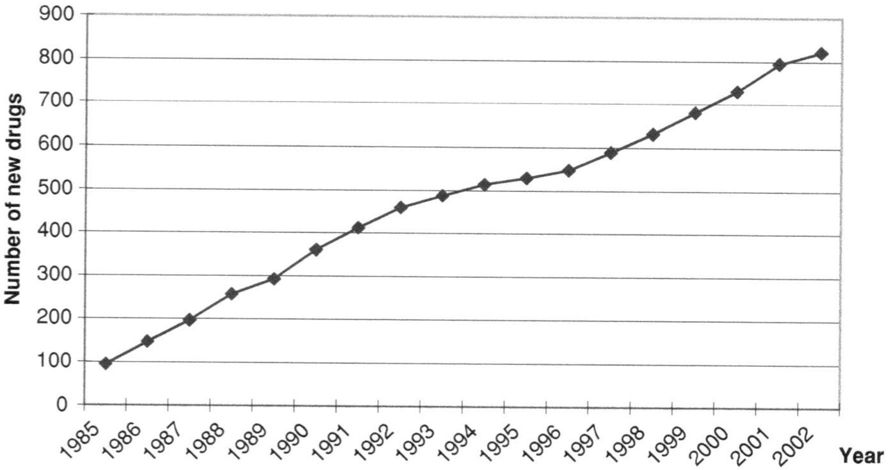

Figure 13.2. Cumulative number of NMEs in Taiwan, 1985–2002.

Health Outcomes

The intertemporal (annual) and cross-sectional (therapeutic classes) variation in the cumulative number of drugs with NMEs allowed us to evaluate the contribution of pharmaceutical innovation to health outcomes empirically. Specifically, we explored whether greater improvements in health outcomes were realized for those diseases for which the stock of innovative drugs

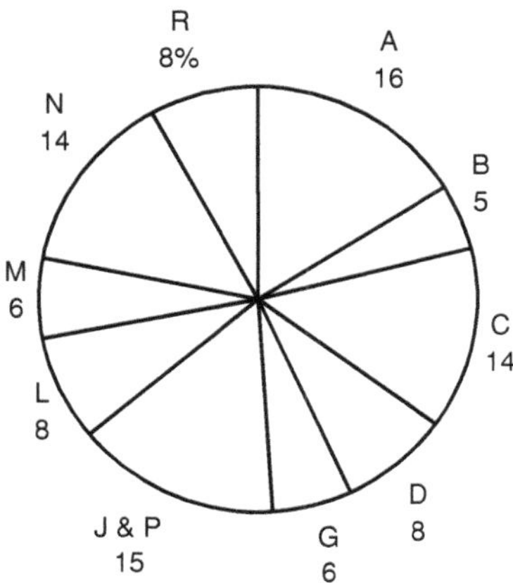

Figure 13.3. Frequency distribution of NMEs in Taiwan's pharmaceutical market, 1985–2002 (%).

increased more rapidly. For this purpose, it was necessary to have disease-specific health outcome measures.

Although life expectancy is the best available general measure of health outcomes, no life tables exist by disease. We constructed an alternative measure of disease-specific life expectancy by computing the proportion of deaths that occurred above certain ages, such as 65, using data on deaths by disease category from a time series of mortality data obtained from the Department of Health in Taiwan.[5]

This measure is likely to be a reasonable proxy for disease-specific health outcomes for two reasons. First, the proportion of deaths occurring above a certain age can be interpreted as the probability of survival until that age, for example, age 65 (Lichtenberg 2005b). Second, there is a statistically positive relationship between life expectancy at birth and the proportion of deaths occurring above a specific age, based on comparisons of time series data within a country or cross-sectional data across countries. For example, with life expectancy at birth on the vertical axis and the proportion of deaths occurring above age 65 for the whole population at the horizontal axis using time series data from Taiwan for 1971–2002, there is a significantly positive relationship, for both males and females (Fig. 13.4). Life expectancy at birth increases as the age at death increases.

In Taiwan the ratio of deaths occurring above age 65 of total deaths for a category varied widely. In 1985 the ratio ranged from 33% for diseases of the nervous system to 70% for diseases of the respiratory system. In 2002 the corresponding ratios for these two categories increased

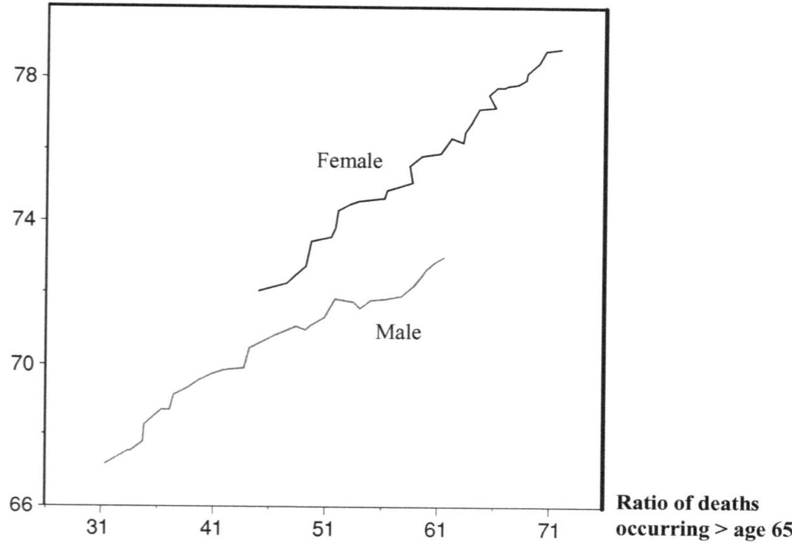

Figure 13.4. Relationship between life expectancy and ratio of deaths occurring above age 65, 1971–2002.

to 63% and 88%, respectively. Thus, in spite of variations among different disease groups, the probability of survival until age 65 increased for almost all disease groups, exceptions being diseases of the skin and subcutaneous tissue and diseases of the musculoskeletal system and connective tissue. This upward trend is also apparent from a comparison of the disease-specific health outcomes in 2002 with those in 1985 (Fig. 13.5). Each point represents a specific disease group. With the exception of the musculoskeletal system (disease Group M), every point in Figure 13.5 lies above the 45-degree line, implying an appreciable improvement in health outcomes during 1985–2002, but with considerable variation among disease groups.

Model Specification

Using the above measures for pharmaceutical innovation and health outcomes, we constructed panel data for disease-specific health outcomes and the cumulative number of NMEs for each disease category. We hypothesized that diseases associated with a higher rate of pharmaceutical innovations would experience greater improvements in health outcomes.

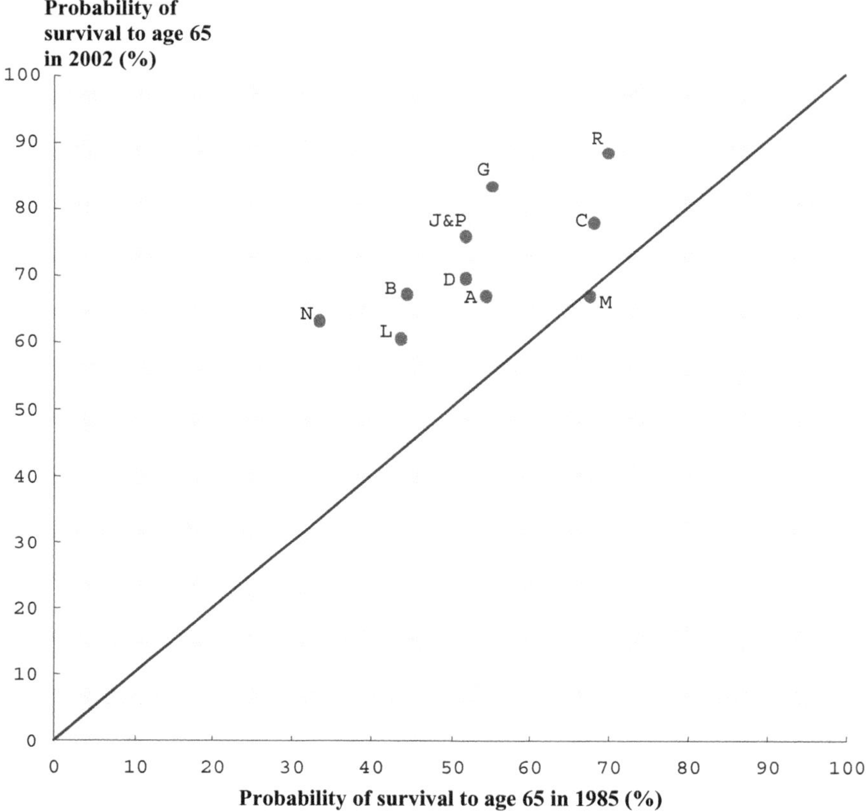

A: Alimentary tract and metabolism
B: Blood and blood-forming organs
C: Cardiovascular system
D: Dermatological
G: Genitourinary system and sex hormones
J & P: General anti-infectives, systemic; parasitology
L: Cytostatics
M: Musculoskeletal system
N: Central nervous system
R: Respiratory system

Figure 13.5. Probability of survival to age 65 in 2002 vs. in 1985, by disease category.

We acknowledge that other factors than pharmaceutical innovation may account for improved health outcomes. Omitting relevant explanatory variables may result in biased parameter estimates if the omitted variables are correlated with included explanatory variables. Since we used

Table 13.2. *Regression results in panel data models*

	Fixed-effect model			Random-effect model			Hausman test
Lag periods	β	t-Value	Overall R^2	γ	t-Value	Overall R^2	Probability > χ^2
0 (N= 180)	0.142	15.43	0.1571	0.141	15.43	0.1571	0.3078
1 (N= 170)	0.125	13.64	0.1359	0.124	13.64	0.1359	0.4291
2 (N= 160)	0.112	11.97	0.1179	0.111	11.97	0.1179	0.5160
3 (N= 150)	0.096	10.19	0.1004	0.096	10.20	0.1004	0.6294
4 (N= 140)	0.089	8.93	0.0903	0.088	8.94	0.0903	0.6828
5 (N= 130)	0.078	7.84	0.0844	0.078	7.87	0.0844	0.7790

Note: N indicates the number of observations.

disease-specific data in our analysis, we could use the fixed-effect and, alternatively, random-effect models to at least partly deal with the potential problem of omitted variables bias. Using fixed effects, we could at least control for time-invariant omitted variables. However, a shortcoming of fixed effects is that the estimated parameters may be inefficient. An alternative technique, which also yields consistent (unbiased) but more efficient estimates, is random effects. Fixed- and random-effect models as used in this study are of the general form:

$$\text{Fixed-effect model}: \ln(Y_{it}) = \alpha_i + \beta \ln(X_{i,t-k}) + \mu_{it} \quad (13.1)$$

$$\text{Random-effect model}: \ln(Y_{it}) = \alpha + \gamma \ln(X_{i,t-k}) + \mu_i + \varepsilon_{it} \quad (13.2)$$

where Y_{it} is the probability of survival to age 65 for disease group i at time t, $X_{i,t-k}$ is the cumulative number of NMEs launched since 1985 for disease group i at time $t-k$, and ε_{it} and μ_{it} are random error terms. Lagging the stock by k years allowed for a delay between the year in which drugs are introduced and the year during which the new drug affected health outcomes. We conducted Hausman tests to determine the model specification most appropriate for this analysis.[6]

IV. Results

Results based on both fixed effects and random effects, with P-values from the Hausman tests, are shown in Table 13.2. The Hausman tests indicated that, in this context, a random-effect framework was more appropriate.

Overall, increases in the stock of pharmaceutical innovation led to statistically significant improvements in health outcomes, which support our study hypothesis. Because both the dependent and explanatory variables were expressed in logarithms, the parameter estimates are elasticities: that

Table 13.3. *Regression results with mean household income and time trends*

	Fixed-effect model		Random-effect model	
Explanatory variable	1	2	1	2
Cumulative NME	0.090	0.075	0.086	0.073
	(3.29)	(3.23)	(3.27)	(3.22)
Mean household income	0.142	—	0.151	—
	(1.98)		(2.17)	
Time trend	—	0.008	—	0.008
		(3.07)		(3.22)
Constant	−2.691	−0.795	−2.797	−0.710
	(−3.06)	(−13.43)	(−3.26)	(−10.11)
Overall R^2	0.19	0.20	0.19	0.20

Note: Asymptotic *t*-statistics are in parentheses.

is, a 1% change in the explanatory variable (pharmaceutical innovation) leads to an x% change in the dependent variable (probability of survival) according to the size of the parameter estimate on the variable for pharmaceutical innovation. All estimates were statistically significant in the models with different period of lags, with the estimated coefficient decreasing as the lag duration lengthened.

Specifically, we found that a 10% increase in the stock of pharmaceutical innovation led to a 0.8–1.4% increase in the probability of survival to age 65. These results are consistent with findings in the recent literature that medical research in specific and technological change in medicine in general have a significant contribution to health outcomes (e.g., Cutler and McClellan 2001a, b; Murphy and Topel 2003b; Cutler 2004).

Parallel to the advance of pharmaceutical innovation, other determinants of health outcome may also change over time, such as income level and personal health care expenditures on other types of care. Because of the limitation of data sources, we are unable to construct the disease-specific data for health care expenditure and income. Rather, we use the average annual household income and time trend to control the influence of social and economic factors on health outcome. For simplicity, we assume that the health effect of pharmaceutical innovation occurs without lag when we extend our regression to include other explanatory variables.

As shown in Table 13.3, the pharmaceutical innovation remains to have significantly positive impact on the probability of survival to age 65 after controlling for the effect of economic and social trends. However, the magnitude of health gain attributed to the pharmaceutical innovation decreases about 40% when average household income or time trend is added into the regression model. The results indicate that a 10% increase in the stock of pharmaceutical innovation leads to a 0.8 to 0.9% increase in the probability of survival to age 65.

Although the lack of a disease-specific life table is an impediment to investigating a direct causal relationship between pharmaceutical innovation and life expectancy, we further explored this relationship with two alternative approaches. First, we used an indirect two-step approach to estimate the effect of pharmaceutical innovation on life expectancy at birth. That is, we first estimated the average effect of change in pharmaceutical innovation on the change in probability of survival to age 65 from a disease-specific panel database (as shown in Tables 13.2 and 13.3). We then estimated the mean effect of change in the probability of survival to 65 for the whole population on the change in life expectancy at birth using time series data. By multiplying these two estimates, we obtained the mean effect of change in pharmaceutical innovation on the change in life expectancy at birth.

Using data shown in Figure 13.4, we used ordinary least squares to estimate the effect of the probability of survival to age 65 on life expectancy at birth and found a significantly positive association between these two measures: a 10% increase in probability of survival to age 65 was associated with a 1.3% increase in life expectancy. This result, combined with the estimates in Tables 13.2 and 13.3, implies that a 10% increase in the stock of pharmaceutical innovation would lead to an increase in life expectancy at birth by 0.10% (i.e., 0.8% × 1.3%) to 0.18% (1.4% × 1.3%).

Second, one could directly estimate the effect of pharmaceutical innovation on life expectancy at birth by regressing life expectancy at birth on pharmaceutical innovation. Since we did not have disease-specific life expectancy tables, we used ordinary least squares with a variable for all NMEs introduced in Taiwan during 1985–2002, the explanatory variable, and with the dependent variable being life expectancy at birth. The disadvantage of this approach is that we had to rely on time series data with only 18 observations. With such a short time period, our regression results must be interpreted with caution. However, the advantage of this approach is that the life table data in Taiwan are available for males and females in 19 age groups. Thus, we could have different measures of the dependent variable in the regression model, and this in turn permitted us to assess whether the effect of pharmaceutical innovation on health outcome differs by age groups.

Table 13.4. *Estimates of life expectancy by age and gender*

Life expectancy age groups	Males			Females		
(yrs)	Estimate	Standard error	*t*-Value	Estimate	Standard error	*t*-Value
Birth	0.0139	0.0019	7.37	0.0194	0.0016	11.82
0–4	0.0100	0.0023	4.30	0.0153	0.0021	7.41
5–9	0.0142	0.0021	6.92	0.0199	0.0018	11.01
10–14	0.0146	0.0021	6.77	0.0211	0.0019	11.11
15–19	0.0152	0.0022	6.80	0.0226	0.0020	11.30
20–24	0.0153	0.0020	7.62	0.0243	0.0021	11.64
25–29	0.0155	0.0019	7.94	0.0259	0.0022	11.83
30–34	0.0163	0.0019	8.58	0.0281	0.0023	12.11
35–39	0.0289	0.0101	2.87	0.0305	0.0025	12.22
40–44	0.0212	0.0021	10.33	0.0377	0.0031	12.09
45–49	0.0241	0.0022	10.87	0.0338	0.0027	12.30
50–54	0.0269	0.0024	11.17	0.0417	0.0034	12.35
55- 59	0.0310	0.0024	12.69	0.0463	0.0038	12.31
60–64	0.0373	0.0027	13.49	0.0518	0.0044	11.71
65–69	0.0464	0.0036	12.97	0.0568	0.0051	11.22
70–74	0.0572	0.0047	12.13	0.0601	0.0057	10.58
75–79	0.0719	0.0074	9.71	0.0613	0.0064	9.38
80–84	0.0969	0.0137	7.06	0.0686	0.0083	8.24
85+	0.1667	0.0217	7.67	0.1100	0.0185	6.35

Table 13.4 reports the estimated effect of pharmaceutical innovations on life expectancy by gender and age. The elasticity of life expectancy at birth with respect to pharmaceutical innovation is 0.014 for males and 0.019 for females, implying that a 10% increase in the stock of pharmaceutical innovation would lead to an increase in the life expectancy at birth by 0.14% years for males and by 0.19% years for females. Although the results reported in Table 13.4 are very preliminary, these results closely resemble results obtained from an indirect approach.

Also, according to results presented in Table 13.4, the "productivity" of pharmaceutical innovation increased with age. For life expectancy at birth, the elasticity of pharmaceutical innovation was less than 0.02, but rose to 0.17 for the life expectancy of men at age 85 and over. This trend in estimated effects suggests that the marginal contribution of pharmaceutical innovations in prolonging life was higher for persons at higher ages. Moreover, the productivity of pharmaceutical innovation for females was greater than that for males until after age 75, at which point the pattern reversed.

V. Discussion

The research reported in this chapter has examined the association between pharmaceutical innovations and health outcomes, using the cumulative number of NME launches in Taiwan as a measure of innovations. Based on a disease-specific panel, we found a statistically significant, positive relationship between the stock of pharmaceutical innovation available in Taiwan's market and the probability of survival to age 65, after accounting for the economic and social trends. We investigated the effect of pharmaceutical innovation on life expectancy with two different approaches. Both approaches yielded similar results. Our low bound or conservative estimate suggests that a 10% increase in the stock of pharmaceutical innovation led to an increase in life expectancy at birth by about 0.1%.

We also found that the impact of pharmaceutical innovation on increased longevity was larger for the elderly than for younger persons. The productivity of pharmaceutical innovation was higher for females than for their male counterparts until age 75; for persons older than this, productivity of innovation was higher for men. This pattern suggests that pharmaceutical innovation may decrease the difference in life expectancy between men and women. On the other hand, the larger impact found in men aged 75 and above may be attributed to sample selection. That is, given a longer life expectancy among women, men who survived beyond the mean life expectancy for their gender may have been healthier than women in the same age range.

The research findings reported here, together with the existing literature reviewed here and in Chapter 12, increase our understanding of the benefit of pharmaceutical innovation as a whole. Compared to costs, benefits are more difficult to quantify because benefits are multiple-dimensional and are more variable over time. For these and possibly for other reasons as well, the existing literature provides more empirical documentation on the effects of pharmaceutical innovation on health care costs than on health benefits (e.g., Dubois et al. 2000; Addis and Magrini 2002; Morgan 2002; Duggan 2005). Our study adds a new insight on the benefits of pharmaceutical innovation and hence makes a contribution to balance the view on the benefits and costs of adopting new pharmaceutical products.

Specifically, our result provides an empirical basis for quantifying the contribution of pharmaceutical innovation to increase in life expectancy. As shown in Figure 13.2, the cumulative number of NME in Taiwan increased about 50%, from 548 in 1996 to 821 in 2002. Based on our study findings, this increase should have increased life expectancy by 0.5% (50 × 0.01). In 1996 life expectancies for males and females in Taiwan were 71.89 and 77.77, respectively (ROC Department of Health 2005). Thus, predicted longevity gains resulting from new drug launches were 0.36 (71.89 × 0.005) and 0.39 (77.77 × 0.005) years for males and females, respectively. During 1996–2002, the actual increase in life expectancy was 1.33 years for males and 1.17 years for females (ROC Department of Health 2005). We thus infer that new drug launches accounted for about 27% (0.36/1.33) to 33% (0.39/1.17) of the observed longevity gain in Taiwan. The mean annual increase in life expectancy of the Taiwanese population resulting from new drug launches was about three weeks (52 × 0.36/6), similar to the estimates by Lichtenberg (2005b).

Our results on benefits can be used with estimates of costs to calculate the incremental cost-effectiveness ratio (ICER). The ICER, which could be interpreted as cost per life year gained resulting from introduction of new drugs in this group of studies, provides a standard metric with which to compare the productivity of health care across different types of products and different countries. Thus, the calculation of ICER provides useful information for improving the efficiency of resource allocation in a country. In addition, international comparison of ICERs for the same product provides useful information for better understanding performance of health care systems in different countries.

For example, Lichtenberg (2005b) estimates that the ICER is about U.S. $6,750 (1997 dollars) for new drug launches in the OECD countries. By combining the benefit estimation reported in this chapter with the estimation on costs, Hsieh and Sloan (2006) find that the ICER for new drug launches in Taiwan is U.S.$1,704 (2003 dollars). As noted above, health benefits of new drugs launches in Taiwan are almost the same as in other countries, but the per capita expenditure spent on new drugs in Taiwan is lower than that for the mean of OECD countries used in Lichtenberg's calculations. One reason that Taiwan has a lower per capita expenditure in new drugs is that its government, as single payer, imposes price regulation on pharmaceuticals. Countries imposing the price regulation on pharmaceutical products capture a larger consumer surplus arising from pharmaceutical innovation and hence have a lower ICER. However, as noted by Danzon, Wang, and Wang (2005), earning a larger consumer surplus by regulatory force comes at a cost of the delay in launching a new drug.

There are several limitations in our study as well as in previous studies that have sought to quantify the health benefits of pharmaceutical innovation. First, we measured health outcomes only in terms of deaths averted. As documented by Cutler (2004) and others, pharmaceutical innovation may also increase quality of life and labor force productivity. For this reason, our study underestimates the contribution of pharmaceutical innovation to improved health outcomes.

Second, we may have overestimated the benefit of longevity gains resulting from the launches of new drugs given that the determinants of mortality reduction are very complex (Cutler, Deaton and Lleras-Muney 2006), and our analysis may not have sufficiently accounted for this complexity. Other factors, such as changes in life style and living environments, may also have important impacts on individuals' health. Although we partially controlled for these other factors with the fixed-effect and random-effect models, there may still be unobservable characteristics not accounted for in our analysis. In particular, Lichtenberg (2005b) noted that other technological advances other than in the pharmaceutical sphere may have co-occurred and were not explicitly captured by the analysis. Thus, the longevity gain resulting from new drug launches may be overestimated if the researcher simply uses the cumulative number of drugs approved with NMEs as a measure of pharmaceutical innovation. To correct the potential bias in quantifying benefits, Lichtenberg (2005b) and Hsieh and Sloan (2006) took only one-third of the estimated effect of new drugs on longevity gain to calculate the cost per life year gained from the launch of new drugs. This correction was based on the evidence that U.S. pharmaceutical R&D expenditure accounts for about one-third of national health R&D expenditure (Lichtenberg 2005b). Thus, it is plausible that the remaining two-thirds of the estimated effect of new drugs on longevity gain may be attributable to other medical innovations.

Third, we assumed that the productivity or quality of pharmaceutical innovation was homogeneous across disease/therapeutic groups. However, according to ratings of U.S. Food and Drug Administration, therapeutic advances varied significantly among NMEs. Such ratings were not available for Taiwan. Thus, we could not control the variation in the extent of innovativeness among NMEs in our study.

Fourth, this and other studies focusing on aggregate-level productivity present an average effect of pharmaceutical innovation on health outcomes. Although, in the aggregate, pharmaceutical innovation as a whole is beneficial relative to its costs, this does not imply that every new drug is cost effective. There is plausible considerable heterogeneity in health benefits among new drugs. The mean or average effect is not likely to be equal to the effect for any particular drug. Thus, an aggregate study like ours provides useful information on overall decision about resource allocation, but it is not a good information source for reimbursement decisions for individual drugs.

VI. Conclusion

This study used data obtained from Taiwan to estimate the impact of pharmaceutical innovation on health outcomes. Overall, our analysis provides evidence consistent with existing literature, namely, that pharmaceutical innovations have a significantly positive impact on life expectancy. Most of the pharmaceutical innovations that occurred during our study period were imported from other countries, such as the United States, Japan, and various European countries. In contrast to these countries, Taiwan, because of both its size and lower level of economic development than the countries where most pharmaceutical research and development is taking place, has limited capacity for such research and development. For an innovation to occur in Taiwan, not only must the drug be introduced in one of the large highly developed countries, but the new technology also must be adopted by Taiwan. Given the higher price of new drugs, there is considerable pressure against adoption. However, our finding on the positive association between pharmaceutical innovation and health suggests that not only is cost higher, but benefits are often likely to be high as well.

An important policy implication of our findings is that focusing on cost containment is not a wise strategy for health policy. Rather, as noted by Cutler (2004), the goal of health policy is on increasing the value of the system. To achieve this goal, the key policy challenge is setting the optimal balance between improving the health of the population and controlling the health care budget. In Chapter 11 Drummond indicates that more than 10 countries in the world have formally adopted economic evaluation research as an important input in reimbursement decisions. By contrast, Taiwan and several other countries reliant on price regulation of pharmaceutical products have not yet formally implemented this approach. Such evaluation represents a promising approach for boosting the value of public spending still further.

As emphasized by Reinhardt in Chapter 2, public investment on valuing pharmaceutical products is an important step toward balancing power between the demand and supply sides of pharmaceutical markets. A lesson from this and previous studies is that excluding new drugs to save money is likely to be unwise, but so is writing a blank check for all new drugs. Thus, careful, but expeditious, analysis of the costs versus benefits of individual new drugs before introduction represents a prudent course for public policy in this field.

FOURTEEN

Conclusions and Policy Implications

Frank A. Sloan and Chee-Ruey Hsieh

I. Introduction

This final chapter summarizes key findings and conclusions of the previous chapters and explores their policy implications. More specifically, we discuss eight policy issues that arise as governments seek to promote pharmaceutical innovation in their countries as well as to cope with the consequences of such innovation on public and private budgets, distinguishing between new innovations that are worth the extra cost from those that are not. The issues, which have implications for public decision making ranging from industrial to health policy, are (1) whether or not a country without a well-developed pharmaceutical sector can successfully promote developing such a sector with an industrial policy, (2) strategies for promoting pharmaceutical innovation, (3) incentives for development and production of vaccines, (4) public provision of information on pharmaceutical cost and effectiveness, (5) policies to promote competition in markets for pharmaceutical products, (6) differentials in prices of pharmaceutical products among countries, (7) health benefits of pharmaceuticals, and (8) how governments cope with pharmaceutical innovation.

II. Is an Industrial Policy Aimed at Promoting Development of a Pharmaceutical Industry Likely to Succeed?

Government policy makers wear two hats vis-à-vis the pharmaceutical sector: (1) seeking to promote economic growth by increasing national employment and income, key objectives of industrial policy, and (2) promoting personal health and life expectancy and averting the spread of pandemics, key objectives of health policy, the latter being more likely to succeed as a consequence of the widespread availability and use of innovative pharmaceutical products (Sloan and Hsieh, Chapter 1). Facing wage competition in the manufacturing sector from less well-developed countries, many newly industrialized countries seek to promote economic growth, using the pharmaceutical and biotech industries as means toward this end. The major technological advances such as those occurring in genomics have, if anything, made this path to economic growth even more attractive. However, the critics argue that the high R&D cost and knowledge capital in this industry, which may not be easily imported, constitute effective barriers to entry, making a public policy emphasis on developing local pharmaceutical and biotech industries inherently risky.

One trend that favors such as emphasis is that pharmaceutical R&D is no longer as monolithic as it once was (Comanor, Chapter 3). In recent years the research process in the pharmaceutical industry has become increasingly disintegrated. An increasing share of pharmaceutical research is being carried out in small biotechnology companies that limit their businesses to one or a small number of products. Increasingly, the major drug companies enter the process only at the development and testing phases. The structure of discovering and developing new drugs having shifted from highly integrated firms to a much more disintegrated process is allowing greater division of labor among firms that can be located in different countries. And once drugs have been developed, pharmaceutical products tend to have high value relative to weight and space required for shipment. Thus, transportation cost is less of a factor than in other industries, which manufacture heavier and bulkier products. Given that location decisions of pharmaceutical research and development (R&D) are not driven by the distance to market, small firms in newly industrialized countries, including the less populous ones, increasingly have opportunities to participate in discovering and developing new drugs.

Nevertheless, the R&D process for pharmaceuticals is a lengthy and expensive one. The newly developed countries will not be able to make advances on their own, but rather in collaboration with firms in countries that have had leading roles in this sector historically.

One author (Reinhardt, Chapter 2) predicts that, over the next several decades, pharmaceutical research will increasingly shift from Europe and the United States to Asia, where many of these newly industrialized countries are located, as has manufacturing in many other industries, ranging from motor vehicles to electronics to computer software.

Overall, there is reason to be optimistic about the role of the local pharmaceutical firms as engines of economic growth. But for this to occur, to promote favorable climates for such firms, governments will have to forego public policies that restrict availability of innovative drugs to their populations, which in turn may have adverse consequences for health budgets (Sloan and Hsieh, Chapter 1). There is no such thing as a free lunch.

III. Strategies for Promoting Pharmaceutical Innovation

Although entrepreneurial opportunities in the pharmaceutical sector in quite a number of countries are, if anything, increasing, countries' specific strategies for promoting pharmaceutical R&D differ. The choice between strategies depends in part on market size, which reflects both the population with a particular disease and income levels in the country, especially among persons with the disease (Hollis, Chapter 4; Lichtenberg, Chapter 7). In countries with larger market sizes, market mechanisms often provide a sufficient base demand to provide adequate incentives for pharmaceutical R&D to occur without resorting to some form of government intervention. Therefore, it is generally preferable to rely on private firms that tend to be more efficient in discovering, developing, producing, and distributing pharmaceutical products than are public enterprises (Chapter 7). Further, public investment is likely to crowd out private investment.

By contrast, in countries with a small market size, domestic demand is likely to be insufficient to justify large private outlays for R&D. Pharmaceutical companies and equity flows available to such companies appear to be attracted to countries in which there is a sizable domestic market or, at least, public policies are favorable to the sale of pharmaceutical products. Thus, smaller countries, which inevitably have smaller domestic markets, tend not to be as well positioned to attract pharmaceutical companies and investment. In addition, such countries are more vulnerable to shortages in the event of national emergencies, such as pandemics. For this reason, some form of government intervention may be required, including government subsidy, public investment in pharmaceutical research, and even direct public production.

Two chapters (Hollis, Chapter 4; Maurer, Chapter 5) describe specifically how governmental agencies or international sponsors can use various forms of subsidy or rewards to promote pharmaceutical innovation. Hollis compares three proposals designed to stimulate private investment in pharmaceutical R&D for effective treatments for heretofore neglected diseases. After considering the pros and cons of several alternative payment arrangements, he concludes that the Optional Reward system, in which the sponsoring agency would pay rewards annually based on the therapeutic effectiveness of drugs, is both a feasible and efficient approach. The Optional

Reward system makes profitability of a drug innovation dependent on therapeutic impacts rather than on consumer ability to pay. Thus, this payment plan provides an incentive to guide R&D resources into drugs that have large health impacts rather than products demanded by relatively affluent persons.

Success of any payment plan lies in the details of implementation, such as whether the measures of treatment effects are valid and reliable, and whether the commitment of payment for innovative drugs is regarded as credible by the firms that do the investing (Sloan and Eesley, Chapter 6; Drummond, Chapter 11). Several countries have adopted a system of economic evaluation to measure the effectiveness of drugs (Chapter 11). In Chapter 10 Pauly is critical of how drug cost is typically measured in cost-effectiveness analysis. This chapter clearly shows that there is ample room for further refinement of existing methodologies. Although the methodologies have shortcomings and many practical issues remain, international experience suggests that the policy on measuring therapeutic effect has proved workable, and, to date, no country formally adopting economic evaluation has abandoned the policy. Much of the opposition to formal evaluations of medical technologies probably reflects the business interests of enterprises that seek to avoid scrutiny rather than a serious analysis of the methodological approaches being used (see Reinhardt, Chapter 2).

There will be learning by doing. Some mistakes must be made for progress against some major diseases to be realized. Various proposals for making payment a function of both therapeutic impact and the number of persons affected should be implemented. We are not persuaded by the argument that such ideas such as the Optional Reward system "are untested." Many implementation issues remain to be resolved (Sloan and Eesley, Chapter 6). Yet to use this excuse for lack of attention to incentives will only lead to loss from disease, disability, and death that pharmaceutical innovations could avert. In the end, the issue is whether governments and the world community more generally have the willingness to incur the cost of investments in the more immediate future to be able to enjoy a substantial return in the more distant future.

IV. The Special Case of Vaccines

In contrast to pharmaceuticals in general, the market for vaccines is small, despite the fact that a sizeable part of the gains in health and longevity realized during the twentieth century are attributable to introduction of new vaccines (Sloan and Eesley, Chapter 6). Unlike drugs to treat most chronic diseases, most vaccines aim to prevent infections. Thus, there are clear external benefits in consumption of vaccines, which are not taken into consideration when a person decides to be vaccinated. Absent some form of government intervention in the market for vaccines, consumption of vaccines will be less than socially optimal.

The market for vaccines is not working well currently. In recent years shortages of vaccines have occurred with alarming frequency. Moreover, there is a widespread view among the experts that existing levels of investment in vaccine R&D are insufficient to exploit the many opportunities that exist for vaccine innovation that could save millions of lives as well as reduce losses from morbidity that could potentially be averted. Concerns about insufficient investment and ultimately suboptimal levels of vaccine production have led to two major proposals, which represent substantial departures from current practice: (1) policies to encourage entry of nonprofit vaccine manufacturers and (2) new financial incentives to elicit innovative activity.

The rationale for substituting nonprofit for for-profit enterprise is that nonprofit organizations' decisions may tend to be more responsive to social objectives than those of their private counterparts. New financial incentives may be desirable because persistent shortages and lack of innovation in vaccines seem to reflect the lack of a profit incentive to make investments in vaccine R&D currently. The possibility that financial incentives may be inadequate is taken as almost an article of faith by economists in markets in which persistent shortages occur. In the vaccine market, it is quite clear that vaccines are less profitable than most drugs (Lichtenberg, Chapter 7). Low profits may be expected to affect output and hence raise the probability of shortages, as well as reduce vaccine R&D in the short run; in the longer run, low profitability should lead to lower rates of product innovation.

Previous analysis of vaccine policy has distinguished between "pull" policies that stimulate innovation by increasing demand for vaccines and "push" policies that accomplish this objective by shifting the supply of vaccine curve to the right (Kremer and Glennester 2004; Chapters 4–6). Hollis (Chapter 4) and Maurer (Chapter 5) discuss how government or international sponsors can use various forms of subsidy or reward to promote pharmaceutical innovation for neglected diseases, which are pull policies.

Such policies face potential opposition from various camps. In the United States, a proposal for advanced purchase of vaccines coupled with a mandate that vaccines with high potential benefit be covered faced substantial opposition from three sources: (1) from the U.S. pharmaceutical industry, which seems to have feared that the plan would lead to price controls in a country lacking price regulation of pharmaceuticals; (2) from insurance companies, which contended that a mandate funded with public dollars would in the end not receive public monies, that is, become an unfunded mandate; and (3) from a government agency, which preferred a program with its direct involvement to one in which much of the decision making remained in the private sector (Sloan and Eesley, Chapter 6). Much of the opposition reflected the importance of the private sector in financing and provision of personal health care services in the United States. But this is the largest single market for health care in the world. If a pull policy applied to one country is to succeed, it is likely to succeed in the United States. Multicountry pull policies, especially those involving provision of vaccines in developing countries, will be highly reliant on private philanthropy as they are currently. By contrast, single smaller newly industrialized countries have reason to place relative emphasis on push policies.

The last few decades have witnessed the spread of new viruses, most notably HIV/AIDS and, to a much lesser extent, SARS. The prospect of a bird flu pandemic looms on the horizon. In the event of a pandemic, developed countries may possess only sufficient capacity to produce vaccines for domestic use. To ensure an adequate domestic supply, governments may restrict exports of vaccines by private manufacturers. Restrictions on export of vaccines would in turn create shortages in other countries, particularly those without ample domestic vaccine capacity. This threat, in spite of the empirical evidence indicating that private enterprises are relatively efficient on average (Lichtenberg, Chapter 7), may justify sponsoring public enterprises for vaccine manufacturing in countries with small domestic markets.

Ironically, while vaccines in general have had difficulty attracting public funding, the threat of bioterrorism following the attack on the United States on September 11, 2001, has led to rapid and large-scale increases in funding for vaccines to counter such threats. In the United States, the desire to increase funding led to the implementation of some questionable policies, which are described by Maurer in Chapter 5.

V. Public Provision on Pharmaceutical Information

There is ample support for the notion that innovation rates are greater when market forces are allowed to operate. However, a prerequisite for a competitive market to function is adequate consumer knowledge. In this market for pharmaceutical products, physicians function as agents for their patients (Sloan and Hsieh, Chapter 1). But even physicians may have difficulty in gauging the value of specific drugs in absolute terms and relative to their cost. The rapid pace of technological change in this sector has led to entry of many new drugs each year. Information on whether the quality of a new product exceeds an old one in its therapeutic class on average is often lacking. As of the 1990s, objective head-to-head comparisons have been few (Sloan, Whetten-Goldstein, and Wilson 1997). One reason for the lack of such comparisons is that they are not typically required by public regulatory authorities. Long-term effects, either favorable or adverse, cannot be known from randomized controlled trials that precede regulatory approval. Additional applications of the new are often discovered in practice. Heterogeneity among individual patients in the beneficial effects and adverse side effects only complicates the information problem, and some amount of individualized learning on the part of patients and their physicians occurs (see Crawford and Shum [2005] for analysis of learning in the context of drugs and Ackerberg [2003] for analysis of learning in the cost of food consumption) but can be costly in terms of health and use of health care resources.

The lack of information on quality as it applies to groups of consumers reduces the effectiveness of market mechanisms in ensuring that the most valuable drugs command the highest prices, that is, that high quality receives financial rewards. Because of a lack of good comparative information on drug quality, demand-side constraints in pharmaceutical markets are insufficiently effective currently (Reinhardt, Chapter 2), which has led a few countries to implement formal public economic evaluation processes (Drummond, Chapter 11).

One issue is that if consumers are ill-informed that effective products exist for treating a disease that they have, they will not seek treatment and will forego some potentially valuable therapies. One potential source of information in two countries, the United States and New Zealand, is direct-to-consumer advertising (DTCA) of prescription drugs. In Chapter 9 Berndt provides a comprehensive review of evidence on DTCA, finding that, in general, DTCA has focused on those diseases for which the market for the pharmaceutical product is large relative to the actual market, for those drugs for which the United States Food and Drug Administration has assigned a "priority" status. DTCA typically describes a disease and then the product of the sponsor used to treat the disease. Thus, DTCA can have two potential effects, first, to increase the demand for all drugs in the therapeutic class of drugs used to treat the disease and, second, to increase the market share of the advertised product within the class. Both nonexperimental and experimental studies reveal that while DTCA increases the size of the overall sales of a particular therapeutic class, brand-specific DTCA does not have a statistically significant impact on the share of any particular brand within the therapeutic class.

The evidence to date thus suggests that as an instrument promoting public health, DTCA has considerable potential, particularly in mitigating undertreatment of important illnesses, for example, major depressive disorders, by increasing consumer awareness of these illnesses and the fact that some effective therapies exist. It can also result in inappropriate utilization of drugs, not only possibly exposing patients to health risks, but also by increasing demand for expensive drugs for treatment of conditions that could be adequately or even equally well treated with less expensive products. As with other forms of advertising, DTCA both informs and persuades. Its effects on consumer welfare are complex and ambiguous. Regulating the communication content of advertisements and other promotions that attempt to balance information on risks and benefits is inherently very difficult and challenging, particularly since consumers plausibly differ in their abilities to process such information. And such ability probably varies over the life course. Our knowledge of consumer drug-information-processing ability is lacking.

In addition to DTCA, payers, physicians, and some consumers may learn information on prescription drugs from the studies of the cost effectiveness of pharmaceuticals. However, up to now, the majority of studies on cost effectiveness of pharmaceutical products are funded by and conducted on behalf of pharmaceutical firms; particularly since negative findings may not be made public, such studies may not merit the trust of the medical community, payers, and the public more generally. For this reason, a case may be made for public provision of information on the cost effectiveness of drugs (Reinhardt, Chapter 2). Unbiased information on pharmaceuticals, both existing and newly introduced, is a public good and therefore is likely to be undersupplied by the private sector. Although the methodologies of cost-effectiveness and cost-benefit analysis are by no means perfect (see Pauly, Chapter 10), as already noted, there is ample evidence from the experience in several countries that such evaluations are workable as guides for pharmaceutical policy (Drummond, Chapter 11).

In Chapter 11 Drummond offers specific suggestions to countries that have used cost-effectiveness and cost-benefit approaches in the context of pharmaceutical decision making as well as those that are considering using these approaches. For countries using these approaches, he urges that the decision-making process be made as transparent to interested outsiders as possible. Also, sound and independent analysis realistically requires a commitment of resources. To not make such a commitment would result in undue reliance on pharmaceutical companies for information. For countries that are considering using these approaches, it is important to learn from the experiences of those countries that have been conducting such economic evaluations of pharmaceuticals for several years.

In Chapter 2 Reinhardt suggests establishing nonprofit PharmacoEconomics Research Institutes (PERIs), as opposed to government-run organizations, to produce systematic information on the relative cost effectiveness of rival pharmaceutical products. Individual countries may benefit from information, whether or not they contribute to the information dissemination process. For this reason, the feasibility of multicountry efforts is worth exploring.

VI. Price Competition and Incentives to Innovate

The patent system is a double-edge sword (Chapters 4–6). On the one hand, by conferring market power on the innovator, patents provide a financial incentive for firms to invest in R&D that would not exist under competitive conditions. On the other hand, at least in the absence of externalities, competition has the desirable property of forcing price to marginal cost of production and consumption levels to the point at which the marginal benefit of consumption equals the marginal cost of producing and distributing the good or service, which is the socially optimal level of consumption. By establishing entry barriers, patents lead to higher prices and lower use than would prevail under competition. After patent expiration, products chemically equivalent to the formerly patented drug can enter the market.

In Chapter 8 Grabowski provides a comprehensive review of the experience of the generic industry in the United States. Although the U.S. experience is somewhat idiosyncratic in that health systems and legal contexts differ between it and those of other countries, the U.S. experience does offer some lessons for other countries.

In the United States, the mean effective patent life for new drugs is about 12 years since the 17-year statutory patent life tolls before drugs are approved by the FDA. After patents expire, generic drugs enter the market and prices fall toward marginal cost as the number of generic competitors increases. The Hatch-Waxman Act, passed by the U.S. Congress in 1984, and the rise of managed care in general and managed care formularies in particular in the 1990s have been two key drivers of the growth of the generic drug industry in the United States. Since generics now account for over 50% of prescriptions in the United States, savings from generic substitution for brand-name products have been substantial. Although generic competition drives out economic profits on brand-name products post patent expiration, rather than rest on their laurels, such competition forces brand-name pharmaceutical manufacturers to invest in new products and maintain a healthy pipeline of products under development. For this reason, pharmaceutical R&D has continued to grow at a substantial rate in the United States since the passage of the 1984 Act, which was designed to promote use of generics. This evidence, in combination with Chapter 8's review of the international experience in generic competition, suggests that generic competition per se does not necessarily hurt the pharmaceutical innovation and may even increase it.

VII. Price Differentials between Countries

Pharmaceutical R&D is clearly an international public good since its output has made and can make a potential to make significant contribution to human health around the world in the future. However, there are major disparities between countries in their ability to pay for pharmaceuticals and other medical technologies. The potential system implicitly assumes that lives of poor persons around the globe are worth little (see Maurer, Chapter 5). While generics make effective drugs available to patients in low- and middle-income countries that cannot afford branded products, they do so with a lag. How best to share the cost of pharmaceutical R&D and of drugs more generally is one of the most pressing issues in global health policy.

Even between high-income countries, there are appreciable differences in prices of pharmaceutical products (Danzon and Furukawa 2003). Such differentials have led to some price arbitrage as occurs with parallel imports: for example, manufacturers in Country A, with high retail prices for pharmaceutical products, exports to Country B these products with lower prices because of government regulation of the prices of such products or price discrimination, and Country B in turn exports to Country A but at the prices of Country B.

There are two sides to the controversy over parallel imports. Aside from the arguments that parallel imports pose risks to patient safety in the importing countries, a concern that should be highly dependent on which country is the exporter, one side argues that such arbitrage reflects regulatory policy in Country B and provides an important disincentive for private investment in pharmaceutical R&D. On the other hand, there is the argument that high prices in Country A discourage consumption of new products in such countries and, moreover, that it is unfair for patients in such countries to bear a disproportionate share of the cost of pharmaceutical R&D, allowing patients in Country B and other countries without a major pharmaceutical manufacturing presence to free ride on the citizens of countries like Country A. As a result, price differentials of pharmaceutical products between countries often become the source of friction in international relations.

Prices of brand-name pharmaceuticals do not reflect marginal cost, but rather reflect a combination of ability to pay, regulatory policy, and bargaining power of purchasers of drugs (see, e.g., Berndt 2002; Reinhardt, Chapter 2; Grabowski, Chapter 8). Pharmaceutical manufacturers engage in price discrimination. Although objectionable to many on equity grounds, in terms of economic efficiency, price discrimination may lead to improvements in the allocation of goods and services under certain circumstances, that is, when the alternative is sales at a single monopoly price. In countries where there is a substantial government or third-party payer payment for drugs, the buyers are likely to have considerable bargaining power relative to sellers of drugs. By contrast, in countries where buyers have little or no market power, such as individual patients paying for their own drugs out of pocket, pharmaceutical firms with patent protection are likely to possess market power, and hence buyers will be charged the high retail drug prices.

In Chapter 2 Reinhardt raises several points that run counter to the thinking of many policy makers. First, using the threat of trade sanctions to force other countries to raise pharmaceutical prices will not necessarily increase total pharmaceutical R&D because pharmaceutical firms on average spend only about 13–14% of their revenue on R&D. Second, a lesson from the microeconomic theory of price-discrimination monopolies is that increases in other countries' prices will not necessary lead to a price decrease in the home country because the domestic price for a pharmaceutical product depends on the relative market power of sellers in the domestic market, not on the prices in foreign markets. Third, location decisions of pharmaceutical manufacturing facilities is determined not only by the country's prices for drugs, but by other factors as well, including availability and cost of scientific research personnel and government regulations directly affecting the R&D enterprise.

VIII. Health Benefits of Pharmaceuticals

The new structure of pharmaceutical research has not led to increased productivity or decreased costs, at least in terms of the number of new products introduced (Comanor, Chapter 3), although it may have influenced the therapeutic properties of the new drugs. The new structure for discovery and development of new pharmaceutical products has not improved efficiency if one measures R&D output by the number of new molecular entities. However, prescription drugs are potentially important inputs in the production of good health (Sloan and Hsieh, Chapter 1; Cremeiux et al., Chapter 12; Hsieh et al., Chapter 13). Thus, the efficiency of pharmaceutical research is more appropriately evaluated in terms of its contribution to improvements in health outcomes. Placed in perspective, technological change in the pharmaceutical sector is only one determinant of improvements in health and longevity. Over the past 160 years, the life expectancy of women in most countries with the highest levels of health care has improved by three months a year on average, an impressive rate of improvement by any standard (Oeppen and Vaupel 2002). Drugs, including the introduction of anti-infectives, have contributed to this increase, but much of the improvement predates the modern pharmaceutical era.

In Chapter 12 Cremieux and his coauthors, based on a systematic review of the empirical evidence, conclude that international and country-specific studies as well as analyses of individual diseases all indicate that, since about 1950, the period covered by their review, investments in pharmaceutical products have generally been worthwhile investments. With rates of return over 10 to 1 based on measures of increased life expectancy alone, not even considering improved quality of life, pharmaceutical research has successfully provided developed countries with better health at a cost that has been far exceeded by the value of improved longevity. Not considering the value of improvements in quality of life, such as from reductions in pain, emotional health, and symptoms from short-term illnesses, should lead to a substantial underestimate of the value of health.

In Chapter 13 Hsieh and his coauthors reinforce this conclusion by specifically focusing on the role of new drug introduction on health outcomes. Using the cumulative number of new molecular entity launches in Taiwan as a measure of innovations, they find a significantly positive relationship between the stock of pharmaceutical innovation available in Taiwan's market and the probability of survival to age 65, after accounting for the economic and social trends. The positive association between the adoption of pharmaceutical innovation and health suggests that excluding new drugs to save money is likely to be unwise. Although the adoption of new drugs often increases health care spending, the empirical evidence indicates that their benefits are likely to be high as well. This, however, does not mean that all new technologies are equally beneficial relative to their costs. Clearly, careful, but expeditious, analysis of the costs versus benefits of new drugs before drug introduction is warranted.

In sum, in Chapters 12 and 13, this book, in combination with previous research by others, such as Murphy and Topel (2003), Cutler (2004), and Lichtenberg (2004b), provides systematic evidence that pharmaceutical spending in general and introduction of new drugs in particular have a significantly positive impact on life expectancy. An increase in access to new drugs can provide a valuable contribution to the improvement of population health. Cast in less positive language, this result also implies that the difference in the access to new drugs between countries or between population groups within countries will increase already sizeable disparities in population health and longevity.

Two chapters in our book (Pauly, Chapter 10; Drummond, Chapter 11) add to an existing economic literature that has attempted to quantify the monetary value of observed gains in longevity. Overall, this research concludes that the economic value of increases in longevity over the last half century is about as large as the value of measured growth in nonhealth goods and services (Nordhaus 2003). The value of improved health and longevity does not appear in accounts of national income. To adjust for this, Becker, Phillipson, and Soares (2005) added the monetary gain from increases in longevity to Gross Domestic Product and termed the sum "national full income." Their empirical analysis revealed that during the period 1965–1995 world inequality in income, as measured by GDP per capita, increased as technological change and innovation became the major engine of economic growth. However, world inequality in full income, the sum of GDP and monetary value of longevity gain, decreased during this period. Their result suggests that investment in health is an important vehicle for closing the gap of world inequality between countries, but of course, historical relationships may not hold in the future, especially if the fruits of R&D are not widely available.

IX. Coping with Pharmaceutical Innovation

Along with the prospect of improved health and longevity come increases in spending, both private and public, with the private-public mix highly dependent on the health care financing system in the country. There are pressures on public budgets and to some extent on private budgets from the aging of populations, especially in high-income countries, that will occur, irrespective of the pace of technological change in the pharmaceutical sector. In theory, people should be willing to pay for favorable outcomes, but the cost of raising public funds is far from negligible.

The benefits of some drugs, such as those to control hypertension or cholesterol, have effects only over decades, a time horizon far longer than that of elected officials who face higher health care costs but not some additional benefits over the "run" that is most relevant to them.

In countries highly reliant on private-sector financing such as the United States, even if employees ultimately pay for most or even all of the cost of employer-provided health benefits (Pauly 1998), adjustments in wage compensation to rapid increases in outlays for health benefits may take years to achieve, with disemployment being the predominant response in the short run. Also, in the United States, persons uninsured for pharmaceutical expenses do not have any bargaining power vis-à-vis the companies and must pay list prices.

Residents of countries in which prevailing prices of pharmaceuticals are high will probably have to wait some time, if ever, before countries with lower prices are willing to raise prices to bear a larger proportion of global pharmaceutical R&D cost. Similarly, the prospect of countries joining together to provide Advanced Purchase Commitments for innovative drugs to be developed is indeed in the far distant future. Books such as ours serve a role in communicating the potential benefits from such arrangements, but realistically actual implementation is at best likely to occur only in the far distant future. In the more immediate time horizon, it is important that public policies not inadvertently harm an innovative industry.

Countries differ appreciably in having centralized command-and-control policies on the one hand and relying on decentralized market mechanisms on the other. The latter approach seems more consistent with promoting innovation and perhaps less consistent with cost control and achieving equity in access to health care. In the latter types of countries, where government controls of pricing have been weak or nonexistent, it will be important for governments to truly implement pro-competitive policies that include a combination of better information provision and patient cost sharing, either through copays or reference pricing (Reinhardt, Chapter 2), coupled with a stop loss to protect families against catastrophic out-of-pocket expense. Just paying lip service to the value of free markets but allowing demand to grow in an unconstrained fashion would likely lead to unacceptable increases in expense and poor allocations of scarce resources. Conversely, those countries with stringent controls on prices will both reduce the rate of productive innovation worldwide below what it would be in the absence of such controls and, in terms of more narrow self-interest, deny access of their populations to recent and important innovations.

A more balanced approach is to balance the added cost burden against the benefits of the new drugs. Because some health benefits accrue long after the added costs are incurred, there is admittedly a conflict between the time horizon of an elected official, which may be from two to eight years, and the time horizon over which innovative drugs may have their full effects.

X. Limitations and Extensions

All of the chapters in this book focus on experiences of high-income countries or propose public policies most relevant for pharmaceutical policy in such countries. To date, virtually all pharmaceutical innovation has occurred in such countries. This may be changing as such large countries as India and China achieve economic development. Furthermore, the major part of the world population lives in countries with middle or low per capita incomes. In many low-income countries in particular, such communicable diseases as HIV/AIDS, tuberculosis, and malaria are major causes of death and disability. And when and if such diseases are conquered, the chronic diseases that plague more affluent countries, such as cardiovascular disease and cancer, will become more dominant in these countries as well. Given the populations of these countries, even today, these diseases are already major burdens.

For low- and middle-income countries, lack of access to many existing pharmaceutical products is more pressing than lack of access to products to be developed in the future (Hollis, Chapter 4). Yet there is no effective vaccine to prevent HIV/AIDS or malaria. Vaccines for these diseases would have very large health benefits. At present, resources for R&D on such vaccines must compete with very large markets for other products that potentially represent improvements on existing therapies available to persons in high-income countries. The problem of lack of ability to pay for important discoveries of potential benefit to populations in low- and middle-income countries has been well noted. Practical solutions are lacking.

While this book has emphasized innovation in pharmaceuticals, there are many other inputs in the production of good health, including other medical interventions. In reducing the burden of cancer for example, innovations include new methods of preventing, detecting, and treating cancers and of providing palliation in the event that the treatment was not successful. Pharmaceuticals provide important roles, but so do imaging, surgery, radiotherapy, and organizational innovations that improve the productivity of resources employed in cancer care. To improve health and increase longevity and to reduce the burden of illness that does occur, technological improvements are needed on all fronts. In providing incentives for pharmaceutical innovation, it is appropriate to consider incentives for the other technologies as well. Often emphasis should be on other types of innovation, not, or not just, pharmaceutical innovations. The settings in which the other types of innovation occur are different, as are the players. Thus, incentives appropriate for promoting the other types of innovation may differ as well. Research on innovation of these other technologies would clearly be worthwhile.

Our understanding of practical implementation issues is inadequate currently. Such issues encompass (1) a better understanding of how the path for financial incentives translates into actual investments in R&D;

(2) learning about how patients and their physicians make choices about drugs and compliance with drug regimens, including how they process information about drug characteristics; (3) studying the processes according to which organizations make drug formulary decisions, the information they use in making such decisions, and interventions that might be effective in promoting more cost-effective decisions about pharmaceuticals; and (4) further investigations of how cost-effectiveness and cost-benefit analysis of pharmaceuticals really works in countries that use these approaches, leading to recommendations about how the decision-making process could be even more effective than it is currently, building on incidence presented in a symposium issue in the 1990s (Sloan and Grabowski 1997).

As such chapters as Chapter 10 by Pauly make clear, there is much room for redefining analytical approaches for assessing the costs and benefits of new pharmaceutical products. Such research should incorporate advances in other fields of economics, such as public and environmental economics.

Finally, such issues as the adequacy of information available to consumers about our pharmaceutical products should be part of a larger research agenda that involves improved understanding of the consumer's decision-making process, which reflects, among other factors, risk and time preferences, values of life extension and improved quality of life, as well as perceptions of risk and benefit. Thus, we urge research on the pharmaceutical industry to branch out and take advantage of developments in a variety of fields, such as marketing, sociology, psychology, and economics.

Likewise, some innovations in payment have been tested in other contexts, for example, "best entry prizes" in the context of chemical engineering (Maurer, Chapter 5). Such experiences provide potentially valuable evidence for the study of pharmaceutical innovation and policy.

Notes

Chapter 2. The Pharmaceutical Sector in Health Care

1. Although economists may think of their so-called economic welfare analysis as being rooted in individual preferences, in its application the benefit-cost analysis based on that welfare theory is inherently collectivist, evoking the image of a collective farm presided over by a benevolent dictator who seeks to practice the welfare calculus of Benthamite utilitarianism. In this connection, see Reinhardt (2001).

Chapter 3. The Economics of Research and Development in the Pharmaceutical Industry

1. The first therapeutic revolution that created the modern pharmaceutical industry is chronicled in Temin (1980), pp. 58–87.
2. Statement of Haskell J. Weinstein, Director of the Chest Hospital, Duarte, California, in Hearings, Part 18, p. 10243.
3. Industry critics argue that these organizations sacrifice their independence through such relationships. However, that charge presumes a more unbalanced relationship than is often the case.
4. By the end of the millennium, these companies included Amgen, Biogen, Chiron, Genentech, and Genzyme.
5. See Aghion and Tirole (1994) for a discussion of the underlying theoretical considerations.
6. Although Vernon and Gusin (1974) acknowledge the possibility of this factor, they reject it by reestimating one of their equations using data for the earlier period. However, these latter results are inconclusive.
7. These amounts describe worldwide research and development spending by member companies of the Pharmaceutical Research and Manufacturers of America and are expressed in constant 2002 dollars using the National Institutes of Health Biomedical R&D Price Deflator. See Cockburn (2004), p. 11.
8. For an interesting discussion of these issues, see Cockburn (2004).

Chapter 4. Drugs for Neglected Diseases

1. Even noncommunicable diseases have worse health impacts in low-income countries because of inadequate diagnosis and treatment, but their share of lost DALYs is not as high because communicable diseases are responsible for so many lost DALYs in low-income countries.
2. The inefficiency Spence was referring to is described by economists as the "deadweight loss" caused by pricing above the marginal cost of production. What this means is that consumers who value the product at above the cost of producing it may still not buy it because of the high price. There is a loss to society's aggregate welfare from this misallocation of resources.
3. Dennis Kucinich, Congressman from Ohio, introduced a bill in the U.S. Congress (Free Market Drug Act of 2004, 108th Session, HR 5155) proposing a method for allowing government to participate in drug commercialization. His approach involves funding several institutes, which would compete for government funds and which, if they failed to deliver useful medicines, would be terminated. The idea is to allow for competition for financing, rather than competition for market success, where the financing is determined by some measure of value created for consumers. The critical issue is whether there would likely be significant competition for institute funding from previously unfunded institutes: it would likely be very difficult for an unfunded organization to compete for funding against an already well-funded organization.
4. Federal Food, Drug, and Cosmetic Act.
5. Letter from Roy Widdus to Commission on Intellectual Property Rights, Innovation and Public Health: "(Hopefully) clarifying the discussion on 'advanced purchase commitments,' 'advanced market' mechanisms for early stage vaccines, and the IFFIm" (May 10, 2005).
6. There is limited evidence on the effectiveness of most drugs at the time they are introduced. For example, many drugs are granted marketing authorization based on surrogate endpoints, such as reduction in lipid levels, as the actual effects on health may take a very long time to be measured. The rewards authority would therefore have to make its best estimate as to the risk-benefit profile of the product, and would presumably update the reward level as new information became available.
7. In principle, the Advanced Purchase Commitment proposal can also use this approach, since if the subsidy paid by the sponsors is very large, it will attract more firms to compete to develop an eligible vaccine, thus dissipating the available profits. However, to the extent that vaccines are substitutes for each other, there may be a substantial increase in costs without an accompanying increase in therapeutic impact.
8. One of the criticisms raised against the Optional Reward plan is that the measurement of DALYs is imperfect. A system of Transferable Intellectual Property Rights avoids this criticism by replacing imperfect measurement with uninformed guesses as to therapeutic importance.

Chapter 5. When Patents Fail

1. Consistent with this challenge, I will focus on finding mechanisms that obtain the desired level of R&D at the lowest possible cost to sponsors. This focus on

cost containment is very different from analyses that argue on sound analytical grounds that the "best strategy" for sponsors would be to ignore possible overpayments and "err on the high side" (Institute of Medicine, p. 176). No matter how sound, such strategies are cold comfort to neglected disease sponsors trying to operate within straitened budgets. In this world of the second best, rigid cost containment lets sponsors do more with what they have.

2. Conceptually, the most convincing strategy would be for governments to announce a budget for new drugs and then destroy any unspent currency at the end of every year. Alternatively, sponsors could pay some fraction of current budgets into a reserve fund. The problem with these procedures is that they divert resources from current needs. Paying high prices for existing drugs yields present benefits while still encouraging industry to develop new products.
3. Commercial pharmaceutical companies frequently use pay-as-you-go strategies. Examples include buying R&D ideas from biotech companies ("external innovation") and paying outside contractors to conduct experiments and clinical trials. Some "virtual pharma" companies purchase almost all of their R&D from outside vendors (see Maurer [2005] for a detailed description.)
4. Examples include The Institute for One World Health, The Drugs for Neglected Diseases Initiative, and The Medicines for Malaria Venture.
5. An R&D production function would (by definition) pass through points corresponding to (a) current rich nation per-drug R&D costs, and (b) a hypothetical "bare bones" discovery program. In what follows, I discuss sponsors' ability to estimate these values from available evidence. McGuire's approach faces the additional difficulty that production functions depend on institutional choices. For example, a production function for patent-driven research must include the effects of intrafirm racing and duplication (Kitch 1977). Applying this function to grant- or contract-based research could prove misleading.
6. Like all incentive mechanisms, contract R&D has strengths as well as weaknesses. I argue below that the benefits outweigh drawbacks for preclinical and human trials. These programs reportedly account for three-quarters of all drug development costs (Global Alliance 2001).
7. In principle, sponsors can slowly raise the reward over time as long as growth does not substantially exceed normal corporate rates of return (Kremer and Glennerster 2004). Unfortunately, this process takes a long time. Depending on how fast R&D costs rise, sponsors could wait 10 to 20 years before R&D started. In some scenarios, R&D never starts at all (Maurer 2005).
8. I assume that sponsors seek to elicit R&D activity with certainty and that probabilities are symmetrically distributed within the quoted range.
9. Berndt et al. (2005) argue that per-drug R&D costs should on average be equal to reported sales figures less marketing costs. Since marketing costs are unknown, their method effectively replaces uncertainty over one unknown (R&D expense) with another (marketing costs). They also make two ad hoc adjustments. First, they assert that published estimates of marketing costs, which vary from 15% to 30%, are overstated and therefore adopt a 10% figure instead. This yields a high estimate of \$2.56 billion, which is 140% of the low estimate that they would have obtained by using the 36% figure. They then adjust their estimate to \$3 billion on the ground that "a malaria vaccine may be more difficult to develop than the typical new chemical entity." This \$3 billion estimate was 117%

of their unadjusted $2.56 billion figure. Both adjustments are made on the basis of qualitative judgments without citation to specific data.

10. DiMasi, Hansen, and Grabowski (2003) find evidence for this behavior in their data.
11. Some commentators have criticized the MMV estimate on grounds that it assumes small clinical trial sizes, nonmarket cost data, and "highly conjectural" failure rates (Calfee 2004). More generally, private public partnership budget estimates show "enormous variability" for reasons that are poorly understood. Commentators warn that they require "great caution" (Towse, Mestes-Fernandez, and Renowden 2004).
12. Companies competing in an end-to-end system would presumably use these same strategies. The main difference between end-to-end and pay-as-you-go strategies lies in who pockets the savings.
13. Lack of financing is the main reason why prizes are disfavored. Historically, academic prizes have elicited many new discoveries.
14. The corresponding drawback of using volunteers is that the supply is more or less fixed. Paying researchers to volunteer turns open source into a grant model.
15. This solution breaks down where the market is too small to support more than one or two entrants. In this case, sponsors should award competitively bid contracts to whichever manufacturer offers to sell drugs at the lowest price.
16. In principle, Private-Public Partnerships can ameliorate the effect by improving their monitoring and bargaining practices, pooling purchases, and finding small vendors who are more likely to value their business. Sponsors can also make Private-Public Partnerships' buying power more credible by providing long-term funding.
17. Quoted margins are for the chemical industry. Margins for other industries might be different, although most R&D services seem to be competitively supplied (Maurer 2005).
18. One variant of the "picking winners" argument is that pay-as-you-go sponsors might produce drugs that society has no use for. By contrast, end-to-end systems are tied to market signals. The problem with this analysis is that end-to-end markets are massively subsidized. This means that market signals are fairly weak. Furthermore, infectious diseases have large externalities. This suggests that public health authorities, and pay-as-you-go solutions, may be able to judge the social value of drugs better than markets can.

Chapter 6. Implementing a Public Subsidy for Vaccines

1. The Stratton, Durch, and Lawrence (2000) Institute of Medicine report, along with detailed examples for individual vaccines, is available online at www.iom.edu/report.asp?id=5648.
2. Danzon, Pereira, and Tejwani (2005) argued that in the United States vaccine producers face high fixed, sunk costs and relatively concentrated demand. As a result, having one or very few producers of a vaccine is a likely outcome. But they also noted that such concentration of vaccine production does not exist in several other developed countries.
3. For example, in contrast to vaccines consumed by persons without the disease, persons with cancer are easily identified by sellers of pharmaceutical products

(Anand 2004). This is illustrated by pricing of the drug thalidomide. Birth defects from this drug provided a rationale for greater public scrutiny of drug safety by the U.S. Food and Drug Administration in the early 1960s. Later the drug was found effective for treating AIDS. But fear of protests of AIDS activists kept the price reasonably low. However, when the drug was found to be effective in treating some cancers, the price rose considerably. In contrast to potential vaccine recipients, cancer patient demand for drugs to treat this disease is likely to be relatively inelastic.

4. Based on a series of four doses: www.cdc.gov/mmwr/preview/mmwrhtml/mm5336a8.htm#tab and www.cdc.gov/nip/vfc/cdc_vac_price_list.htm, accessed Dec. 1, 2004; update on Dec. 10, 2004.
5. According to one study, children were undervaccinated a mean of 172 days for all vaccines combined during the first two years of life and more than one-third of children were undervaccinated for more than six months. Among factors associated with the delay were having two or more vaccination providers and using public vaccination provider(s) (Luman et al. 2005).
6. ACIP wields power, however, beyond its mission or design. For example, when ACIP voted to recommend the pneumococcal conjugate vaccine in 2000, its actions increased federal expenditures by half a billion dollars over two years (Freed and Cowan 2002).
7. The committee recommended a change in ACIP membership and procedures to link vaccine coverage to social benefits and costs. Currently, ACIP considers only benefits and then not in dollar terms, as would be required under the committee's proposal.
8. Grabowski (2005) was also critical of aspects of the IOM report. He noted "One potentially serious flaw in the IOM proposal is the time inconsistency problem. The R&D process for new vaccines and drugs generally takes more than 10 years, requires high up-front spending, and is subject to higher rates of project attrition. The proposal therefore raises the problem of how to precommit future government bodies to a pricing process that is credible to current R&D investors" (pp. 697–698). He expressed the view that precommitment devices such as placing public funds for future vaccine purchases in an escrow fund would work given the scale of the IOM proposal. Grabowski also identified problems with "push" strategies that provide public subsidies for vaccine R&D. This time inconsistency problem arises in virtually all demand-oriented policy strategies, not just in the IOM proposal.
9. As an alternative to the IOM proposal, NVAC recommended new public subsidies such as rapid appropriation of new funds through the Section 317 program when new vaccines are recommended. See Hinman (2005). However, this proposal is subject to the same time inconsistency problem as the IOM proposal (see previous note). Why should the manufacturers believe that such funds will be allocated to a new vaccine when they undertake investments in R&D far in advance of the date at which such an allocation of government funds might take place? Even the case for public production of vaccines is weakened by the time inconsistency problem (Pauly 2005). If there is a tendency to reduce prices to the marginal cost of production, once a new vaccine has been developed, then a public vaccine manufacturer would also operate at a loss and require a public subsidy to survive.

10. Of course, the VFC was untested as well at the time it was implemented. The citizens' groups noted that substantial legislative effort would be required to implement the IOM proposal.
11. PhRMA questioned whether financial barriers are the major reason people are not immunized but "recommended encouragement of 'first dollar' insurance coverage" (p. 4).
12. For a more general discussion of health insurance markets, including the roles of moral hazard and adverse selection, see Cutler and Zeckhauser (2000).
13. An actuarial study by Milliman & Robertson estimated the costs of 12 of the most common insurance mandates and found that they could increase the cost of insurance by from 15% to 30%. However, for 7 of the 12 mandates, the individual mandate increased the cost of coverage by less than 1% (www.ncpa.org/ba/gif/estimate.gif, accessed Nov. 10, 2004). Jensen and Morrisey (1999) provide a critical review of actuarial studies of mandates. However, the conclusion that mandates tend to increase the cost of coverage seems to be uncontroversial.
14. Sloan and Conover (1998) found that the number of state health insurance mandates decreased the probability of having any private health insurance, including group health insurance coverage. The probability of being covered fell by 0.004 for each mandate added. Their analysis implied that removing 11 mandates (the sample mean) would increase the proportion of adults covered by over 0.04. Given that 18% of their sample was uninsured, this result implied that between one-fifth and one-quarter of the uninsured could be attributed to mandates, a finding consistent with an earlier study by Goodman and Musgrave (1987), who concluded that 14% of individuals lacked health insurance coverage because of mandates.
15. Gruber (1994) found that the employee groups affected by the mandates paid the full cost of the mandates in terms of reductions in wages. For example, wages of married women in the childbearing ages were 4.3% lower in states mandating maternity coverage than in other states. More generally, see Currie and Madrian (1999) and Gruber (2000) for a review of the empirical literature on the relationship between health insurance and wages.
16. An underlying assumption is that insurance mandates improve health of the covered population. Klick and Markowitz (2003) did not find that mandating mental health benefits improved the mental health of the covered population, but this result may not generalize to vaccinations.
17. This concern was raised by Hinman (2004), who used this argument to oppose the IOM proposal. That other factors than price may be important is not a valid reason to oppose the proposal. More than one policy may be needed to boost vaccination rates to optimal levels. Brito, Sheshinski, and Intriligator (1991) have challenged the notion that the presence of externalities means compulsory vaccination is necessary to reach optimal vaccination levels.
18. There is evidence that the health and financial externalities of vaccination even extend to the unborn. Relative to other birth cohorts, those *in utero* during the 1918 flu pandemic demonstrate accelerated adult mortality, increased rates of physical disability, reduced educational attainment, lower income, and lower socioeconomic status (Almond 2003). This effect has not been incorporated into cost-effectiveness analyses.

19. Various scenarios for calculating the cost effectiveness can be explored interactively at http://post.economics.harvard.edu/faculty/kremer. For example, a malaria vaccine would be cost effective to develop even if the risk and expense of R&D required a price of $40 per person vaccinated.
20. Stratton, Durch, and Lawrence (2000) and the spreadsheets available at www.iom.edu/report.asp?id=5648 serve to show that valuing benefits is very doable.
21. Some research has been conducted in other fields, such as for the marginal discovery costs for oil and gas (Livernois 1988). However, in contrast to pharmaceuticals and vaccines, data were available on oil and gas exploration inputs and on discoveries.
22. There is a large regulatory economics literature on problems a cost-of-service regulator as in determining *c*. See, e.g., Breyer (1982), Kahn (1971), Schmalensee (1979), and Spulber (1989).
23. The IOM proposal did not make a distinction in payment method between new and existing vaccines, only to note in general terms that there might be a difference. Kremer and Glennerster (2004) argued that paying a higher price for existing vaccines may be an inefficient method for stimulating R&D in new vaccine products.
24. This is not the only sector in which regulation is subject to supply disruptions. The electrical power industry is another example (Joskow 1989). In general, a solution is to set payment over *c* to the extent that quality is a concern (Laffont and Tirole 1993: p. 233). Ceteris paribus, this will raise the returns to the manufacturers relative to the consumer surplus.
25. For further discussion, see, e.g., Gallini and Scotchmer (2002). In spite of the potential moral hazard problem (firms conducting R&D receive tax subsidies even if the research is not successful, thereby potentially reducing the firm's effort), they are often recommended. See e.g., Offit (2005).
26. Orphan compounds were generally barred from patentability under section 102 of the patent law because they were typically discovered during research on a different disease and their potential use for the rare disease was often discussed in printed publications (Clissold 1995).
27. The Department of Defense (DoD) uses three phases – a design phase, selection of the sole source of production, and production. In the initial phases, the DoD alleviates the hold-up problem by funding the research directly and allowing firms to add their own funds in a design competition (Rogerson 1989). In the production phase prices are fixed under annual contracts and are based on both projected and historic costs. DoD officers are obligated by regulations to negotiate a "fair" price, based on costs, but to preserve innovation by not obtaining the lowest possible price (Rogerson 1994). In this way, prizes for innovation are built into the procurement process.
28. According to Finkel and Buron (2001), 69% of households receiving a voucher actually used it.
29. These include enforcing waiting periods before one can enter the public program, cost-sharing, and using application questions to monitor recent health insurance status (Davidson et al. 2004). Also, anti-crowd-out measures can be targeted to specific groups, such as persons who are employed or have higher

incomes (Kronick and Gilmer 2002). While estimates of crowd-out vary widely, a State Children's Health Insurance Program crowd-out of private health insurance was estimated to be 50%, and waiting periods were found to significantly affect crowd-out as well as participation rates (Lo Sasso and Buchmueller 2004). We have emphasized the potential effect of a voucher for vaccine program on demand for private health insurance. Another potential form of crowd-out is in private savings and labor supply (see, e.g., Hubbard, Skinner, and Zeldes 1995). High marginal tax rates on earnings and private savings can trap people in poverty (Bradford and Shaviro 2000).

Chapter 7. Ensuring the Future Supply of Vaccines

1. Unfortunately, reliable data on prices paid for vaccines by nonfederal purchasers are not available.
2. The Veterans Administration publishes current contract prices on its Web site: www.vapbm.org/PBM/prices.htm. The Veterans Administration honored my request to provide unpublished historical price data.
3. Each package size of a given brand is a different product.
4. Value- or quantity-weighted estimation is preferable, but we lack data on quantities purchased.
5. The CDC provided information about both the price including excise tax and the price excluding excise tax. We will analyze the behavior of the price excluding excise tax.
6. The "capture" theory was introduced by the late George Stigler, a Nobel laureate who did not work mainly in the public choice field.
7. Data on the occupational distribution of employment in the vaccine industry – a subset of the pharmaceutical industry – are not available.
8. This is taken from the National Science Foundation's "National Expenditures for R&D, from Funding Sectors to Performing Sectors," available at www.nsf.gov/sbe/srs/nsf03313/tables/tab1b.xls.
9. Kremer (2000) argues that government-directed research programs may be well suited for basic research, but for the later, more applied states of research, committing to compensate successful private vaccine developers has important advantages.
10. The third policy, the Vaccine Injury Compensation Fund, introduced a government-run, no-fault product liability system that reduced the mean and variance of product liability costs associated with four childhood vaccines: polio, diphtheria-tetanus, measles-mumps-rubella, and pertussis.
11. Wright (1983) proved that, theoretically, if the government sets the prize properly, the optimal number of firms race to win it
12. According to the theory, Tobin's q is equal to the ratio of the marginal benefit of capital to the marginal (user) cost of capital. When Tobin's q is high (greater than 1), the firm should invest. We hypothesize that changes in the environment affect the (marginal) expected benefits and costs of "knowledge capital," hence the incentives to invest in R&D.
13. Hassett and Hubbard (1996, p. 31) argue that "determining the response of investment to [q] is easiest during periods in which large exogenous changes in

the distribution of structural determinants occur, as during tax reforms" – or, in our context, changes in the regulatory or legal environment.

14. OOPD Program Overview, www.fda.gov/orphan/progovw.htm, accessed 15 June 2006.
15. Brief History of the Office of Orphan Drug Development, www.fda.gov/orphan/History.htm, accessed 15 June 2006.

Chapter 8. Competition between Generic and Branded Drugs

1. One notable exception to this situation involved antibiotic drugs. These drugs did not have to conduct any new safety and efficacy trials because FDA approval of generic antibiotics was governed by the reference monograph approach. Specifically, generic antibiotic products had to show only therapeutic equivalence to the corresponding branded entity.
2. H.R. 98–857 (I) at 16 (1984), reprinted in 1984 U.S.C.C.A.N. 2647, 2649.
3. Preface to the 22nd edition of FDA's *Approved Drug Products with Therapeutic Equivalence Evaluations,* commonly known as the "Orange Book."
4. Orange Book, preface.
5. This list is also available on line at www.express-scripts.com/ourcompany/pressroom/mediakit/generics/docs/laws.pdf, accessed June 27, 2006.
6. PhRMA (2000), p. 66, based on original data from IMS® Health 2000.
7. Capitation is a method of payment in which a physician receives a fixed amount for each person eligible to receive services (dollar/participant/month).
8. See, e.g., Grabowski and Vernon (1996), Masson and Steiner (1985), and Bloom, Wiertz, and Pauly (1986).
9. Ironically, this can lead to the government's paying a higher price for the generic product compared to its branded version when generics first enter the market. This can occur because brand manufacturers are required to give Medicaid discounts based on their "best price" to any buyer and, in any case, a minimum discount of 15.1%. The comparable requirement for generics is 11%. For example, the state of Maine, in 2001, initially paid 17% more for the generic fluoxetine than it had been paying for Prozac prior to automatically switching Medicaid users to the generic (Caffrey 2002).
10. Data audits of IMS Health as reported in PhRMA 2000 *Pharmaceutical Industry Profile* and subsequent IMS news releases.
11. For a simultaneous equation analysis of these various market variables, see Saha et al. (2006).
12. Richard Frank and David Salkever (1992, 1997) find the impact was positive, consistent with specific conditions on a brand firm's demand curve becoming more inelastic after generic entry. More recently, Saha et al. (2006), focusing on the 1990s, found that the net impact of generics on the rate of change in prices was negative, but relatively small in magnitude. In particular, they found that it takes 16 or more generic entrants to cause brand prices to actually decline in value in the first full year after generic entry.
13. One key assumption is that total sales of the molecule remain constant in terms of units in the face of generic competition (zero elasticity of demand). This can lead to an overstatement of savings, but studies of the effect of generic competition

on the sales of the molecule indicate this is a reasonable first approximation (IMS generic spectra product summaries in 2002).

14. The sample involves a regression analysis framework that estimates the effect on price of the number of generic products of the same molecules. Danzon and Chao (2000) also control for the number of therapeutic substitutes, first-mover advantages, molecule age, and several other factors.
15. In a related approach involving a multicountry study, Hudson (2000) found that the impact on brand sales from generic entry is much greater in the case of the United States compared to the United Kingdom, Germany, or France.
16. For example, Edwin Mansfield (1986) surveyed the chief research officers of 100 U.S. corporations and found that 60% of the innovations commercialized in 1981–1983 by the pharmaceutical firms would not have been developed without patent protection. The mean for all industry was 14%.
17. This framework was originally employed by Grabowski and Vernon (1986) to simulate the potential effects of the Act on R&D returns when the Act was first passed.
18. Another formulation strategy for the life cycle management is to combine a drug product subject to patent expiration with a newer product that has a much longer effective patent. In this case one needs to demonstrate to the FDA that the product, in combination, has a synergistic effect. According to IMS (2004), fixed combinations have become an important life cycle management approach in recent years.
19. Any agreements among ANDA applicants and brand name companies, or involving other ANDA applicants, must be filed with the Federal Trade Commission and the Department of Justice within 10 days of execution (Padden and Jenkins 2004).
20. AZT was originally developed unsuccessfully as a cancer remedy and remained as an unapproved drug candidate until its antiviral activity was discovered in the mid-1980s. For a case history, see Emmons and Nimgade (1991).
21. When a new indication is approved, only that indication receives three years of additional exclusivity under the Act. However, there is no effective way to prevent a less expensive generic firm from being used for all indications during this three-year exclusivity period, since physicians do not specify an indication when they write a prescription. This will be the case unless the brand firm utilizes an alternative delivery system or formulation that has exclusivity or patent protection.
22. In addition the EU law also allows for one year of additional data exclusivity for the whole compound if additional indications of significant overall therapeutic value are approved within the eight-year period (Towse 2004).

Chapter 9. The United States' Experience with Direct-to-Consumer Advertising of Prescription Drugs

1. For an interesting history of detailing in the United States, see Greene (2004).
2. See Berndt (2005) and the references cited therein.
3. See, e.g., in the context of the United States, Angell (2004), Avorn (2003, 2004), Batchlor-Laouri (2003), Berndt (2005), Calfee (2002, 2003), Dubois (2003), and

Gahart et al. (2003); recently the U.S. Pharmaceutical Research and Manufacturers of America issued guideline principles for its members regarding DTCA; see PhRMA (2005). For a discussion of policy debates in New Zealand, and a comparison of the United States and New Zealand controversies, see Hoek, Gendall, and Calfee (2004).

4. For a review of this literature and principal findings, see Aikin (2003) and Calfee (2002); the most recent survey is that by Weissman et al. (2004), who provide extensive references.
5. For discussion, see Temin (1980).
6. See Pines (1999), Calfee (2002), and Donohue (2003) for more detailed historical discussion of the marketing of prescription drugs to physicians and consumers.
7. Hollon (1999).
8. For a discussion of DTCA on antiulcer drugs, see Ling, Berndt, and Kyle (2002).
9. Rosenthal et al. (2002) report DTCA spending by media through 2001, the last year for which data are publicly available. Data here from Nielsen Monitor-Plus.
10. Palda (1969).
11. In the context of prescription pharmaceuticals, see, e.g., Hurwitz and Caves (1988), Leffler (1981), and Vernon (1981).
12. Carlton and Perloff (1994), p. 625.
13. For empirical evidence on consumers' search costs for acute vs. chronic medications, and impacts on retail pricing of drugs, see Sorenson (2000). Bagwell (2001) provides a useful collection of economics articles dealing with the theoretical foundations and empirical analyses of advertising as information vs. persuasion, and the relationships among advertising, product quality, and market structure.
14. Data from IMS Health, accessed online at www.imshealth.com/ims. Nominal figures converted to 2000 dollars using the implicit GDP price deflator.
15. A list of current PhRMA member companies can be obtained by accessing their Web site, www.phrma.org.
16. Data from IMS Health, Competitive Media Reports, and PhRMA.
17. For a discussion of what one should expect regarding promotional intensity in pharmaceuticals compared to that in other industries, and for some empirical comparisons, see Berndt (2001, 2002).
18. Neslin (2001); see also Wittink (2002).
19. The 2000 and 2003 data are from IMS Health and Competitive Media Reports, while that for 2004 is from Nielsen Monitor-Plus.
20. This line of reasoning is typically attributed to Nelson (1970, 1974), who argues that when a product is of high quality, the value to its manufacturer of informing potential buyers of its availability and attributes is also high.
21. A corresponding literature has emerged that surveys patients' and physicians' perceptions of DTCA, and how it has affected relationships between physicians and patients. These surveys are discussed in detail in, among others, Aikin (2003) and Calfee (2002). The most recent of these is that by Weissman et al. (2004), who also reference earlier *Prevention* magazine and FDA surveys.
22. See Berndt et al. (2002) for further discussion.
23. For discussion, see, for example, Berndt, Kyle, and Ling (2003).
24. Unfortunately, the evidence on this is based on the author's informal conversations with industry personnel and is not in the public domain.

25. Calfee, Winston, and Stempski (2002), p. 673.
26. Iizuka and Jin (2005a) distinguish between the accumulated stock of DTCA and the current-period DTCA efforts. This is done by specifying a DTCA stock having a constant geometric rate of depreciation, which they estimate along with other parameters using nonlinear estimation methods. They estimate the monthly depreciation rate to be about 3%, which is about 33% on an annual basis.
27. Iizuka and Jin (2005b) was originally the latter portion of Iizuka and Jin (2003).
28. Stocks of detailing and medical journal advertising depreciate much more slowly than does the DTCA stock. When a price term is interacted with DTCA stock, the resulting coefficient estimate is positive but statistically insignificant, indicating that DTCA does not significantly reduce price sensitivity
29. Kravitz et al. (2005), pp. 1995–1996.
30. Kravitz et al. (2005), p. 1997.
31. Kravitz et al. (2005), pp. 1996–1998.
32. Kravitz et al. (2005), p. 2000.
33. Weissman et al. (2004), p. W4–224.
34. For further discussion, see Weissman et al. (2004) and Berndt (2005).
35. For a further decomposition, see Pomerantz et al. (2004), who find that patients seen by psychiatrists were most likely to receive appropriate treatment duration, patients seen by primary care and internal medicine physicians were less likely to receive appropriate treatment duration, and patients seen by specialists other than psychiatrists, primary care physicians, or internists were least likely to receive appropriate treatment duration.
36. Some of the material here is taken from Hoek, Gendall, and Calfee (2004), as well as from informal correspondence with Janet Hoek at Massey University.
37. An influential legal precedent in the United States is the case *Central Hudson Gas & Electric vs. Public Service Commission,* which was considered by the U.S. Supreme Court in 1997. The Supreme Court justices ruled that the First Amendment protects consumers' "right to receive information," but that regulations affecting commercial free speech do not violate the First Amendment if (1) the regulated speech concerns an illegal activity, (2) the speech is misleading, or (3) the government's interest in restricting the speech is substantial, the regulation in question directly advances the government's interest, and the regulation is no more extensive than necessary to serve the government's interest. Additional Court rulings invalidated state laws prohibiting price advertising prescription drugs and alcohol and laws banning news racks for primarily commercial publications, such as real estate guides. For further information, see "Government Regulation of Commercial Speech. The Issue: How Far May Government Go in Regulating Speech That Proposes an Economic Transaction?" available online at www.law.umkc.edu/faculty/projects/ftrials/conlaw/commercial.htm, last accessed May 2, 2005.
38. Hoek, Gendall, and Calfee (2002), p. 204.
39. See New Zealand Ministry of Health (2000a, b).
40. In addition to Hoek, Gendall, and Calfee (2002), see Toop et al. (2003) (a report from faculty at various Schools of Medicine in New Zealand arguing for the banning of DTCA) and Saunders (2003) (a report commissioned by

the Advertising Standards Authority, supporting continued self-regulation of DTCA).

41. Hoek, Gendall, and Calfee (2002), Table 3, p. 214.
42. Hoek, Gendall, and Calfee (2002), pp. 206–209.
43. Much of the information in this paragraph emanates from e-mail correspondence with Professor Janet Hoek, J.A.Hoek@massey.ac.nz. Additional information is available from the Web site of the Joint Therapeutics Agency, www.jtaproject.com, the Advertising Standards Authority, www.asa.co.nz, and the Researched Medicines Industry ("RMI," analogous to PhRMA in the United States, although not all pharmaceutical companies are members of RMI), www.rmianz.co.nz.

Chapter 10. Measures of Costs and Benefits for Drugs in Cost-Effectiveness Analysis

1. For cost-benefit analysis, the perspective is automatically that of welfare economics, unless specified to the contrary.
2. For example, Dennis Mueller's (1986) study of the persistence of high profits across industries found U.S. drug firms to be the most consistent garners of apparently above-normal returns. There are some measurement issues in calculating a proper return on capital measure for drug firms, precisely because R&D investment is not treated as part of the firm's capital stock for tax purposes. Further, there do not seem to be high barriers to entry into the market for new products, as the recent success of some small new firms in biotech relative to other larger and more established firms has shown.
3. There are some qualifications to this argument about extra-normal profits. First, if the owners of a firm in a given country are not all citizens of that country even if the firm is headquartered there, a societal perspective that defined "society" as citizens only would not treat profits for noncitizen owners as transfers, but would rather treat them as true costs to that society. Second, actually calculating the profit cannot be done by obtaining data on R&D costs for a given successful drug and trying to determine the excess of the present value of revenues for that drug over these costs plus its production costs. Prospective investment decision needs to take into account the quite large probability of failure to develop a marketable product. Trying to base evaluation on the realized profits of successful products is a fool's errand. Instead, it is the expected profit that ought to be taken into account, with appropriate adjustment for the beta a measure of risk that is not eliminated by asset diversification, applicable to drugs.

Chapter 12. Pharmaceutical Spending and Health Outcomes

1. In this analysis, pharmaceutical spending includes spending on prescription drugs dispensed outside of hospitals. Drugs prescribed in hospitals are part of hospitals' budgets and cannot be distinguished from other hospital services. Over-the-counter drugs are also excluded.
2. Murphy and Topel (2005) cite Viscusi (1993) and Viscusi and Aldy (2003) as leading sources.

Chapter 13. Pharmaceutical Innovation and Health Outcomes

1. There are many forms of new prescription drugs, including NME, new formulation, new combination, new indication, and new manufacturer. This chapter discuss new drugs in the form of NMEs only. During the period 1990–2004, NMEs account for about one-third of the total new drugs approved by U.S. Food and Drug Administration (FDA). For details, see the FDA Web site (www.fda.gov/cder/rdmt/pstable.htm).
2. In Chapter 3, William Comanor has pointed out that pharmaceutical firms in the United States have spent a large share of their research and development expenditures on finding new indications for existing drugs. Berndt, Cockburn, and Grepin (2000) describe the effort for finding new indications as an incremental innovation.
3. Taiwan established a compulsory national health insurance program in March 1995 by integrating three existing health insurance programs and by expanding the program to cover the remaining 43% of the uninsured population.
4. The annual number of NMEs introduced into the Taiwan market is larger than that approved by U.S. Food and Drug Administration. This is because the sources of import for new drugs include not only the United States but also Japan and many European countries, such as United Kingdom, France, Germany, Switzerland, and Sweden.
5. We use age 65 as the cutoff point because age 65 is a traditional threshold point for aging. In Taiwan, the ratio of population age 65 and above was 5.06% in 1985. This figure increased to 9.04% in 2002.
6. The Hausman test was used to test the null hypothesis that the coefficients estimated by the efficient random-effect model are the same as the ones estimated by the consistent fixed-effect model. If this null hypothesis cannot be rejected (insignificant *P*-value; in general, it is larger than 0.05), then the random-effect model is more appropriate.

References

Abramocicz, M. 2003. "Perfecting Patient Prizes." *Vanderbilt Law Review* 56(1):114–236.

Acemoglu, D., and J. Linn. 2004. "Market Size in Innovation: Theory and Evidence from the Pharmaceutical Industry." *Quarterly Journal of Economics* 119(3):1049–1090.

Ackerberg, D. 2003. "Advertising, Learning, and Consumer Choice in Experience Good Market: A Structure Examination." *International Economic Review* 44:1007–1040.

Addis, A., and N. Magrini. 2002. "New Approaches to Analysing Prescription Data and Transfer Pharmacoepidemiological and Evidence-Based Reports to Prescribers." *Pharmacoepidemiology and Drug Safety* 11:721–726.

Ades, A. 2003. "A Chain of Evidence with Mixed Comparisons: Models for Multi-parameter Syntheses and Consistency of Evidence." *Statistics in Medicine* 22:2995–3016.

Advanced Markets Working Group. 2005. *Making Markets for Vaccines: A Practical Plan to Spark Innovation for Global Health.* Washington, DC: Center for Global Development & Global Health Policy Research Network. Available at www.cgdev.org/section/initiatives/_active/vaccinedevelopment/chapters.

Aghion, Philippe, and Jean Tirole. 1994. "The Management of Innovation." *Quarterly Journal of Economics* 109:1185–1209.

Aikin, Kathryn J. 2003. "The Impact of Direct-to-Consumer Prescription Drug Advertising on the Physician-Patient Relationship." PowerPoint presentation. Available at www.fda.gov/cder/ddmac/aikin/sld001.htm.

Almond, D. 2003. "Is the 1918 Influenza Pandemic Over? Long-Term Effects of Utero Influenza Exposure in the Post-1940 U.S. Population." Available at www.nber.org/~almond. Last accessed January 21, 2005.

American Psychiatric Association. 2003. *Practice Guidelines for the Treatment of Patients with Major Depression.* Available at www.psych.org/psych_pract/treatg/pg/Depression2e.book.cfm. Last accessed July 18, 2004.

Anand, G. 2004. "How Drug's Rebirth as Treatment for Cancer Fueled Price Rises; Once-Demonized Thalidomide Boosts Celgene's Sales; Patients See Costs Soar; Avoiding AIDS Activists." *Wall Street Journal*, November 15, 2004.

Anderson, G. F., and P. S. Hussey. 2001. "Comparing Health System Performance in OECD Countries." *Health Affairs* 20(5):219–232.

Anderson, G. F., U. E. Reinhardt, P. S. Hussey, and Varduhi Petrosyan. 2003. "It's the Prices, Stupid: Why the United States Is So Different from Other Countries." *Health Affairs* 22(3):89–105.

Angell, Marcia. 2004. *The Truth about the Drug Companies: How They Deceive Us and What to Do about It*. New York: Random House.

Anis A. H., and Y. Gagnon. 2000. "Using Economic Evaluations to Make Formulary Coverage Decisions: So Much for Guidelines." *PharmacoEconomics* 18:55–62.

Anon, N. D. 2005. "The History of the Pasteur Institute." Paris: Pasteur Institute. Available at www.pasteur.fr/english.html.

Anton, J. J., and D. A. Yao. 1987. "Second Sourcing and the Experience Curve: Price Competition in Defense Procurement." *Rand Journal of Economics* 18(1):57–76.

Anton, J. J., and D. A. Yao. 1989. "Split Awards, Procurement, and Innovation." *Rand Journal of Economics* 20(4):538–552.

Arnould, R., and L. DeBrock 2002. "An Overview of the Market for Vaccines in the United States." Unpublished. Available from the Institute of Medicine, Washington, DC.

Arrow, Kenneth J. 1963. "Uncertainty and the Welfare Economics of Medical Care." *American Economic Review* 53(5):941–973.

Avorn, Jerry. 2003. "Advertising and Prescription Drugs: Promotion, Education, and the Public Health." *Health Affairs – Web Exclusive* W3:104–108.

Avorn, Jerry. 2004. *Powerful Medicines: The Benefits, Risks, and Costs of Prescription Drugs*. New York: Alfred A. Knopf.

Azoulay, Pierre. 2004. "Capturing Knowledge within and across Firm Boundaries: Evidence from Clinical Development." *American Economic Review* 94 (5):1591–1612.

Babazono, Akira, and Alan L. Hillman. 1994. "A Comparison of International Health Outcomes and Health Care Spending." *International Journal of Technology Assessment in Health Care* 10(3):376–381.

Bagwell, Kyle, ed. 2001. *The Economics of Advertising*. International Library of Critical Writings in Economics, vol. 136. Cheltenham, U.K.: Edward Elgar Publishing.

Bain & Company. 2005. "The Pharma Innovation Divide: The High Cost of Europe's 'Free Ride.'" Available at www.bain.com/bainweb/Consulting_Expertise/hot_topics/detail.asp?id=22. Last accessed October 28, 2005.

Baines, Darrin L, Keith H. Tally, and David K. Whynes. 1997. *Prescribing Budgets and Fundholding in General Practice*. London: Office of Health Economics.

Batchlor, Elaine, and Marianne Laouri. 2003. "Pharmaceutical Promotion, Advertising, and Consumers." *Health Affairs – Web Exclusive* W3:109–115.

Bear Stearns. 2002. "Attack of the Clones: 18 Years past Waxman-Hatch." October 2. New York: Bear Stearns.

Becker, Elizabeth. 2003. "U.S. Is Battling for Higher Drug Prices Overseas." *New York Times*, November 28.

Becker, Gary S., Thomas J. Phillipson, and Rodrigo R. Soares. 2005. "The Quantity and Quality of Life and the Evolution of World Inequality." *American Economic Review* 95(1):277–291.

Benkler, Y. 2004. "Commons Based Strategies and the Problems of Patents." *Science* 305:1110–1111.

Berndt, Ernst R. 2001. "The U.S. Pharmaceutical Industry: Why Major Growth in Times of Cost Containment?" *Health Affairs* 20(2):100–114.

Berndt, E. R. 2002. "Pharmaceuticals in U.S. Health Care: Determinants of Quality and Price." *Journal of Economic Perspectives* 16(4):45–66.

Berndt, Ernst R. 2005. "To Inform or Persuade? Direct-to-Consumer Advertising of Prescription Drugs." *New England Journal of Medicine* 352(4):325–328.

Berndt, Ernst R., Ashoke Bhattacharjya, David Mishol, Almudena Arcelus, and Thomas Lasky. 2002. "An Analysis of the Diffusion of New Antidepressants: Variety, Quality, and Marketing Efforts." *Journal of Mental Health Policy and Economics* 5(1):3–17.

Berndt, Ernst R., Iain M. Cockburn, and Karen A. Grepin. 2005. "Biopharmaceutical R&D: Is the Productivity Decline Overstated?" Working paper, Conference on Health Reform in Europe and the U.S., Tufts Center, Talloues, France, July 2005.

Berndt, E., R. Glennerster, M. R. Kremer, J. Lee, R. Levine, G. Weizsacker, and H. Williams. 2005. "Advanced Markets for a Malaria Vaccine: Estimating Costs and Effectiveness." National Bureau of Economic Research Working Paper 11288.

Berndt, E. R., and J. A. Hurwitz. 2005. "Vaccine Advance Purchase Agreements for Low-Income Countries: Practical Issues." *Health Affairs* 24(3):653–665.

Berndt, Ernst R., Margaret K. Kyle, and Davina C. Ling. 2003. "The Long Shadow of Patent Expiration: Generic Entry and Rx to OTC Switches." Chapter 8 in *Scanner Data and Price Indexes*, NBER Series on the Conference on Research in Income and Wealth, vol. 61, ed. by Robert C. Feenstra and Matthew D. Shapiro, 229–267. Chicago: University of Chicago Press for the National Bureau of Economic Research.

Beutels, P., W. J. Edmunds, F. Antoñanzas, G. A. de Wit, D. Evans, R. Feilden, A. M. Fendrick, et al. 2002. "Economic Evaluation of Vaccination Programmes: A Consensus Statement Focusing on Viral Hepatitis." *PharmacoEconomics* 20:1–7.

Birch, S., and A. Gafni. 2002. "On Being NICE in the UK: Guidelines for Technology Appraisal for the NHS in England and Wales." *Health Economics* 11:185–191.

Black, Douglas J., Cyril Smith, and Peter Townsend. 1982. *Inequalities in Health: The Black Report*. New York: Penguin Books.

Bloom, B. D. J. Wiertz, and M. Pauly. 1986. "Cost and Price of Comparable Branded and Generic Pharmaceuticals." *Journal of the American Medical Association* 256(18):2523–2530.

Boardman, Anthony, Ruth Freedman, and Catherine Eckel. 1986. "The Price of Government Ownership: A Study of the Domtar Takeover." *Journal of Public Economics* 31(3):269–286.

Boardman, Anthony E., and Aidan R. Vining. 1989. "Ownership and Performance in Competitive Environments: A Comparison of the Performance of Private, Mixed, and State-Owned Enterprises." *Journal of Law and Economics* 32(1):1–33.

Boswell, C. 2003. "InnoCentive and Web-Based Collaborative Innovation." *Chemical Market Reporter*, April 14.

Bradford, D. F., and D. N. Shaviro. 2000. "The Economics of Vouchers," in *Vouchers and the Provision of Public Services*, ed. by C. E. Steuerle, Van Doorn Ooms, George Peterson, and Robert D. Reischauer, 606–607. Washington, DC: Brookings Institution Press.

Branstetter, Lee G., Raymond Fisman, and C. Fritz Foley. 2003. "Do Stronger Intellectual Property Rights Increase International Technology Transfer? Empirical Evidence from U.S. Firm-Level Panel Data." Unpublished paper, Columbia University Business School.

Breyer, S. 1982. *Regulation and Its Reform.* Cambridge, MA: Harvard University Press.

Brito, D. L., E. Sheshinski, and M. D. Intriligator. 1991. "Externalities and Compulsory Vaccinations." *Journal of Public Economics* 45:69–90.

Caffrey, Andrew. 2002. "Why Generics Can Cost States More Money." *Wall Street Journal,* February 13.

Calfee, John E. 2002. "Public Policy Issues in Direct-to-Consumer Advertising of Prescription Drugs." *Journal of Public Policy & Marketing* 21(2):174–193.

Calfee, John E. 2003. "What Do We Know about Direct-to-Consumer Advertising of Prescription Drugs?" *Health Affairs – Web Exclusive* W3:116–119.

Calfee, John E. 2004. "Paying for the Pills: How Much Does It Really Cost to Put a New Drug on the Market?" *Nature* 429: 807.

Calfee, John E., Clifford Winston, and Randolph Stempski. 2002. "Direct-to-Consumer Advertising and the Demand for Cholesterol-Reducing Drugs." *Journal of Law and Economics* 14(2):673–690.

Carlton, Dennis W., and Jeffrey M. Perloff. 1994. *Modern Industrial Organization.* 2nd ed. New York: HarperCollins College Division.

Caro J., W. Klittich, A. McGuire, and I. Ford. 1997. "The West of Scotland Coronary Prevention Study: Economic Benefit Analysis of Primary Prevention with Pravastatin." *British Medical Journal* 315:1577–1582.

Caves, R. E., M. D. Whinston, and M. Hurwitz. 1991. "Patent Expiration, Entry, and Competition in the U.S. Pharmaceutical Industry." *Brookings Papers on Economic Activity Microeconomics* (1991):1–66.

Center for Global Development Advanced Market Commitment Working Group. 2005. "Making Markets for Vaccines: Ideas to Action." Available at www.cgdev.org/Publications/vaccine/_files/MakingMarkets-complete.pdf. Last accessed April 28, 2005.

Claxton K., L. Ginnelly, M. Sculpher, Z. Philips, and S. Palmer. 2004. "A Pilot Study on the Use of Decision Theory and Value of Information Analysis as Past of the National Health Service Technology Assessment Programme. *Health Technology Assessment* 8(31) (whole issue).

Clissold, D. B. 1995. "Prescription for The Orphan Drug-Act: The Impact of the FDA's 1992 Regulations and the Latest Congressional Proposals for Reform." *Food and Drug Law Journal* 50(1):125–147.

Cochrane, A. L., A. S. St. Leger, and F. Moore. 1978. "Health Service 'Input' and Mortality 'Output' in Developed Countries." *Journal of Epidemiology and Community Health* 32(3):200–205.

Cockburn, Iain M. 2004. "The Changing Structure of the Pharmaceutical Industry." *Health Affairs* 23:10–22.

Cockburn, Iain, and Rebecca Henderson. 1994. "Racing to Invest? The Economics of Competition in Ethical Drug Discovery." *Journal of Economics and Management Strategy* 33:481–519.

Cockburn, Iain, and Rebecca Henderson. 1996. Scale, Scope, and Spillovers: The Determinants of Research Productivity in Drug Discovery. *Rand Journal of Economics* 27: 32–60.

Cockburn, Iain M., and Rebecca M. Henderson. 1998. "Absorptive Capacity, Co-Authoring Behavior, and the Organization of Research in Drug Discovery." *Journal of Industrial Economics* 46:157–182.

Cockburn, Iain, and Rebecca Henderson. 1999. "The Economics of Drug Discovery," in Ralph Landau et al., eds., *Pharmaceutical Innovation*, 308–330. Philadelphia: Chemical Heritage Press.

Cockburn, Iain, and Rebecca Henderson. 2001. "Scale and Scope in Drug Development: Unpacking the Advantages of Size in Pharmaceutical Research." *Journal of Health Economics* 20(6):1033–1057.

Cockburn, Iain M., Rebecca Henderson, and Scott Stern. 1999. "The Diffusion of Science Driven Drug Discovery, Organizational Change in Pharmaceutical Research." National Bureau of Economic Research Working Paper 7359.

Cohen, J. 2002. "US Vaccine Supply Falls Seriously Short." *Science* 295(5562):1998–2001.

Cohen, J. 2004. "Vaccine Policy: Immunizing Kids against Flu May Prevent Deaths among the Elderly." *Science* 306(5699):1123.

Cohen, W. M., and S. A. Merrill. 2003. *Patents in the Knowledge-Based Economy: Committee on Intellectual Property Rights in the Knowledge-Based Economy*. Washington, DC: National Academies Press, National Research Council (U.S.).

Cohen, Wesley M., Richard R. Nelson, and John P. Walsh. 2002. "Protecting Their Intellectual Assets: Appropriability Conditions and Why U.S. Manufacturing Firms Patent (Or Not)." National Bureau of Economic Research Working Paper 7552.

Comanor, William S. 1964. "Research and Competitive Product Differentiation in the Pharmaceutical Industry in the United States." *Economica* 31:372–384.

Comanor, William S. 1965. "Research and Technical Change in the Pharmaceutical Industry." *Review of Economics and Statistics* 47(2):182–190.

Conroy, Robert, Robert Harris, and Thomas Massaro. 1992. "Assessment of Risk and Capital Costs in the Pharmaceutical Industry." Unpublished paper, University of Virginia, Darden School, June 30.

Corrigan, J. M., A. Greiner, and S. M. Erickson, eds. 2002. *Fostering Rapid Advances in Health Care: Learning from System Demonstrations*. Washington, DC: National Academies Press.

Covert, N. 2000. "Cutting Edge: A History of Fort Detrick." Frederick, MD: Self-published. Available at www.detrick.army.mil/detrick/cutting_edge/index.cfm?chapter12.

Crawford, Gregory S., and Matthew Shum. 2005. "Uncertainty and Learning in Pharmaceutical Demand." *Econometrica* 73(4):4.

Cremieux, Pierre-Yves, Marie-Claude Meilleur, Pierre Ouellette, Patrick Petit, Martin Zelder, and Ken Potvin. 2005. "Public and Private Pharmaceutical Spending as Determinants of Health Outcomes in Canada." *Health Economics* 14:107–116.

Cremieux, Pierre-Yves, Pierre Ouellette, Marie-Clause Meilleur, Stephanie Leong, Paul Greenberg, and Howard Birnbaum. 2001. "Pharmaceutical Spending and Health Outcomes in the United States," in *Investing in Health: The Social and Economic Benefits of Health Care Innovation*," ed. by Irina Farquhar, Kent Summers, and Alan Sorkin, 59–76. Oxford: Elsevier Science.

Cremieux, Pierre-Yves, Pierre Ouellette, and Caroline Pilon. 1999. "Health Care Spending as Determinants of Health Outcomes." *Health Economics* 8:627–639.

Currie, J., and Brigitte C. Madrian. 1999. "Health, Health Insurance and the Labor Market," in *Handbook of Labor Economics*, ed. by Orley Ashenfelter and David Card, 3309–3415. Amsterdam: Elsevier Science.

Cutler, David M. 2004. *Your Money or Your Life: Strong Medicine for America's Health Care System.* New York: Oxford University Press.

Cutler, David M., Angus S. Deaton, and Adriana Lleras-Muney. 2006. "The Determinants of Mortality." *Journal of Economic Perspective* 20(3):97–120.

Cutler, David M., and Srikanth Kadiyala. 2003. "The Return to Biomedical Research: Treatment and Behavioral Effects," in *Measuring the Gains from Medical Research: An Economic Approach*, ed. by Kevin M. Murphy and Robert H. Topel, 110–162. Chicago: University of Chicago Press.

Cutler, David M., and Mark McClellan. 2001a. "Is Technological Change in Medicine Worth It?" *Health Affairs* 20(5):11–29.

Cutler, D. M., and M. McClellan. 2001b. "Productivity Change in Health Care." *American Economic Review* 91(2):281–286.

Cutler, David, Mark McClellan, and Joseph Newhouse. 1997. "The Costs and Benefits of Intensive Treatment for Cardiovascular Disease." Paper presented at AEI-Brookings Conference on Measuring the Prices of Medical Treatments, December 12.

Cutler, David, and Elizabeth Richardson. 1997. "Measuring the Health of the U.S. Population." *Brookings Papers on Economic Activity: Microeconomics* (1997):217–271.

Cutler, David M., and R. Zeckhauser. 2000. "The Anatomy of Health Insurance," in *Handbook of Health Economics*, ed. by Antony J. Culyer and Joseph P. Newhouse, 563–643. Amsterdam: Elsevier.

Danzon, Patricia M. 2000. "Pharmaceutical Benefit Management: An Alternative Approach." *Health Affairs* 19(1):24–25.

Danzon, Patricia M. 2001. "Reference Pricing: Theory and Evidence," in *Reference Pricing and Pharmaceutical Policy*, ed. by G. López-Casasnova and B. Jönsson, 86–126.

Danzon, P. 2002. *Pharmaceutical Price Regulation: National Policies versus Global Interests.* Washington, DC: AEI Press.

Danzon, Patricia M., and Li-Wei Chao. 2000. "Does Regulation Drive Out Competition in Pharmaceutical Markets?" *Journal of Law and Economics* 42(2):311–357.

Danzon, Patricia M., and Michael Furukawa. 2003. "Prices and Availability of Pharmaceuticals: Evidence from Nine Countries." *Health Affairs – Web Exclusive* W3:521–536.

Danzon, Patricia M., Sean Nicholson, and Nuno Sousa Pereira. 2005. "Productivity in Pharmaceutical-Biotechnology R&D: The Role of Experience and Alliances." *Journal of Health Economics* 24:317–339.

Danzon, P. M, N. S. Pereira, and S. S. Tejwani. 2005. "Vaccine Supply: A Cross-National Perspective." *Health Affairs* 24(3):706–717.

Danzon, Patricia M., Y. Richard Wang, and Liang Wang. 2005. "The Impact of Price Regulation on the Launch Delay of New Drugs: Evidence from 25 Markets in the 1990s." *Health Economics* 14:269–292.

Davidson, G., L. A. Blewett, K. T. Call, and SHADA Center. 2004. "Public Program Crowd-out of Private Coverage: What Are the Issues?" Research Synthesis Report No. 5. Available at www.rwjf.org/publications/synthesis/reports_and_briefs/issue5.html.

Davis, M. M., S. M. Ndiaye, G. L. Freed, C. S. Kim, and S. J. Clark. 2003. "Influence of Insurance Status and Vaccine Cost on Physicians' Administration of Pneumococcal Conjugate Vaccine." *Pediatrics* 112(3):521–526.

Davis, M. M., J. L. Zimmerman, J. R. C. Wheeler, and G. L. Freed. 2002. "Childhood Vaccine Purchase Costs in the Public Sector: Past Trends, Future Expectations." *American Journal of Public Health* 92(12):1982–1987.

DeLaat, E. A. A. 1997. "Patents or Prizes: Monopolistic R&D and Asymmetric Information." *International Journal of Industrial Organization* 15(3):369–390.
Depression Guideline Panel. 1993. *Depression in Primary Care: Treatment of Major Depression.* Rockville, MD: U.S. Department of Health and Human Services, Public Health Service, Agency for Health Care Policy and Research.
Dickson, Michael, and Jean Paul Gagnon. 2004. "Key Factors in the Rising Cost of New Drug Discovery and Development." *Nature Reviews* 3:417–428.
DiMasi, J. A., R. W. Hansen, and H. G. Grabowski. 2003. "The Price of Innovation: New Estimates of Drug Development Costs." *Journal of Health Economics* 22(2):151–185.
DiMasi, J. A., R. W. Hansen, H. G. Grabowski, and L. Lasagna. 1991. "Cost of Innovation in the Pharmaceutical Industry." *Journal of Health Economics* 10(2):107–142.
Dion, M. R., and L. Pavetti. 2000. *Access to and Participation in Medicaid and the Food Stamp Program: A Review of the Recent Literature.* Washington, DC: Mathematica Policy Research.
Donaldson C., G. Currie, and C. Mitton. 2002. "Cost-Effectiveness Analysis in Health Care: Contraindications." *British Medical Journal* 325:891–894.
Donohue, Julie M. 2003. "The Evolving Roles of Consumers and Consumer Protection: The History of Prescription Drug Advertising." *Milbank Quarterly* 84(4):659–694.
Donohue, Julie M., and Ernst R. Berndt. 2004. "Effect of Direct-to-Consumer Advertising on Medication Choice: The Case of Antidepressants." *Journal of Public Policy & Marketing* 23(2):115–127.
Donohue, Julie M., Ernst R. Berndt, Meredith Rosenthal, Arnold M. Epstein, and Richard G. Frank. 2004. "Effects of Pharmaceutical Promotion on Adherence to Guideline Treatment of Depression." *Medical Care* 42(2):1176–1185.
Dorfman, Robert, and Peter O. Steiner. 1954. "Optimal Advertising and Optimal Quality." *American Economic Review* 44(5):826–836.
Dornbusch, Rudiger, and Stanley Fischer. 1994. *Macroeconomics.* 6th ed. New York: McGraw-Hill.
Downs, Anthony. 1957. *An Economic Theory of Democracy.* New York: HarperCollins College Division.
Drummond, M. F., and F. Pang. 2001. "Transferability of Economic Evaluation Results." In *Economic Evaluation in Health Care: Merging Theory with Practice*, ed. by M. F. Drummond and A. McGuire, 256–327. Oxford: Oxford University Press.
Drummond, M. F., and M. J. Sculpher. 2005. "Common Methodological Flaws in Economic Evaluations." *Medical Care* 43(4):5–14.
Drummond, M. F., M. J. Sculpher, G. W. Torrance, B. J. O'Brien, and G. L. Stoddart. 2005. *Methods for the Economic Evaluation of Health Care Programmes.* 3rd ed. Oxford: Oxford University Press.
D'Souza, Juliet, and William L. Megginson. 1999. "The Financial and Operating Performance of Privatized Firms during the 1990s." *Journal of Finance* 54(4):1397–1438.
Dubois, Robert W. 2003. "Pharmaceutical Promotion: Don't Throw the Baby Out with the Bathwater." *Health Affairs – Web Exclusive* W3:96–103.
Dubois, Robert W., Anita J. Chawla, Cheryl A. Neslusan, et al. 2000. "Explaining Drug Spending Trends: Does Perception Match Reality?" *Health Affairs* 19:231–239.
Duggan, Mark. 2005. "Do New Prescription Drugs Pay for Themselves? The Case of Second-Generation Antipsychotics." *Journal of Health Economics* 24:1–31.

Ehrlich, Isaac, Georges Gallais-Hamonno, Zhiqiang Liu, and Randall Lutter. 1994. "Productivity Growth and Firm Ownership: An Analytical and Empirical Investigation." *Journal of Political Economy* 102(5):1006–1038.

Ellison, G. S., and F. Ellison. 2000. "Strategic Entry Deterrence and the Behavior of Pharmaceutical Incumbents Prior to Patent Expiration." Working paper, MIT, Cambridge, MA.

Ellison, Sara Fisher, and Wallace P. Mullin. 1997. "Gradual Incorporation of Information into Stock Prices: Empirical Strategies." National Bureau of Economic Research Working Paper 6218.

Emmons, Willis A., and Ashok Nimgade. 1991. "Burroughs Wellcome and AZT." Harvard Business School Case No. 9-792-004, Cambridge, MA.

Enserink, M. 2004. "Influenza: Crisis Underscores Fragility of Vaccine Production System." *Science* 306(5695):385.

EPIC Investigators. 1994. "Use of Monoclonal Antibody Directed against the Platelet Glycoprotein lib/111a Receptor in High-Risk Coronary Angioplasty." *New England Journal of Medicine* 330:956–961.

Fama, E. F. 1980. "Agency Problems and the Theory of the Firm." *Journal of Political Economy* 88(2):288–307.

Fama, E. F., L. Fisher, M. Jensen, and R. Roll. 1969. "The Adjustment of Stock Prices to New Information." *International Economic Review* 10(1):1–21.

Farber, Henry S., and Max H. Brazerman. 1986. "The General Basis of Arbitrator Behavior: An Empirical Analysis of Conventional and Final-Offer Arbitration." *Econometrica* 54:819–844.

Farlow, A. 2004. "Analysis of the Problems of R&D Finance for Vaccines and an Appraisal of Advance Purchase Commitments." Preprint. Oxford: University of Oxford. Available at www.economics.ox.ac.uk/members/andrew.farlow/VaccineRD.pdf#search='farlow%20and%20analysis%20of%20the%20problems.

Farlow, Andrew, Donald W. Light, Richard T. Mahoney, and Roy Widdus. 2005. "Concerns Regarding the 'Making Markets for Vaccines' Submission to the Commission on Intellectual Property Rights, Innovation and Public Health." Available at www.who.int/intellectualproperty/en/. Last accessed May 10, 2005.

Farquhar, Irina, Kent Summers, and Alan Sorkin, eds. 2001. *Benefits of Health Care Innovation*. Oxford: Elsevier Science.

Federal Trade Commission. 2002. *Generic Competition Prior to Patent Expiration: An FTC Study*. Washington, DC: Federal Trade Commission.

FinFacts. *Global/World Income per Capita/Head 2005*. 2005. Available at www.finfacts.com/biz10/globalworldincomepercapita.htm. Last accessed October 20, 2005.

Finkel, M., and L. Buron. 2001. *Study on Section 8 Voucher Success Rates*. Cambridge, MA: Diane Publishing.

Finkelstein, A. 2004. "Static and Dynamic Effects of Health Policy: Evidence from the Vaccine Industry." *Quarterly Journal of Economics* 119(2):527–564.

Forbes, Steve. 2005. "Rich Freeloader Countries – France, German, Canada – Rob America on Health Care." USA Next. Available at www.usanext.org/full_story.cfm?areticle_id=16&category_id=3. Last accessed October 30, 2005.

Fortune Magazine. 2005. *The 2005 Fortune 500: Most Profitable Industries: Return on Revenues*. Available at www.fortune.com/fortune/subs/fortune500/topperformers/industrysnapshot/0,23619,prof_pct_rev,00.html.

Frank, John W., and J. Fraser Mustard. 1998. "The Determinants of Health from a Historical Perspective." The Founders' Network. Available at www.founders.net/fn/papers.nsf.

Frank, R. G., C. Dewa, E. Holt, et al. 1995. "The Demand for Childhood Immunizations: Results from the Baltimore Immunization Study." *Inquiry* 32(2):164–173.

Frank, R. G., and D. S. Salkever. 1992. "Pricing, Patent Loss and the Market for Pharmaceuticals." *Southern Economic Journal* 59:165–179.

Frank, R. G., and D. S. Salkever. 1997. "Generic Entry and Pricing of Pharmaceuticals." *Journal of Economics and Management Strategy* 6(1):75–90.

Frech, H. E., III, and Richard D. Miller, Jr. 1999. *The Productivity of Health Care and Pharmaceuticals: An International Comparison.* Washington, DC: AEI Press.

Freed, G. L., S. J. Clark, D. E. Pathman, R. Schectman, and J. Serling. 1999. "Impact of North Carolina's Universal Vaccine Purchase Program by Children's Insurance Status." *Archives of Pediatric and Adolescent Medicine* 153(7):748–754.

Freed, G., and A. Cowan. 2002. "State-Level Perspectives on Vaccine Purchase Financing." Unpublished. Available from the Institute of Medicine, Washington, DC.

Freed, G. L., M. M. Davis, M. C. Andreae, S. Bass, and H. Weinblatt. 2002. "Reimbursement for Prevnar: A Modern-Day Version of Hercules and the Hydra." *Pediatrics* 110(2):399–400.

Fuchs, Victor R., and Richard Zeckhauser. 1987. "Valuing Health: A 'Priceless' Commodity." *American Economic Review* 77(2):263–268.

Gafni A., and S. Birch. 1993. "Guidelines for the Adoption of New Technologies: A Prescription for Uncontrolled Growth in Expenditures and How to Avoid the Problem." *Canadian Medical Association Journal* 148(6):913–917.

Gahart, Martin T., Louise M. Duhamel, Anne Dievler, and Roseanne Price. 2003. "Examining the FRDA's Oversight of Direct-to-Consumer Advertising." *Health Affairs – Web Exclusive* W3:120–123.

Gallini, N., and S. Scotchmer. 2002. "Intellectual Property: When Is It the Best Incentive Mechanism?" in *Innovation Policy and the Economy*, ed. by A. Jaffe, J. Lerner, and S. Stern, 2:51–78. Cambridge, MA: MIT Press.

Gambardella, Alfonso. 1995. *Science and Innovation: The U.S. Pharmaceutical Industry during the 1980s.* Cambridge: Cambridge University Press.

George, B., A. Harris, and A. Mitchell. 2001. "Cost-Effectiveness Analysis and the Consistency of Decision-Making: Evidence from Pharmaceutical Reimbursement in Australia (1991 to 1996)." *PharmacoEconomics* 19(11):1103–1109.

Georges, P., A. Ann Margaret, P. D. Jeffrey, D. D. Michael, et al. 2003. "Strengthening the Supply of Routinely Recommended Vaccines in the United States: Recommendations from the National Vaccine Advisory Committee." *Journal of the American Medical Association* 290(23):3122–3128.

Giaccotto, Carmelo, Rexford E. Santerre, and John A. Vernon. 2005. "Drug Prices and Research and Development Investment Behavior in the Pharmaceutical Industry." *Journal of Law and Economics* 48(1):195–214.

Giffin, R., K. Stratton, and R. Chalk. 2004. "Childhood Vaccine Finance and Safety Issues." *Health Affairs* 23(5):98–111.

Glassman, James K. 2005. "Free Riding Isn't Free." Available at www.techcentralstation.com/022304F.html. Last accessed October 28, 2005.

Glied, Sherry. 2003. "Health Care Costs: On the Rise Again." *Journal of Economic Perspective* 17(2):125–148.

Global Alliance for TB Drug Development. 2001. *Economics of TB Drug Development*. New York: Global Alliance for TB Drug Development. Available at http://66.216.124.114/pdf/Economics%20Report%20Full%20(final).pdf.

Global Health Policy Research Network. 2004. "Making Markets for Vaccines." Pull Mechanisms Working Group. Available at www.cgdev.org/globalhealth/proj_pull.cfm.

Gold, M., J. E. Siegel, L. B. Russell, and M. C. Weinstein, eds. 1996. *Cost Effectiveness in Health and Medicine.* Oxford: Oxford University Press.

Goodman, J. C., and G. L. Musgrave. 1987. *Freedom of Choice in Health Insurance.* Dallas: National Center for Policy Analysis.

Goolsbee, Austan. 1988. "Does Government R&D Policy Mainly Benefit Scientists and Engineers?" *American Economic Review* 88(2):298–302.

Grabowski, Henry. 2004. "Are the Economics of Pharmaceutical R&D Changing? Productivity, Patents and Political Pressures." *PharmacoEconomics* 22(Suppl. 2):15–24.

Grabowski, Henry. 2005. "Encouraging the Development of New Vaccines." *Health Affairs* 24(3):697–700.

Grabowski, Henry, Iain Cockburn, and Genia Long. 2006. "The Market for Follow-On Biologics: How Will It Evolve." *Health Affairs* 25(5):1291–1301.

Grabowski, Henry, and Margaret Kyle. 2006. "Generic Competition and Market Exclusivity Periods in Pharmaceuticals." *Managerial and Decision Economics*, forthcoming.

Grabowski, Henry, and C. Daniel Mullins. 1997. "Pharmacy Benefit Management Cost-Effectiveness Analysis and Drug Formulary Decisions." *Social Science and Medicine* 45(4):535–544.

Grabowski, Henry, and John Vernon. 1986. "Longer Patents for Lower Imitation Barriers: The 1984 Drug Act." *American Economic Review: Papers and Proceedings* 76(2):195–198.

Grabowski, Henry, and John M. Vernon. 1990. "A New Look at the Return and Risks to Pharmaceutical R&D." *Management Science* 36:804–821.

Grabowski, Henry, and John Vernon. 1992. "Brand Loyalty Entry and Price Competition in Pharmaceuticals after the 1984 Act." *Journal of Law and Economics* 35(2):331–350.

Grabowski, Henry, and John M. Vernon. 1994. "Returns on New Drug Introductions in the 1980s." *Journal of Health Economics* 13:383–406.

Grabowski, Henry, and John Vernon. 1996. "Longer Patents for Increased Generic Competition: The Waxman-Hatch Act after One Decade." *PharmacoEconomics* 10 (Suppl. 2):110–123.

Grabowski, Henry, and John Vernon. 2000. "Effective Patent Life in Pharmaceuticals." *International Journal of Technology Management* 19(1–2):98–120.

Grabowski, Henry, John M. Vernon, and Lacy Glenn Thomas. 1978. "Estimating the Effects of Regulation on Innovation: An International Comparative Analysis of the Pharmaceutical Industry." *Journal of Law and Economics* 21(1):133–163.

Grabowski, Henry, and Richard Wang. 2006. "The Quantity and Quality of Worldwide New Drug Introductions:1982–2003." *Health Affairs* 25(2):452–460.

Greene, Jeremy A. 2004. "Attention to 'Details': Etiquette and the Pharmaceutical Salesman in Postwar America." *Social Studies in Science* 34(2):271–292.

Gruber, J. 1994. "The Incidence of Mandated Maternity Benefits." *American Economic Review* 84(3):622–642.

Gruber, J., ed. 2000. "Health Insurance and the Labor Market," in *Handbook of Health Economics*, ed. by Antony J. Culyer and Joseph P. Newhouse, 645–706. Amsterdam: Elsevier Science.

Guedj, Ilan, and David Scharfstein. 2004. "Organizational Scope and Investment: Evidence from the Drug Development Strategies of Biopharmaceutical Firms." National Bureau of Economic Research Working Paper.

Gupta, Nandini. 2002. "Partial Privatization and Firm Performance." Unpublished working paper, Columbia University. August. Available at www-1.gsb.columbia.edu/divisions/management/seminar/papers/gupta.pdf.

Hall, Bronwyn H. 1993, "R&D Tax Policy during the Eighties: Success or Failure?" in *Tax Policy and the Economy* 7, ed. by James Poterba, 1–35. Cambridge, MA: MIT Press.

Hall, Bronwyn H., and John van Reenen. 2000. "How Effective Are Fiscal Incentives for R&D? A New Review of the Evidence." *Research Policy* 29:449–469.

Hall, Robert E., and Charles I. Jones. 1999. "Why Do Some Countries Produce So Much More Output per Worker than Others?" *Quarterly Journal of Economics* 114(1):83–116.

Hansen, Ronald W. 1979. "The Pharmaceutical Development Process: Estimates of Development Costs and Times and the Effects of Proposed Regulatory Changes," in *Issues in Pharmaceutical Economics*, ed. Robert I. Chien, 151–187. Boston: Lexington Books.

Hart, Oliver D., Andrei Shleifer, and Robert W. Vishny. 1997. "The Proper Scope of Government: Theory and an Application to Prisons." *Quarterly Journal of Economics* 112(4):1126–1161.

Hassett, Kevin, and R. Glenn Hubbard. 1996. "Tax Policy and Investment." Unpublished paper, Federal Reserve Board of Governors and Columbia University Business School.

Heffler, Stephen, Sheila Smith, Sean Keehan, Christine Borger, M. Kent Clemens, and Christopher Truffer. 2005. "U.S. Health Spending for 2004–2014." *Health Affairs – Web Exclusive* W5:74–85.

Henderson, Rebecca, and Iain Cockburn. 1996. "Scale, Scope and Spillovers: The Determinants of Research Productivity in Drug Discovery." *RAND Journal of Economics* 27(1):32–59.

Hill, S. R., A. S. Mitchell, and D. A. Henry. 2000. "Problems with the Interpretation of Pharmacoeconomic Analyses: A Review of Submissions to the Australian Pharmaceutical Benefits Scheme." *Journal of the American Medical Association* 283:2116–2121.

Hinman, A. 2004. "Institute of Medicine Report on Financing Vaccines in the 21st Century: National Vaccine Advisory Committee/National Vaccine Program Office Response." Available at www.hhs.gov/nvpo/nvac/NVAC-IOM100604.htm.

Hinman, A. 2005. "Addressing the Vaccine Financing Conundrum." *Health Affairs* 24(3):701–704.

Hoek, Janet, Philip Gendall, and John Calfee. 2004. "Direct-to-Consumer Advertising of Prescription Medicines in the United States and New Zealand: An Analysis of Regulatory Approaches and Consumer Responses." *International Journal of Advertising* 23:197–227.

Hollis, A. 2005a. "An Efficient Reward System for Pharmaceutical Innovation." Preprint. Available at http://econ.ucalgary.ca/fac-files/ah/drugprizes.pdf#search='hollis%20and%20an%20efficient%20reward%20system.

Hollis, A. 2005b. "An Optional Reward System for Neglected Disease Drugs." Mimeo, University of Calgary.

Hollon, Matthew F. 1999. "Direct-to-Consumer Prescription Drugs: Creating Consumer Demand." *Journal of the American Medical Association* 281(4):382–384.

Holmstrom, Bengt, and Jean Tirole. 1993. "Market Liquidity and Performance Monitoring." *Journal of Political Economy* 101:678–709.

Hotz, J., A. Ahituv, and T. Philipson. 1996. "The Responsiveness of the Demand for Condoms to the Local Prevalence of AIDS." *Journal of Human Resources* 21(4):869–897.

Hsieh, Chee-Ruey, and Frank A. Sloan. 2006. "Adoption of Pharmaceutical Innovation and the Growth of Drug Expenditure: The Taiwanese Experience." Working Paper, Duke University.

Hsu, J. C., and E. S. Schwartz. 2003. "A Model of R&D Valuation and the Design of Research Incentives." National Bureau of Economic Research Working Paper 10041.

Hubbard, R. G., J. Skinner, and S. P. Zeldes. 1995. "Precautionary Saving and Social Insurance." *Journal of Political Economy* 103:360–399.

Hudson, John. 2000. "Generic Take-Up in the Pharmaceutical Market Following Patent Expiry: A Multi-Country Study." *International Review of Law and Economics* 20:205–221.

Hume, C., and W. Schmitt. 2001. "Pharma's Prescription." *Chemical Week*, April 11, 21.

Hurwitz, Mark A., and Richard E. Caves. 1988. "Persuasion or Information? Promotion and the Shares of Brand Name and Generic Pharmaceuticals." *Journal of Law and Economics* 31, no. 5:299–320.

Huskamp, H. A., M. B. Rosenthal, R. G. Frank, and J. P. Newhouse. 2000. "The Medicare Prescription Drug Benefit: How Will the Game Be Played?" *Health Affairs* 19(2):8–23.

Iglehart, John K., ed. 2004. "Variations Revisited: A Supplement to Health Affairs." *Health Affairs – Web Exclusive* 23:3–4.

Iizuka, Toshi. 2004. "What Explains the Use of Direct-to-Consumer Advertising of Prescription Drugs?" *Journal of Industrial Economics* 52(3):349–379.

Iizuka, Toshi, and Ginger Z. Jin. 2003. "The Effects of Direct-to-Consumer Advertising in the Prescription Drug Markets." Unpublished working paper, Vanderbilt University, Owen Graduate School of Management, September 29.

Iizuka, Toshi, and Ginger Z. Jin. 2005a. "The Effect of Prescription Drug Advertising on Doctor Visits." *Journal of Economics and Management Strategy*, forthcoming.

Iizuka, Toshi, and Ginger Z. Jin. 2005b. "Direct to Consumer Advertising and Prescription Choice." Working paper, Vanderbilt University, Owen Graduate School of Management.

IMS. 2004. *Global Pharmaceutical Review*. October. London.

IMS Intelligence. 2005. Chart 1. PowerPoint Presentation Supplied via e-mail by Raymond Hill of IMS, May 21.

Institute of Medicine. 2000. *Calling the Shots: Immunization Finance Policies and Practices*. Washington, DC: National Academies Press.

Institute of Medicine. 2003. *Hidden Costs, Value Lost: Uninsurance in America*. Washington, DC: National Academies Press, 2003.

Institute of Medicine. 2004. *Financing Vaccines in the 21st Century: Assuring Access and Availability*. Washington, DC: National Academies Press.

Institute of Medicine, J. Corrigan, A. Greiner, and S. M. Erickson. 2002. *Fostering Rapid Advances in Health Care: Learning from System Demonstrations*. Washington, DC: National Academies Press.

Ives, D., J. Lave, N. Traven, and L. Kuller. 1994. "Impact of Medicare Reimbursement on Influenza Vaccination Rates in the Elderly." *Preventive Medicine* 23:134–141.

Jensen, Elizabeth J. 1987. "Research Expenditures and the Discovery of New Drugs." *Journal of Industrial Economics* 36:83–95.

Jensen, G. A., and M. A. Morrisey. 1999. "Employer-Sponsored Health Insurance and Mandated Benefit Laws." *Milbank Quarterly* 77(4):425–459.

Jewkes, John, David Sawyers, and Richard Stillerman. 1958. *The Sources of Invention.* London: Macmillan.

Jones, Charles. 1998. *Introduction to Economic Growth.* New York: W. W. Norton.

Joskow, P. L. 1989. "Regulatory Failure, Regulatory Reform, and Structural-Change in the Electrical-Power Industry." *Brookings Papers on Economic Activity* (1998):125–208.

Juhl, R. P. 2000. "Prescription to Over-the-Counter Switch: A Regulatory Perspective." *Clinical Therapeutics* 20(Supp. C):111–117.

Kahn, A. 1971. *The Economics of Regulation: Principles and Institutions.* New York: Wiley.

Kaiser Family Foundation. 2001. *Prescription Drug Trends: A Chartbook Update* Washington, DC.

Kaiser Family Foundation. 2002. *Employer Health Benefits: 2002 Annual Survey.* Washington, DC.

Kaiser Family Foundation. 2005. *Prescription Drug Coverage for Medicare Beneficiaries: A Summary of the Medicare Prescription Drug, Improvement, and Modernization Act of 2003.* Available at www.kff.org/medicare/6112.cfm. Last accessed November 5, 2005.

Kanavos, Panos, and Uwe E. Reinhardt. 2003. "Reference Pricing For Drugs: Is It Compatible with U.S. Health Care?" *Health Affairs* 22(3):16–30.

Kettler, Hannah E. 1999. "Updating the Cost of a New Chemical Entity." London: Office of Health Economics.

Keynes, John Maynard. 1936. *The General Theory of Employment, Interest, and Money.* London: Macmillan.

Kim, Jong-Il, and Lawrence J. Lau. 1994. "The Sources of Economic Growth of the East Asian Newly Industrialized Countries." *Journal of the Japanese and International Economies* 8:235–271.

Kitch, E. W. 1977. "The Nature and Function of the Patent System." *Journal of Law and Economics* 10:265–290.

Klein, Daniel B. 2005. "Policy Medicine versus Policy Quackery: Economists against the FDA." *Knowledge, Technology, and Policy* 31(1):92–101.

Klick, J., and Sara Markowitz. 2003. "Are Mental Health Insurance Mandates Effective? Evidence from Suicides." National Bureau of Economic Research Working Paper 9994.

Kobelt, G., L. Jönsson, A. Young, and K. Eberhardt. 2003. "The Cost-Effectiveness of Infliximab (Remicade) in the Treatment of Rheumatoid Arthritis in Sweden and the United Kingdom Based on the ATTRACT Study." *Rheumatology* 42:326–335.

Kravitz, Richard I., Ronald M. Epstein, Mitchell D. Feldman, Carol E. Franz, Rahman Azari, Michael S. Wilkes, Ladson Hinton, and Peter Franks. 2005. "Influence of Patients' Requests for Direct-to-Consumer Advertised Antidepressants: A Randomized Controlled Trial." *Journal of the American Medical Association* 293(16):1995–2002.

Kreling, D. H., T. Collins, H. Lipton, and K.C. Hertz. 1996. "Assessing the Impact of Pharmacy Benefit Managers." HCFA Contract Report, HCFA 95-023/PW, September 30.

Kremer, M. 1998. "Patent Buyouts: A Mechanism for Encouraging Innovation." *Quarterly Journal of Economics* 113(4):1137–1167.

Kremer, M. 2000a. "Creating Markets for New Vaccines Part I: Rationale." National Bureau of Economic Research Working Paper 7716.

Kremer, M. 2000b. "Creating Markets for New Vaccines Part II: Design Issues." National Bureau of Economic Research Working Paper 7717.

Kremer, M., and R. Glennerster. 2004. *Strong Medicine: Creating Incentives for Pharmaceutical Research on Neglected Diseases.* Princeton, NJ: Princeton University Press.

Kremer, M., and C. M. Snyder. 2003. "Why Are Drugs More Profitable than Vaccines?" National Bureau of Economic Research Working Paper 9833.

Kronick, R., and T. Gilmer. 2002. "Insuring Low-Income Adults: Does Public Coverage Crowd Out Private?" *Health Affairs* 21(1):225–239.

Laffont, J.-J., and J. Tirole. 1993. *A Theory of Incentives in Procurement and Regulation.* Cambridge, MA: MIT Press.

Landau, Ralph, et al. 1999. *Pharmaceutical Innovation: Revolutionizing Human Health.* Philadelphia: Chemical Heritage Press.

Lanjouw, J. 2004. "Outline of Foreign Filing License Approach." Washington, DC: Center for Global Development & Global Health Policy Research Network. Available at www.cgdev.org/docs/FFLOutline.pdf.

Lanjouw, J. O., and M. MacLeod. 2005. "Statistical Trends in Pharmaceutical Research for Poor Countries." Available at www.who.int/intellectualproperty/studies. Last accessed May 10, 2005.

Learner, Josh, and Robert P. Merges. 1998. "The Control of Technology Alliances: An Empirical Analysis of the Biotechnology Industry." *Journal of Industrial Economics* 46:125–156.

Learner, Josh, and Alexander Tsai. 2000. "Do Equity Financing Cycles Matter? Evidence from Biotechnology Alliances." National Bureau of Economic Research Working Paper W7464.

Leffler, Keith B. 1981. "Promotion or Information? The Economics of Prescription Drug Advertising." *Journal of Law and Economics* 24(2):45–74.

Levin, Richard C., Alvin K. Klevorick, Richard R. Nelson, and Sidney G. Winter. 1987. "Appropriating the Returns from Industrial Research and Development." *Brookings Papers on Economic Activity* 3:783–820.

Lichtenberg, Frank R. 1984. "The Relationship between Federal Contract R&D and Company R&D." *American Economic Review* 74(2):73–78.

Lichtenberg, Frank R. 1986. "Energy Prices and Induced Innovation." *Research Policy* 15:67–75.

Lichtenberg, Frank R. 1987. "Changing Market Opportunities and the Structure of R&D Investment: The Case of Energy." *Energy Economics* 9(3):154–158.

Lichtenberg, Frank R. 1988. "The Private R&D Investment Response to Federal Design and Technical Competitions." *American Economic Review* 78(3):550–559.

Lichtenberg, Frank R. 1996. "The Effect of Pharmaceutical Utilization and Innovation on Hospitalization and Mortality." National Bureau of Economic Research Working Paper 5418.

Lichtenberg, Frank R. 2001a. "The Allocation of Publicly Funded Biomedical Research," in *Medical Care Output and Productivity*, Studies in Income and Wealth vol. 62, ed. by Ernst Berndt and David Cutler, 565–589. Chicago: University of Chicago Press.

Lichtenberg, Frank R. 2001b. "The Effect of New Drugs on Mortality from Rare Diseases and HIV." National Bureau of Economic Research Working Paper 8677.

Lichtenberg, Frank R. 2003a. "Pharmaceutical Innovation, Mortality Reduction, and Economic Growth." In *Measuring the Gains from Medical Research: An Economic Approach*, ed. by Kevin M. Murphy and Robert H. Topel, 74–109. Chicago: University of Chicago Press.

Lichtenberg, Frank R. 2003b. "The Effect of New Drugs on HIV Mortality in the U.S., 1987–1998." *Economics and Human Biology* 1:259–266.

Lichtenberg, Frank R. 2003c. "The Benefits to Society of New Drugs: A Survey of the Econometric Evidence." *Proceedings of the Federal Reserve Bank of Dallas* (September):43–59.

Lichtenberg, Frank R. 2004a. "Public Policy and Innovation in the U.S. Pharmaceutical Industry," in *Public Policy and the Economics of Entrepreneurship*, ed. by Douglas Holtz-Eakin and Harvey S. Rosen, 83–113. Cambridge, MA: MIT Press.

Lichtenberg, Frank R. 2004b. "Sources of U.S. Longevity Increase, 1960–2001." *Quarterly Review of Economics and Finance* 44(3):369–389.

Lichtenberg, Frank R. 2005a. "Pharmaceutical Innovation and the Burden of Disease in Developed and Developing Countries." *Journal of Medicine and Philosophy* 30(6):663–690.

Lichtenberg, Frank R. 2005b. "The Impact of New Drug Launches on Longevity: Evidence from Longitudinal Disease-level Data from 52 Countries, 1982–2001." *International Journal of Health Care Finance and Economics* 5(1):47–73.

Lichtenberg, Frank R., and Suchin Virabhak. 2002. "Pharmaceutical Embodied Technical Progress, Longevity, and Quality of Life: Drugs as "Equipment for Your Health." National Bureau of Economic Research Working Paper 9351.

Lichtenberg, F., and J. Waldfogel. 2003. "Does Misery Love Company? Evidence from Pharmaceutical Markets before and after the Orphan Drug Act." National Bureau of Economic Research Working Paper 9750.

Light, Donald W., and Rebecca N. Warburton. 2005. "Extraordinary Claims Require Extraordinary Evidence." *Journal of Health Economics* 24(5):1030–1033.

Ling, Davina C., Ernst R. Berndt, and Margaret K. Kyle. 2002. "Deregulating Direct-to-Consumer Marketing of Prescription Drugs: Effects on Prescription and Over-the-Counter Product Sales." *Journal of Law and Economics* 14:691–723.

Livernois, J. R. 1988. "Estimates of Marginal Discovery Costs for Oil and Gas." *Canadian Journal of Economics* 21(2):379–393.

López-Casasnovas, G., and B. Jönsson, eds. 2001. *Reference Pricing and Pharmaceutical Policy*. Barcelona: Springer Verlag Ibéria.

López-Casasnovas, G., and J. Puig-Junoy. 2001. "Review of the Literature on Reference Pricing," in *Reference Pricing and Pharmaceutical Policy*, ed. G. López-Casasnovas and B. Jönsson, 1–41. Barcelona: Springer Verlag Ibéria.

Lo Sasso, A. T., and T. C. Buchmueller. 2004. "The Effect of the State Children's Health Insurance Program on Health Insurance Coverage." *Journal of Health Economics* 23(5):1059–1082.

Luman, E. T., L. E. Barker, K. M. Shaw, et al. 2005. "Timeliness of Childhood Vaccinations in the United States: Days Undervaccinated and Number of Vaccines Delayed." *Journal of the American Medical Association* 293(10):1204–1211.

Lurie, N., W. G. Manning, C. Peterson, et al. 1987. "Preventive Care: Do We Practice What We Preach?" *American Journal of Public Health* 77:801–804.

Mackenbach, J. P. 1991. "Health Care Expenditure and Mortality from Amenable Conditions in the European Community." *Health Policy* 19:245–255.

Manca, A., P. Lambert, S. Hahn, M. J. Sculpher, and N. Rice. 2004. "Exploring the Generalisability by Location of Multilevel Trial-Based CEA Results: The Case of Bayesian Hierarchical Linear Modeling," in *5th European Conference of Health Economics*, 542. London: Open Mind Journals.

Mansfield, Edwin. 1977. *The Production and Application of New Industrial Technology*. New York: W. W. Norton.

Mansfield, Edwin. 1986. "Patents and Innovation: An Empirical Study." *Management Science* 32(2):173–181.

Masson, A., and R. Steiner. 1985. "Generic Substitution and Prescription Drug Prices: Economic Effects of State Drug Product Selection Laws." Staff Report of the Bureau of Economics, FTC, Washington, DC, October.

Maurer, S. 2005. "The Right Tool(s): Designing Cost-Effective Strategies for Neglected Disease Research." Geneva: WHO Commission on Intellectual Property Rights, Innovation, and Public Health. Available at www.who.int/intellectualproperty/studies/research_development/en/.

Maurer, S., A. Rai, and A. Sali. 2004. "Finding Cures For Tropical Diseases: Is Open Source an Answer?" *PLOS: Medicine* 1:183–186. Available at http://medicine.plosjournals.org/perlserv/?request=get-document&doi=10.1371/journal.pmed.0010056.

Maurer, S., and S. Scotchmer. 2004. "Procuring Knowledge," in *Advances in the Study of Entrepreneurship, Innovation and Growth*, ed. by G. Libecap, 15:1–31. Greenwich, CT: JAI Press.

McCarran, E. 1991. "Rx to OTC Switches: Promises and Pitfalls." *Medical Marketing and Media* 13–26.

McGuire, T. G. 2003. "Setting Prices for New Vaccines (in Advance)." *International Journal of Health Care Finance and Economics* 3(3):207–224.

Megginson, William L., and Jeffry M. Netter. 2001. "From State to Market: A Survey of Empirical Studies on Privatization." *Journal of Economic Literature* 39(2):321–389.

Meltzer, M. I., N. J. Cox, and K. Fukuda. 1999. "The Economic Impact of Pandemic Influenza in the United States: Priorities for Intervention." *Emerging Infectious Disease* 5(5):659–671.

Menzin J, G. Oster, L. Davies, M. F. Drummond, W. Greiner, C. Lucioni, J. L. Merot, F. Rossi, V. D. Schulenberg, and E. Souetre. 1996. "A Multinational Economic Evaluation of rhDNase in the Treatment of Cystic Fibrosis." *International Journal of Technology Assessment in Health Care* 12(1):52–61.

Merrill, S. A., R. C. Levin, and M. B. Myers. 2004. *A Patent System for the 21st Century*. Washington, DC: National Academies Press.

Millenson, Michael L. 2004. "Getting Doctors to Say Yes to Drugs: The Cost and Quality Impact of Drug Company Marketing to Physicians." Chicago: Blue Cross Blue Shield Association. Available at www.bcbs.com/coststudies/reports/Drug_Co_Marketing_Report.pdf. Last accessed November 20, 2005.

Miller, Richard D., Jr., and H. E. Frech III. 2004. *Health Care Matters: Pharmaceuticals, Obesity, and the Quality of Life*. Washington, DC: AEI Press.

Mitchell, V. S., N. M. Philipose, and J. P. Sanford, eds. 1993. *The Children's Vaccine Initiative: Achieving the Vision*. Washington, DC: National Academy Press.

Morgan, Steven G. 2002. "Quantifying Components of Drug Expenditure Inflation: The British Columbia Seniors' Drug Benefit Plan." *Health Services Research* 37:1243–1266.

Mueller, D. 1986. *The Persistence of Profits*. Cambridge: Cambridge University Press.

Murphy, Kevin, and Robert H. Topel. 2003a. "The Economic Value of Medical Research," in *Measuring the Gains from Medical Research: An Economic Approach*, ed. by Kevin M. Murphy and Robert H. Topel, 41–73. Chicago: University of Chicago Press.

Murphy, Kevin M., and Robert H. Topel. 2003b. *Measuring the Gains from Medical Research: An Economic Approach*. Chicago, IL: University of Chicago Press.

Murphy, Kevin M., and Robert H. Topel. 2005. "The Value of Health and Longevity." University of Chicago Working Paper.

Myers, Stewart. 1999. "Measuring Pharmaceutical Risk and the Cost of Capital," in *Risk and Return in the Pharmaceutical Industry*, ed. by Jon Sussex and Nick Marchant, 59–76. London: Office of Health Economics.

Nace, N., C. Larson, T. Lester, and J. Kosinski. 1999. "Perceived Barriers to Childhood Immunization: A Physician and Parent Survey in a Southeastern Urban/Rural Community." *Tennessee Medicine* 92(7):265–268.

National Association of Boards of Pharmacy. 2004. *Survey of Pharmacy Law for 2003–2004*. Park Ridge, IL: NABC.

National Institute for Clinical Excellence (NICE). 2000. "Guidance on the Use of Zanamivir (Relenza) in the Treatment of Influenza." *Technology Appraisal Guidance No. 15*. London: NICE.

National Institute for Clinical Excellence (NICE). 2004. *Guide to the Methods of Technology Appraisal*. London: NICE.

National Science Council (Taiwan). 2004. *Indicators of Science and Technology*. Taipei: NSC.

National Science Foundation. 2006. "National Expenditures for R&D, from Funding Sectors to Performing Sectors." Available at www.nsf.gov/sbe/srs/nsf03313/tables/tab1b.xls.

Nelson, Philip K. 1970. "Information and Consumer Behavior." *Journal of Political Economy* 78(2):311–329.

Nelson, Philip K. 1974. "Advertising as Information." *Journal of Political Economy* 82(4):729–754.

Neslin, Scott A. 2001. *ROI Analysis of Pharmaceutical Promotion (RAPPP)*. Unpublished study, Hanover, NH, Amos Tuck School of Business, Dartmouth College. Available at www.rxpromoroi.org/rapp.

Neumann, P. J. 2004. "Why Don't Americans Use Cost-Effectiveness Analysis?" *American Journal of Managed Care* 10:308–312.

Newhouse, Joseph P. 2004. "How Much Should Medicare Pay for Drugs?" *Health Affairs* 23(1):89–102.

New Zealand Ministry of Health. 2000a. "Direct to Consumer Advertising of Prescription Medicines under Review." Media release, December 1. Available at www.moh.govt.nz/moh.nsf. Last accessed April 30, 2005.

New Zealand Ministry of Health. 2000b. "Direct-to-Consumer Advertising of Prescription Medicines in New Zealand: A Discussion Paper." November. Available as dtcaDiscussionDoc.pdf at www.moh.govt.nz/moh.nsf. Last accessed April 30, 2005.

Nexoe, J., J. Kragstrup, and T. Ronne. 1997. "Impact of Postal Invitations and User Fee on Influenza Vaccination Rates among the Elderly: A Randomized Controlled Trial in General Practice." *Scandinavian Journal of Primary Health Care* 15(2):109–112.

Nicholson, S., Patricia M. Danzon, and Geoffrey McCullough. 2002. "Biotech-Pharmaceutical Alliances as a Signal of Asset and Firm Quality." National Bureau of Economic Research Working Paper 9007.

Nordhaus, William D. 2003. "The Health of Nations: The Contribution of Improved Health to Living Standards," in *Measuring the Gains from Medical Research: An Economic Approach*," ed. by Kevin M. Murphy and Robert H. Topel, 9–40. Chicago: University of Chicago Press.

Oeppen, J., and J. W. Vaupel. 2002. "Demography: Broken Limits to Life Expectancy." *Science* 296(5570):1029–1031.

Offit, P. A. 2005. "Why Are Pharmaceutical Companies Gradually Abandoning Vaccines?" *Health Affairs* 24(3):622–30.

Ohmit, S. E., A. Furumotodawson, A. S. Monto, and N. Fasano. 1995. "Influenza Vaccine Use among an Elderly Population in a Community Intervention." *American Journal of Preventive Medicine* 11(4):271–276.

Or, Zeynep. 2003. "Determinants of Health Outcomes in Industrialised Countries: A Pooled, Cross-Country, Time-Series Analysis." OECD Economic Studies No. 30, 2000/I. Available at www.oecd.org.

Organization for Economic Cooperation and Development. 2004. "Table 1. Life Expectancy in Years," in *OECD Health Data 2004*, 3rd ed. Available at www.oecd.org.

Outterson, Kevin. 2004. "The U.S.-Australian Free Trade Agreement's Unfortunate Attack and Good Healthcare Policy." Comments Submitted to the U.S. Congress, House of Representatives, Committee on Ways and Means, June 22, 2004. Available at www.ita.doc.gov/td/chemicals/phRMA/Outterson%20Response1.pdf. Last accessed October 20, 2005.

Padden, Michael, and Thomas Jenkins. 2004. "Hatch-Waxman Changes." *National Law Journal*, February 23, p. 13.

Palda, Kristian. 1969. *Economic Analysis for Marketing Decisions*. New York: Prentice-Hall.

Palmer, S., M. Sculpher, M. Robinson Philips, L. Ginnelly, and D. Gary. 2005. "Management of Non-ST-Elevation Acute Coronary Syndromes: How Cost-Effective Are Glycoprotein IIb/IIIa Antagonists in the UK National Health Service?" *International Journal of Cardiology* 100(2):229–240.

Pauly, M. V. 1998. *Health Benefits at Work: An Economic and Political Analysis of Employment-Based Health Insurance*. Ann Arbor: University of Michigan Press.

Pauly, M. V. 2005. "Improving Vaccine Supply And Development: Who Needs What?" *Health Affairs* 24(3):680–689.

Pauly, M. V., P. Danzon, P. Feldstein, and J. Hoff. 1991. "A Plan for 'Responsible National Health Insurance.'" *Health Affairs* 10(1):5–25.

Pharmaceutical R&D Policy Project. 2005. "The New Landscape of Neglected Disease Drug Development." London: London School of Economics. Available at www.lse.ac.uk/collections/pressAndInformationOffice/PDF/Neglected_Diseases_05.pdf.

Pharmaceutical Research and Manufacturers of America. 2000. *Pharmaceutical Industry Profile*. Washington, DC: Pharmaceutical Research and Manufacturing Association.

Pharmaceutical Research and Manufacturers of America. 2005. *PhRMA Guiding Principles: Direct to Consumer Advertisements about Prescription Medicines.* Washington, DC, August 2005. Available at www.phrma.org.

Philipson, T. 2000. "Economic Epidemiology and Infectious Diseases," in *Handbook of Health Economics*, ed. by A. J. Culyer and J. P. Newhouse, 1B: 1761–1769. Amsterdam: Elsevier Science.

Pines, Wayne L. 1999. "A History and Perspective on Direct-to-Consumer Promotion." *Food and Drug Law Journal* 54:489–518.

Pleis, J., and J. Gentleman. 2002. "Using the National Health Interview Survey: Time Trends in Influenza Vaccinations among Targeted Adults." *Effective Clinical Practices* 5(3 Suppl.):E3.

Plotkin, S. A. 2005. "Why Certain Vaccines Have Been Delayed or Not Developed at All." *Health Affairs* 24(3):631–634.

Pogge, T. 2005. "Human Rights and Global Health: A Research Program." *Metaphilosophy* 36(1/2):182–209.

Poikoilainen, K., and J. Eskola. 1988. "Health Services Resources and Their Relation to Mortality from Causes Amenable to Health Care Intervention: A Cross-national Study." *International Journal of Epidemiology* 17(1):86–89.

Pomerantz, Jay M., Stan N. Finkelstein, Ernst R. Berndt, Amy W. Poret, Leon E. Walker, Robert C. Alber, Vidya Kadiyam, Mitali Das, David T. Boss, and Thomas H. Ebert. 2004. "Prescriber Intent, Off-Label Usage, and Early Discontinuation of Antidepressants." *Journal of Clinical Psychiatry* 65(3):395–404.

Popp, David. 2001. "Induced Innovation and Energy Prices." National Bureau of Economic Research Working Paper 8284.

Poulson, David, and Sarah Kellogg. "Private Labs' Ability to Deliver Vaccines Questioned." Available at www.newhouse.com/archive/story1c110501.html.

Rappuoli, Rino, Henry I. Miller, and Stanley Falkow. 2002. "The Intangible Value of Vaccination." *Science* 297(5583):937–938.

Rawlins, M. D., and A. J. Culyer. 2004. "National Institute for Clinical Excellence and Its Value Judgments." *British Medical Journal* 329:224–227.

Reichert, T. A., N. Sugaya, D. S. Fedson, et al. 2001. "The Japanese Experience with Vaccinating Schoolchildren against Influenza." *New England Journal of Medicine* 344(12):889–896.

Reiffen, David, and Michael R. Ward. 2005. "Generic Drug Industry Dynamics." *Review of Economics and Statistics* 87(1):37–49.

Reiffen, David, and Michael Ward. 2006. "Branded Generics as a Strategy to Limit Cannibalization of Pharmaceutical Markets." *Managerial and Decision Economics*, forthcoming.

Reinhardt, Uwe E. 1996. "Rationing in Health Care: What It Is, What It Is Not, and Why We Cannot Avoid It," in *Strategic Choices for a Changing Health System*, ed. by Stuart H. Altman and E. Uwe, 63–100. Chicago: Health Administration Press.

Reinhardt, Uwe E. 1997. "Making Economic Evaluations More Respectable." *Social Science and Medicine* 45(4):555–562.

Reinhardt, Uwe E. 2001. "Can Efficiency in Health Care Be Left to the Market?" *Journal of Health Politics, Policy and Law* 26(5):967–992.

Reinhardt, Uwe E. 2004. "An Information Infrastructure for the Pharmaceutical Market." *Health Affairs* 23(1):107–112.

Rice, Thomas H. 2002. *The Economics of Health Reconsidered.* Chicago: Health Administration Press.
Ridley, R. G. 2004. "Product Development Public-Private Partnerships for Diseases of Poverty," in *Combating Diseases Associated with Poverty*, ed. by R. Widdus and K. White. Geneva: Initiative on Public-Private Partnerships for Health.
Riordan, M. H., and D. E. M. Sappington. 1989. "Second Sourcing." *Rand Journal of Economics* 20(1):41–58.
ROC Department of Health. 2005. *Health and Vital Statistical.* Taipei: Department of Health.
Rodewald, L., E. Maes, J. Stevenson, et al. 1999. "Immunization Performance Measurement in a Changing Immunization Environment." *Pediatrics* 103(4):889–897.
Rogerson, W. P. 1989. "Profit Regulation of Defense Contractors and Prizes for Innovation." *Journal of Political Economy* 97(6):1284–1305.
Rogerson, W. P. 1994. "Economic Incentives and the Defense Procurement Process." *Journal of Economic Perspectives* 8(4):65–90.
Romer, Paul. 1990. "Endogenous Technological Change." *Journal of Political Economy* 98:71–102.
Rosenthal, Meredith B., Ernst R. Berndt, Julie M. Donohue, Arnold M. Epstein, and Richard G. Frank. 2003. "Demand Effects of Recent Changes in Prescription Drug Promotion," chapter 1 in *Frontiers in Health Policy Research*, vol. 6, ed. Alan M. Garber, 1–26. Cambridge, MA: MIT Press for the National Bureau of Economic Research.
Rosenthal, Meredith B., Ernst R. Berndt, Julie M. Donohue, Richard G. Frank, and Arnold M. Epstein. 2002. "Promotion of Prescription Drugs to Consumers." *New England Journal of Medicine* 346(7):498–505.
Rosso, R. 2001. "Trends in Food Stamp Program Participation Rates: 1994 to 1999." Alexandria, VA: United States Department of Agriculture, Food and Nutrition Service.
Rubin, Robert, Ann Hawk, and Elisa Cascade. 1998. "PBMs: A Purchaser's Perspective," in *PBMs: Reshaping the Pharmaceutical Distribution Network*, ed. by Sheila Shulman, Elaine Healy, and Louis Lasagna, 30. Binghamton, NY: Pharmaceutical Products Press.
Saha, Atanu, Henry Grabowski, Howard Birnbaum, Paul Greenberg, and Oded Bizan. 2006. "Generic Competition in the U.S. Pharmaceutical Industry." *International Journal of the Economics of Business* 13(1):15–38.
Salkever, D., and R. Frank. 1996. "Economic Issues in Vaccine Purchase Agreements," in *Supplying Vaccine: An Economic Analysis of Critical Issues*, ed. by M. Pauly, C. A. Robinson, S. Sepe, M. Sing, and M. K. Willian. Amsterdam: IOS Press.
Satterthwaite, P. 1997. "A Randomised Intervention Study to Examine the Effect on Immunisation Coverage of Making Influenza Vaccine Available at No Cost." *New Zealand Medical Journal* 110(1038):58–60.
Saunders, Barrie. 2003. "Direct to Consumer Advertising of Prescription Drugs in New Zealand: Professors' Protest to Government Placed under the Microscope." Wellington, New Zealand: Saunders Unsworth. Available at www.sul.co.nz.
Scharfstein, D. 1988. "The Disciplinary Role of Takeovers." *Review of Economic Studies* 55(2):185–199.
Scherer, F. M. 2000. "The Pharmaceutical Industry," in *Handbook of Health Economics*, vol. 1, ed. by A. J. Culyer and J. P. Newhouse, 297–336. Amsterdam: Elsevier Science.
Scherer, F. M. 2001. "The Link between Gross Profitability and Pharmaceutical R&D Spending." *Health Affairs* 20:216–220.

Scherer, F. M., and D. R. Ross. 1990. *Industrial Market Structure and Economic Performance*. 3rd ed. Boston: Houghton-Mifflin.

Schmalensee, R. 1979. *The Control of National Monopolies*. Lexington, MA: D. C. Heath, Lexington Books.

Schmookler, Jacob. 1966. *Invention and Economic Growth*. Cambridge, MA: Harvard University Press.

Schwartzman, David, and Antonio Cognato. 1996. "Has Pharmaceutical Research Become More Scientific?" *Review of Industrial Organization* 11:841–851.

Schweitzer, Stuart. 1997. *Pharmaceuticals, Economics, and Policy*. New York: Oxford University Press.

Scotchmer, S. 2004. *Innovation and Incentives*. Cambridge, MA: MIT Press.

Scott Morton, F. M. 1999. "Entry Decisions in the Generic Pharmaceutical Industry." *RAND Journal of Economics* 30(3):421–440.

Scott Morton, F. M. 2000. "Barriers to Entry Brand Advertising, and Generic Entry in the U.S. Pharmaceutical Industry." *International Journal of Industrial Organization* 18(7):1085–1104.

Scriabiane, Alexander. 1999. "The Role of Biotechnology in Drug Development," in *Pharmaceutical Innovation: Revolutionizing Human Health*, ed. by Ralph Landau, Basil Achilladelis, and Alexander Scriabine. Philadelphia: Chemical Heritage Foundation Press.

Sculpher, M. J., F. S. Pang, A. Manca, M. F. Drummond, S. Golder, H. Urdahl, L. M. Davies, and A. Eastwood. 2004. Generalisability in Economic Evaluation Studies in Health Care: A Review and Case Studies. *Health Technology Assessment* 8(49) (whole issue).

Shavell, S., and T. Van Ypersele. 2001. "Rewards versus Intellectual Property Rights." *Journal of Law and Economics* 44(2):525–547.

Shaw, James W., William C. Horrace, and Ronald J. Vogel. 2005. "The Determinants of Life Expectancy: An Analysis of the OECD Health Data." *Southern Economic Journal* 71(4):768–783.

Shleifer, Andrei. 1998. "State versus Private Ownership." *Journal of Economic Perspectives* 12(4):133–150.

Shleifer, A., and R. Vishny. 1994. "Politicians and Firms." *Quarterly Journal of Economics* 109:995–1025.

Siegel, Jonathan B. 2004. "Financial Aspects of 180-Day Generic Exclusivity." Presentation to the Food and Drug Law Institute Conference on Two Decades of Hatch-Waxman, December 1–2, Washington, DC.

Sinclair, G., S. Klepper, and W. Cohen. 2000. "What's Experience Got to Do with It? Sources of Cost Reduction in a Large Specialty Chemicals Producer." *Management Science* 46(1):25–28.

Skinner, J., and J. E. Wennberg. 2000. "How Much Is Enough? Efficiency and Medicare Spending in the Last Six Months of Life," in *The Changing Hospital Industry: Comparing Not-for-Profit and For-Profit Institutions*, ed. by David Cutler, 169–193. Chicago: University of Chicago Press.

Sloan, Frank A., and Chris J. Conover. 1998. "Effects of State Reforms on Health Insurance Coverage of Adults." *Inquiry* 35:280–293.

Sloan, Frank A., and Henry G. Grabowski. 1997. "Introduction and Overview." *Social Science and Medicine* 54(4):505–510.

Sloan, Frank A., K. Whetten-Goldstein, and A. Wilson. 1997. "Hospital Pharmacy Decisions, Cost Containment, and the Use of Cost-Effectiveness Analysis." *Social Science and Medicine* 54(4):525–536.

Smith, J. S. 1990. *Patenting the Sun*. New York: Morrow.

Song, F., D. G. Altman, A. M. Glenny, and J. Deeks. 2003. "Validity of Indirect Comparison for Estimating Efficacy of Competing Interventions: Empirical Evidence from Published Meta-Analyses." *British Medical Journal* 326:472–478.

Sorenson, Alan T. 2000. "Equilibrium Price Dispersion in Retail Markets for Prescription Drugs." *Journal of Political Economy* 108(4):833–850.

Spence, M. 1984. "Cost Reduction, Competition, and Industry Performance." *Econometrica* 52:101–121.

Spulber, D. 1989. *Regulation and Markets*. Cambridge, MA: MIT Press.

Stapleton, S. 2004. "Project BioShield." *American Medical News* 47(31):19.

Statistics Canada. 1974. *Life Tables, Canada and Provinces, 1970–1972*. Ottawa: Minister of Industry.

Statistics Canada. 2002. *Life Tables, Canada, Provinces and Territories, 1995–1997*. Ottawa: Minister of Industry.

Stein, J. C. 1988. "Takeover Threats and Managerial Myopia." *Journal of Political Economy* 96(1):61–80.

Stern, Scott, Michael E. Porter, and Jeffrey L. Furman. 2000. "The Determinants of National Innovative Capacity." National Bureau of Economics Research Working Paper 7876.

Stinnett, A. A., et al. 1996. "The Cost Effectiveness of Dietary and Pharmacologic Therapy for Cholesterol Reduction in Adults," in *Cost Effectiveness in Health and Medicine*, ed. by M. Gold, J. E. Siegel, L. B. Russell, and M. C. Weinstein, 349–391. Oxford: Oxford University Press.

Stratton, K. R., J. S. Durch, and R. S. Lawrence. 2000. *Vaccines for the 21st Century: A Tool for Decision-Making*. Washington, DC: Institute of Medicine, National Academy Press.

Summers, L. H. 1989. "What Can Economics Contribute to Social Policy?" *American Economic Review* 79(2):177–183.

Tan, Litjen, and the American Medical Association. 2006. "Strengthening the Supply of Routinely Recommended Vaccines in the United States: A Perspective from the American Medical Association." *Clinical Infectious Diseases* 42(Suppl. 3):S121–S124.

Taylor, C. R. 1995. "Digging for Golden Carrots: An Analysis of Research Tournaments." *American Economic Review* 85(4):872–890.

Temin, Peter. 1980. *Taking Your Medicine: Drug Regulation in the United States*. Cambridge, MA: Harvard University Press.

Thomas, P. 2002. "The Economics of Vaccines." *Harvard Medical International (HMI) World*, September/October.

Tobin, James. 1969. "A General Equilibrium Approach to Monetary Theory." *Journal of Money, Credit, and Banking* 1(1):15–29.

Toop, Les, Dee Richards, Tony Dowell, Murray Tilyard, Tony Fraser, and Bruce Arrol. 2003. "Direct to Consumer Advertising of Prescription Drugs in New Zealand: For Health or for Profit?" Report to the Minister of Health Supporting the Case for a Ban on DTCA, February. Available at www.chmeds.ac.nz/report.pdf. Last accessed April 30, 2005.

Towse, A. 2004. "Developing the Idea of Transferable Intellectual Property Rights (TIPP) to Incentivize R&D in Drugs and Vaccines for Neglected Diseases." Office of Health Economics, London, March 2, Appendix I, 22–24.

Towse, A., and H. Kettler. 2005. "Review of IP and Non-IP Incentives for R&D for Diseases of Poverty: What Type of Innovation Is Required and How Can We Incentivise the Private Sector to Deliver It?" Available at www.who.int/intellectualproperty/studies/health_innovation/en. Last accessed May 10, 2005.

Towse A., J. Mestre-Fernandez, and O. Renowden. 2004. "Estimates of the Medium Term Financial Resource Needs for Development of Pharmaceuticals to Combat 'Neglected Diseases,'" in *Combating Diseases Associated with Poverty*, ed. by R. Widdus and K. White. Geneva: Initiative on Public-Private Partnerships for Health.

Tufts Center for the Study of Drug Development. 2003. "Total Cost to Develop a New Prescription Drug, Including Cost of Post-Approval Research, Is $897 million." Press release, May 13, 2003. Available at www.csdd.tufts.edu.

Turner, Margaret A. 2003. "Strengths and Weaknesses of the Housing Voucher Program." Congressional Testimony prepared for the Committee on Financial Services, Subcommittee on Housing and Community Opportunity, U.S. House of Representatives, June 17, 2003. Available at www.urban.org/url.cfm?ID=900635.

U.S. Centers for Disease Control and Prevention. 1999. "An Ounce of Prevention . . . What Are the Returns?" 2nd ed. Available at www.cdc.gov/epo/prevent.htm.

U.S. Centers for Disease Control and Prevention. 2002a. "Influenza and Pneumococcal Vaccination Levels among Persons Aged > 65 years, United States, 2001." *Morbidity and Mortality Weekly Report* 51(45):1019–1024.

U.S. Centers for Disease Control and Prevention. 2002b. "National, State, and Urban Area Vaccination Coverage Levels among Children Aged 19–35 Months: United States, 2001." *Morbidity and Mortality Weekly Report* 3:664–666.

U.S. Centers for Disease Control and Prevention. 2003. "National, State, and Urban Area Vaccination Coverage Levels among Children Aged 19–35 Months: United States, 2002." *Morbidity and Mortality Weekly Report* 52(31):728–732.

U.S. Centers for Disease Control and Prevention. 2004. "Influenza Viruses." Available at www.cdc.gov/flu/avian/gen-info/flu-viruses.htm. Last accessed March 2, 2005.

U.S. Centers for Disease Control and Prevention. 2005a. "Influenza Pandemics." Available at www.cdc.gov/flu/avian/gen-info/pandemics.htm. Last accessed March 2, 2005.

U.S. Centers for Disease Control and Prevention. 2005b. "Avian Influenza Infection in Humans." Available at www.cdc.gov/flu/avian/gen-info/avian-flu-humans.htm. Last accessed March 2, 2005.

U.S. Centers for Medicaid and Medicare Services. 2003. "The Nation's Health Care Dollar: 2001." Washington, DC: Government Printing Office.

U.S. Committee on Ways and Means, U.S. House of Representatives. 2003. *Background Material and Data on the Programs within the Jurisdiction of the Committee on Ways and Means.* (Informally known as the "Green Book.") WMCP 108–6. Washington, DC: Government Printing Office.

U.S. Congressional Budget Office. 1998. "How Increased Competition Has Affected Prices and Returns in the Pharmaceutical Industry." July, 38. Washington, DC: Government Printing Office.

U.S. Department of Health and Human Services. 2002. *"Payment by Results" Breakthrough Ends Years of Uncertainty for MS Patients: Agreement Follows Recommendation from NICE.* Washington, DC: Government Printing Office.

U.S. Department of Health and Human Services. 2004. "Pandemic Influenza Preparedness and Response Plan," 1–54. Washington, DC: Government Printing Office.

U.S. Food and Drug Administration. 1999. "Creating a Risk Management Framework: Report to the FDA Commissioner from the Task Force on Risk Management." Washington, DC: Government Printing Office.

U.S. Food and Drug Administration. 2005. "CDER NDAs Approved in Calendar Years 1990–2204 by Therapeutic Potential and Chemical Type." Available at www.fda.gov/cder/rdmt/pstable.htm.

U.S. Senate. 1960–. *Administered Prices in the Drug Industry*. Hearings before the Sub-Committee on Antitrust and Monopoly, 86th Congress, 1959 and 1960, Part 18. Washington, DC: Government Printing Office.

U.S. Senate, Republican Policy Committee. 2005. "Pharmaceutical Price Controls Abroad: An Unfair Trade Policy." Available at www.kyl.senate.gov/legis_center/rpc_110603.pdf. Last accessed October 20, 2005.

Vernon, John M. 1981. "Concentration, Promotion, and Market Share Stability in the Pharmaceutical Industry." *Journal of Industrial Economics* 19(3):246–266.

Vernon, J., and H. Grabowski. 2000. "The Distribution of Sales Revenues from Pharmaceutical Innovation." *PharmoEconomics* 18(1):21–32.

Vernon, John M., and Peter Gusen. 1974. "Technical Change and Firm Size: Pharmaceutical Industry." *Review of Economics and Statistics* 56:294–302.

Viscusi, W. Kip. 1993. "The Value of Risks to Life and Health." *Journal of Economic Literature* 31:1912–1946.

Viscusi, W. Kip. 1995. "Discounting Health Effects for Medical Decisions," in *Valuing Health Care*, ed. Frank Sloan, 125–147. Cambridge: Cambridge University Press.

Viscusi, W. Kip, and Joseph E. Aldy. 2003. "The Value of a Statistical Life: A Critical Review of Market Estimates throughout the World." *Journal of Risk and Uncertainty* 27(1):5–76.

Vistnes, G. 1994. "An Empirical Investigation of Procurement Contract Structures." *Rand Journal of Economics* 25(2):215–241.

Walsh, J. P., A. Arora, and W. M. Cohen. 2003. "Working through the Patent Problem." *Science* 299(5609):1021.

Weissman, Joel S., David Blumenthal, Alvin J. Silk, Michael Newman, Kinga Zapert, Robert Leitman, and Sandra Feibelmann. 2004. "Physicians Report on Patient Encounters Involving Direct-to-Consumer Advertising." *Health Affairs – Web Exclusive* W4: 219–233.

WHO. 2004. *World Health Report, Revised Global Burden of Disease 2002 Estimates.* London: WHO.

WHO Collaborating Centre for Drug Statistics Methodology. 2004. "Guidelines for ATC Classification and DDD Assignment." Oslo: Norwegian Institute.

Widdus, Roy, and Katherine White. 2004. "Combating Diseases of Poverty: Financing Strategies for Product Development and the Potential Role of Private-Public Partnerships." Geneva: Initiative on Private-Public Partnerships for Health.

Wilby, J., A. Kainth, N. Hawkins, D. Epstein, C. McDaid, et al. 2003. *A Rapid and Systematic Review of the Clinical Effectiveness, Tolerability and Cost-Effectiveness of Newer Drugs for Epilepsy in Adults.* Report to the National Institute for Clinical Excellence, forthcoming.

Willan, A. R., E. M. Pinto, B. J. O'Brien, et al. 2005. "Country Specific Cost Comparisons from Multinational Clinical Trials Using Empirical Bayesian Shrinkage Estimation: The Canadian ASSENT-3 Economic Analysis." *Health Economics* 14(1):327–338.

Wittink, Richard R. 2002. "Analysis of ROI for Pharmaceutical Promotions," September, video presentation, Association of Medical Publications. Available at www.vioworks.com/clients/amp.

Wosinska, Marta. 2002. "Just What the Patient Ordered? Direct-to-Consumer Advertising and the Demand for Pharmaceutical Products." Harvard Business School, Marketing Research Paper Series, No. 02-04.

Wosinska, Marta. 2005. "Direct-to-Consumer Advertising and Drug Therapy Compliance." *Journal of Marketing Research* 42(3):323–332.

Wright, Brian D. 1983. "The Economics of Invention Incentives: Patents, Prizes, and Research Contracts." *American Economic Review* 73:691–707.

Zucker, Lynne E., Michael R. Darby, and Marilynn B. Brewer. 1998. "Intellectual Human Capital and the Birth of U.S. Biotechnology Enterprises." *American Economic Review* 88(1):290–306.

Index

www.ingramcontent.com/pod-product-compliance
Ingram Content Group UK Ltd.
Pitfield, Milton Keynes, MK11 3LW, UK
UKHW022000190125
453752UK00006B/30

9 780521 874908